D1356785

DECANTATIONS

A TRIBUTE TO MAURICE CRAIG

EDITED BY AGNES BERNELLE

THE LILLIPUT PRESS

First published in 1992 by
THE LILLIPUT PRESS LTD
4 Rosemount Terrace, Arbour Hill,
Dublin 7, Ireland.

A CIP record for this
title is available from
The British Library.

ISBN   0 946640 64 5

Acknowledgments
The publisher is most grateful for the
assistance and design skills of John O'Regan
of Gandon Editions during the course of
this work's lengthy gestation.

Jacket design by Jarlath Hayes
Layout & typeset by Gandon Editions
(10 on 11.75 Garamond)
Printed in Dublin by ßetaprint

CONTENTS

WORDS – VISIONS

A. B.

WHEN Maire de Paor asked me if anyone had considered publishing a FESTSCHRIFT for Maurice on his seventieth birthday I thought it a very good idea and immediately set about organizing one. I did not, at the time, know exactly what this involved. I still think it a very good idea, but in retrospect I feel a little like a relative of mine must have done after tobogganing merrily down an inviting-looking Alpine slope on her small homemade sledge only to discover afterwards that she had survived a dangerous Olympic run.

I asked at the time how I should proceed and was told by those who knew that before all else I would have to find a co-ordinator, a publisher and some sponsors. I was lucky enough to find a publisher straightaway, and luckier still that it happened to be the very publisher I had been anxious to have. The sponsorship response came to over seventy per cent. Finding a co-ordinator, however, proved much more difficult. People I approached all said that a FESTSCHRIFT was a time-consuming undertaking, for which none of them had sufficient leisure, and suggested that I should think of some other way to celebrate the occasion. This was a challenge I could not resist, and, with the help of two co-editors, Professor Kevin Nowlan and the architect Sean Rothery, and with Antony Farrell, the publisher, I went ahead.

It has been a most rewarding experience. I could not have done it, of course, without the help of Maurice's colleagues and friends – who sent in their contributions with the minimum fuss and delay – and without the assistance of more than 170 of our mutual Friends – the subscribers – not to mention the professional organizations who helped out financially towards the end. It is some time since the inception of this FESTSCHRIFT. I have heard of others that took seven years to appear in print! But for me the most rewarding aspect has been the correspondence I entered into with so many interesting and brilliant people. This very correspondence made it difficult at times to keep the plan secret from Maurice until the actual birthday. 'Why is Sir John Summerson writing to *you*' he would ask, and 'What is he saying? Can I see?' It was the same with Sir Steven Runciman, who sent several charming letters, though he was ultimately unable to find anything suitable amongst the charred ruins of his tragically burnt papers. I had sometimes to find excuses. My regular communion with Lilliput was also problem and had to be heavily disguised. I could hardly believe my luck when none of the many friends who were involved gave the show away, although there were a number of near misses.

When the whole operation was finally unveiled, I believe Maurice was somewhat taken aback. He had never, he says, come across a FESTSCHRIFT that was organized by the subject's wife, be she legal or otherwise. And as a meticulous, and at times pedantic man, he found it difficult to adjust to this unusual situation. Another aspect that puzzled him was the catholic nature of the publication. A FESTSCHRIFT, he explained to me, comprises erudite essays by the recipient's peers, almost always on his or her own specialist subject. In this case I had decided early on to make it slightly different. I endeavoured to have all Maurice's diverse interests represented: not only architectural history, but archaeology, art, poetry, literature, humour, photography, graphics and model engineering. You will find in these pages experts writing about their own subjects, an eminent speleologist writing on ship-modelling and an architect on computer usage, and also poems along with sketches, photographs and a chapter of a yet unpublished novel. I devoutly hope that Maurice will nevertheless accept this kaleidoscopic offering from so many of his friends in the spirit in which it is presented to him – the spirit of love.

A.B.
Dublin, October 1992

THE CELESTIAL STEAM PACKET[1]

C.E.B. BRETT

THE BOY, James Waldron,[2] had often been puzzled by the faded sign attached to the wall of Dun Laoghaire pier, on which was painted 'D. & I.O.B. Steam Packet Coy.[3] Times of Sailing'. No times were specified; no hint was given as to the meaning of the initials; never had he seen a passenger vessel moored to this stretch of quay. On this particular afternoon of late summer, however, he was surprised to notice that a printed slip had been pasted onto the board. It read:

Alteration in Service
Owing to lack of patronage the Company are regretfully compelled to suspend the weekly service, and to retain only the
Special Sailings
which will depart punctually at sunrise on the fifth Saturday of every month that has one. Return Tickets, available for the weekend only, may be obtained on board from the purser. As an extra inducement, every ticket will be valid for *two* round trips, provided that not less than fifty years elapses between the first and the second.
By Order of the Board.'

Tomorrow, he realized, would be not only the last, but also the fifth, Saturday of the month. He resolved to rise very early, and come to see. But, in his heart, he feared that it was all a hoax, and that he should see nothing.

To his delight, however, as he clambered down the steep steps in the minutes before dawn, he saw the masts, funnel and bowsprit of a surprisingly large vessel silhouetted against the fading stars. At the foot of the gangway stood a tall, handsome man with a large hand-bell in one fist, a turnip watch in the other. The Purser or Bursar – for it was he, as he was also the ship's Bellman[4] – made haste to issue, and punch, a large and ornate ticket, nicely printed like an invitation-card, which he pressed into the fingers of young James Waldron, refusing payment (despite his faintly Scottish accent) on the grounds that it was not the Company's policy to contract with minors, whom it preferred to carry free of charge and free of liability. It seemed there was to be no other passenger. In a trice,[5] James and the Purser were standing on the quarter-deck; the gangway had been shipped; the energetic clanging of the hand-bell had been echoed by the ringing of the ship's engine-room telegraphs; the Blue Peter had been smartly hauled down from the yard-arm; the sun had leaped up over the eastern horizon; and the ship was moving, at a startling pace, away from the quay.

As she passed between the pierheads, young James took time to inspect her. He was, for his tender years, surprisingly conversant with the technicalities of nautical equipment and usage.[6] She was a most delightful vessel, neat and shipshape, every pintle revolving snugly in its gudgeon, and so forth. Like a model railway train, she had all the expected organs in the expected places.[7] He would have explored her from truck to keelson, but that the former was out of reach, the latter underwater; nevertheless, he explored her from bowsprit to fanal – for she had a stern-light above her scrolled counter. Her elegant lines displayed no fewer than three discrepant kinds of sheer.[8] Of her name, he could discover no hint; but he did, at any rate, learn from various builders' plates that she had been built by Samuda Bros of Poplar in 1865; reconstructed by Inglis of Glasgow in 1905; refitted at Portsmouth Dockyard in 1920; and that she was propelled by three Parsons turbines driving three screws, with five main and one auxiliary Inglis multi-tubular boilers.[9] This information gave him as much gratification as if she had been a D.8. 4-litre Delage motor car with Figoni coachwork.[10]

It seemed that he had the ship almost to himself. There was accommodation for many passengers; a manifest pinned up in a mess-room listed 'a captain, two lieutenants, master, bursar, boatswain, gunner, carpenter, master's mate, coxswain, boatswain's mate, and carpenter's mate'.[11] Yet the lack of patronage seemed to have reduced the crew to a point where it comprised only – apart from the Bursar – the Captain, a tiny leprechaun-like figure; the Boatswain, a burly man of lawyer-like mien with a spreading bushy beard and a silver whistle; the Engineer, a slim, brisk, curly-bearded fellow of vaguely Assyrian appearance; and a francophone ship's parrot, of a uniquely republican shade of green, which answered to the name of Laverdure with cries, almost invariably, of 'Tu causes, tu causes, c'est tout ce que tu sais faire.'[12]

Not long after leaving port, a single piercing blast on the ship's steam-whistle was followed by a sharp turn to starboard.[13] With trepidation, James climbed the steep companionway leading to the wheel-house, and knocked on the door. After inspecting his ticket, the Captain admitted him. 'Excuse me, Sir, please,' said James, 'but where are we going?' 'Why, my boy, to the Islands of the Blest, of course.' 'And please Sir, where are they?' 'Why, boy, look at the chart.' And indeed, upon the chart-table was spread out a large map representing the sea without the least vestige of land – a perfect and absolute blank. 'Other maps are such shapes, with their islands and capes: this, you can *all* understand.'[14] Then the Captain pulled down, from a shelf above the compass, the ship's Almanack, a volume most handsomely bound in green vellum, the binding incorporating cottage-design returns, featherwork, tongues of flame, and chains of vesicae: evidently the work of Parliamentary Binder B.[15] Having consulted it, he continued: 'To make it quite plain to you, I shall turn sharp to starboard again when we pass the Tuskar Rock; and sharp to starboard yet again when we are past Cape Clear; and we shall find the Islands of the Blest, just where they ought to be, far out in the Atlantic to the west of the Skelligs.'

The sun was soon well up, the ship was racing along through the solemn Buzz of the still sea,[16] and the boy derived great pleasure from the stir and swing of the sea-lit air and the movement of the morning.[17] He was leaning on the rail, admiring the wake, when he was joined by the engineer, who introduced himself as Eddie. 'Tell me about these islands,' said James. 'There is a whole Archipelago,' the Engineer replied. 'First, there are the Gothic Isles, also known as the Barbarides. There are the Princes' Islands, or Byzantinisles. There are the Spice Islands of Araby. Then there is a group of very mediocre islands of the middle class, the Vernaculars, with strangely unsuburban names however: Hymenstown, Bridestream, Rosegarland; Ballyruin, Ballyseedy, Ballydrain, Ballynahaha, Castle Fish...[18] And last but best of all, there are the incorruptible Capitals, Doric, Ionic and Corinthian.[19] (Naturally, I omit the more obvious *sehenswurdigkeit*.[20]) And there are, strewn along our course, many lesser rocks and islets – why, see, there is one over yonder.'

And indeed, fine on the starboard bow appeared a rock upon which sat a black-haired siren,[21] vastly attractive, holding up a mirror and singing in a husky, magical voice songs of Kurt Weill, Bertold Brecht, and Albert Rechts, learned at her mother's knee in the far-off inland waters of Balaton and the Tihany peninsula ... 'May I not go to her?' pleaded James, ravished. 'Not now; perhaps you may go to her some other day'; (and so he did).

Not long after this, Alistair, the purser, rang his bell to signal luncheon. The meal was a modest one of pemmican and ship's biscuit, washed down with ginger ale; but as the Captain remained on the bridge, James was able to spend a useful half-hour reading the labels on the sauce bottles, and picturing the bearded and bewhiskered Mr Lea, Mr Perrins, Mr Crosse and Mr Blackwell competing for gold medals at some Hungarian spa.[22]

When he went up on deck again, it was to find that the wind had freshened, the sea was rising, and the ship was now well out in the open Atlantic. It seemed to James that a storm was coming, for the sea, luminous grey and angry, curled up to show white teeth, its petulant upper lip.[23] Not long after, he was startled by a crash of thunder and a bolt of lightning. He was not alone in being startled: from Laverdure's cage in the saloon came a screech: 'Pare à virer! Chasse à tribord! Hissez les hublots! Patinez la dunette! Récoltez le cacatois!'[24] Alistair was not slow to rebuke the parrot, and remind him that the days when he had sailed before the mast with the Comte de Bonfils Lablènie[25] were past; and that nowadays there was no other cockatoo on board. Quite quickly the squall abated; a rainbow appeared; and the first of the Islands came into sight on the horizon.

These turned out to be the Gothic Islands. The ship did not halt there, but sailed very close to land in the deep water below the cliffs. The Captain passed James an enormous pair of opera-glasses, through which he could see clearly the principal inhabitants, luxuriously abounding in solecisms and anachronisms.[26] They were lined up on the cliff-top beside the lighthouse, their surplices, cassocks, stoles and Trinity College hoods flapping in the stiff breeze: Saint Werburgh, Saint Stephen, Saint Olaf, Saint Michan, Saint Michael-le-Pole, Saint Marie del Dam,[27] Saint Luke, Saint Kevin, Saint

Bride,[27] and last but not least the formidable squinting Saint Audoen:[28] the ends of his stole bearing the spurious but colourable date 1194 in Arabic numerals.[29] Poor fellow, he appeared unable to look his fellow-saints in the eye on account of suffering from a blocked hagioscope.[30]

Soon, to port, they saw a low-lying islet of sexual allure and somewhat vulgar appearance ('eldorado banal de tous les vieux garçons').[31] Its occupants, said Nicholas Boatswain, displayed a distressing amalgam of gothic and of artisan mannerism;[32] and spent one day of each week in residence in each of their seven mansions, Jigginstown, Sigginstown, Gigginstown, Zinckinstown, Smokingstown, Jinglestown, and Xigginstown.[33] Nearby, a rather larger island, called Romanesque, seemed almost completely covered in an urban maze of spirit-groceries, ball-alleys, and round towers [34] resembling the campanili of Ravennate churches[35] (all bearing the inscription 'IMPORTANT IF TRUE'[36]), their environment rendered fragrant by the occasional gleu yard.[37] The ship passed also some Canary Islands, but on these Laverdure looked with understandable disdain.

At this point, the vessel slowed to permit the Purser dexterously to recover a Message floating by in a bottle. James was astounded to discover that the label, embossed with gold medallions,[38] was addressed to himself; and bore a stamp portraying, at actual size, the minuscule thatched cottage recently discovered by archaeologists under a shamrock-leaf in Borris-in-Ossory.[39] The Message itself, to the gratification of the entire crew (not excluding Laverdure), comprised a whole litre of Powers' Gold Label whiskey: the Medium was the Message.

It soon became evident that they were approaching the Byzantinisles, for, as James observed with surprise, the sea hereabouts was being torn to shreds by dolphins; and at the same time, tormented by gongs;[40] similar to those which had boomed from end to end of University Square, Belfast, at supper-time in his earlier childhood. Criss-crossed and tortured as it was, the surface of the sea sparkled with diamond-hard brilliance. 'ποντιων τε κυματων ανηριθμον γελασμα,' [41] cried the polyglot Captain Kevin. He spake in Greek, which Britons speak, seldom, and circumspectly; nonetheless James, who had received a sound classical grounding, translated it correctly.[42] Once again, they skirted the islands, admiring the anachronistic interplay of domes, minarets, squinches, pendentives, mihrabs, mimbars, and the antique Plataean column of serpents in the Maidan,[43] all to the accompaniment of the sonorous but melancholy music[44] of the golden horn: which moved Laverdure to comment – 'dieu, que le son du boa est triste au fond du cor'.[45]

Now, to port, were the low-lying Vernaculars; to starboard, the Isles of Araby, where Aflatun and Aristu and King Iskander are Plato, Aristotle and Alexander;[46] surmounted by a Great Mosque evidently closely modelled on St Anne's, Shandon, by observant Phoenicians;[47] ahead, their destination, the Capital Islands. On every side rose noble buildings nobly laid out, in accordance with Vitruvian rule, and in accordance also with 'la chiara predilezione degli irlandesi per la sistemazione delle masse in lunghezza, piuttosto che in profondità'.[48] They included the Nuova Dogana; the

Quattro Tribunali; the Collegio della Trinità; the Palazzi della Borsa and delle Poste; and the Armeria del Castello;[49] many of them with reposeful pediments.[50] The very harbour was stately and imposing; from such a quay-side embarked Ursula and the ten thousand virgins in the visions of Carpaccio; [51] from such a quayside set forth, never to return, the Bateau hopelessly Ivre.[52] As the ship slipped between twin moles, they saw that a reception party was waiting for them.

In front, a double row of the Commissioners for making Wide and Convenient Streets,[53] drawn up with particular care as to their disposition and intervals, *faisaient la haie*, backed by the members of the Paving Board.[54] To their rear, in meticulous order of precedence, half-mounted gentlemen; gentlemen every inch of them; and gentlemen to the backbone;[55] then the six grades of poets, and one of satirists.[56] And behind them again, the holders of honorific sinecures: the Jerquer, the Craner and Wharfinger, the Taster of Wines, the Prothonotary, the Cursitor, the Philizer, the Exigenter, the Filacer, the Summonister, and the Alnager of Ireland.[57]

Beside them, a military band played like mad with fife and drum, flam, drag and paradiddle, till the very judges were wakened from their slumbers on the benches of the four courts;[58] and Serjeant Arabin rushed onto the quay, admonishing the Wide Street Commissioners – 'No man is fit to be a cheesemonger who cannot guess the *length* of a street';[59] and William Caldbeck cried out 'Not guilty, my lords, except just once at Newtownards'; [60] and all the litigants turned out to see the fun, including Thomas Charles Druce the furniture dealer and his *alter ego*, the fifth Duke of Portland.[61] The populace cheered wildly; even the official Greeks moved their lips.[62] The members of the Reform Club made faces out of their windows,[63] and the Christy's Minstrels performed on Leinster Lawn.[64] A merry peal chimed out from the tower at the rear of No.64 Eccles Street, where Francis Johnston had installed the clock and eight bells of St George's for his own amusement.[65] Everyone who was, or had been, or ever would be, anyone, came down to the quayside to welcome the steam packet and its passenger: Dean Swift; Sir Edward Lovett Pearce, and his innumerable cousins; [66] James Gandon, Thomas Cooley, Richard Cassels, and Thomas Ivory; the Morrisons, all three of them, *grand-père, père,* and *fils;* Lord Charlemont, hot-foot and sandy from his regular Saturday sea-bathing,[67] and Dr Achmet Borumbarad (alias Patrick Joyce) wet and salty from his Hot and Cold Sea Water Baths;[68] Sir William Chambers, Sir Boyle Roche, Sir John Betjeman, Sir Jonah Barrington, Sir Nikolaus Pevsner, the author of this article, and the Knight of Glin; C.J. Haughey and Garrett the Good; d'Aviso de Arcort, Placido Columbani, and the brothers Francini; George and Mercy MacCann, Florence Irwin and Mariga Guinness; Daniel Robertson in his wheelbarrow, clutching his bottle of sherry;[69] the corpulent Francis Grose, his breath recovered, leaning on the arm of that young helper who answered equably either to the name of 'Guinea-pig', or to that of 'Badger'[70] ... And so on, almost ad infinitum ... And they all, in a rout, escorted the bewildered young James to the welcoming lodging-house of Signora Morandi,[71] where he was to spend the night.

And what a night that was! It was with infinite wistfulness and reluctance that, next day, he climbed the gangway for the return voyage. 'Come again!' they cried ... 'you cannot come again for fifty years; but after that, come again; and in the meanwhile, keep our memory (in every sense of the word) green!' Humbly, he promised to do so.

———

He kept both promises. Yet it was well over fifty years before he was to step again on board the Dublin and Isles of the Blest Steam Packet. Nothing had changed in the interval. He landed once again at the sea-steps: once again, the whole island was en fête to greet him. There was the touch of fresh leaves on his forehead. Someone had crowned him.

ΤΕΛΟΣ

NOTES

[1] Cf. E.M. Forster, *The Celestial Omnibus* (London 1911).

[2] Postcard from M.J. Craig (hereafter 'M.J.C.') to author, 8 September 1986: 'Ces deux noms m'ont été donnés au moment de mon baptême, autrement peu efficace, parce que mon père s'appelait Jacques, et ma mère est née Waldron. Veuillez agréer, cher Monsieur, mes sentiments les plus distingués. Seamus de Bhaldruinn.' (See also reference to James Fitzmaurice in note 62.)

[3] See M.J.C. on the City of Dublin Steam Packet Company in 'S.S. Kilkenny', *Sunday Miscellany 2* (Dublin 1976), p.48.

[4] See L. Carroll, *The Hunting of the Snark* (London 1876), Fit the Second.

[5] A pulley or windlass *(OED)*.

[6] Like the youthful Lord Charlemont: M.J.C.: *The Volunteer Earl* (London 1948), p.61.

[7] M.J.C.: *The Architecture of Ireland* (London and Dublin 1982), p.315, ref. St Finn Barre's Cathedral, Cork.

[8] M.J.C.: *The Elephant and the Polish Question* (hereafter *E.&P.Q.*) (Dublin 1990), p.114.

[9] Cf. 'Mahroussa', *Jane's Fighting Ships* (London 1940), p.152.

[10] M.J.C.: *E. & P.Q.*, p.196.

[11] M.J.C.: *Dublin, 1660-1860* (Dublin 1952), p.92. These were the officers of the Ouzel Galley Society, a body incorporated for the dual purposes of promoting arbitration and conviviality.

[12] R. Queneau, *Zazie dans le Métro* (Paris 1959), *passim*.

[13] *A Seaman's Pocket-Book* (Admiralty, London 1943), p.40: 'A steam vessel sounds on whistle or syren: one short blast means 'I am directing my course to starboard.'

[14] L. Carroll, *The Hunting of the Snark*, Fit the Second.

[15] Cf. M.J.C., *Irish Bookbindings 1600-1800* (London 1954), pp.8-11 and 14-15.

[16] Lord Charlemont, in M.J.C., *The Volunteer Earl*, p.63.

[17] J.E. Flecker, 'Epithalamion', *Collected Poems* (London 1916).

[18] M.J.C.: *Classic Irish Houses of the Middle Size* (London 1976) p.49.

[19] M.J.C.: *Some Way for Reason*, poems (London 1948), p.31.

[20] M.J.C. and Knight of Glin: *Ireland Observed* (Cork 1970), p.5.

[21] 'She whose Genius never enter'd Literature's gin-palaces'; W.S. Landor, *Miscellaneous Poems*, CCXXVI.

[22] M.J.C.: 'Labels on bottles', *Sunday Miscellany 2*, p.125.

[23] M.J.C.: *Some Way for Reason*, p.55.

[24] R. Queneau, *Les Oeuvres Complètes de Sally Mara* (Paris 1962), p.264.

[25] The naval historian: author of *Histoire de la Marine Française* (1845).

[26] M.J.C.: *The Personality of Leinster* (Dublin 1961), p.26.

[27] The Church of Ireland has displayed somewhat less alacrity in recognizing the eligibility of persons of the feminine gender for holy orders, than their eligibility for sanctification; but

has got there in the end.

[28] H.A. Wheeler and M.J.C.: *The Dublin City Churches of the Church of Ireland* (Dublin 1948), *passim*.

[29] *Ibid.*, p.13.

[30] *Ibid.*, p.14.

[31] C. Baudelaire, 'Le Voyage à Cythère' in *Fleurs du Mal* (Paris 1857).

[32] M.J.C.: *The Architecture of Ireland*, p.138.

[33] *Ibid.*, p.138.

[34] *Ibid.*, p.7.

[35] M.J.C.: *The Personality of Leinster*, p.17.

[36] M.J.C.: *E.&P.Q.*, cit. A.W. Kinglake, p.89.

[37] M.J.C.: *The Legacy of Swift* (Dublin 1948), p.36.

[38] M.J.C.: 'Labels on Bottles', *Sunday Miscellany 2*, p.125.

[39] Designed by Michael Craig.

[40] 'That dolphin-torn, that gong-tormented sea': W.B. Yeats, 'Byzantium'.

[41] Aeschylus, *Prometheus Bound*, p.88.

[42] J.E. Flecker, '*The Ballad of Hampstead Heath*'.

[43] M.J.C.: *E.&P.Q.*, p.79.

[44] Naturally, the horn solo from H. Berlioz, *Les Troyens*, part II (Chasse Royale et Orage) (Paris 1858).

[45] N. Mitford, *The Pursuit of Love* (London 1945), cap.17; and cf. the punch-line of A. de Vigny, *Le Cor* (Pau 1825).

[46] J.E. Flecker, 'The Ballad of Iskander'.

[47] See M.J.C., *The Architecture of Ireland*, p.207, where the author perversely advances the contrary argument, *viz*, that St Anne's, Shandon, may be modelled on the Great Mosque of Kairouan in Tunisia.

[48] M.J.C.: *L'architettura di ispirazione Palladiana in Irlanda*, Bolletino del Centro Internazionale di studi d'Archittetura Andrea Palladio (iii), (1961) p.34.

[49] *Ibid., passim*.

[50] M.J.C.: *The Legacy of Swift*, p.37.

[51] V. Carpaccio, Ciclo di Sant'Orsola, Venezia, Accademia.

[52] A. Rimbaud.

[53] M.J.C.: *Dublin*, p.172.

[54] *Ibid.*, p.173.

[55] *Ibid.* (per Sir Jonah Barrington), p.268.

[56] M.J.C.: *The Personality of Leinster*, p.11.

[57] *Ibid.*, pp.207-8. Other Republics are not afraid to confer honours; might not these ancient Irish titles, long antedating the Act of Union, be revived, with or without honoraria? Would it not be fitting if M.J.C. were appointed Alnager of Ireland?

[58] M.J.C.: *The Architecture of Ireland*, p.240.

[59] M.J.C.: 'Serjeant Arabin', *Sunday Miscellany 2*, p.27.

[60] M.J.C.: 'The Account-Book of William Caldbeck, Architect' in *Design and Practice in British Architecture* (1984), p.423.

[61] M.J.C.: 'The Druce-Portland Case', *Sunday Miscellany 2, passim* and *E.&P.Q.*, p.214 *sqq*.

[62] R. Peyrefitte: *Les Ambassades;* tr. as *Diplomatic Diversions* by James Fitzmaurice (orse M.J.C.) (London 1953), p.57.

[63] M.J.C.: 'Academy House and its Library' in *The Royal Irish Academy* (Dublin 1985), p.320.

[64] M.J.C.: in J. Meenan and D. Clarke, *The Royal Dublin Society* (Dublin 1981), p.68.

[65] H.A. Wheeler and M.J.C.: *The Dublin City Churches*, p.20.

[66] M.J.C., in H.M. Colvin and M.J.C., *Architectural Drawings in the Library of Elton Hall by Sir John Vanbrugh and Sir Edward Lovett Pearce* (Oxford 1964), pp.xl, xliv.

[67] M.J.C.: 'James Gandon' in *The Bell*, XVII (April 1951), p.27.

[68] M.J.C.: *Dublin*, p.271.

[69] M.J.C.: *Dublin*, p.295.

[70] M.J.C.: 'Francis Grose', *Irish Book Lover*, XXX (November 1947), p.56.

[71] Piazza dell' Annunziata 14, Firenze.

THE PARTY

LENINGRAD IN 1932

HUBERT BUTLER

'NINE MILLION tons of pig-iron is the estimate for 1932,' said a Soviet official, adding weakly: 'Yes, we have made great progress in education and theatre and the films are all excellent, but we haven't enough to eat.' There was nothing very surprising about this admission (indeed, it was self-evident) except that an official should have made it. Never till this winter have the Communists been so frank about the hardships that the Five Year Plan is imposing on the Russian people. It is now nearing its end and the strain is at its greatest. Never since 1920 have the people been called on to face a more cheerless winter; if they endure it without collapse there seems to be no limit to what can be borne. Whatever we may think of the goal they are striving towards, the chances are that they will stay the course.

There are plenty of inducements dangled in front of them, it is true. The next Five Year Plan is to develop the light industries and to raise the standard of living. Many of the great industrial undertakings will already be working at full capacity and there will be less need for foreign capital and foreign brains. They will not have to export food, but the finished products of their new factories and the collective farms will be under way. Because of this there will be butter and eggs and sugar and tea and bacon in plenty for the housewives.

This is an old story and the Russian citizen does not question its truth – but the prospect of good dinners a few years hence is cold comfort for any empty stomach. What sort of meals will the average Russian be sitting down to this winter?

If you walk down Nevsky Prospekt, looking in at the shop windows, you will get some notion of what he can hope to buy. Certainly there is not much variety. There are bread shops and vodka shops and Torgsins where the foreigners buy, and co-operatives where the Russians buy, and the odd dairy where there is cheese and products of sour milk and cream called smetana and tvorog. There are three or four small restaurants and an occasional small shop where hot pies filled with cabbage or jam are dispensed over the counter. Shop windows display enticing chocolate boxes with pretty lids tied with gorgeous ribbons – but, alas, there are no chocolates inside; behind the tempting facades there is nothing but scarlet paprikas like elongated tomatoes and chicory coffee. It is the same with the little pots of luscious-looking honey and cranberry jam. They are real right enough but they are not for sale. They are there just to remind one of the pots and pots of honey and jam that were on sale a month or two ago. It was

10

excellent and it wasn't very dear, but in one night it vanished like snow in Leningrad. Has it too gone away to Germany to buy machinery? 'They might have spared us the honey,' think the housewives.

Torgsin, the foreigners' shop, is the most splendid of all the food stores. Cotton curtains hide the display from the street, and the doorway is barred by an old man who says, 'Only foreign currency or gold.' It is a great privilege to be able to shop there, even a walk round provides the simple with a thrill. When our maid, Masha, went to buy eggs and butter there, she tied a clean red hand-kerchief round her head, and took a friend. Once through the door, except for the long queues and the seething crowds, one might be in Liptons or the Home and Colonial. There are mountains of butter and eggs and white loaves, cheese – and tins of fish and fruit, cream cakes, pear drops and strawberry jam. One can hear English spoken with an American accent, German, Italian, Czech, and the cashier has drawers full of dollars and shillings, lire and marks, in which she fumbles distractedly and seldom produces the right change. It is a foreigners' shop yet the mass of the customers are Russian. The Russians are of two types. There are stocky peasant women who have probably exchanged a gold cross or their wedding ring for Torgsin bonds. A prosperous peasant in the old days sel-dom invested his money in anything but gold ornaments for his wife. Banks break, currency becomes worthless, but gold never loses its value. The Soviet government has always been aware of the wealth of gold in private hands and has tried to extract it in various ways. It has used laws and threats, violence, even torture, but endurance is one of the lessons that Russia has learnt from the past. Torgsin is a more humane mode of extracting it – you may not get a great deal for your gold, but you get something, and even the thriftiest find it hard to resist the temptation of the well-filled shelves.

The other class of Russian who shops in Torgsin has seen better days. Though they are bourgeois, a few have married into Communist families or used their brains to get positions of trust. Others are too old or too deeply com-mitted to the old order of things to adapt themselves to the new. They belong to a liquidated class yet they have a certain value to the Soviets for their relations, who emigrated, send them foreign money for Torgsin bonds. But bad times in Paris and Prague, Berlin and Belgrade and all the haunts of refugees have checked the flow of gold to Russia; the geese have stopped laying the golden eggs, it is time to sell them. A few weeks ago it became possible to ransom one's relations from Russia.

But in spite of the crowds only a very small proportion of the inhabitants of Leningrad can hope to shop in Torgsin – for the others there remain the co-oper-atives with their various categories. Third Category workers can be sure of little but bread and vegetables, the Second may count on rice, buckwheat and millet, macaroni and sugar and butter, while the First Category can often get such deli-cacies as sausage or dried fruit. The prices are very low but the quantities allowed on each ticket very small. The majority of people supplement their tick-ets by purchasing in the open market. Prices may be ten times as high there as in the co-operatives, but purchasers are usually found.

There is a big market building filled with stalls not far off the Nevsky where the produce of the collective farms is sold – the surplus which the government has not commandeered. It is moderately filled, but to reach it one must pass through a narrow lane seething with excited traders. It is in this small lane and not in the spacious official hall that the bulk of the business is transacted. Rows of countrywomen stand holding slabs of butter or meat, while some are reselling at a profit sugar and meal and delicacies purchased at Torgsin or the co-operatives. Not far away stand others, haggling over galoshes or old leather coats.

To get regular meals in Leningrad, if you are not a factory worker with a factory dining-room, needs ingenuity and patience. It is sometimes too much of a bother, and to save trouble one misses a supper. Yet for a special occasion, for a marriage or a name-day or a big party, no effort will be spared. For weeks beforehand the whole family will be collecting and contriving for delicacies. A cousin who is on the stage will get them a cake through the theatrical co-operative, relations in the First and Second categories will bring gingerbread and sausages and smoked herring and pickled cucumber. A German engineer will be asked to bring sprats and Caucasian wine and Marie biscuits from Torgsin. The maid will be sent home on a holiday to bring back a couple of chickens or some home-cured bacon, and her work of waiting in the bread queue will have to be undertaken by the members of the family.

The party is the blossoming of weeks of effort. The tables groan with food and drink. There are toasts and jokes and songs and laughter. At two or three o'clock some of the guests go home, while the rest go to bed on the floor and tiptoe out in the early morning – but the family sleep on, in no hurry to awake. Food achieved, they sleep replete. Pinching, planning and privation are over – till tomorrow.

THE CHUB

MICHAEL CRAIG

There is a fine stuffed chavender,
A chavender or chub,
That decks the rural pavender,
The pavender or pub,
Wherein I eat my gravender,
My gravender or grub.
How good the honest gravender!
How snug the rustic pavender!
From sheets as sweet as lavender,
As lavender or lub,
I jump into my tavender,
My tavender or tub.

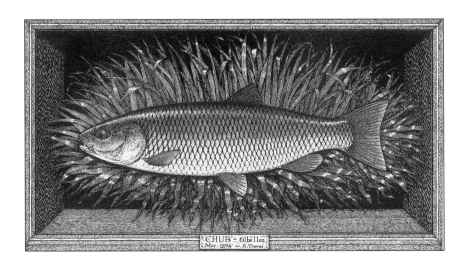

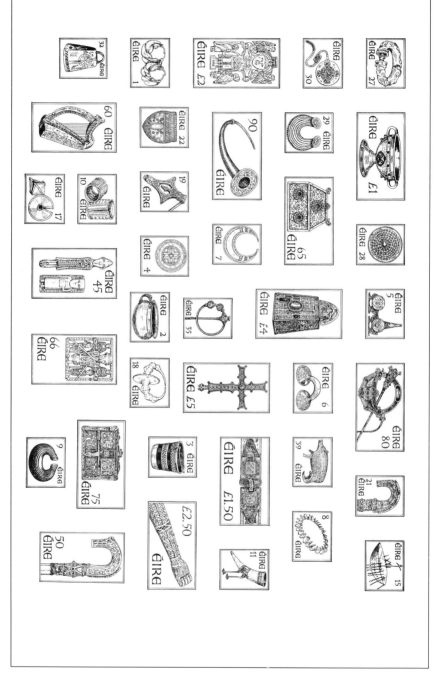

Michael Craig – Postage stamp designs

14

SONNET 26

from THE END OF THE MODERN WORLD

———————

ANTHONY CRONIN

My ancestors were wise, they dug and trenched,
Plumbing foundations in the quaking soil,
Raising the chaste, severe and classical
Column, entablature and pediment,
Reproving nature with proportion's stare
And showing man a measurer for joy.
So let stand thus forever stylobate,
Podium, portico and colonnade,
Organic artlessness acknowledged in
The thin acanthus leaf but now transcended.
Who tumbles, burns or tarnishes beware,
How rare is balance, brought about in mass,
Rightness which none can rectify, dispute,
The threatened made enduring, lines in air.

THE CONVERSATION PIECE

IN IRISH PAINTING IN THE EIGHTEENTH CENTURY

ANNE CROOKSHANK

NOT ALL the gaps in Irish painting can be explained by the great losses it has suffered through destruction and reattribution. Admittedly one has to accept there were once many horse paintings by Irish artists in this country, so dedicated as it is to the horse, but in the social upheavals of the last hundred years most have disappeared, perhaps with their owners to England, where they may languish under other artists' names. But this explanation does not fit every case. For instance, there are a mere dozen or so Irish conversation pieces * painted in oil, none certainly dated before 1760, and not that many in pastel either. This is very strange and must indicate that they were never commonplace. In England the great period for this genre was undoubtedly the 1730s and 40s, the period of Hogarth who created its greatest examples, showing how much life and character can be fitted into a small canvas by a great artist. His works, which were well known in Ireland due to his engravings, had surprisingly little influence.

From the early period there are three surviving Irish examples. Two are by an Englishman, James Worsdale, *The Limerick Hell Fire Club, c.*1735/6, and the *Dublin Hell Fire Club* of much the same date. The third is by a Dutch artist, Willem van der Hagen. He painted a *Ball at Dublin Castle* in 1731 which can also be claimed as a conversation piece. It is suggested that this is a work of 1757 by Joseph Tudor though the costume dates it fairly firmly to the earlier period, and even if it is proven to be a Tudor it would still date before 1760. After this date the genre is occasionally found, usually in the work of artists who are known to have English links; for instance of the three works of this type attributed to Philip Hussey, 1713-83, all come from the latter part of his career from the 1760s onwards. Two are large, *The Bateson Family* (Ulster Museum), and *The Greg Family* (the National Trust), and would be more correctly called portrait groups as the figures are nearly life size and, in the former, not particularly informal. Only one is a true example of the conversation piece, the family group in the NGI, which, in its stiffness, is closer to Arthur Devis than to Hogarth. It is recorded by Strickland, from an unnamed source, that Hussey visited England twice, and this may account for his use of the format.

* Joseph Burke *(English Art, 1714-1800* (Oxford 1976), pp. 108-9) defines the conversation piece as 'an informal portrait group in a familiar private and proprietary setting, with an emphasis on recreation'.

Thomas Hickey, *fl.* 1756-1816, sometimes uses the conversation piece as in his *Stephen, first Earl and Helen, Countess of Mountcashell, with four of their children* and in his *Charles Boddam with his Persian teacher and his hooker-burdar,* painted in 1787 in Calcutta. Hickey lived for some years in England, in London and in Bath, where he probably painted the Mountcashells, and later travelled to India, where he died. John Trotter, d.1792, whose small painting of *A Group of Gentlemen of the Blue-coat School* dates somewhat earlier in the 1770s, also painted some small double portraits of the Ponsonby family which might be called conversation pieces. These were later added to by the American visitor, Gilbert Stuart. Trotter had spent many years out of Ireland, mostly in Italy, and had probably picked up the genre from English painter friends. A group of the Wyse family seated in their print room, which is painted on copper, may be by George Mullins, *fl.* 1763-75, who is better known as a landscape painter but who according to Pasquin 'worked at Mr Wyse's manufactory at Waterford; and painted snuff-boxes and waiters, in imitation of the Birmingham ware.' Presumably this was early in his career, before he went to England, possibly in 1768 when he is recorded as showing 'A conversation' in the exhibition held by the Society of Artists in Ireland. The splendid conversation piece by Herbert Pugh, *fl.* 1758-88, of *George, fifth Earl of Granard having his wig powdered,* which is a deliberate Hogarth pastiche, must date from the late 1770s. Pugh, though Irish, lived and exhibited most of his life in London.

Apart from these examples one could count Irish oil conversation pieces in single figures, and I doubt that you would actually find five more painted in the eighteenth century. There is no such work by James Latham, by Thomas Frye or Nathaniel Hone despite the fact that the latter two both lived most of their lives in England; and there are no oil examples by Hugh Douglas Hamilton. Indeed the list could be extended to cover most Irish artists. Fortunately some visiting English painters, like Francis Wheatley, fill the gap and give us a few paintings of Irish people at home.

However, in the field of pastels and watercolours conversation pieces are found rather more often, though apart from Matthew William Peter's drawing of himself and his teacher Robert West, dated 1758, again there is nothing surviving before 1760. The conversation pieces by Hugh Douglas Hamilton were painted in England or Rome, not in Ireland, though his masterpiece *Canova in his Studio with Henry Tresham RA,* about 1789, must count as one of the best pastels painted by an Irishman in this period. The most famous and charming examples are the set of pastels by Robert Healy done in 1768 for Lady Louisa Conolly. These are particularly interesting as they are documented. Lady Louisa wrote to her sister Lady Sarah Bunbury on 29 February mentioning that they had a number of guests staying at Castletown and adding that the 'day is so bad that they can't stir out ... there is a man [presumably Healy] in the House, who draws very good likeness's, in black and white Chalk, we have made him draw some of the Company which is good entertainment'. Healy must have used these portraits as the basis of the faces in his series of pastels of the house party out skating, walking and hunting together with several horse and groom portraits. Lady Louisa had been included in a Stubbs painted about 1760 for her brother the third Duke of Richmond, which shows racehorses belonging to the Duke exercising at Goodwood watched by the Duke, Duchess and Lady Louisa. The obvious stylistic links between Healy and Stubbs have never been fully explained and one cannot help speculating that Healy may have known Stubbs or his work through his patroness and that the reason for the commission was Lady Louisa's knowledge of such paintings. Apart from the Castletown set no other conversation pieces or horse pictures by Healy are now known.

Francis Robert West
Members of the Vesey Family taking tea

The only Irish artist who really made the genre his own is the son of Robert West, the founder of the Dublin Society Schools, Francis Robert West, *c.*1749-1809, whose chalk drawings are mostly conversation pieces. His series of the Vesey family in scenes from everyday life shows them drinking tea, the first occasion that this homely occupation appears in Irish art. They are also seen playing cards and other indoor games like billiards and the series also includes some outdoor scenes. Two other drawings from the Malahide Castle sale may have been illustrations more than conversation pieces as the figures are shown in exotic dress and in one, a man in a Russian outfit is pushing a lady in a sleigh, which is hardly likely to represent contemporary Irish life though it could be a fancy dress party. All of these are in ovals and totally relaxed in atmosphere. Even when West paints a single figure, as in the charming study of a man in a library (Pierpont Morgan Library) which is dated 1771, the informality of the scene, with papers pushed into the crown of the sitter's hat and the untidy books behind, give it quite a different air to Hugh Douglas Hamilton's more formal pastels. West is recorded in the catalogue of the 1772 exhibition of the Society of Artists as showing 'portraits in conversation', perhaps the Vesey set. Charles Forrest, *fl.* 1765-80, also a Dublin Society School pupil, now known only for his single figures and one conversation piece of the Fish family, is recorded in the exhibition catalogue of the Society of Artists in 1771 as showing 'a portrait of a gentleman, his servants, horses and dogs, a hunting piece, in chalk', which sounds like a Healy. He showed other chalk conversation pieces in 1772 and 1773. John James Barralet, *c.*1747-1815, also a Dublin Society trained artist and a contemporary of Hamilton, Healy, Forrest and Francis West, signed a watercolour conversation piece of Speaker Foster and his family outside Oriel temple in 1786. One or two other artists are recorded in the exhibition catalogues as occasionally using the form.

The reasons for the lack of popularity of the conversation piece in Ireland are hard to find. Possibly if you had the money to pay for a portrait you expected the artist to immortalize you, and sitters might have been worried that the informality of the genre might reveal the undoubtedly rough-and-ready social existence to be found in many Irish great houses in the eighteenth century. One has however to qualify this as the conversation pieces by that English master of the genre, Arthur Devis, show many English provincial families sitting in imaginary rooms, far grander than those they owned. Patrons may also have thought that the small format lacked the dignity of the single portrait, even the single portrait in small (a popular form if one looks at the Society of Artists catalogues). The Irish artist was allowed to show character and sometimes later in the century to place his sitter in an unconventional setting, but generally speaking pose, costumes, etc. had to conform to upper-class ideals of propriety as was of course the case elsewhere. Robert Hunter is an Irish artist who exhibits this well. For instance informality was allowed in Hunter's portrait of his friend, Samuel Madden, where Madden is *en déshabillé* wearing a cap, but this was altered when the picture was engraved. Then Madden appears in a wig and more formally clothed. When Hunter painted a series of portraits of the young Lord Kingsborough and his brothers and sisters in the late 1740s, the men are shown carrying guns but dressed for the drawing-room, though later in his career when he paints a member of the La Touche family resting when out shooting (NGI), the sitter is more suitably dressed and altogether more at ease sitting on the ground. Hunter's group of Sir Robert Waller and his son (NGI) where the boy, standing on the table, is pulling books out of the bookcase, is a curious stiff conversation piece in which the relationship of the remonstrating father and his son is not convincingly shown. It is almost as though Sir Robert asked for a 'playful' theme to illustrate his son's youth and his interest in him, but would not allow the artist the freedom to convey his just irritation at his son's behaviour. As a result Sir Robert looks as though he was dancing and not stopping the boy throwing books out of the shelf.

It is obvious from the exhibition catalogues that the number of conversation pieces was small. As they were cheap it seems odd that they are not more commonplace and that they are not found in the collections of professional families where their price should have made them popular. One possible explanation is that despite the political ties with England, it was to the Continent that Irish patrons looked when considering artistic matters in the first half of the century. Even as early as 1700 three Irishmen, Howard, Trench and Jervas, were training as artists in Italy. The conversation piece, though it owes much to French art, is not a genre much employed in France or in Italy. Educated Irish sitters may have felt it brought them greater prestige to maintain a difference from English modes. In this case the conversation piece would never have become part of their artistic consciousness. It is notable that French and Italian engravings are the source of the plasterwork which Irishmen patronized and that the executants were sometimes Italian or French; the Dublin Society Drawing School employed as teachers artists trained in France, and many patrons in the first half of the century, Protestant as well as Catholic, had family links with France either as Huguenots or as 'Wild Geese'. In the second half of the century the scene changes and not only as regards pictures. The furniture made in Ireland and the plasterwork in its houses in the last quarter of the eighteenth century is much closer to English examples. By the end of the century most Irish artists visited England, many lived there and the ties with the Continent lessened, partly due to the foundation in 1768 of the Royal Academy Schools which were used by many Irish artists as a post-graduate institution after their years at the Dublin Schools, which never taught oil painting. Earlier they had gone to France, Antwerp or Italy for further training. The Napoleonic Wars must have helped finally to turn the Irish student towards England and it was only in the 1850s that they began to return to France for their education and inspiration. As a result the charming genre of the conversation piece, with its heyday in the 1730s and 40s, nearly passed Ireland by unheeded.

NOTES

[1] Strickland, Walter G., *A Dictionary of Irish Artists*, 2 vols (Dublin 1913).
[2] Pasquin, Anthony [i.e. John Williams], *Memoirs of the Royal Academicians and an Authentic History of the Artists of Ireland* (London 1796), reprinted with an introduction by R.W. Lightbown (London 1970).

SAMUEL MADDEN
AND THE SCHEME FOR THE ENCOURAGEMENT OF USEFUL MANUFACTURES

MAIREAD DUNLEVY

DR JOHNSON said of Samuel Madden that his was a name that Ireland ought to honour: the same should be said of Maurice Craig. These two northern men, separated by centuries, attended the same university, were closely associated with the Royal Dublin Society, and have both encouraged an interest in Ireland's applied arts and architecture.

That I shall give some little Method to what I shall lay before you — I shall reduce what hints I shall offer to ye Under the following heads, and be as short on all, as the Importance of the subject will allow me.

First the Necessity that there appears to me of Enlarging your Fund and the Number and Weight of your members.

2ndly the probability of getting this done if proper means be used.

3rdly the several methods and regulations necessary to be entered on when this is Accomplisht.

And lastly to what useful and excellent purpose, your Fund may be applied when it is thus Enlarg'd.

Such was the introduction made by the Rev. Dr Samuel Madden in his letter to the Dublin Society, 23 June 1739, a letter which he said was prompted by the Society's uncomfortable financial state, as well as by its ambition to improve Ireland's economic well-being, its agriculture, 'new Arts' and 'methods of Industry'. This was required, he said, because

a great part of this kingdom languishes under a long habit of sloth and sleep (but the Society) will in the best manner Rouze them from their long dreaming Indolence and not only open their Eyes, but direct and Employ the hands of our people and at the same time, by shortening the Stages, and levelling the Roads of the Laborious, prevent the Industrious part of our Natives from spending double toil and pains in performing half work for quarter profit by distributing all to their proper Classes.[1]

The Rev. Dr Samuel Madden (1686-1765) inherited his family's estates at Manor Waterhouse near Newtownbutler, Co. Fermanagh, in 1703 and on being ordained became, at first, rector of Galloon and then of Drummully, parishes serving Newtownbutler and its vicinity. Madden was a man of his time at a period when many gentlemen sought methods of developing 'this poor country of ours'. Men of his ilk founded the Dublin Society in 1731 with the aim of improving husbandry, manufactures and other Useful Arts. At this time too Arthur Dobbs, Thomas Prior, George Berkeley and Jonathan Swift contributed pamphlets on the country's economic development, generally promoting a protectionist attitude.

Madden was a man of many interests and has a right to be remembered for each of them. His literary contributions, opinions on land management, absentee landlords and education, as well as his proposals for the training of Ireland's artists and sculptors and the encouragement of manufactures, have all been considered elsewhere.[2] Madden's contributions were such, though, that they can stand further attention. His premium scheme for manufactures, for example, is of interest since, amongst other things, it shows the wide variety of small industries existing and being encouraged in Ireland at that time and the methods in which new expertise was found for them.

THE DUBLIN SOCIETY

On its foundation in 1731 The Dublin Society addressed itself to the difficulty of making Ireland's manufactures more competitive, and as early as 18 September of that year agreed that their Committee of Arts should convene once a fortnight and, taking the advice of artists, tradesmen and husbandmen, find out

what foreign improvements may be introduced here, or new Inventions set on foot, by what means and at what Expense; and that Models of Instruments of every art be procured, more especially of such instruments which are made use of in other countries and not known here, and of such complicated Engines whose use and formation cannot easily be discovered by the figure thereof.[3]

This became the accepted development plan for some time. The practical approach which the Society adopted was such that they quickly requested dissertations on dyestuffs and on submission of a full account on saffron, their Committee of Experiments grew the plant and built a kiln for it. To obtain new information on madder they sent a questionnaire to madder-growers in Holland and then ordered madder sets from there. They continued this support through the 1740s by offering premiums regularly for dyeing cloth scarlet, black and saffron.

In a similar practical manner the Committee considered the mining and refining of silver (1732), addressed themselves to selecting new spinning-wheels (1734 and 1740), and experimented with a different mould material for pewterers (1734), with local materials for glass (1738) and with uses for Irish clay (1741). They examined numerous ideas considered to have potential for the linen industry – going even as far as to erect a damask broad-loom in the Parliament House (1741). In the same year they paid Alexander Atkinson to travel to Lancashire and bring back 'several instruments made use of at Manchester in the Fustian Manufacture'. On his return Atkinson was given further funding to carry on his business, seemingly because he discovered their new methods of spinning, weaving and cutting fustian (coarse twilled cloth of cotton and linen) as well as 'recipes for dying Fustians which we were strangers to here, and kept a Secret there and that he is now ready to put every part of that Art in execution'.[4] This enthusiasm of the Society members for encouraging industry is not surprising since the range of new industries introduced in the seventeenth century must have tempted hope for a development which would parallel that taking place in Britain. The increase in population and in general prosperity also created a market for many of these products. The change in industrial approach of the late seventeenth century can be seen in, for example, the removal of glass factories, which probably concentrated on the production of bottles, from forest to port locations, due partly to the change from charcoal to coal as fuel. About that time, too, the preference for glass rather than leather bottles is reflected in the emergence of a new bottle shape. The discovery of the recipe and method of manufacture for flint or crystal glass in the late seventeenth century gave rise to a demand for that robust, clear table glass which local manufacture attempted to satisfy. The development of an industrial approach is seen also in the establishment of the first factory for the mass-manufacture of white ceramics – that making blue and white delft (tin-glazed earthenware) in imitation of Chinese porcelain and of Dutch Delft.

In 1733 the Society asked their Committee to examine the progress being made by a number of manufacturers and how they could be helped. We will ignore here their study of agriculture, horticulture, silviculture and the production of textiles and sugar but look at the smaller industries[5] because the Belfast pottery which seems to have opened in 1698 may have existed only up to about 1724, yet delftware was becoming increasingly fashionable. The glass factories in Dublin and Waterford were in an infant state. There was a new approach to ironwork design also as the court of Louis XIV and followers of William III gave preference to a much lighter, cleaner and often more vigorous design in metalwork. The increase in the use of paper for print as well as for wallpaper would have recommended attention there too. As lace was so important as a trimming on both men and women's clothing at that time it is not surprising that the Society encouraged it, particularly in charity schools.

The Dublin Society would seem to have attempted to identify industries worthy of support and studied their specializations and requirements. They took particular interest in imported items which were either not made here at all, or whose manufacture was considered capable of improvement. Because of lack of funds, though, they were unable to give much practical support to any of these industries.

MADDEN'S PREMIUMS

The importance of the Dublin Society's project, but the general failure to achieve much, may have prompted Madden to a practical involvement in the country's development. The plan which he recommended in *A Letter to the Dublin Society,* signed 23 June 1749, was a system of monetary rewards for achievement. This incentive, he claimed, would unleash 'a force of Energy [which would] make us another sort of people than to our sorrow (and I wish I could not add to our Reproach) we now appear'. The proposal was similar to that which he had made earlier at Trinity College in which he argued that the incentive for study, which students would appreciate best, was a monetary award.[6] Madden's attitude to the nation's well-being was similar to that held by the Society; his aim being to encourage manufacture here and to make the country self-reliant. He, however, counselled gentlemen against starting new industries themselves as that was 'too low and hazardous a risk', but just as the Society had said previously, he recommended that they attract workmen from abroad through 'moderate and settled' annual salaries as well as 'premiums to help them settle and introduce their business here'. It was such experts, he claimed, who would 'help skilled Irish people to increase their skills and improve their industry'. In this context he recommended that the glass bottle industry should look for skilled hands in Great Britain or Holland, that workers from Birmingham and other places in the north of England be brought over to set up 'new-style iron works for tools, pots, knives, scythes and hardware', and that teachers for lace schools should be sought in Stony Stratford, Salisbury, Newport Pagnell, Brussels and Mechlin. On the other hand he recommended that much could be learnt in England about flint glass production. He was less specific when dealing with the delft and paper industries, saying that they needed the injection simply of more able hands and 'improvements'. Apart from these industries which the Society had identified as those which already upset our balance of payments, Madden was able to add others because, in the interim, there had been considerable enthusiasm about the furnishing of the new Parliament House. Because of this he suggested that there were trades which were

so little thought on in England, that it seems left Entirely open for us, and might with a little care and Expense be nurst up here to very considerable advantage and the Employing of Many idle hands, who would soon enable us to Export large quantities.

In this context he considered tapestry, 'flowered carpets', as well as silk and gilt leather for wall-hangings. An underlying point which he made regularly was the need to develop our coalfields and to improve the method of transporting that coal to the industrial centres.

Madden offered to give £130 per annum for life if the Society collected £500 a year for premiums for the encouragement of 'Sundry Arts, Experiments and Several Manufactures not yet brought to perfection in this Kingdom'.[7] He proposed that the Society should distribute the premiums in such a way as to help particular manufactures and then when they were strong enough, to move the support to another. Madden collected the money himself and, in spite of at least one dramatic interview in which an unwilling subscriber was naked on Madden's arrival,[8] yet he was able to report in February 1739 that he had secured £900 (including his own contribution). He was relieved of this money-collecting task later when William Hawker, who seems also to have worked for the Parliament House, was appointed to collect subscriptions.[9] Hawker's remuneration was sixpence in the pound for the first £300 and one shilling and sixpence (7.5p) for the remainder. Two members also went surety for him to the value of £1000.

On 13 December 1739 Samuel Madden laid his plan for the improvement of the Dublin Society scheme before its Board. On the following 31 January the Secretaries reported that he had followed that with his financial offer and so a committee was established to select the manufactures 'not yet brought to perfection in this Kingdom', yet fit to be encouraged. At the meeting of 27 March 1740 it was ordered that the proposed scheme and a list of selected commodities be advertised in newspapers. On 6 November 1740 applications were received from John Chambers, World's End (for delft), Elizabeth Roberts, Lazer's Hill (lace), Elizabeth Atkinson, The Coombe (fustian), Richard Brennan, Cavan Street (crêpe), Samuel Emery, New Copper Alley (glass and watch-spring maker), and Stephen Jovamer, Anglesea Street (lamp black).

Madden, while contributing annually and exercising considerable control, was not a member of the Board and, indeed, not even a member of the Society until 1759.[10] His influence and the respect held for him in the Society, though, was great. It was obviously he who directed that his and the Society's premiums were kept separate. Madden exercised direct influence on painting, sculpture, lace and some industries – those for which his money was employed. Although the first three mentioned remained constant, he varied the others annually, to the extent that, for example, in 1744, there were premiums for the importation of the best stallion, bull and heifer.

INITIAL DIFFICULTIES

The Society made every effort to ensure that there would be no misappropriation of the funds within their establishment and that the money was spent wisely. A panel decided on the premiums and judged the standards of applications and from 1741 Thomas Prior frequently went to check the work places themselves. The Society experienced initial difficulties, though, because they ambitiously sought 'inventions'. As a result Francis Coleman's claim for making thimbles in 'his own way' was discounted as it was contended that he had been making them in that way for a decade.[11] On the other hand Richard Brennan's application for crêpe weaving was rejected because it was not sufficiently well established on 18 June 1741, but in April 1743 it suffered the same fate – then because it was not an invention of the previous year. There were other unusual judgments.

About 1735 John Chambers established the White Pothouse at the World's End (Store Street region), the site which became the Dublin pottery area for fine ceramics for the following decades. He imported skilled workmen and, on the evidence of two plates of his manufacture still extant, would seem to have attracted those men from Liverpool. Chambers claimed that he made blue and white defltware for general use and for apothecaries which was 'equal in goodness in every respect to any imported from Delft or England and will be sold 25 per cent cheaper than any imported from abroad'.[12] Although Chambers applied for 'encouragement' from the Society in February 1739, for financial aid from the Dublin

Parliament in November 1739 and for a Madden premium in January 1740, he received nothing.

However, on 19 November 1741 the premium of £10 was given to William Bright of Charles Street 'for making the best set of Earthenware consisting of nine Dishes and three dozen plates'. The following spring there were two contenders: William Lake whose set was considered to be of a good colour, and the same William Bright who won the premium because of the quality of the pieces.[13] Bright was the proprietor of the delft-ware pottery in Rostrevor but Lake does not seem to have been involved in any pottery!

Another surprise is the failure to give 'encouragement' to John Brooks.[14] His boast that he introduced 'the art of Graving into this Kingdom' was in his character but his claim that he had an improvement which was an 'invention' may have had substance. Brooks tried vainly to have this method of printing on enamel or ceramics accepted in his native city and on failure there, tried also in Birmingham, 1751. His innovation, which was of major importance for the cheap and uniform decoration of products, received little attention until he was employed in the Battersea (London) enamel factory in 1753. Credit for the discovery is often now given to John Sadler of Liverpool, whose first recorded use of transfer-printing was in 1756.

Another enigma is the claim for the invention of making twilled stock-ings. In January 1740 Nicholas Bean's application was considered 'not of sufficient importance to be put up for the Premium'. In April 1741 Michael Bean – a man who from an earlier application would seem to have been an investor rather than a hosier – won the Madden premium for the 'invention of weaving rib'd stocking in the twilled way', i.e. twilled 'on the inside to render them more serviceable' and a method in which the stocking fitted the leg better. There seems to be an injustice in that Bean's modification of the stocking-frame machine is equated with a contemporaneous invention in France which produced fancy hose stitches.[15] The Society, however, appreciated that there was some importance in Michael Bean's modifica-tion and voted eighteen pounds to him to purchase and adjust a stocking-frame. It was directed that he should be allowed to use the frame for a 'month or two' so that the Society could judge the 'usefulness of the Invention'. Obviously satisfied, they gave him an extra £7 a fortnight later on condition that he

carry on the said Manufacture in this Kingdom for Seven Years if he so long lives and instruct such Stocking weavers in said Art as shall be recommended to him by the Society at any time from and after Michelmas next.[16]

Whether Michael Bean acted as a hosier himself or employed an artifi-cer is less important here than the fact that the Society was active in the supervision of his work.

The style of supervision might be judged from that exercised on Arthur Atkinson (fustian-maker) mentioned above and on John Roche, producer of 'Birmingham' or brass ware. In the latter case the committee met in

Roche's home and workhouse on Usher's Quay, at 11.00 a.m on 6 April 1741, and

saw his men go through the whole work of making Buckles, Buttons etc. from mixing the Metal in Furnace and Casting them and after Stamping, filing the edges, drilling, Polishing and finishing the same, that he has furnished himself with all the Instruments and Conveniencys from Bermingham and brought with him several Workmen and Apprentices.

They were so satisfied with his work that in spite of opposition from importers they continued to support him for a few years and recommended his wares to 'all Agents of Regiments or Others who have occasion for large quantities of Bermingham Wares'. They made the usual proviso, though, that he had to employ apprentices and that he had to carry on the business 'effectually' for some years.

PARLIAMENTARY INVOLVEMENT

The premium scheme was well established within a few years and considered an undoubted success. The increase in generous subscriptions made to the fund annually and in the applications for awards meant a substantial growth in the number and range of premiums offered. Through this system the Society influenced not only the development of industry but also design attitudes as, for example, lace-makers were directed to copy Brussels, Mechlin and Point (French and Italian) lace, 1744, while the delft-ware factory, 1750, was directed away from the staid styles of Chinese porcelain – a ware which was more easily available then – and towards the more colourful wares of Rouen and 'Burgundy' as well as Dutch Delft.

The frequent publication of lists of imported items which could be made here must have raised public awareness and may have been the reason for the production of such novel items as Spanish leather dressing (1742), 'warm and fine' stockings made of a combination of beaver fur and Spanish wool (1743), and in 1744 the introduction of premiums for gooseberry, currant, cowslip, elderflower and elderberry wines, and incentives for destroying Norway rats, discovering mines, making beaver hats and producing plans for buildings.

The success of the scheme is shown in that in 1746 the Lord Lieutenant, Lord Chesterfield, gave the Society an annual grant of £500 and in 1761 the Irish Parliament made their first large annual grant. This was £2000 to increase the premiums for agriculture and manufactures and £10,000 for distribution among petitioners for premiums. The Society established a large committee, one of whom was Samuel Madden, to adjudicate on the distribution of those premiums.[17] The petitions made give an idea of the development of the style of industries which we have been following. Although the system of importing expertise had been shown to have expensive drawbacks the petitioners were careful to emphasize that they continued the practice and that they employed apprentices. The industries in general, though, were larger and seemingly well established. The range was great, varying from gold and silver lace manufacture to carpets and japanned tin. Although some industries blamed their weakness on the emergence of combinations, there were others, such as that of window and bottle glass, which were so market-orientated that they could change styles according to fashion and public demand and were able to compete effectively with imports.

NOTES

[1] Samuel Madden, *A Letter to the Dublin Society on the Improving their fund and the Manufactures and Tillage of Ireland* (Manor Waterhouse 1739).

[2] James Meenan and Desmond Clarke (eds), *The Royal Dublin Society 1731-1981* (Dublin 1981), pp.5-9; J.C. Beckett, 'Literature in English 1691-1800' in T.W. Moody and W.E. Vaughan (eds), *A New History of Ireland*, Vol. IV, *Eighteenth Century Ireland* (Oxford 1986), pp.424-67; L.M. Cullen, *The Emergence of Modern Ireland 1600-1900* (London 1981), pp.46-9; John Turpin 'The School of Ornament of the Dublin Society in the 18th Century', *Journal of the Royal Society of Antiquaries of Ireland,* Vol. 116 (1986), pp.40-2.

[3] I am deeply indebted to Mary Kelleher, Librarian of The Royal Dublin Society, for her generosity with information and for the help which she and all of the library staff kindly gave me in the preparation of this article. It is based on information taken from the Society's minute books.

[4] Minute Book of The Dublin Society, 21 May and 18 June 1744.

[5] *Ibid.,* 5 July 1733.

[6] Samuel Madden, *A Proposal for the General Encouragement of Learning in Dublin College* (1731), pp.9-14.

[7] Minute Book of the Dublin Society, 31 January 1739.

[8] Samuel Burdy, *The Life of the late Rev. Philip Skelton with some curious anecdotes* (1792), p.38.

[9] Minute Book of The Dublin Society, 11 December 1740.

[10] I am grateful to Mary Kelleher for this information prior to publication.

[11] Minute Book of The Dublin Society, 4 February 1741.

[12] M.S.D. Westropp, *Irish Pottery and Porcelain, General Guide to the Art Collections,* National Museum of Ireland (1935), pp.10-11.

[13] Minute Book of The Dublin Society, 25 March and 1 April 1742.

[14] *Ibid.,* 14 January and 4 February 1941.

[15] William Felkin, *A History of the Machine-Wrought Hosiery and Lace Manufactory* (London 1867), pp.84-92.

[16] Minute Book of The Dublin Society, 14 May 1741.

[17] *The Proceedings of the Dublin Society on the several Petitions of sundry Manufactures and others and the Disposition of the sum of Ten Thousand Pounds, committed to their determination by Order of the Rt. Honble. the Knight, Citizens and Burgesses in Parliament assembled.* Session 1761-2, Royal Dublin Society manuscript.

1898 Lace

THE ORMONDE INVENTORIES
1675-1717

A STATE APARTMENT AT KILKENNY CASTLE

JANE FENLON

Fig. 1 – Francis Place, Kilkenny Castle and City, Co. Kilkenny from Wind Gap Hill, 1690 (detail), ink and wash on paper, 27.5x64cm (National Gallery of Ireland)

'IT WAS intended as a beautiful Palace and such it must have been about 30 years since',[1] wrote a visitor to Kilkenny Castle in the mid-eighteenth century. The 'beautiful Palace' was the seventeenth century residence of James Butler, 1st Duke of Ormond, which had been allowed to fall into decay. Several views of Kilkenny, particularly those by Francis Place, provide a fair record of the appearance of the Castle at that time. Some details of the interiors are contained in a series of inventories which were taken at the Castle during the period 1675-1717.[2] Today, little remains of that building, just the north-facing wall, some of the western boundary wall and portions of the original thirteenth-century towers. The rest is mainly of nineteenth century construction. The central block, now a bleak and empty shell,* occupies approximately the same site as an earlier structure which housed the principal apartments. Of the splendid interiors, there is no trace. Any attempt, therefore, to locate the principal apartments, in particular a State Apartment, has to be made with evidence gathered from illustrations and various documentary sources.

Place's view of the Castle, taken from the south-east (fig.1), was executed in 1690, just two years after the death of the 1st Duke of Ormond. In this drawing a rambling collection of buildings of various ages can be seen, sit-

* The OPW has commenced an extensive programme of restoration on this building.

Fig. 2 – The Courtyard at Kilkenny Castle, *c*.1814
Miller/Robertson Papers, Royal Society of Antiquaries of Ireland
watercolour on paper, 13x21cm actual drawing (RSAI)

uated on high ground to the west of the river Nore. Ranged around four
sides of a trapezoidal space, several of these buildings can be identified. In
the centre of the picture stands the Waterhouse, No.1 in the background
and to the right, on the northern boundary, is the central block with dorm-
ers and tall chimneys on the roof No.2 This central block penetrates a
square Towerhouse structure No.3 and adjoins the north-east circular
tower, No.4. A Great Hall, No.5 on the eastern boundary abutting the
square Towerhouse,[3] and several other buildings, are shown on the slope
going down the riverbank No.6. To the left and behind the Waterhouse on
the southern boundary, stands a double towered Gatehouse No.7. The
large south-west tower No.8 is shown with dormers, tall chimneys and a
balustrade on the roof. (The north-western circular tower cannot be seen in
this drawing by Place, as it is obscured by the western gable end of the
central block.)

As the central block and flanking circular towers housed the principal
apartments, it is desirable to look closely at these buildings. A more
detailed view of the central block (before it was altered in the nineteenth
century) is available in a drawing of the courtyard of the Castle, executed in
1814.[4] This drawing (fig.2) clearly shows a three-storied building with
dormers in the roof, adjoining the north-west tower, with a 'new' gatehouse
in the western boundary wall and to the left, the south-west tower. Another
view of the Castle of approximately the same date (fig.3) taken from the
eastern bank of the river, shows the gable-end of the central block, where it
joins the north-east tower. In the background, is a section of the west wall
and among the trees on the left is the south-west tower.

A major programme of renovation and refurbishment was begun at the
Castle *c*.1661,[5] at the time of the Duke's return to Ireland as Lord

Lieutenant. During this phase of building, work continued at the Castle for over twenty years and a veritable army of craftsmen was employed and lived there. Rooms were provided for stone carvers, painters, gilders, carpenters, upholsterers and various other skilled men.[6] Prior to this renovation, the central block had been essentially an Elizabethan building, with interiors organized in the old-fashioned manner of the previous generation. An inventory taken there in 1630 names a Great Chamber, a Gallery and a Drawing Chamber among the rooms listed.[7] By mid century a new form of interior planning, which Girouard calls 'the Formal Plan',[8] had become popular. In keeping with this, efforts were made to formalize the existing structure and the former room arrangements were adapted to suit the needs of the new planning. Apartments were the key to formal planning and a State Apartment was the most important feature of this. Such an apartment would have been planned to conform to contemporary etiquette, for the reception and housing of important visitors, with a strong emphasis on the processional character of the rooms. For this, a sequence of four or five rooms, consisting of a State Bedroom, preceded by two or three rooms and followed by one or two small closets, situated on the first floor, would be required. As this formalizing arrangement had to be made within the constraints of the older structure at Kilkenny, it will be seen that there were difficulties in accommodating the required sequence of rooms on one floor.

According to information available from inventories taken at the Castle in the late seventeenth century, the most lavishly furnished rooms were to be found mainly on the first floor of the central block. Because of their distinctive shapes the position of two of these rooms can still be identified. Both were situated in the flanking circular towers: the Great Dining Room

Fig. 3 – Kilkenny Castle, *c.*1814
Miller/Robertson Papers, Royal Society of Antiquaries of Ireland
pen and ink on paper, 37x43cm, actual drawing (RSAI)

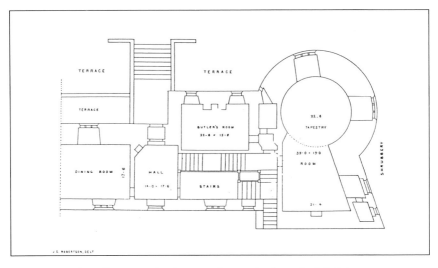

Fig. 4 – Kilkenny Castle, diagram of NE angle, drawn by J.G. Robertson
copied from an old drawing once in the possession of the Marquis of Ormond.
This is a confusing diagram as it shows two floor levels (see fig. 5)
reproduced from JRSAI, Vol. 2, 1852-3 (RSAI)

was in the north-east tower a little below the first floor level of the central
block, and the Duchess's Closet in the north-west tower at slightly above
first-floor level. Several visitors to the Castle made comments which have
proved useful in locating these rooms. John Dunton, who was there in
1686,[9] writes of the Great Dining Room, '...the Doctor had me up one pair
of stairs, where, on the left hand, was the room where the Duke of
Ormond dines; it was high roofed, very large and hung all round with gild-
ed leather'. Later, in the eighteenth century, another visitor describes this
room as '...a fine Dining room of a circular form.'[10] These observations sug-
gest a circular dining room, hung with leather, up two flights of stairs. On a
diagram taken from an old drawing (fig.4) the Great Staircase (prior to the
nineteenth century remodelling) can be seen rising from a 'hall', to a circu-
lar room in the north-east tower. An inventory of 1684 confirms the location
and the leather wall-coverings, when it lists in a sequence of rooms off the
great Stairs... 'the Great Dining Room, hung and fitted with gilt leather'.[11]
Also remarked upon was the Duchess's Closet, 'The principal bed chamber
with a beautiful octagonal closet, has been the finest I ever saw.'[12] This
octagonal shape of the Duchess's Closet can be seen on a floor plan of the
nineteenth century remodelled Castle[13] where a room, situated in the north-
west tower, is still called by that name. Several inventories include the
phrase, 'the staircase from the Alcove to her Grace's closet', describing a
definite link between these two rooms, which in turn would suggest that
the Alcove, a large, lavishly furnished room, containing a bed, was in fact
the 'principal bedroom'.[14] The staircase was required to bridge the gap
between the Alcove situated at the western end of the first floor and the
Duchess's Closet in the north-west tower. Also, from the inventories, we

learn that a Drawing Room always preceded the Alcove. A sketch plan of the Castle (fig.5) shows the suggested position of these two rooms and their relationship to the Duchess's Closet in the flanking tower; also shown is the Great Dining Room situated in the north-east tower. Thus far it has been possible to locate four rooms in sequence and mainly on the first floor. Such a combination of rooms could be said to fulfil the requirements for a State Apartment and an examination of their furnishings may help to to verify this.

As a State Bedroom was the principal prerequisite of a State Apartment, it is necessary to establish that the Alcove, which was the 'principal bed chamber', served this function. An inventory taken in 1684 records that splendid bedchambers for the ducal pair already existed at the Castle.This would certainly indicate that the Alcove was reserved for important visitors, thus fulfilling the main requirement of a State Bedroom. Several other features of the Alcove serve to confirm this opinion. Firstly, the lavish furnishings; the bed, in a curtained alcove, was fitted with 'Furniture of green damask with a rising tester', and stood on a 'Tangier mat fitted to the alcove'.[15] A similar arrangement can be seen in the State Bedroom at Powis Castle, where the State bed is placed in an alcove, though it is also behind a balustrade in the French manner. The walls of the Alcove at Kilkenny were hung with matching green silk, 'fitted and edged with silver and gold fringe and lined with canvas'.[16] Seating was provided by 'Four elbow chairs, and eight back chairs to match with gilded frames'.[17] Secondly, as it was the third room in a sequence of four, only visitors of the highest quality would have progressed this far, given the hierarchical etiquette of the period and, very significantly, the tapestry-hung Drawing Room, which preceded it,

Fig. 5 – A sketch plan of part of Kilkenny Castle in the seventeenth century, showing the central block, NE angle, and western towers. The four rooms of the State Apartment are in thick outline. The Great Dining Room was located up two flights of stairs, between the ground and first floor levels. (Drawing Fran Lyons)

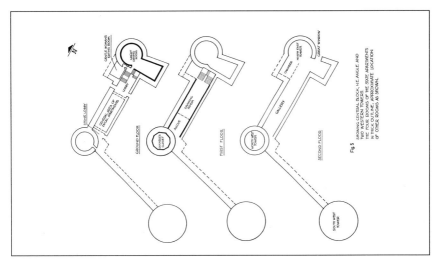

contained a chair of state. This item is described in an inventory as a 'great easy chair, fringed about with silver and gold fringe, the cushion with four tassels and edged with galoon', standing on a dais.[18] The presence of this important piece of furniture confirmed the dual function of the room as Presence Chamber/Drawing Room, preceding the State Bedroom/Alcove. Cornforth and Fowler,[19] when writing about chairs of state, make the observation that 'no other single object emphasizes so clearly the pre-18th century sense of hierarchy and the processional character of a great house'. The absence of this chair from the Drawing Room in the eighteenth century and the presence of 'a large hazard Table of Dansick Oake'[20] certainly points to a less formal attitude and lends substance to their assertion.

The Duchess's Closet was a small room, approximately eighteen feet in diameter.[21] An inventory taken in 1675[22] gives a vivid description of the contents. A couch or day bed with a carved and gilt headboard had blue damask bed furniture and the walls were hung with matching blue fringed silk. Several squab frames with cushions provided the seating. The closet housed a remarkable collection of paintings. Some sixty were listed, hanging in the window reveals and covering most of the available wall space. Pictures are also described hanging on eight pedestals ranged around the room. Most of the paintings would have been small Dutch paintings; several are described as such in the inventories. A small glass cuboard was also used to display pictures, probably miniatures. As the final room in the sequence, the closet was by this definition the most exclusive. Entrance here would have been reserved for family, the grandest visitors and intimate friends.[23] At the other end of the sequence of rooms, the Great Dining Room, which was the first room of the Apartment, was approached up the Great Staircase. Two eighteenth-century commentators are at odds about this particular feature. One says, 'The staircases are grand, and well adorned with Fresco'[24] while the other describes the stairs as 'mighty ugly'.[25] The entrance to the the Great Dining Room led off the second landing on the staircase. Although furnished with large tables for dining, it is probable that this room also served as an Ante Room. Here, visitors would gather, sometimes to eat, before progressing further along the line of rooms. These four rooms, then, constituted a seventeenth-century State Apartment at Kilkenny Castle, providing as they did, a State Bedroom/Alcove, preceded by a Presence Chamber/Drawing Room and an Ante Room/Great Dining Room and followed by a closet, the Duchess's Closet.

In 1684 there were almost one hundred rooms and named passageways at Kilkenny Castle. Information from a number of sources can be used to locate apartments and rooms other than the State Apartment. Inventories provide a certain amount of useful material, but it is to the various visitors that we turn for further evidence. For instance, when John Dunton came to write about the Gallery he first of all describes how he approached it: 'We ascended two pairs of stairs which brought us into a noble gallery.'[26] A second visitor, after referring to rooms on the first floor, goes on to add that 'Over this whole wing runs a Gallery above an hundred feet long and thirty broad. There are six large Casement windows on one side; with a noble one at the end, which commands a fine prospect of the River and adjacent country.'[27] These two observations place the Gallery on the second floor. Drawings add more detail to these descriptions. The six windows referred to can be counted, on the second floor of the central block, in a drawing of the courtyard (fig.2). In a second drawing, of the eastern gable end (fig.3), it can be seen that the large window on the second floor does indeed overlook the river.[28] Dunton goes on to describe the Gallery in the following terms: '... for length, variety of gilded chairs and curious pictures that adorn it, [it] has no equal in the three kingdoms and perhaps not in Europe'.[29] It must, indeed, have been a spectacular sight, the walls hung with pictures in elaborate carved and gilded frames. Lighting was provided by three crystal chandeliers suspended on chains and twelve carved gilded sconces. Dunton's comments about the paintings and the gilded chairs are borne out by the inventories. In 1684[30] sixty-five paintings were listed hanging in the Gallery; as one emerged from the Great Staircase, a dozen or so of the most important full-length portraits were ranged on either side. Among these were works by Van Dyck, Lely, Wissing and John Michael Wright, the foremost portrait painters of the age. With regard to the 'gilded chairs', there were in fact over three dozen of them – all are described as having gilded frames and coverings of crimson- and yellow-figured velvet.

Downstairs on the ground floor of the main block, a series of six rooms was arranged, as Entrance Lobby, Supping Room and three-roomed Ducal Apartment, with another Lobby at the end.[31] As the Great Staircase rose from this last lobby, which was situated towards the eastern end of the house, the Ducal Apartment must therefore have been sited in the area between the central doorway and the western end of the block (see fig.5 for approximate position). It is possible that the Supping Room was situated in the north-west tower, but there is no way of confirming this. One other room, 'the Gentlewoman's Eating Room', can be placed with some accuracy off the second landing on the Great Staircase. In fig.4 it can be seen that entry to this room (called the Butler's Room on the diagram) was made through a narrow passage set in the thickness of the wall of the north-east tower. Throughout the central block and flanking circular towers there were several other chambers and closets which cannot be located with any accuracy. For instance, the Duchess's Bedchamber and Dressing Room, an apartment for the Earl of Arran's family, rooms for the senior staff, all are named but cannot be traced as yet. The large south-west tower, or 'Round' tower, which stood apart from the main buildings, housed an apartment. This was situated on the first floor. It consisted of 'a Council chamber, Ducal Closet and Dressing Room, with several other rooms on floors above and below'.[32]

The State Apartment described in this essay was constructed between the years 1661-84, at the behest of the 1st Duke of Ormond and his Duchess, Elizabeth Preston. An extensive correspondence exists between both the Duke and Duchess of Ormond and their agents and builders concerned with various aspects of building.[33] Their grandson, James Butler, 2nd

Duke of Ormond, apparently concerned himself little with Kilkenny Castle. As early as 1705 signs of neglect and dilapidation were already visible.[34] By 1717 decay had spread and an amusing comment in an inventory of that date tells of the ducal bed having 'part of the Curtains cut and carried away by Thieves'.[35] Even though existing structures at the Castle were being neglected, new buildings were still being erected there. At some time before 1709 a new Gateway was built in the west wall.[36] Also by that date the Great Hall had been demolished and a building erected on the site. This was described by Dr Thomas Molyneux as 'mighty ugly, crooked and very expensive, tho not yet finished'.[37] After the 2nd Duke was impeached for treason and a Bill of Attainder passed against him in 1715, the Irish properties were seized by the Forfeited Estates Commissioners and eventually sold back to his brother, Charles Earl of Arran. In 1721 a report describing the 'ruinous state' of the Castle was sent to the Earl by a Mr Clayton[38] who tells us that the Castle was now in the hands of two agents, who were living 'in the part near the garden' and 'in the Round Tower'. By 1748 'the beautiful palace' was being compared to 'a weather-beaten ship in a storm, after a long voyage with all her cargo thrown overboard'.

ACKNOWLEDGMENTS – My thanks to those who encouraged me to write this article, especially Paddy Friel OPW, Kilkenny Castle, and Desmond Fitz-Gerald, Knight of Glin. Also, to Siobhain de hOir, of the RSAI, Ann Simmons of the Irish Architectural Archive and Adrian Le Harivel NGI for their help in obtaining photographs. Fran Lyons of 'Stylos' for the drawing; the staff of the National Library of Ireland, and the MSS Department, Library of TCD. To Edward McParland, Catherine Marshall, Noreen Casey and Anne Crookshank for all their help and comments.

NOTES

* Spelling of the name Ormond. The original title was Earl of Ormond, when the Dukedom was conferred in 1660 it was as Ormonde. However, the first Duke always signed documents Ormond and is referred to as Ormond. The spelling Ormonde does not come into common usage until the eighteenth century.

[1] Wm. R. Chetwood [in NLI catalogue], *A Tour through Ireland by Two English Gentlemen* (1748), p.179.
[2] All of the inventory material quoted is taken from the following manuscripts. At the National Library of Ireland, Ms.2552 [1630], Ms.2527 [1675], Ms.2554 [1684], Ms.2524 [1705], Ms.2525 [1713]. At the Public Record Office, Kew, London, FEC 1/876. As several of the inventories are made up of separate documents, the pagination is confused. I have not given page references to the NLI material. There is no published index to any of the inventories.
[3] Similar architectural arrangements of square towerhouse, with abutting Great Hall, were to be found in other Butler properties, such as Cloughgrenan and Kilcash.
[4] Figs 2 & 3 are from the Miller/Robertson papers, RSAI It seems that George Miller was employed by William Robertson to make some of the drawings in this collection. A number of these were eventually engraved and used in *Antiquities and Scenery of the County of Kilkenny*, published in 1851, by James George Robertson, a relative of William Robertson. Figs 2 & 3 are not by the same hand. I am indebted to Mary Pat O'Malley for information about these drawings.
[5] Letter regarding repossession and condition of Kilkenny Castle and other properties, from

Sir William Flower and John Bruden to the Duchess of Ormond in 1660. H.M.C., Ormonde Papers, Vol. 3. N.S. p.6. It is unlikely that work began at the Castle before this date. A series of letters dated *c.*1681, in Ms.2417, NLI, is concerned with various projects still going on at the Castle.

[6] NLI, Ms. 2527 (1675).

[7] NLI, Ms. 2552 (1680).

[8] See Mark Girouard, *Life in the English Country House*, Chapter 5, 'The Formal House 1630-1720', for a comprehensive study of this subject.

[9] John Dunton's *The Life and Errors of John Dunton* (incl. Dunton's Conversation in Ireland) (London 1818), p.592.

[10] Chetwood, *op.cit.,* Note 1 above, p.186.

[11] NLI, Ms. 2554 (1684).

[12] Chetwood, *op.cit.,* Note. 1, above, p.186.

[13] The Irish Architectural Archive has a series of nineteenth-century drawings, which show floor plans of the remodelled interiors of Kilkenny Castle. The Duchess's Closet, located in the north-west tower, is clearly marked on a plan of the drawing-room floor.

[14] NLI, Ms. 2554 (1684).

[15] *Ibid.*

[16] *Ibid.*

[17] *Ibid.*

[18] Ormond had access to three 'great chairs', from the Great Wardrobe in London. NLI, Ms.2326, Doc.1439, Great Wardrobe London, 1661. This document is part of the Ormonde Papers, and is a note of various items from the Great Wardrobe in London which lists among other items, 'three clothes of Estate ... and to each of them and [sic] great chair, two high stools, one foot stool and two cushions', for use 'for his Majestie's Service in the Kingdom of Ireland in the year 1661'.

[19] J. Fowler and J. Cornforth, *English Decoration in the Eighteenth Century* (London 1974), p.58.

[20] NLI, Ms.2524 (1705).

[21] This measurement is given in fig.4, and as the closet retained its octagonal shape within the massive walls, it is reasonable to suggest that the size remained as it had been in the seventeenth century.

[22] NLI, Ms.2527 (1675).

[23] Girouard, *op.cit.,* at note 8, pp.145-7, for a discussion on the subtleties of etiquette associated with a visitor's progress along the sequence of State Rooms.

[24] Chetwood, *op.cit.,* at note 1, above p.186.

[25] TCD. Ms. 883/2, p.92.

[26] Dunton, *op.cit.,* at note 9, above p.593.

[27] Chetwood, *op.cit.,* at note 1, above p.186.

[28] This window is also mentioned in the inventories. Paintings in gallery are described as hanging to the north or south of the great window.

[29] Dunton, *op.cit.,* at note 9, above p.593.

[30] NLI, Ms.2554 (1684).

[31] This lobby was situated inside the central door, that can be seen in fig.2. In 1684 the Ducal Apartment consisted of three rooms, referred to as His Grace's Drawing Room, Bed Chamber and Closet.

[32] Public Record Office, Kew, London, FEC1/876, pp.11-18. This large tower had 14 or15 named rooms and passages. (The number listed changes from inventory to inventory.)

[33] This correspondence is to be found in both manuscript and published sources. NLI, Ms.2417, Ducal letters, Ms.2503, extensive correspondence of Duchess of Ormond with Captain George Mathews, 1668-73. H.M.C., Ormonde Papers, N.S., Vols 3, 6, 7. See also note 5 above.

[34] NLI, Ms.2524 (1705).

[35] Public Record Office, Kew, London, FEC 1/876, p.2.

[36] *Op.cit.,* at note 24, above p.92. Dr Thomas Molyneux.

[36] *Ibid.,* p.92.

[37] NLI, Ms. 2512, p.7.

[38] Chetwood, *op.cit.,* note 1, above p.179.

Joseph Edmonson engraving (details)

ENMORE CASTLE

MARK GIROUARD

In 1764 Joseph Edmondson, who combined the occupations of herald and coach-painter, published *Baronagium Genealogicum,* containing the family trees of the English peerage in five folio volumes. Page after page of somewhat dubious genealogy was interlarded, in the case of some of the families, with full-page coats of arms engraved at the expense of the holder of the titles. In the whole run of five volumes only one peer paid for more than this. He was John Perceval, 2nd Earl of Egmont, an Irish Earl whose right to feature in the volumes derived from his grant of an English title, as Baron Lovel and Holland, two years before the *Baronagium* was published. In addition to a full-page engraving, in the same style as all the others, he paid for a double-page spread 17 by 20 inches in size. The centre of this impressive display was occupied by a hatchment containing 32 quarterings. Around it were arranged engravings of the three castles which he owned in Ireland, and three floor plans and a general view of the very large castle which he had recently completed at Enmore in Somerset.

Vanbrugh's Vanbrugh Castle at Greenwich (1717) was too small and too suburban to count as a country house. Clearwell Castle in Shropshire (1728) is barely a castle, in spite of its name. Inveraray Castle, which was started in 1745, is generally accepted as the founding father of revived country-house castles. Enmore Castle was started in 1751, and ran it a close second; and equipped as it was with proper machicolations and a working drawbridge, its castle character was rather more thoroughgoing than that of Inveraray. Because the greater part of it was demolished in the 1830s, it has been virtually ignored by architectural historians, and little written about by anybody else.[1] Its nature and background are worth resurrection.

The Perceval family had been of some importance in Somerset since the Middle Ages; by the seventeenth century they had split into two main branches, the junior one of which had its main seat at a house called Sydenham just outside Bridgwater.[2] Richard Perceval, head of the junior branch, was a protégé of the Cecil family and had a post in the English Court of Wards in Ireland. Any connection with wardship was likely to be extremely profitable, and Perceval built up a sizeable Irish estate, mainly in County Cork. He increased it by selling the greater part of his English properties, including Sydenham, and reinvesting the proceeds in Ireland.

His son, Sir Philip Perceval (1605-47), besides succeeding to his father's registrarship, became an adept at finding defects in the land-titles of Catholic Irish families, and if possible obtaining transfer of the resulting forfeited lands to himself. By 1641 he owned around 100,000 acres of good Irish land, in Cork, Tipperary and Wexford. But as a result of the Irish rebellion and the Civil War, his Irish revenues collapsed, and in 1644 he was compelled to sell the remaining Perceval estates in Somerset. His son recovered most of the Irish properties after the Restoration, and was made a baronet in 1661; in 1733 his grandson was granted an Irish title, as Earl of Egmont in the county of Cork.[3]

The first Earl of Egmont was active in both English and Irish politics. His son, the second Earl, operated mainly in England. He was an able man but not a likeable one, and he had a streak of eccentricity which prevented him from getting further than he did. Even so, he obtained a considerable reputation when, as a supporter of Frederick, Prince of Wales, he led the opposition in the House of Commons between 1748 and 1751. By the 1760s he was a supporter of the government, was Paymaster-General in 1762-3, and First Lord of the Admiralty in 1763-6. He died in 1770, aged fifty-nine.

According to Horace Walpole, Egmont was never known to laugh, and only smiled when playing chess.[4] Samuel Johnson described him as 'a man whose mind was vigorous and active, whose knowledge was extensive and whose designs were magnificent, but who had somewhat vitiated his judgment by too much indulgence of romantic projects and airy speculations'.[5] As a young man, he is said to have had a scheme for assembling the Jews and making himself their king.[6] But his most marked eccentricities derived from his obsession with his family and with the feudal age.

He and his father collaborated on commissioning and, one suspects, paying for the two-volume *Genealogical History of the House of Yvery* by James Anderson, published in 1742. This work was concerned with all possible, and some impossible, aspects of the Perceval family and its connections, from the earliest days. Included in the second volume were engravings of the family's remarkable clutch of castles in Cork. There were three of these: Liscarroll, a great rectangular curtain-wall castle, moated and towered, which was said to date from the fifteenth or early sixteenth century; Loghort, or Lothart, a single massive tower, also moated, which probably dated from a little later; and Kanturk, which survives in ruin as one of the most impressive Elizabethan castles in Ireland. The Egmonts' pride in these is also shown by their featuring them in their titles; in addition to being Earls of Egmont, they held the title of Viscount Perceval of Kanturk; and in 1770 the second Earl's second wife was given a title in her own right, as Baroness Arden of Lothart Castle.

In England the second Earl owned or rented a house at Charlton, near Greenwich, but in 1748, after his father's death, he began to consider acquiring a sizeable English estate. In October of that year he was interested in the possible purchase of Herstmonceux Castle, from Mrs Naylor.[7] On the back of a letter to him, giving details of the size and cost, is a pencil sketch of the castle, possible by Egmont himself. It was then still relatively intact, and one of the most remarkable late medieval castles in England.

But instead of Herstmonceux Lord Egmont purchased, in 1750, the Enmore estate, near Bridgwater in Somerset.[8] The attraction of buying a medieval castle had given way to that of re-establishing a broken link and acquiring an estate in the county in which the Percevals had lived until they moved to Ireland. Enmore had never belonged to the Percevals; it had been a seat for many centuries of the Malet family, had passed by inheritance to Sir Edward Baynton Rolt, and been sold by him in 1742 to James Smyth of St Audries, from whom Lord Egmont purchased it. But it was only a few miles from Sydenham, the ancient seat of the Percevals. The estate was a sizeable one; when it was sold in 1833 (by when it may have been increased by further purchases) it amounted to 7160 acres.[9]

Lord Egmont's correspondence with his Somerset bailiff, John Gooding, survives for the years 1751 and 1752.[10] It makes clear that only a fragment of the Malet house at Enmore remained in 1750, in the form of a two-towered gatehouse, and possibly a small range adjoining; Gooding's references suggest the surviving portion of a medieval courtyard house, perhaps not dissimilar to the fragment that still exists, also incorporating a gatehouse, a few miles from Enmore at West Bower Manor. The building at Enmore was lived in by a farmer who, to begin with, was moved into a corner so that the rest could be made habitable for Lord Egmont.

But by at least June 1751, preparations were being made for a very much larger house, the building of which had probably been envisaged by Lord Egmont from the start. The result was Enmore Castle. Lord Egmont may have decided against buying a medieval castle in Sussex; but instead he built a modern castle, almost as large as Herstmonceux, in Somerset.

The new castle measured 157 feet by 150, and was built round a courtyard 86 feet by 78.[11] There were single ranges of rooms to north, south and east of the courtyard, and a double range to the west, which contained the main entrance and principal rooms. The whole building was three storeys high, including the basement, except for the towers and the courtyard half of the double western range, which rose a storey higher. Entrance to the courtyard was through the remodeled gatehouse, which was incorporated into the eastern range. The main reception rooms were up on the first floor, with access by way of a two-storey hall, opening onto the courtyard. The kitchen and main offices were on the ground floor. The basement contained cellars, servants' bedrooms, a confectionery, a laundry, and an evidence room. This last room was in the portion of the building which still exists, and contains the remains of a hypocaust heating system.

Apart from the two round towers of the gatehouse, further round towers projected from the middle of the north, west and south fronts, and the four corners of the square were raised a storey to form four square towers. All these towers were surmounted by machicolated battlements. The castle was surrounded by a dry moat, sixteen feet deep and forty feet wide. Access to the gatehouse was by a causeway and a drawbridge. The principal windows were round-headed, with simple classical mouldings. The basement was lit from the moat by rows of narrow, single-light windows. One of the building's most distinctive features was an outer ring of basement rooms, letting onto the outer side of the moat, and similarly lit. At the four corners of the moat were four sizeable L-shaped rooms, with double stone vaults supported on ranges of stone piers. These were linked along the intervening portions of the moat by narrow galleries. The moat was connected to the outside world by a tunnel, which came out in a sunken courtyard, surrounded by further underground rooms, a little to the northeast of the castle.[12] Seen from the park, the castle had, as a result, no visible offices, service wings or back entry.

The moat is always referred to as the 'ditch' in the surviving correspondence. It is called 'ditch' or 'fosse' on the engraved plans; in addition to those in Edmondson's *Baronagium* a further undated set, with minor variations from the other, was engraved separately. 'Ditch' or 'fosse' were terms used in eighteenth-century military architecture, and the dry moat, together with the vaulted rooms along it, were features adapted from contemporary usage; the simple classical detailing seems to relate, too, to the style inaugurated by Vanbrugh for military and naval buildings.

John Gooding's letters start in April 1751, and to begin with are concerned with fitting up and altering the existing building. The 'ditch' is first mentioned in an undated letter probably written in July. In August arrow-slits, described as 'spike-holes', are being inserted in the gatehouse. The 'ditches' are being dug out in September, and Gooding hopes that enough stone will be found in them to give 'a full sufficiency for your Lordship's purposes' – a hope that was not to be realized. On 4 October Robert Parsons, a Bath mason, gave a piece-work estimate for stonework, including the basement windows and the battlements. A similar undated estimate supplied by John Pilcher is interesting because of its detailed description of the make-up of the battlements:

To the Block Corbles in one stone solid 4 foot into the walls 2 foot high 14 inches wide, the Corble part for sustaining parapet to project 13 inches from the main wall pr Corbel. The openings between Corbel and Corble to be exactly 3 feet.

To the transom stones lying from Corbel to Corbel to support the Parapet wall being each stone four feet two inches long 9 inches high and 9 inches wide.[13]

The results were probably the first archaeologically correct machicolations to be built in the eighteenth century, for earlier castles have, at best, a corbel table under the battlements, with no open gap between battlement and wall. The working drawbridge at Enmore was another archaeological pioneer, and Lord Egmont was proud enough of it to have an engraving made to show its elaborate system of cogged wheels, flywheels, and counterweights.[14]

In October 1751, 'the ditch goes on but slowly at present' since 'all the hands' are employed in wheat sowing. Gooding's surviving correspondence ends in this month, but letters between Edward Thomas of Wenvoe Castle in Glamorganshire and Lord Egmont describe 'operations at Enmore' as going well in April 1752, and Lord Egmont as about to come there on 3 September 1752: 'I mean to try to amuse myself with my workmen ... the accommodation will be now worse than ever, tho' I hope in order very soon to be extremely good, for I have not at present one room in my whole house that I can use.' That is the end of the surviving correspondence in the Egmont papers. There is nothing in them to show when the castle was completed.

Its careful detailing fully justified Horace Walpole's comment on the castle and Lord Egmont: 'He mounted it round and prepared it to defend itself with crossbows and arrows against the time in which the fabric and use of gunpowder shall be forgotten.' Walpole wrote this in his *Memoirs of the Reign of George III*, in the context of Lord Egmont's unsuccessful bid for the island of St John's (today Prince Edward Island) in the Gulf of St Lawrence, Canada. This episode forms a curious tailpiece to the building of his castle.

The bid took the form of a printed Memorial 'to the King's most Excellent Majesty', made in December 1763. In it Lord Egmont asks for the grant of the island, estimated to contain two million acres, in order to establish it as a county: 'the said Earl proposes to hold the said County by the tenure of finding one thousand two hundred men for the defence of the said county'. He proposes that the island be divided into fifty Hundreds (or 'Baronies, as in Ireland'), ten to be reserved in an Earl's Demesne, the remainder to be granted to forty Lords of Hundred. Each Hundred in its turn is to be divided into twenty manors of 2000 acres, ten of which are to be reserved to the Lord of Hundred, and each of the remaining ten to be granted to ten Lords of the Manor. These in their turn are each to establish two 200-acre freeholders on their manor. All holdings are to be held by a combination of quit rent and military tenure. The four hundred Lords of the Manor and eight hundred freeholders make up the one thousand two hundred men ready for military service, on the strength of which Egmont petitioned for the grant.

Egmont envisaged that he himself would build a county town on his demesne, and each Lord of Hundred a market house on his. In addition he, as Earl or Lord of the County, would provide on his demesne, 'a large and strong Block-house, or House of Defence, mounted with ten pieces of cannon ... with a circuit round the same of three miles every way ... to be kept in hand or leased in short terms only ... for the greater security of the same ... as the capital seat of the Lord of the said county for ever, and as a place of general retreat and protection ... upon any alarm of sudden danger'. Each Lord of Hundred was to provide a smaller eight-cannon block-house on his demesne, and each Lord of the Manor a 'strong house'.

An engraving in the Egmont papers appears to show the Earl's block-house. This is, as it were, a reduced Enmore Castle with the medieval trimmings left off; a compact ten-sided building, embrasured for cannon, and surrounded by a dry moat giving access to basement rooms along its outer sides, as at Enmore.[15]

Egmont defended his proposal as follows: 'The Authority and Power being thus territorial and not hereditary and personal, by this plan; but sub-ject to complete alienation. The Benefits from both the principles of aristocracy and democracy conjoined, are preserved and reconciled – the respective evils of both avoided, and the real source of contention between these two Orders extinguished.' In the light of this statement Enmore Castle can be seen as a symbolic declaration that feudalism, suitably adapted, was still valid in Georgian England.

According to William Watt's *Seats of the Nobility and Gentry* (1779-86), 'the Castle was built by John, the last Earl of Egmont, who himself designed and planned the whole'. Certainly, no architect features in the surviving Egmont MSS, and the castle's internal planning is so unlike contemporary practice as to suggest an amateur. Some reasonably competent draughts-man must, however, have been employed to draw out the designs – perhaps the same individual as made the survey drawings of Loghort and Liscarol castles, which are now in the Egmont MSS.[16]

Several loose sheets of sketch designs for castles, also in the Egmont MSS, are probably by Lord Egmont himself.[17] They are full of variety: geo-metric castles, based on a right-angled triangle with towers added, and one square superimposed diagonally over another; a towered gatehouse, per-haps a first idea for converting the old building at Enmore; a formidable symmetrical castle, with a Rochester-style keep rising from a walled and towered courtyard; a rectangular castle with tower attached to opposite angles of the rectangle; an irregular L-shaped castle, with a fortified court-yard in the arm of the L, a little reminiscent of Vanbrugh Castle.

Had Enmore grown out of the last sketch, it would have been a pioneer in the development of the Picturesque castles of later Georgian days. Instead, Lord Egmont opted for a grand symmetrical design, a solution, incidentally, with good medieval precedents, such as at Herstmonceux, which he had considered buying, and Bodiam, which he could well have known of, for it is not far from Herstmonceux, or from Tunbridge Wells, where at one period he had a house.

Lord Egmont's own Irish castles may have made him castle-proud, but they exerted little if any influence on the planning or detail of Enmore. Nor did he show the slightest interest in the Gothic style. If he did have a pro-fessional co-adjutor in the design, he is more likely to have found him among military engineers than pioneer Gothicists.

His sketch (if it is by him) of a plan made up of two super-imposed squares is similar to the plan of the remarkable 'house at Inveraray designed in the castle style' drawn up by the military engineer Dugal Campbell in about 1744.[18] This too, like Enmore, was to have been elaborately castellated and turreted, but the detail was otherwise classical; it was designed for serious defence, with a ditch or *fossée* and a drawbridge, precautions not unreasonable in the Highlands at that date.

This resemblance may be accidental, but those between Enmore and Inveraray as it was built to the designs of Roger Morris seem too close to be coincidence. These do not relate to the main buildings, which are altogether different from each other, but to the treatment of the ditch. Both Enmore and Inveraray have an arrangement of underground rooms around the outside of the ditch; both have or had access to the ditch. On the Inveraray plans the rooms are called 'casemates', the technical term among military engineers for underground rooms letting onto a ditch; on the Enmore plan they are 'underground offices'.

Influence was clearly flowing, but in which direction? The ditch at Enmore was started in 1751; there is no specific reference to the underground offices in the 1751-2 correspondence, but ditch and rooms seem all of a piece. The ditch at Inveraray was only started, along with the casemates and the approach, in 1755, after the main structure of the castle had been finished; there must, however, have been some kind of area from the start, to give access and light to the basement. But was the final arrangement designed by Morris but executed later, or was it an improvement introduced by John Adam, who took over when Morris died in 1749? Two sets of plans at Inveraray, which show the final arrangement, have been attributed to Morris and to 1745, but seem at least as likely to have been drawn by Adam in 1754.[19]

There is a possibility, then, that the ditch at Inveraray was enlarged in 1755 in imitation of that at Enmore, but whichever way the influence was running, a second problem remains, as to how it travelled between Somerset and Argyll. There is no clear-cut link through engraved or published sources. The Inveraray plans were engraved for *Vitruvius Scoticus,* which was not published until about 1812, although the engravings were in preparation, and possibly in circulation, from at least 1733. One or the three sets of engraved Enmore plans dates from 1764, the other two are undated. Of course the original plans may have been shown around in London, or there may have been some direct contact between individuals of which we do not know; one is left with the impression that Enmore and Inveraray form two pieces in a castle-puzzle which would make more sense if other pieces came to light.

In terms of subsequent influence there can be no question as to which of the two castles was the more important. Inveraray, by translating the compact central staircase plan into neo-feudal and Gothic language, provided a formula that was to be copied or adapted for large numbers of later eighteenth- and early-nineteenth-century castles. Enmore's courtyard plan bore more relationship to medieval castles, but was inconvenient by eighteenth-century standards, and found no imitators.

The 2nd Earl's grandson, the 4th Earl, was improvident. The Enmore estate was sold in 1833, by order of the Court of Chancery, and most of the castle pulled down shortly afterwards; an Esdaile, of nearby Cothelstone, described it in a commonplace book at the time as 'a very ugly ill-built concern'.[20] All that was kept by the new owner was the western range. The machicolations were removed, the roof apparently replaced by a new one of steeper pitch, and a two-storey loggia added to the eastern front. Then or later most of the ditch and a large part of the underground rooms were demolished or filled in. The house was further reduced in size between the wars in this century. What survives today is the middle portion of the western range, the western stretch of the ditch, the underground rooms up to a point about half way across the original courtyard, and the sunken approach courtyard together with about half the tunnel. The surviving underground rooms which originally looked onto the north and south moats have, accordingly, lost their source of daylight, and become an eerie sequence of unlit spaces, exploration of which makes Lord Egmont's castle fantasies seem even more eccentric than in fact they were.

NOTES

[1] There is an inadequate notice in N. Pevsner, *Buildings of England: South and West Somerset* (1958). A fuller account will be appearing in the next Wiltshire volume of the Victoria County History. For contemporary descriptions see J. Collinson, *History and Antiquities of the County of Somerset* (1791) I, p.94; W. Watts, *Seats of the Nobility and Gentry* (1779-86), Pl. 54 and accompanying text; engraving and description in J. P. Neale, *Views of the Seats of Noblemen and Gentlemen* 2nd series (1824-9), IV; Stebbing Shaw, *A Tour in the West of England in 1788*. When I wrote the article I was unaware that Tim Mowl was working on another study of Enmore for the Autumn 1990 issue of *Architectural History*.

[2] Collinson, *op. cit.*, III, p.86.

[3] There are useful entries on Richard and Philip Perceval, and the 1st and 2nd Earl of Egmont, in the *Dictionary of National Biography*.

[4] R. Sedgwick (ed.), *The House of Commons 1715-54*, under Egmont.

[5] *Ibid.*

[6] Horace Walpole, *Memoirs of the Reign of George II* (1882) I, p.35.

[7] Letter from M. Shelley, British Library, Additional MS 47010, f.132. This is part of a very large collection of Egmont papers, mostly unrelated to Enmore.

[8] Add. MS 47011.

[9] Printed Sales particulars, Somerset County Record Office, Taunton, DD/PLE 64.

[10] Add. MS 47011.

[11] Watts, *op. cit.;* engraved in *Baronagium Genealogicum*, and two undated sets, also engraved, in British Library King's Maps XXVII, 14 and Bodleian Library, Oxford, Gen. Top. 60 f. 251-4, also Graph Maps 29, f. 23b. The Bodleian set includes elevations.

[12] The blocked tunnel appears to be intended to connect with the ditch, but is not shown on any of the surviving plans.

[13] Add. MS 47011, f.137.

[14] British Library, King's Maps XXVIII, 14 lc.

[15] Add. MS 47213 B.

[16] Add. MS 47157.

[17] Add. MS 47213 B, ff.110, 122; Add. MS 47157.

[18] Reproduced I.G. Lindsay and Mary Cosh, *Inveraray and the Dukes of Argyll* (Edinburgh 1973), Fig. 19.

[19] Lindsay and Cosh assign them to Morris, but they appear to be undated and show the bridge and main entrance door in a form which seems more likely to date from after Morris's death.

[20] Cothelstone House Estate commonplace book, 1830-67, Somerset County Record Office, Taunton, T/PH/es.

A DIRECTORY OF
THE DUBLIN FURNISHING TRADE
1752-1800

THE KNIGHT OF GLIN

Illus 1 – Mahogany George III centre table by G. O Connor, Dublin 1775.

IT IS a little ironic to offer this particular subject to Maurice in his Festschrift. I have known and admired him for so long and happily collaborated with him on a number of occasions in the past. I therefore realize only too well that it is the more formal aspects of architectural history that he really loves and writes about so lucidly. His concern with the niceties of interior decoration, Irish mahogany furniture, gilt mirrors and consoles, is, as he is the first to admit, not in the forefront of his mind. However, the furnishing trade of eighteenth-century Dublin is still a neglected field of study, so he will have to forgive this dry offering.

I have published elsewhere two studies on Dublin directories, trade labels and ephemera.[1] The list of names presented here gathers together the furniture trade, culled from a number of sources: the most important being Peter Wilson's publication which lists the merchants and traders of Dublin, first published as a pamphlet in 1751. No craftsmen's names are recorded in this first edition. In the next year, 1752, Wilson's pamphlet was bound in Watson's Almanack and included the names of craftsmen. A third edition was published in 1753, but none in 1754. From 1755 it was published annually, although the next surviving edition is that of 1761 and no copy for 1763 has yet been found. The availability of these Directories has not changed since Joseph Dennan studied them over fifty years ago.[2]

Illus 2 – Mahogany Dressing/Work Box. Private Collection, Washington D.C.
Illus 3 – Trade Label of George Austin, Cabinet Maker. He was at 7 Andrew St in 1829-30.

As this is a directory of the Dublin furnishing trade, it includes only those craftsmen associated with house furnishing. It excludes Musical Instrument makers, who have been carefully studied elsewhere.[3] Members of crafts who were associated with the actual building and decoration of houses have been omitted. Happily, a compilation of names of architects and craftsmen involved in the building trade, is well under way.[4] The following list includes, upholders/upholsterers, cabinet makers, carvers and gilders, glass grinders and looking glass sellers. The upholder was the chief agent in organizing the furnishing of a new house and it was he who often employed the other craftsmen/tradesmen. These arrangements are conveniently rehearsed in R. Campbell's *The London Tradesman* of 1747.[5] The carvers were divided into two distinct groups, chair carvers and frame carvers. The latter specialized in mirror frames, pier tables and stands, and they were often good draftsmen. By the early nineteenth century the craft of frame carver was killed off by the introduction of moulded composition and machine made decoration. The niceties and division of labour in the London furniture trade are excellently summarized by Pat Kirkham [6] and Dublin would have followed London's example. Of course, the trade in London was vast by comparison, with its population of about 675,000, in contrast to Dublin's 150,000 or so in the mid-eighteenth century. Still, as this directory of 298 names proves, Dublin had a vigorous trade, patronised by a wealthy and often extravagant nobility and gentry, whose elaborately decorated town houses and country seats were frequently being refurbished in the latest styles.

It is regrettable that so little original furniture still remains in any of these houses and connecting maker's and individual pieces is a fairly rare occurrence. However, when it has been possible to do so, I have added references to makers and their labels after each entry. This largely applies to mirrors and frames, for craftsmen's labels safely adhered to their backs, and do turn up from time to time. A very good example of a labelled piece, (though dating from after 1800, therefore we are stretching the case) is the Dressing/Work Box in a private collection in Washington D.C., that bears the label inside of 'GEO. AUSTIN CABINET MAKER. 7 St Andrew St' [Dublin]. From our complete index of furniture makers, we know that he was at this address from 1828-29 and therefore this dates the box very exactly (illus 2). His label tells us that he made portable writing desks, dressing cases, work boxes, military canteens and plate chests (illus 3). The interior has beautifully inlaid rosettes and is furnished with bottles for lavender water and eau-de-cologne, mother-of-pearl spools etc. By chance the lady of the house has left two of the keys for the coach house and butler's pantry from her chatelaine in the box.

The Directory entries have been supplemented with additional names taken from lists of the Freemen of Dublin.[7] It also includes pupils of the Blue Coat School in Dublin, where many young men were educated before being apprenticed to their trade. We have not been able to add craftsmen who went through the Dublin Society Drawing Schools as lists of these students have yet to be published.[8] An interesting addendum to these sources, are the subscriber's names to Levi Hodgson's work on measuring, published in a number of editions in the late eighteenth century.[9] This manual includes the names of many craftsmen involved in the building and furniture trade. It is hoped that the identification of these craftsmen will lead to further interest in the fine work of Dublin's furniture makers in the eighteenth century.

¹

SOURCES

[1] The Knight of Glin, 'Dublin Directories and Trade Labels', *Furniture History*, XXI (1985), pp.258-82; 'Early Irish Trade-Cards and other Eighteenth Century Ephemera', *Eighteenth Century Ireland*, II (1987), pp.115-32.

[2] Joseph Dennan, 'The First Hundred Years of the Dublin Directory', *The Bibliographical Society of Ireland*, Vol. I., No.7 (1920), pp.91-108. A useful update on this subject is Rosemary ffolliott and Donal F. Begley, 'Guide to Irish Directories', *Irish Genealogy & Record Finder*, 1981, pp.75-106.

[3] Brian Boydell, *A Dublin Musical Calendar, 1700-60*, Dublin (1989).

[4] Mary Colley, 'A List of Architects, Builders...', extracted from Wilson's *Dublin Directories 1760-1837*, *Irish Georgian Society Bulletin*, XXXIV (1992).

[5] Reprint, Newton Abbot 1969, pp.169-75.

[6] Pat Kirkham, 'The London Furniture Trade 1700-1820', *Furniture History*, XXIV (1988), pp.11-27.

[7] 'An Alphabetical List of the Freemen of the City of Dublin, 1774-1824', *The Irish Ancestor*, Nos. 1 and 2, 1983. Genealogical Office, Ms.490-93, A manuscript list of Dublin Freemen, prior to 1774. Compiled by G. Thrift. Rolf Loeber (ed), An alphabetical list of artists who worked in Dublin during the seventeenth and eighteenth centuries (covering crafts/trades such as carvers, upholsterers, cabinet makers and related trades). Copy available at the Irish Architectural Archive. This list includes names extracted from the List of Pupils of the Blue Coat Hospital, Dublin, 1675-1819. The lists of names from the sources in note 7, were compiled by Donal and Jane Fenlon.

[8] A complete list of these students up to 1800 has been compiled by Mr & Mrs Robert Raley, Wilmington, Delaware. It is as yet unpublished.

[9] *The Complete Measurer* (Dublin 1779). I am indebted to Christine Casey for the reference.

AYCKBOUM, (John Ded.), GLASS SELLER, 15 Grafton Street, 1784-1809; 16 Grafton Street, 1810; AYCKBOUM, William, GLASSWARE HOUSE, 1812-14; AYCKBOUM, Son and MURPHY, 1815; AYCKBOUM, MURPHY & Co., 1816-18; MURPHY & Co. 1819. An oval looking glass and hanging sconce, signed on the back 'John D. Ayckboum', was illustrated by Martin Mortimer in *Country Life*, 16 December 1971.

ADAMS, Philip, CARVER & GILDER, 14 Marlborough Street, 1790.

ASHWORTH, Nathaniel, CARVER, Little Booter Lane, 1768-76; 34 Little Booter Lane, 1777-9.

ATKINSON, Andrew, CABINET MAKER, 2 Bride's Alley, 1787.

BAILIE, Robert, CARVER & GILDER, LOOKING GLASS MANUFACTURER, 15 Henry Street, 1790-3. Freeman of the City of Dublin as a CARVER by service, Easter 1780.

BAKER, Thomas, CABINET MAKER, 4 Temple Lane, 1784-6.

BAMBRICK, Edward, UPHOLDER & CABINET MAKER, 50 Exchequer Street, 1787-8; 89 William Street, 1789.

BANKS, Henry, CABINET MAKER, 66 Aungier Street, 1791-1803.

BARBER, Thomas & William, JOINER & UPHOLDER, 64 South Great George's Street, 1782-9; BARBER, William, 1790-7. Subscriber to Levi Hodgson, 1779.

BARKER, James, CARVER & GILDER, 6 E. Arran Street, 1784-8.

BARKER, Robert Johnson, UPHOLDER, Stephen's Street, 1773-4; College Street, 1774; 6 College Street, 1775-9.

BARNE, John, TRUNK MAKER, 40 Fishamble Street, 1788-95; BARNES, Edward, 1796-1807.

BARNWALL, Andrew, UPHOLDER, Church Lane, College Green, 1765-74; 2 Church Lane, 1776-7.

BARRY, Edward, LOOKING GLASS SELLER, 10 Poolbeg Street, 1797.

BASTIVILLE, Richard, CABINET MAKER, 83 Capel Street, 1786; CABINET MAKER & UPHOLDER, 83 Capel Street, 1790-4.

BEATTY, Richard, CARVER, 24 Henry Street, 1768-83.

BECKFORD, William, UPHOLDER & AUCTIONEER, 1 Coppinger's Lane, 1775-8; 10 South Anne Street, 1779-80. Freeman of the City of Dublin by Act of Parliament, Midsummer 1772.

BERGAN, Timothy, UPHOLDER & AUCTIONEER, 39 Bride's Alley, 1788-92.

BIBBY, William, GLASS GRINDER, Essex Bridge, 1761-3; BIBBY, Joseph & William, GLASS SELLER, 1764-71; BIBBY, Joseph, 1772-4; 4 Essex Street, 1775. Freeman of the City of Dublin as a GLASS GRINDER by fine, Midsummer 1760.

BIDDULPH, Nicholas, UPHOLDER, Henry Street, 1766.

BLAIR, Humphrey, UPHOLDER, Upper Ormond Quay, 1762-5. Freeman of the City of Dublin as a UPHOLSTERER by service to BLAIR, Richard, Midsummer 1713. DUNBAR, Robert, Freeman of the City of Dublin as UPHOLDER by service to BLAIR, Humphrey, Midsummer 1753. BLAIR, Humphrey, UPHOLDER, master to WORTHINGTON, Joseph from 1763. BLAIR, Mark Anthony, Freeman of the City of Dublin as UPHOLDER by birth (son of BLAIR, Humphrey), Easter 1767.

BOLTON, Peter, CABINET MAKER, 5 North King Street, 1784-7.

BOOKER, Francis & John, GLASS GRINDERS, Essex Bridge, 1761-3; GLASS SELLERS, 1764-73; BOOKER, John, LOOKING GLASS SELLER, 6 Essex Bridge, 1774-86; 4 Jervis Street, 1787-9; BOOKER, John, Freeman of the City of Dublin as a GLASS GRINDER by birth (son of Francis Booker), Christmas 1760. See my 'Dublin Directories and Trade Labels', *Furniture History*, Vol. XX1, 1985., pp.261-2, and my 'Family of Looking Glass Merchants', *Country Life*, 28 January 1971, pp.195-9.

BOSWELL, Henry, CARVER & GILDER, 26 Abbey Street, 1804-10; 34 Abbey Street, 1811-16. A pupil of the Blew Coat Hospital, Dublin, 1781. Apprenticed to GALLAGHER, Richard, CARVER, 1786; CARVER & GILDER, master to CURTIS, William, 1809. Freeman of the City of Dublin as JOINER by service, Easter 1815.

BOURKE, Edward, CARVER, GILDER & GLASS SELLER, 50 College Green, 1785.

BRADSHAW, William, CABINET MAKER, 23 Aungier Street, 1790-1814; BRADSHAW, H. & Wm., 1815-30.

BRANGAN, Richard, CARVER & GILDER, 16 Lwr Ormond Quay, 1787-1815; 37 Abbey Street, 1816-21.

BRERETON, Francis, UPHOLDER, 77 Capel Street, 1785-6; 4 Coleraine Street, 1787-8.

BRICE, James, CABINET MAKER, Liffey Street, 1793-4; BRICE, Joseph, 7 Strand Street, 1795-7; 21 Aungier Street, 1806.

BROWN, George, UPHOLDER, Strand Street, 1771-4.

BURKE, Edward, LOOKING GLASS SELLER, 50 College Green, 1783-4;

BURKE, Edward, CARVER, GILDER & GLASS SELLER, 1785.

BURKE, Mary, CABINET MAKER, 3 Angelsea Street, 1784-5; BURKE, Mary & Son, 35 Henry Street, 1786-9; CABINET MAKER & UPHOLDER, 1790-6; 6 Sackville Street, 1797.

BURKE, Patrick, CARVER & GILDER, 53 Grafton Street, 1797-1800; 18 St Stephen's Green, 1801-9; 17 St Stephen's Green, 1810-14.

BURKE, William, CABINET MAKER & UPHOLDER, 6 Drogheda Street, 1790-96.

BURNETT, Peter, CARVER & GILDER, 43 Cuffe Street, 1793-5; 44 Cuffe Street, 1796-1817. Freeman of the City of Dublin as a CARVER by service with CRANFIELD, Richard, Christmas 1767.

BURNETT, Thomas, UPHOLDER, Jervis Street, 1765-9. Freeman of the City of Dublin as UPHOLSTERER by birth, Easter 1754.

BUTTERTON, Peter, UPHOLDER, George's Lane, 1766-9; Great George's Street, 1770-2; 3 South Great George's Street, 1773.

BUTTERTON, Abraham, UPHOLDER, Chequer Lane, 1769-73; Brock Lane, 1774; 27 Mary's Abbey, 1775-83. Freeman of the City of Dublin as UPHOLSTERER by service with BUTTERTON, Peter, Michaelmas 1754. BUTTERTON, Peter, a Freeman of the City of Dublin as an UPHOLDER by birth, Midsummer 1737 (son of BUTTERTON, Abraham). BUTTERTON, Abraham, Freeman of the City of Dublin as an UPHOLDER by service, Pas. 1799.

BYRNE, John, see under GRACE, Reeves, below.

CAIN, Patrick, CARVER, GILDER & HAIR CLOTH MANUFACTURER, 137 Francis Street, 1794-7.

CALDER, John, TURNER, Fisher's Lane, 1766-70.

CAMPBELL, St George, UPHOLSTERER, 25 Dawson Street, 1790-1800; 35 Grafton Street, 1801-10. Freeman of the City of Dublin as UPHOLDER by service, Michaelmas 1798.

CAREY, Anthony, CABINET MAKER, 181 Abbey Street, 1797. Freeman of the City of Dublin as a JOINER by service, Michaelmas 1792.

CARROLL, John, TRUNK MAKER, 6 Swift's Row, 1793-1811. Freeman of the City of Dublin as CARPENTER by birth, Midsummer 1797. Freeman of the City of Dublin as JOINER by birth, Michaelmas 1792.

CHARGE, Joseph, CARVER & GILDER, 30 William Street, 1786-7; 1 South Great George's Street, 1788-90; 86 South Great George's Street, 1791-4; 89 South Great George's Street, 1795-1800; 88 South Great George's Street, 1801-5; CHARGE, Monica, 89 South Great George's Street, 1806-9; 86 South Great George's Street, 1810-13; CHARGE, William, 135 Abbey Street, 1814-15; CHARGE, Monica, 137 Abbey Street, 1816-20; CHARGE, Joseph, Freeman of the City of Dublin as CARVER by Grace Especial, Easter 1789.

CLARKE, John, GLASS SELLER, Middle Liffey Street, 1764; CLARKE, John, 29 Mary Street, 1765-94. Freeman of City of Dublin as MERCHANT by Grace Especial, Christmas 1768.

CLAYTON, Christopher, LOOKING GLASS MANUFACTURER, 62 Bride Street, 1784-90.

COLEMAN, Charles, UPHOLDER, Suffolk Street, 1753. Freeman of the City of Dublin as an UPHOLSTERER by birth, Midsummer 1733. Master to MARLOW, John, as an UPHOLSTERER, 1744.

CONNER, Matthew, TRUNK MAKER, 34 Wood Quay, 1799.

CONNER, Patrick, CABINET MAKER, 27 Great Britain Street, 1784-9; 38 Great Britain Street, 1790; 41 Great Britain Street, 1791-9; UPHOLDER & CABINET MAKER, 55 Henry Street, 1800.

CONNOLLY, Edmond, UPHOLDER, Bachelor's Quay, 1765-9; Freeman of the City of Dublin as an UPHOLSTERER by Grace Especial, Midsummer 1770.

CONNOLLY, Thomas, CARVER & GILDER, 79 Aungier Street, 1773-83; Freeman of the City of Dublin as a MERCHANT by service, Easter 1767.

CONWAY, Henry, CABINET MAKER, 15 Abbey Street, 1793-5.

CONWAY, John, CABINET MAKER, 88 Pill Lane, 1789-91.

COOKE, JOHN, CABINET MAKER, 62 Townsend Street, 1791.

COOPER, William, CARVER & GILDER, 31 Drogheda Street, 1773-87.

CORR, Jas., JOINER, 22 Bride's Alley, 1797-1803; Patrick, CABINET MAKER, 14 Bride's Alley, 1806-10, 1813-15; 22 Bride's Alley, 1816-19; 67 Thomas Street, 1820-3; CORR, Mary & Catherine, 1824-30.

COTTON, William, CABINET MAKER & UPHOLDER, 24 Great Ship Street, 1784-90.

CRANFIELD, John Smith, CARVER & GILDER, 109 Capel Street, 1787-98; CRANFIELD, John S. a Freeman of the City of Dublin as CARPENTER by birth, Michaelmas 1792. See W. G. Strickland, *Dictionary of Irish Artists* (Dublin 1913), Vol. I, p.220.

CRANFIELD, Richard, CARVER & GILDER, Hog Hill, 1765-8; 3 Church Lane, College Green, 1769-98; CRANFIELD, Richard & Son, 1785-98; Freeman of the City of Dublin as a CARVER by Grace Especial, Easter 1758; CRANFIELD, Richard, master to CLARKE, Thomas as a CARVER, 1776. See Strickland, Vol. I, pp.218-20. He carved the Dublin Society's Chair in 1769 and worked at the Provost's House, with James Robinson, *q.v.* He also worked at Castletown etc.

CROFTON, Phillip, CABINET MAKER, 35 Tighe Street, 1796-9; Freeman of the City of Dublin as MERCHANT by service with Alderman Hans Bailie, Michaelmas 1750.

CROSBIE, Thomas, CABINET MAKER, 82 Abbey Street, 1793-6; 12 Bride's Alley, 1796-1807.

CROW, (Crowe) Robert, UPHOLDER, 12 Abbey Street, 1765-8; CROW, Robert & Son, 1769-90; Freeman of the City of Dublin as an UPHOLSTERER by Grace Especial, Midsummer 1744; CROW, Robert, UPHOLDER, 12 Abbey Street, 1791; Freeman of the City of Dublin as an UPHOLSTERER by Grace Especial, Easter 1764. CROW, William, UPHOLDER & AUCTIONEER, 22 Abbey Street, 1791-4; 12 Abbey Street, 1795-1800. Subscriber to Levi Hodgson, 1779.

CURRAN, Thomas, CARVER, Liffey Street, 1768-83.

CURRIN, Humphrey, UPHOLDER, Mary Street, 1767.

DALTON, George, UPHOLDER, Britain Street, 1769-74; 11 Henry Street, 1775-9.

DARTIS, August, CABINET MAKER. Subscriber to Levi Hodgson, 1779.

DAVIS, Anthony, CABINET MAKER, 20 Music Hall, Fishamble Street, 1775-83; CABINET MAKER & AUCTIONEER, 93 Fleet Street, 1784; CABINET MAKER, 1785-92; CABINET MAKER, AUCTIONEER & UPHOLDER, Royal Exchange, 1793-7; UPHOLDER & AUCTIONEER, 1798-1800; DAVIS, Anthony, a Freeman of the City of Dublin as JOINER by Grace Especial, Michaelmas 1773 (admitted Midsummer 1773).

DAVIS, John, CABINET MAKER, UPHOLDER & AUCTIONEER, 62 South Great George's Street, 1779-89; UPHOLDER & AUCTIONEER, 60 South Great George's Street, 1790-1813; DAVIS & ELLIOTT, 1815.

DELANY, Daniel, CABINET MAKER, 1 Crane Street, 1784-96.

DEMPSEY, Luke & Mary, UPHOLDER, Grafton Street, 1766-70; DEMPSEY, Luke, 32 William Street, 1771-91; 20 Cuffe Street, 1791-1814; DEMPSY, Luke, a Freeman of the City of Dublin as an UPHOLSTERER by service, Michaelmas 1755.

DEZOUCHE, James, CABINET MAKERS, 48 Aungier Street, 1787-8.

DEZOUCHE, Isaac, UPHOLDER & AUCTIONEER, 8 Digges Street, 1782-5.

DIXON, Joseph, CABINET MAKER & UPHOLDER, 27 Mary Street, 1791-1810; DIXON, Joseph, a Freeman of the City of Dublin as a JOINER by service, Easter 1790.

DOBBIN, James, UPHOLDER & AUCTIONEER, Great Cuffe Street, 1773-7.

DOBSON, Elizabeth, CARVER & GILDER, Lr Abbey Street, 1773-4.

DOBSON, Henry, UPHOLDER & AUCTIONEER, 80 Capel Street, 1766-1810; DOBSON, Henry, a Freeman of the City of Dublin as UPHOLSTERER by service with EVATT, John.

DOBSON, Samuel, CARVER & GILDER, Capel Street, 1771-3.

DODD, John, UPHOLDER, 49 Bolton Street, 1790-5; UPHOLDER & AUCTIONEER, 1796-1808.

DOOLITTLE, Robert, JOINER & CABINET MAKER, York Street, 1770-2: 4 South Great George's Street, 1773-4: 32 South Great George's Street, 1775; 68 South Great George's Street, 1776-81; DOOLITTLE, Robert, a Freeman of the City of Dublin as JOINER by service, Midsummer 1761.

DONELLAN, Patrick, CABINET MAKER & AUCTIONEER, 11 Drogheda Street, 1787-92.

DOUGHERTY, Christopher, CABINET MAKER, 42 Henry Street, 1784-1819.

DOWLING, Patrick, CABINET MAKER, 3 Bride's Alley, 1786-8.

DOWLING, William, CABINET MAKER, 43 William Street, 1784-5.

DUPRE, Nathaniel, CARVER, Angelsea Street, 1768-73; 104 Grafton Street, 1774-80; 87 Grafton Street, 1781-94; DUPRE, Nathaniel, master to DAVIS, Edward, as CARVER & GILDER, 1774.

DURHAM, Barry, UPHOLDER, 25 Bride's Alley, 1794, 25 Bride's Alley, 1798-9; 33 Bride's Alley, 1800-14.

DWYER, Phillip, UPHOLDER, 71 Stafford Street, 1762-80; DWYER, Philip, a Freeman of the City of Dublin as UPHOLSTERER by service, Christmas 1735.

EDWARDS, Richard, UPHOLDER & AUCTIONEER, 9 Ormond Quay, 1775-82.

EGAN, John & Laurence, CARVER, 10 Meeting House Yard, 1770-91; 10 Usher's Court, 1792.

EGGLESO, CABINET MAKER, 4 Gloucester Street, 1787-8.

EGGLESO, Henry, CABINET MAKER & UPHOLDER, 89 Abbey Street, 1796; 12 Abbey Street, 1797-1808; 12 Abbey Street & 41 Stafford Street, 1810; 21 Abbey Street & 41 Stafford Street, 1811; EGGLESO & POWER, UPHOLSTERERS to His Majesty, 11 Abbey Street, 1812-16; EGGLESSO, Henry, UPHOLDER to his Majesty, 11 Abbey Street, 1818

EGGLESO, Peter, CABINET MAKER & UPHOLDER, 41 Stafford Street and 21 Abbey Street, 1790-9; EGGLESO Peter & Co. 1800-5.

ELLIS, Joseph, CABINET MAKER, Mary Street, 1774; 35 Stafford Street, 1775-1800; ELLIS, Joseph, a Freeman of the City of Dublin as JOINER by birth (as the son of ELLIS, John), Easter 1736. Subscriber to Levi Hodgson, 1779.

EVANS, John, a Freeman of the City of Dublin as UPHOLSTERER by service, Michaelmas 1780.

EVANS, Robert, CABINET MAKER, Kevan (sic) Street, 1774-?.

EVATT, Henry, UPHOLDER & AUCTIONEER, 9 Abbey Street, 1770-9.

EVATT, John, UPHOLDER & AUCTIONEER, 9 Abbey Street, 1780; 32 Moore Street, 1781-4; 26 Henry Street, 1785-1813; Summerhill, 1814-15. Subscriber to Levi Hodgson, 1779.

FANNIN, Robert, CABINET MAKER, 15 Bride's Alley, 1786-1800; FANNIN, Richard, CABINET MAKER & AUCTIONEER, 1801-11; CABINET MAKER, 1812, 1814-15, 1818-20; FANNIN, Robert, CABINET MAKER 1822-6. Subscriber to Levi Hodgson, 1779.

FARRELL, (FERREL, FERREL) James, CABINET MAKER, 10 Bride's Alley, 1787-1810; 29 Bride's Alley, 1815;

FAWCETT, Widow, GLASS SELLER, Essex Quay, 1764-9.

FENLAN, Patrick, UPHOLDER, 57 Aungier Street, 1771-9.

FINIGAN, Charles, CABINET MAKER, 11 Bride's Alley, 1796-1817;

FINNIGEN, John, CARVER, Essex Street, 1769.

FINLAY, Christopher, UPHOLDER & CABINET MAKER, 144 Abbey Street, 1782-8; CABINET MAKER, UPHOLDER & AUCTIONEER, 1789-92.

FISHER, Green, UPHOLDER, 1 Strand Street, 1769-82.

FITZGERALD, William, UPHOLDER, Jervis Quay, 1762-9; Freeman of the City of Dublin as UPHOLSTERER by service, Christmas 1747.

FITZSIMONS, Christopher, MERCHANT, George's Hill, 1761-3; GLASS MERCHANT, 1764.

FLANAGIN (FLANEGAN), John, CARVER, Essex Street, 1768-74.

FLEMING, Thomas, UPHOLDER & CABINET MAKER, 26 St Andrew's Street, 1785-1802; Freeman of the City of Dublin as JOINER by service, Michaelmas 1765; Master to BALL, Roger, as a CABINET MAKER, 1769. Subscriber to Levi Hodgson, 1779.

FLOOD, James, CABINET MAKER & UPHOLDER, 40 Grafton Street, 1790-1809; 42 Grafton Street, 1810-22.

FOXALL, Zach., CABINET MAKER. Subscriber to Levi Hodgson, 1779.

GALLAGHER, Richard, LOOKING GLASS MANUFACTURER, 8 Essex Quay, 1790-2; 34 South Great George's Street, 1793-1805; 31 South Great George's Street, 1806-11; CARVER & GILDER, 1812-16. Freeman of the City of Dublin as CARVER by Grace Especial, 1789; GALLAGHER, Thomas, CARVER & GILDER, 31 South Great George's Street, 1817-30. Freeman of the City of Dublin as JOINER by service, Michaelmas 1806.

GARDINER & CO., PRINTSELLERS & GILDERS, 49 Mary Street, 1794-1800;

GARDINER, John, PRINTSELLER & GILDER, 49 Mary Street, 1801-3.

GARDINER, Richard, GILDER, Cole Alley, Castle Street, 1761.

GARDNER, John, CABINET MAKER, 21 Aungier Street, 1790-1805; CABINET MAKER & UPHOLSTERER, 21 Upr Sackville Street, 1806-09; 14 Sackville Street, 1810-16.

GAYNOR, Peter, UPHOLDER, 154 Britain Street, 1771-6.

GIBSON, Richard, CARVER & GILDER, 16 Bridge Street, 1784-1800.

GIBTON, Robert, CABINET MAKER, UPHOLDER & AUCTIONEER, 21 Aungier Street, 1790-3, 28 Aungier Street, 1794-6, 10 Stephen's Street, 1800-6. See *Furniture History*, p.270.

GILLINGTON, John, UPHOLDER & AUCTIONEER, 7 Montague Street, 1794-1800; 51 Stephen's Street, 1800-9; GILLINGTON, John & Sons, 119 Abbey Street, 1811-14; GILLINGTON, Samuel & Son, 1815-16; GILLINGTON, Samuel & George, 119 Abbey Street, 1816-20; 118 Abbey Street, 1820-3; GILLINGTON, George, 1824-30; GILLINTON, Samuel, freeman of the City of Dublin as UPHOLDER by service, Michaelmas 1806. See *Furniture History*, p.266.

GLINN, Bernard, CABINET MAKER, 14 Marlborough Street, 1797-9.

GONNE, Henry, LOOKING GLASS SELLER, 26 Abbey Street, 1775-1800.

GRACE, Reeves, UPHOLDER, Stephen's Street, 1769-89; 65 Stephen's Street, 1790-1805; 57 Stephen's Street, 1806-12. Freeman of the City of Dublin as UPHOLSTERER by service, Michaelmas 1754. BYRNE, John, freeman of the City of Dublin as UPHOLSTERER by service with GRACE, Reeves, 1765.

GRAHAM, John, CABINET MAKER, 70 Capel Street, 1793-4. Freeman of the City of Dublin as a CARPENTER by service, Easter 1769.

GRANT, Benjamin, CABINET MAKER, UPHOLDER & AUCTIONEER, 1 Aungier Street, 1789-98.

GRANT, George, CABINET MAKER, 1 Aungier Street, 1785-8.

GRANT, George, UPHOLDER, Aungier Street, 1762-98.

GRANT, Peter, CABINET MAKER. Subscriber to Levi Hodgson, 1779.

GRAVES, Joseph, UPHOLDER, Marlborough Street, 1765-86.

GREEN, Fisher, UPHOLDER, 1 Strand Street, 1769-82.

GREHAN, John, CARVER & GILDER, 3 Nth Anne Street, 1791-1828.

GREIR, James, UPHOLDER, Joseph's Lane, 1762-9.

GRIFFITHS, William, CABINET MAKER, 14 Upr Ormond Quay, 1782-4; 195 Abbey Street, 1785-92.

GRUNDY, George, CABINET MAKER, 4 W. Cole Street, 1787-95; 1 Bride's Alley, 1796-1803; CABINET MAKER & FEATHER MERCHANT, 1813-16; 15 Bride Street, 1818-19. Freeman of the City of Dublin as JOINER by Grace Especial, Christmas 1790.

GUNSTON, Joshua, UPHOLDER & JOINER, Inns Quay, 1762-75. Freeman of the City of Dublin as a JOINER by birth (son of Thomas Gunston), Christmas 1753. Master to CRUISE, Christopher, as CABINET MAKER, 1755. Master to KATHRENS, Samuel, as JOINER, 1759. Master to COUNTY, John, as JOINER & CABINET MAKER, 1763.

GUNSTON, Thomas, UPHOLDER, May Lane, also Capel Street, 1762-9. Master to HARRISON, Joseph, as JOINER, 1751. Master to WALSH, James, as JOINER, 1749.

HACKETT, Richard, UPHOLDER, 22 Phoenix Park, 1784-90; 5 Bow Lane, 1791-3.

HALE, Edward, CABINET & MACHINE MAKER, 16 Cork Street; 1796-7, 100 Coombe, 1798-1800.

HARDY, Samuel, CABINET MAKER & UPHOLDER, 3 Digges Court, 1784-5; CABINET MAKER, 1786.

HARRICKS, John, CARVER, 23 Denmark Street, 1784-6.

HAWKINS, Thomas, UPHOLDER & CABINET MAKER, 41 South Great George's Street, 1771-81; 68 South Great George's Street, 1782-3; UPHOLDER, 1784-6.

HAWKESWORTH, James, CARVER & GILDER, 12 Duke Street, 1794-1806. See *Furniture History*, p.266.

HAYES, William, UPHOLDER, Henry Street, 1766-70.

HEALY, Elms, UPHOLDER & AUCTIONEER, 1 Suffolk Street, 1776-8. Subscriber to Levi Hodgson, 1779.

HEALY & GRANT, CABINET MAKER, 1 & 18 Suffolk Street, 1779-87.

HEARN, Charles, UPHOLDER & AUCTIONEER, Gt Booter Lane, 1765-8; Great George's Street, 1769-86.

HEARN, Christopher, JOINER, 41 Fishamble Street, 1762-73; JOINER & CABINET MAKER,

1774-80; 13 Dawson Street, 1781-6.

HEARN, William, CABINET MAKER, 47 Henry Street, 1784-98.

HEFFERNON, David, CABINET MAKER, 20 Grafton Street, 1784-5; 16 Hawkins Street, 1786-99; 16 Hawkins Street & 18 Bachelor's Walk, 1800-10; 16 Hawkins Street, 1811-12.

HIGLEY, Nicholas, UPHOLDER, Lr Ormond Quay, 1762-72.

HEVEIN, John, CABINET MAKER, 21 Arran Quay, 1779-83

HOUGHTON, John, CARVER & GILDER, Duke Street, 1761-74. See, Strickland, Vol. I, p.525, and Homan Potterton, *Irish Church Monuments* (Belfast 1975), p.79, and Anne Crookshank, *Irish Sculpture from 1600* (Dublin 1984). There are at least three generations of this family with the same christian name, and work survives in the House of Lords and picture frames in St Patrick's Deanery and the Provost's House, Trinity College Dublin.

HUDSON, John, CARVER & GILDER, 15 Marlborough Street, 1772-6.

HULBERT, George William, CARVER, 29 Grafton Street, 1771-83; HULBERT, George & Robert, CARVER & GILDER, 36 Dawson Street, 1796-8.

HUMPHREYS, Edward, CABINET MAKER, 42 Fishamble Street, 1793-1804.

HUNTER, William, CABINET MAKER, 12 King's Inn Quay, 1780-7. Freeman of the City of Dublin as CARPENTER by Grace Especial, Michaelmas 1775.

INNS, George, CABINET MAKER, 55 South Great George's Street, 1782-92; CABINET MAKER & UPHOLDER, 9 Bishop Street, 1793-95; INNS, Mary, CABINET MAKER, 9 Bishop Street, 1796-1800. Freeman of the City of Dublin as a JOINER by service, Christmas 1782.

JACKSON, Anne & James, GLASS GRINDERS, 5 Essex Bridge, 1761-3; GLASS SELLERS, 1764-74; JACKSON, James & Richard, 1775-85; JACKSON, Richard, 1786-1800; 3 Essex Bridge, 1801-8; CARVER & GILDER, 5 Essex Bridge, 1809-17; CARVER & GILDER & LOOKING GLASS WAREHOUSE, 1818-27. See *Furniture History*, pp.266-7. They traded under the sign of The Golden Frame and Spectacles, see Henry F. Berry, 'House and Shop Signs in Dublin in the seventeenth and eighteenth centuries', *JRSAI* Pt.II, Vol. XL, 1910, p.97.

JACOB, Philip, UPHOLDER, Marlborough, 1769-74; 31 Great Britain Street, 1775-83.

JOLLAND, Charles, UPHOLDER & CABINET MAKER, 31 Mary Street, 1779-90. Subscriber to Levi Hodgson, 1779.

JONES, Theophilus, CABINET MAKER, 33 Mary Street, 1774-7. Freeman of the City of Dublin as a JOINER by service, Michaelmas 1763.

JONES, William, CABINET MAKER, 31 Ormond Quay, 1786-7; 34 Ormond Quay, 1788-1805; 5 Stephen's Green North, 1810, 1812-16; 36 Ormond Quay, 1820, 1822; JONES & SONS, UPHOLSTERERS, 1823-30.

KAVANAGH, Matthew, CABINET MAKER, 4 Bride's Alley, 1792.

KAVANAGH, Miles, CABINET MAKER, 24 Bride's Alley, 1796-1816, 1818-19, 1822; KAVANAGH, Catherine, 1823-6.

KEAM, Patrick, CARVER, Brock Lane, Britain Street, 1768-70.

KEARNEY, Joshua, CARVER & GILDER, 186 Grt Britain Street, 1797-1804; 49 Henry Street, 1805-29. Freeman of the City of Dublin as a CARPENTER by service, Easter 1808. See *Furniture History*, p.269.

KELLY, William, UPHOLDER, 28 Stephen's Street, 1784.

KENNY, Thomas, CABINET MAKER, 7 Henry Street, 1791-2.

KENNEDY, James, UPHOLDER, Abbey Street, 1762-6.

KING, Gilbert, UPHOLDER, Britain Street, 1762-7.

KIRCHOFFER, Francis, CABINET MAKER, 52 Henry Street, 1785-94.

KIRCHOFFER, Hall, CABINET MAKER, 8 Marlborough Street, 1780-1; CABINET MAKER, 15 Nth Earl Street, 1782-4; 17 Henry Street, 1785-8; 15 Nth Earl Street, 1789-94; 62 Henry Street, 1796-1812; HALL KIRCHOFFER & SON, 61-2 Henry Street, 1814-16. Freeman of the City of Dublin as JOINER by birth as a son of KIRCHOFFER, John, Easter 1768. See, Strickland Vol., I, p.581. The family were auctioneers, specializing in the timber trade, see Eileen McCracken, *The Irish Woods since Tudor Times* (Newtown Abbot 1971), p.130.

KIRCHOFFER, Thomas, CABINET MAKER. Subscriber to Levi Hodgson, 1779.

LAGRUE, John, CARVER & GILDER, 10 Stephen's Street, 1791.

LAMBERT, Andrew, LOOKING GLASS SELLER, 11 Suffolk Street, 1785-6; CARVER & GILDER, 1787-91.

LAMBERT & MADDOCK, CABINET MAKERS, 45 South Great George's Street, 1784-8; LAMBERT, John, freeman of the City of Dublin as CARPENTER by Grace Especial, Michaelmas 1759.

LEAHY, Theophilus, CABINET MAKER, 29 William Street, 1781-4.

LE GRANDE, Claude, CARVER & GILDER, 42 Mecklenburgh Street, 1793; 9 Denmark Street, 1794-95. Emigrated to Philadelphia and worked as a carver on the Bank of the United States, see Beatrice B. Garvan, *Federal Philadelphia 1785-1825* (Philadelphia 1987).

LE MAISTRE, Peter, UPHOLDER, South Great George's Street, 1769. Freeman of the City of Dublin as JOINER by birth as son of Le MAISTRE, William, Michaelmas 1752,

LLOYD, Mary, TRUNK MAKER, 1769.

LLOYD, Richard, UPHOLDER, Capel Street, 1769.

LORD, William, UPHOLDER, Angelsea Street, 1769-74. Freeman of the City of Dublin as UPHOLDER by service, Easter 1767.

McALLISTER, John, CABINET MAKER, 26 South Great George's Street, 1784.

McCANN, Patrick, CABINET MAKER, 11 Eustace Street, 1784-92.

McCREADY, John, CABINET MAKER & UPHOLDER, 15 Abbey Street, 1790-1. Freeman of the City of Dublin as UPHOLDER by birth, Midsummer 1783.

McCREADY, William, UPHOLDER, Bride Street, 1762. Freeman of the City of Dublin as UPHOLSTERER by service, Michaelmas 1755.

McCREADY, William, UPHOLDER, 66 Bride Street, 1765-95; McCREADY, William & Thomas, UPHOLDERS, 1796-1800; McCREADY, William, UPHOLDER, 66 Bride Street, 1801- 6; WILLIAM & Son, 1807-10; UPHOLDER & AUCTIONEER, 1811; 43 Bride Street, 1812-14; UPHOLDER, CABINET MAKER & AUCTIONEER, 4 Dawson Street, 1828-30. Freeman of the City of Dublin as UPHOLDER by birth, Christmas, 1783. Subscriber to Levi Hodgson, 1779.

McCUTCHIN, James, CABINET MAKER, 28 Brunswick Street, 1794-1801.

McDANIEL, John, CABINET MAKER, 71 Capel Street, 1790-1.

McDERMOTT, Bernard, CABINET MAKER, 30 Golden Lane, 1793-1803; McDERMOTT, Bernard & Son 1808-10. Freeman of the City of Dublin as CARPENTER by Grace Especial, Michaelmas 1792.

McDONALD, Charles, CABINET MAKER, 3 Mary Street, 1794-1803, 1827.

McDONALD, William, TRUNK MAKER, 17 Smock Alley, 1796-1801, 1804-25.

MacLUNE, Southwell, CABINET MAKER, 185 Abbey Street, 1787-96; CABINET MAKER & AUCTIONEER, 1797-8. Freeman of the City of Dublin as a CABINET MAKER by Grace Especial, Easter 1787.

McOWEN, Richard, CABINET MAKER, 108 Capel Street, 1782-1809, 1816-18, 1829.

MACK, John, CABINET MAKER. Subscriber to Levi Hodson, 1779.

MACK, John, CABINET MAKER, 188 Abbey Street, 1784-1800; MACK & GIBTON, 188 Abbey Street & 39 Stafford Street, 1801-6; 39 Stafford Street, 1807-9; MACK, WILLIAMS & GIBTON, 31 Stafford Street, 1810; 39 Stafford Street, 1811-12; WILLIAMS & GIBTON, 39 Stafford Street, 1813-30; WILLIAMS & GIBTON, CABINET MAKERS, UPHOLDERS & AUCTIONEERS, 39 Stafford Street, 1831-3; 39 & 40 Stafford Street, 1834-45; WILLIAMS & SONS, 42 & 43 Stafford Street, 1845-52. Subscriber to Levi Hodgson, 1779. See *Furniture History*, pp.269-70.

MADDOCKS, Benjamin, CABINET MAKER, 45 South Great George's Street, 1787-8.

MALLET, Robert, CABINET MAKER. Subscriber to Levi Hodgson, 1779.

MALLET, Robert, CABINET MAKER, 62 Capel Street, 1785-1804. Freeman of the City of Dublin as CABINET MAKER by Grace Especial, Easter 1787. Subscriber to Levi Hodgson, 1779.

MARSH, Patrick, UPHOLDER & AUCTIONEER, 33 Bride's Alley, 1782-95; 33 Bride Street & 4 York Street, 1796-7.

MARTIN, William, UPHOLDER & AUCTIONEER, Bolton Street, 1770-4.

MASON, Benjamin, UPHOLDER, William Street, 1769. Freeman of the City of Dublin as a UPHOLSTERER by service, Midsummer 1750.

MASON, Joseph, CABINET MAKER, Queen Street, 1769-72; Gravel Walk, 1773-4; 4 Barrack Street, 1775-8.

MATHEW, John (SPROULE & MATTHEW), CABINET MAKER & UPHOLDER, 2 Coppinger Lane, 1776-83. Freeman of the City of Dublin as CARVER by Grace Especial, 1769.

MATTHEWS, John, CARVER, Temple Bar, 1768-71; 60 Dorset Street, 1772-83.

MAYN, Thomas, UPHOLDER, Ryder Lane, 1769-81.

MAYNE, Richard, UPHOLDER, 10 College Street, 1775-80; MAYNE, Richard, 26 Queen's Street, 1788.

MAYNE, Richard, CABINET MAKER, 24 Bachelor's Walk, 1785-6.

MAYNE, Thomas, UPHOLDER, 44 Henry Street, 1775; UPHOLDER & AUCTIONEER, 1778-82; 44 Henry Street, 1783-5. Freeman of the City of Dublin as a UPHOLDER by service, Midsummer 1767.

MEDCALF, Charles, CABINET MAKER, 28 Bride's Alley, 1792-1815. Apprentice to MEDCALF, Charles, as CABINET MAKER, 1818.

MILLER, Joseph, CABINET MAKER, 42 Coombe, 1781-99.

MOORE, Elizabeth, UPHOLDER, 162 Britain Street, 1790-1; 162 & 184 Great Britain Street, 1792-5; UPHOLDER & CABINET MAKER, 1796-8.

MOORE, John, CABINET MAKER, 12 Nth Anne Street, 1790-95; Freeman of the City of Dublin as CARPENTER by service, Midsummer 1762.

MOORE, Richard, UPHOLDER, Capel Street, 1762-9.

MOORE, William, CABINET MAKER, 22 Abbey Street, 1785-91; 47 Capel Street, 1792-1801, 1804-14. Freeman of the City of Dublin as CARPENTER by service, Michaelmas 1794.

MORGAN, Robert, CABINET MAKER, 16 Henry Street, 1782-9; UPHOLDER & CABINET MAKER, 21 Henry Street, 1790-1807. Freeman of the City of Dublin as a JOINER by service, Michaelmas 1779.

MORLET, Arthur, CABINET MAKER, 59 South Great George's Street, 1790-2.

MOSS, Jacob, CABINET MAKER & UPHOLDER, 22 Grafton Street, 1778-83.

MOUNTGARRET, John, UPHOLDER, Mid Strand Street, 1769; Freeman of the City of Dublin as UPHOLDER by service, Michaelmas 1754.

MOUNTGOMERY, William, CABINET MAKER, 21 Wood Street, 1796; MONTGOMERY, William, 1797-1820.

MUNDEE, Edward, CABINET MAKER, 34 Exchequer Street, 1796-8.

MUNDEE, Robert, CABINET MAKER, 34 Exchequer Street, 1782-4.

MUNDIE (MUNDEE?), Edward, CABINET MAKER. Subscriber to Levi Hodgson, 1779.

MURPHY, James, CHAIR MAKER, 2 Essex Quay, 1790; MURPHY, J., CABINET MAKER, UPHOLDER & AUCTIONEER, 1791-1800; UPHOLDER & AUCTIONEER, 1801-5.

MYLER, (MEYLER) Thomas, GLASS SELLER, Dame Street, 1768-74; 1 College Green, 1775-92; 25 Suffolk Street, 1793-4; MEYLER, Thomas & Son, CARVER & GILDER, 25 Suffolk Street, 1796-1800; MEYLER, John, 25 Suffolk Street, 1801-10.

MEYLER, Thomas, CARVERS & GILDERS, 25 Suffolk Street, 1792-4; MEYLER, Thomas & son, 1795; MEYLER, Thomas & John, 1796-1800; MEYLER, John, CARVER & GILDER, 1801-15; 19 Lr Mount Street, 1816-20. See *Furniture History*, p.271.

NEILL, John, CABINET MAKER, 86 Capel Street, 1787-97.

NEWTON, Isaac, LOOKING GLASS SELLER, 4 Essex Bridge, 1778-81; 88 Grafton Street, 1782-7. Freeman of the City of Dublin as MERCHANT by birth, Midsummer 1777.

NUGENT, Michael, GLASS MAN, Charles Street, 1761-3; GLASS SELLER, 1764-77.

O'BRIEN, Patrick, TRUNKMAKER, 26 Winetavern Street, 1793-5.

O'CONNOR, Owen, CABINET MAKER. Subscriber to Levi Hodgson, 1779.

O'CONNOR, Owen, CABINET MAKER, 20 Blackhall Row, 1793-8; 19 Blackhall Row, 1799.

O'DONNELL, John, UPHOLDER, West Arran Street, 1765-9.

O'DONNELL, Thomas, CARVER, West Arran Street, 1762.

OLDHAM, Thomas, CABINET MAKER, 35 Moore Street, 1768-78.

PARSONS, Thos., CABINET MAKER. Subscriber to Levi Hodgson, 1779.

PARTRIDGE, William, CARVER, Blind Quay, 1768-73; 18 Parliament Street, 1774-83; PAR-TRIDGE, Jane, CARVER, 18 Parliament Street, 1784-6; LOOKING GLASS SELLER, 1787-9. See *Furniture History*, p.271.

PASLEY, William, UPHOLDER, Upr Strand Street, 1762-75; 24 Great Strand Street, 1776-80. Freeman of the City of Dublin as UPHOLDER by service, Midsummer 1739. PASLEY, Jonas. Apprentice to PASLEY, William, as UPHOLDER, Michaelmas 1765.

PHELAN, Simon, UPHOLDER, Inns Quay, 1762-6.

PLUNKETT, Mary, TRUNK MAKER, 26 Fishamble Street, 1779-87.

POPE, Justin, PAINTER, CARVER & GILDER, 44 Stephen's Street, 1792-1802.

POWER, John, CABINET MAKER, 48 Nth King Street, 1784-99. Freeman of the City of Dublin as JOINER by service, Michaelmas 1753.

PRESTON, John, CABINET MAKER & AUCTIONEER, 7 Henry Street, 1793-1803, 1805; PRE-STON, John & Son, 7 Henry St, 1806-12; 6 Henry Street, 1813-14; 8 Henry St, 1815-19; 7 & 8 Henry St, 1820, 1824-5. (Supplied the magnificent Regency furniture at Castle Coole, Co. Fermanagh. See Gervase Jackson-Stops, *Country Life*, 10 April 1986, pp.918-20.)

PROUDFOOT, John, CABINET MAKER, 23 Bride's Alley, 1796-9; 28 Bride Street, 1800-24.

RAINSFORD, James, CABINET MAKER, 62 Aungier Street, 1790-1803, 1812.

REED, Patrick, CARVER & GILDER, 3 Union Street, 1784-93.

REILLY, Thos., CARPENTER, UPHOLDER & AUCTIONEER, 5 Redmond's Hill, 1793-1800. Freeman of the City of Dublin as JOINER by Grace Especial, Easter 1790.

RIDGEWAY, William, JOINER & CABINET MAKER, 31 Bride Street, 1767-9, 1775-93.

RIGG, Matthew, CABINET MAKER, 21 Bride's Alley, 1796-1803; RIGG, Mary, 1804-12.

RIGG, Peter, CABINET MAKER, 3 Bride's Alley, 1787-1803, 1812.

ROBINSON, James, CARVER, Lr Abbey Street, 1761-3; CARVER & GLASS SELLER, 1764-70; 7 Capel Street, 1771-8. (Supplied mirrors to the Great Drawing Room at Newbridge House, Co. Dublin, and worked with Richard Cranfield at the Provost's House, *q.v.*)

ROBINSON, John, CARVER, Kevin Street, 1768.

ROBINSON, John, CARVER & GLASS SELLER, Dame Street, 1775-9; 27 Capel Street, 1780; 34 College Green, 1781-6.

ROGERS, Abraham. CABINET MAKER. Subscriber to Levi Hodgson, 1779.

ROGERS, William, TRUNK MAKER, 5 Smock Alley, 1799-1814.

RUSSELL, George, CABINET MAKER. Subscriber to Levi Hodgson, 1779.

SANDFORD, Patrick, CARVER & GILDER, 110 Grafton Street, 1784-8; LOOKING GLASS MANUFACTURER, 45 Henry Street, 1789-1805; 56 Henry Street, CARVER & GILDER, 1806-13.

SAVAGE, Francis, UPHOLDER & AUCTIONEER, 182 Abbey Street, 1790-2.

SAVAGE, John, UPHOLDER, 85 Capel Street, 1762-76. Freeman of the City of Dublin as CARPENTER by service with Hamilton Bell, Christmas 1768.

SAVAGE, Patrick, GLASS GRINDER, 7 Exchequer Street, 1791-2.

SINNOT & OLDHAM, CARVERS & GILDERS, 48 Henry Street, 1784-90.

SMITH, John, CABINET MAKER, 167 Thomas Street, 1778-83.

SMITH, John, UPHOLDER & AUCTIONEER, 107 Coombe, 1794-7. Freeman of the City of Dublin as UPHOLDER by service, Michaelmas 1780.

SMITH, Roger, UPHOLDER, Stephen's Green, 1762-79; 4 South King Street, 1780-91, 47 Sth King Street, 1792-1800. Freeman of the City of Dublin as an UPHOLSTERER by service, Michaelmas 1758. ANDREW, Christopher. Apprenticed to SMITH, Roger, as UPHOLDER, 1788. (His advertisement in *The Universal Advertiser*, 'At the Sign of the Eagle and Easy Chair', is reproduced in my 'Early Irish Trade Cards and other Eighteenth Century Ephemera, *Eighteenth Century Ireland*, Vol. II, Dublin 1987, p.129.)

SPRING, George, UPHOLDER, Crow Street, 1762-70. Freeman of the City of Dublin as UPHOLDER by service, Midsummer 1733.

SPRING, William, UPHOLDER, Church Lane, College Green, 1771-5. Freeman of the City of Dublin as UPHOLDER by birth (son of George Spring), Easter 1767.

SPROULE, Miller & Matthew, CABINET MAKERS AND UPHOLDERS, 2 Coppinger's Lane, 1773-5.

STACY, George, CABINET MAKER, 20 White Friar Street, 1791-93.

STACY, Richard, CABINET MAKER, 18 Duke Street, 1790-3; STACY, Richard & George, CAB-INET MAKERS, 1794; STACY, Richard, 1795-8; 21 Duke Street, 1799-1800.

STRONG, Henry, CARVER, 39 Jervis Street, 1764-77. Freeman of the City of Dublin as a CARVER by Grace Especial, Easter 1765.

STURGES, John, CARVER, Bow Lane, 1761-4.

SULLIVAN, James, UPHOLDER. Subscriber to Levi Hodgson, 1779.

SULLIVAN, James, CABINET MAKER, 49 Capel Street, 1785-95; UPHOLDER, CABINET MAKER & AUCTIONEER, 1796-1803, 1805, 1814-16.

SUMMERS, Felix, CARVER & GILDER, 21 Aston Quay, 1796-1803.

SWEENY, Francis, CABINET MAKER & UPHOLDER, 118 Great Britain Street, 1794-7.

TARLETON, Edward, CABINET MAKER & UPHOLDER, Stephen's Street, 1770-1. Freeman of the City of Dublin as JOINER by service, Michaelmas 1767.

TENNANT, Charles, TRUNKMAKER, Merchant's Quay, 1765-80.

THEWLES, James, CABINET MAKER, 38 Aungier Street, 1784-92.

TICKELL, George, CABINET MAKER, 14 Bride's Alley, 1790-1810; TICKELL, Mary, 1811-14. Freeman of the City of Dublin as JOINER by Grace Especial, Easter 1790. TICKELL, George apprenticed to TICKELL, George, as a CABINET MAKER, 1817.

TIERNEY, Robert, CABINET MAKER. Subscriber to Levi Hodgson, 1779.

TROY, Mary Ann, CABINET MAKER, 9 Bride's Alley, 1787- 8.

TWIGG, John, CARVER & GILDER, 14 Moore Street, 1784-97.

VIZER, (VIZOR), Thos. & Charles, UPHOLDER & CABINET MAKER, 31 (34) Great Britain Street, 1787-93. Freemen of the City of Dublin as SADDLERS by service, Midsummer 1789. VIZER, Thos. Powell, becomes a Freeman of the City of Dublin as an UPHOLDER by service with Job Burnett, Easter 1768. Subscriber to Levi Hodgson, 1779.

WALPOLE, Robert, UPHOLDER, Bolton Street, 1762-9. Freeman of the City of Dublin as UPHOLDER by service with Charles Dempsey, Easter 1758.

WARMINGHAM, Charles, CABINET MAKER, 30 Angelsea St, 1774-1800; 17 Fleet St, 1801-18.

WARREN, Bartholemew, CABINET MAKER, 1 Cathedral Lane, 1796-7.

WARREN, William, UPHOLDER, 28 Beresford Street, 1789-1800; CABINET MAKER & UPHOLDER, 17 Sackville Street, 1801-04; 29 Sackville Street, 1805-13, 1816-20.

WHITESTONE, Thos., UPHOLDER, 14 Ormond Quay, 1769-80; 35 Dawson Street, 1781-3; 39 Dawson Street, 1784-94.

WHISTLER, Gabriel, UPHOLDER & AUCTIONEER, 66 South Great George's Street, 1769-99; 69 South Great George's Street, 1800-5. Freeman of the City of Dublin as UPHOLDER by birth, Michaelmas 1790. Subscriber to Levi Hodgson, 1779.

WHITE, Edward, UPHOLDER, 3 Fownes Street, 1762-85.

WILKENSON, William, CARVER & GILDER, Chequer Lane, 1761-74; 34 Exchequer Street, 1775-84.

WILLIAMS, Richard & Co., GLASSMAKER, 15 Lwr Ormond Quay, 1784.

WILLIAMSON, Matthew Jun., CARVER & GILDER, 89 Grafton Street, 1790-1800; WILLIAMSON, Matthew, 36 Grafton Street, 1801-2; 93 Grafton Street, 1803; 20 Chatham Street, 1804-10.

WILLIAMSON, William, GILDER, Hoey's Court, 1761.

WILSON, James, CABINET MAKER & AUCTIONEER. Subscriber to Levi Hodgson, 1779.

WILSON, James, UPHOLDER, 55 Stephen's Street, 1783-92.

WISDOM, John, CABINET MAKER, 21 Jervis Street, 1793-5.

WRIGHT, James, CABINET MAKER, 26 Mary's Abbey, 1790-2.

YOUNG, George, CABINET MAKER, 23 Charles Street, 1782-9; YOUNG, John, 57 South Great George's Street 1790-9; 2 Dawson Court, Stephen's Street, 1800-10.

LEINSTER HOUSE
AND ISAAC WARE

DRAWINGS FROM THE COLLECTION OF THE HON. DESMOND
GUINNESS AND THE LATE MRS MARIGA GUINNESS

DAVID J. GRIFFIN

THE PURPOSE of this essay is to discuss in some detail the series of designs
connected with the completion of Kildare House (renamed Leinster House
in 1766) following the death of Richard Castle, its architect, in February
1751.[1]

The majority of these designs are for the first-floor suite of rooms on
the garden front, the design of which has in the past been attributed by
John Harris[2] to Sir William Chambers (1723-96) on the basis of a comment
made by Chambers in a letter to Lord Charlemont dated 5 August 1767:[3] 'I
beg your Lordship will present my humble respects to her Grace's com-
mand on this and on all other occasions on which she shall please to
honour me with them.' But the inclusion of an earl's coronet in a number of
these designs dates them to before 1761 when the Earl was created
Marquess of Kildare, a fact which must rule out any connection between
them and this letter.

Here the authorship of these interiors is attributed to the important sec-
ond-generation Palladian architect Isaac Ware (1707-66).[4] Ware's most
important architectural works are Chesterfield House, London, 1748-9
(demolished 1934), and Wrotham Park, Middlesex, 1754, but it is for his
impeccable translation of Palladio's *Four Books of Architecture* published
in 1738 that he is now remembered. This book is still available by way of a
modern reprint.

I have several reasons for this attribution. Ware was already employed
by the Earl of Kildare by 1756 when in that year he included his designs for
the bridge at Carton in his *A Complete Body of Architecture,* plate 110-11:
'Stone bridge for the Right Hon. the Earl of Kildare Dublin'. This work also
includes a design for a chimneypiece at the home of the Right Hon. Henry
Fox, Albemarle St, London (plate 95 top), brother-in-law to the Earl. A
number of these designs have comments from Fox which would suggest
that he was acting as a kind of middle man. It should be noted that the
depiction of ceiling details in these designs is identical to that used by Ware
in *Some Designs of Inigo Jones and others* c.1735, a method which seems
peculiar to him. The most convincing proof of Ware's involvement is con-
tained in a postscript (in Fox's hand) referring to the great staircase in a
letter from Lady Caroline Fox to the Countess of Kildare dated 13 March
1759:[5] 'I like the Norfolk banister better than either of Mr. Ware's but I think

a handsome plain rail gilt will be at once cheaper and more magnificent, I approve the arches.' The 'Norfolk banister' is clearly a reference to Norfolk House, St James's Square, London, designed by Matthew Brettingham senior (1699-1769) and built between 1748 and 1752 (demolished 1938).[6] No drawings survive for the Leinster House staircase but it is interesting to note its similarity in plan and concept to that at Chesterfield House.

The chimneypiece and overmantels in the Garden Hall and adjoining room to the south can also be attributed to Ware on stylistic grounds.

The work here under discussion has hitherto been thought of as a remodelling of rooms designs by Richard Castle, but recent repairs have confirmed them as a belated completion of the house following Castle's death at Carton while writing a letter to a carpenter employed at Leinster House.[7]

The method which I shall adopt in this essay is to analyse each design separately, their sources and the work as executed.

Design for a chimneypiece and overmantel (plate 1)
Insc: 'For the Earl of Kildare.'

Plate 1 – While the design of this room (formerly the dining room) as a whole cannot be attributed to Ware, the design of the chimneypiece and overmantel must be his. The chimneypiece is shown as executed but with some of its decorative details omitted for clarity. It was removed to 'Carton in 1815 with the sale of the house, and installed in the state dining-room there. It was replaced by a chimneypiece from a first-floor drawing-room. It is worth noting that this splendid chimneypiece is clearly by the same hand as that at Carton. The overmantel was carried out with minor modifications and still exists at Leinster House. The cartouche and earl's coronet shown in the design have since been removed.

Plan, three wall elevations, ceiling plan (showing alternative designs), ceiling and entablature details and elevations of chimneypiece (plate 2)

Plate 2 – Richard Castle's plans show three rooms in this space, a servant's waiting-room with a staircase to the basement to the west, a bow-ended room in the centre with the bow screened by columns, and a parlour to the east. Repairs to this room in 1989 show that such a scheme was carried out and there was evidence of the removal of the two cross walls to form the present room.

The room can be dated to *c*.1759 when blue wallpaper is mentioned in connection with it.[a]

Ware's design shows the room almost as executed. The decoration on the friezes which included an earl's coronet, was not carried out. It may be noted that this drawing shows more columns than now exist. These were removed by the Royal Dublin Society early in the nineteenth century and incorporated in the gallery of the drawing school (now part of the National College of Art and Design).

In the room as executed Ware introduced doors in the north wall to balance those to the south. The room has two chimneypieces based on a design by William Kent published by Ware, *Designs of Inigo Jones and others,* plate 45 (bottom). Another chimneypiece based on this design exists at Phoenix Lodge (now Áras an Uachtaráin), Dublin. The pedimented over-mantels not shown in this design are based on a design attributed to Inigo Jones published by John Vardy in *Some Designs of Mr Inigo Jones and Mr William Kent,* plate 5, a copy of which was in the library at Carton. A similar overmantel formerly existed at Milton Abbey, Dorset,[b] a house on which is Vardy is known to have worked.

The ceiling, for which Ware gives two designs, is based on designs published in Sebastiano Serlio, *The Book of Architecture* (London ed.1611), book 4, folio 69. The central pedimented Ionic doorcase is taken from Ware's *A Complete Body of Architecture,* plate 44.

ᵃ *Correspondence of Emily Duchess of Leinster,* vol. 1, pp. 80, 88 & 95.
ᵇ See *Country Life,* 5 June 1915.

Plate 3 – Insc: 'No.1. Section of the Great Gallery on the principal floor 65ft 3ins by 24ft 6ins' and on an attached piece of paper: 'Mr Fox disapproves the ornament between the capitals of the doorcase and this sketch is in lieu of it and does not like the cornucopias in centre of the frieze, would therefore institute this sketch in its place.'

This design is the first of a set of designs numbered one to five (No.4. is missing) for the first-floor series of parade rooms on the garden or east front.

Castle's plansᵃ show that this space was always intended as a picture-gallery and that its height was to extend into the attic space. Repairs carried out in 1988-9 show that Castle's room was never completed and that the room remained an empty shell until *c.*1775 when the present room was designed by James Wyatt (1746-1813) for the 2nd Duke.

Ware's unexecuted design shows a room divided by screens of columns. These screens are based on a design published in Ware's *Designs of Inigo Jones and others,* plate 23; at Leinster House he changes the order from Corinthian to Ionic. These columns stand on pedestals and support

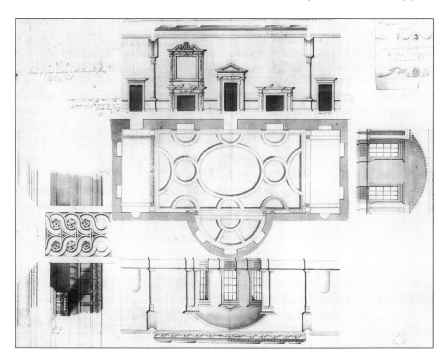

Plan, three wall elevations, ceiling plan and details of ceiling cornice and ceiling (plate 3)

DAVID J. GRIFFIN

segmental pediments with tympanum omitted.[b]

An unusual feature of the design of this room is that the window cases have full entablatures and balustrades under the sills, features more appropriate to the exterior of a building.

The pedimented doorcase to the main staircase of the composite order is flanked by twin chimneypieces, similar in design to that in Ware's *A Complete Body of Architecture*, plate 96. The swan-necked overmantels incorporate the star of the garter in their decoration.

The ceiling is ornamented with oval, circular and semi-circular compartments.

[a] Plans, Collection the Hon. D. Guinness.
[b] Other examples of this type of screen exist in the Cumberland Suite, Hampton Court Palace, by William Kent c.1732, and at No. 59 Lincoln's Inns Fields, London, *c.* 1757.

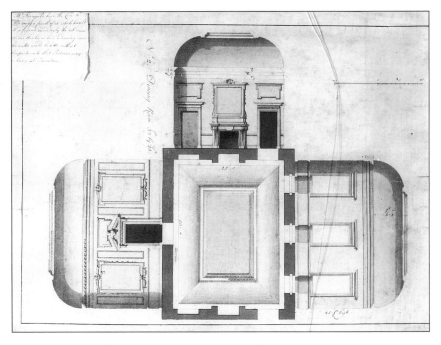

Plan, three wall elevations an a ceiling plan (plate 4)

Plate 4 – Insc: 'No. 2. Dining Room 33 ft by 25ft' and on a piece of paper pasted on: 'Mr Fox would have the cove of this room a fourth of its whole height, it is figured accordingly though it is not drawn so, and thinks as it is a dining-room, the walls would be better without compartments that the pictures may be hung at discretion.'

As with the adjoining picture-gallery it is clear from Castle's plans that it was always intended that this room was to extend in height into the attic floor above.

Ware's design shows a coved ceiling which was not carried out. The present ceiling, no doubt designed by Ware, is in the style of Inigo Jones with an oval central compartment. This ceiling is identical to that in the dining-room at Castletown, Co. Kildare, a room previously attributed, as with these interiors, to Sir William Chambers.

Ware shows two chimneypieces with swan-necked pedimented overmantels, only one of which was carried out (without the overmantel) with only minor modifications to the shape of its central plaque.

Fox's comments about the wall panels were ignored and they were carried out as shown with only minor modifications. The panel above the chimneypieces has been added since 1912.[a] The swagged and beaded mask above this panel is very similar to those above the arches in the small first-floor corridor lobbys at Castletown.

Besides this drawing, the Guinness Collection contained five copies of printed wall elevations of this room, one having MS dimensions.

[a] See *The Georgian Society Records*, vol. IV, plate XXV.

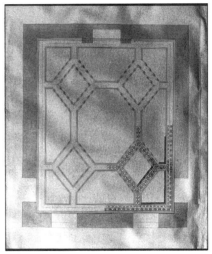

(A) Plan, four wall elevations, ceiling plan and ceiling and cornice details (plate 5). Insc: 'No. 3. Drawing Room 24ft by 20ft 3in.' (B) Plan and ceiling plan (plate 6)

Plates 5 & 6 – These designs show the room almost as executed. The ceiling is of simple compartment type composed of octagonal and diamond-shaped panels with guilloche pattern-enriched ribs. Ware's plain frieze was replaced in execution by one with an enriched Vitruvian scroll. The way in which the cornice and ribs are depicted in this drawing is identical to plate 12 in Ware's *Designs of Inigo Jones and others,* a method which seems peculiar to him. The chimneypiece was executed as shown; it was moved to the former ground-floor dining-room in 1815 to replace that removed to Carton when the house was sold to the RDS. It is not known if the swan-necked pedimented overmantel was executed.

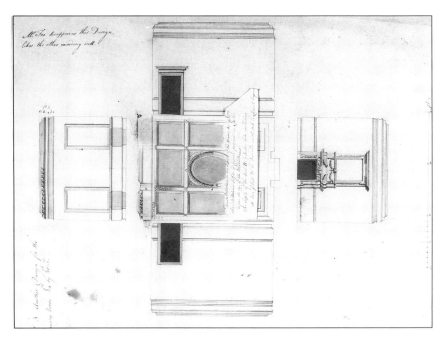

Plan, four wall elevations, ceiling design and cornice details (plate 7)

Plate 7 – Insc: 'No. 3. Another for the Drawing Room 24ft by 20ft 3in.' and 'Mr Fox disapproves this design, likes the other exceedingly well.' Mr Fox got his way and this design was unexecuted. It shows a broken pediment-ed chimneypiece with side panels ending in volutes, above which was a simple overmantel. The ceiling, in the style of Inigo Jones, has a central oval compartment and an attached flap gives the following details: 'Double guilloched upon the soffites of the beam A. 9 inch single guilloche in soffite of cornice projecting 4 inches before the cap of the modillions. The soffite of the oval B 7 inches wide including its two fillets to be enriched with oak or laurel leaves.' A note on the left-hand side of this drawing, '4th Room for hangings', refers to the intended damask wall-hangings.

Plates 8 & 9 (opposite page) – No overall design for this room survives, but it is clear from the numbering of this set of drawings that this room was designed at the same time and would have been No. 4. (The flanking rooms are inscribed No. 3 and No. 5.) As in the adjoining rooms, the ceiling is of compartment type, this time with oval and semi-oval panels. The junctions of these panels are decorated with masks and shells, the masks being similar to those depicted in Ware's *A Complete Body of Architecture*, plate 74: 'a ceiling for a staircase'; and plates 82-83, 'Dining room ceiling at Chesterfield House'.

Two designs for overmantels and chimneypieces exist which seem to relate to this room. Both depict Roman Ionic chimneypieces which differ in

Design for an overmantel and chimneypiece (plate 8)
Alternate design for an overmantel and chimneypiece (plate 9)

minor details. The second design shows the chimneypiece as executed, and it now survives in the Green Drawing-Room at Carton (former Library). It is of white marble with a central plaque of blue malachite. It was moved to Carton with the sale of Leinster House in 1815. Both of these designs show swan-necked pedimented overmantels, the more elaborate of which includes an earl's coronet below the picture frame and the star of the garter above.

Plate 10 (overleaf) – Insc: 'No. 5 Lady's Dressing Room 24ft 6in by 18ft 10in.' This design, which was unfortunately unexecuted, is perhaps the most interesting and important in this series, and can perhaps be considered the most authentically correct French interior of the Irish Rococo.

The ceiling is very close to Ware's engraving of his Music Room ceiling at Chesterfield House, London,[a] 1747-9 as published, in *A Complete Body of Architecture,* plates 81-2. The walls are decorated with carved panels or *boiseries.* They are shown in the arrangement favoured in France with alternating wide and narrow panels with shaped tops and bottoms. The panels below the dado or chair rail are also in this style and similar to those at

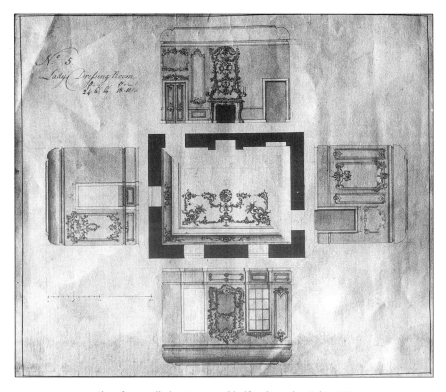

Plan, four wall elevations and half ceiling plan (plate 10)

Chesterfield House. The chimneypiece is also in the French taste as is the overmantel mirror and pier glass opposite. It should be noted that Ware proposed to insert a window in the south wall.

ª For a full discussion of Issac Ware and Chesterfield House, see essays by Roger White in *The Rococo in England*, a symposium edited by Charles Hind (Victoria & Albert Museum 1986).

Plate 11 (opposite page) – Insc: 'No. 5.' Ware's French Rococo design for this room must have been considered either too elaborate or too expensive, and this alternative design shows the room more or less as executed. The ceiling, again of compartmented type, is similar to that in the drawing-room (executed design, insc: 'No. 3'). The frieze as executed is more elaborate being enriched with oak leaves. The chimneypiece and overmantel are shown only in dotted outline suggesting that it may have already been in place. The chimneypiece as executed is taken from Ware's *Designs of Inigo Jones and others,* plate 22, a design attributed to Inigo Jones. Other examples of this survive at Carton, Co. Kildare (wood); Castletown, Co. Kildare, Red Drawing-Room (marble); and at No. 6 South Leinster Street, Dublin, Dining-Room (marble). This design also shows the dimensioned outline of a pedimented breakfront bookcase.

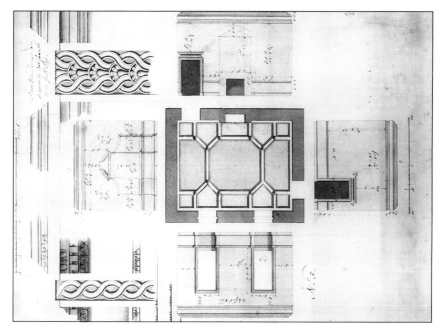

Plan, four wall elevations, ceiling plan and ceiling and cornice details (plate 11)

Plate 12 (overleaf) – Although no documentary evidence exists, it seems likely that this design was intended for Leinster House. The Doric chimney-piece depicted is almost certainly that now installed in the State Dining Room at Carton *c.*1850[a] where it was moved from Kilkea Castle. Another property of the Dukes of Leinster in Co. Kildare, it is most unlikely that it originally belonged there.

[a] See *The Georgian Society Records*, vol. 5. p.60.

Plate 13 (overleaf) – This design, probably intended for Leinster House, depicts a titled head on its central plaque, symbolizing Sleep,[a] which would suggest that this design was intended for a bedchamber.

[a] See Ware's *A Complete Body of Architecture*, plate 92, 'Bed Chamber chimney-piece'.

Acknowledgments – The author would like to thank the following for help in preparation of this essay: The Hon. Desmond Guinness and the late Mrs Mariga Guinness for permission to photograph drawings in their possession; Desmond Fitz-Gerald, Knight of Glin, who kindly provided photocopies of drawings now lost.

I must also thank Mr Frederick O'Dwyer and Mr Geoffrey Johnston, both architects with the Office of Public Works in Ireland, for answering many questions about the building, the staff at Leinster House for permission to visit and photograph the rooms under discussion, and finally my colleagues at the Irish Architectural Archive: Sean O'Reilly for photography and Ann Simmons who showed great patience as usual in typing my untidy manuscripts. – David James Griffin, Dublin 1989-90.

Unidentified Location Design for a chimneypiece and overmantel (plate 12) left

Design for a chimneypiece (plate 13) above

NOTES

[1] For a general account of Leinster House see *The Georgian Society Records,* vol. IV, 1912.
[2] John Harris, 'Sir William Chambers, friend of Lord Charlemont', in the *Quarterly Bulletin of the Irish Georgian Society,* vol. VIII, no.3, and *Sir William Chambers, Knight of the Polar Star* (London 1970).
[3] Royal Irish Academy: Charlemont Manuscripts. Reported in *Historical Manuscripts Commission, 12th Report* (1981).
[4] For a full account of Isaac Ware see Howard Colvin, *A Biographical Dictionary of British Architects,* 2nd ed. (1978).
[5] Brian FitzGerald (ed.), *Correspondence of Emily Duchess of Leinster,* vol.I (1949), pp.199-200.
[6] For Norfolk House see *The Survey of London,* vol. XXIX (1960).
[7] *Anthologia Hibernia* (October 1793), vol. II, pp. 242-3.

BIBLIOGRAPHY

Fitzgerald, Brian, (ed.), *Correspondence of Emily, Duchess of Leinster, 3 vols* (Dublin 1949-57).
The jGeorgian Society Records, 5 vols (Dublin 1909-13).
Harris, John, 'Sir William Chambers, Friend of Lord Charlemont', *Quarterly Bulletin of the Irish Georgian Society,* vol. VIII, no. 3 (1965).
Harris, John, *Sir William Chambers, Knight of the Polar Star* (London 1970).
Hind, Charles, (ed.), *The Rococo in England,* a symposium (London 1986).
Kent, William, *The Designs of Inigo Jones,* 2 vols (London 1727).
Vardy, John, *Some Designs of Mr Inigo Jones and Mr William Kent* (London 1744).
Ware, Isaac, *Designs of Inigo Jones and others* (London c. 1733).
Ware, Isaac, *The Plans, Elevations and Sections of Houghton, Norfolk* (London 1735).
Ware, Isaac, *A Complete Body of Architecture* (London 1756).

THE ABSENTEE

BRYAN GUINNESS

The moss reproaches my feet,
Tenderly under my tread,
As I follow the unwalked path
To the twirls of the garden gate,
Curtained with cobwebs and beaded with dew.

'Put on a necklace,' she said,
Stooping to tell me her tale,
'If the dew-drops hang on the gossamer thread,
Look by the holm-oak tree.'

What was it the visiting lady
Promised that I should see?
A glimmer of vanishing creatures?
Or today's me?

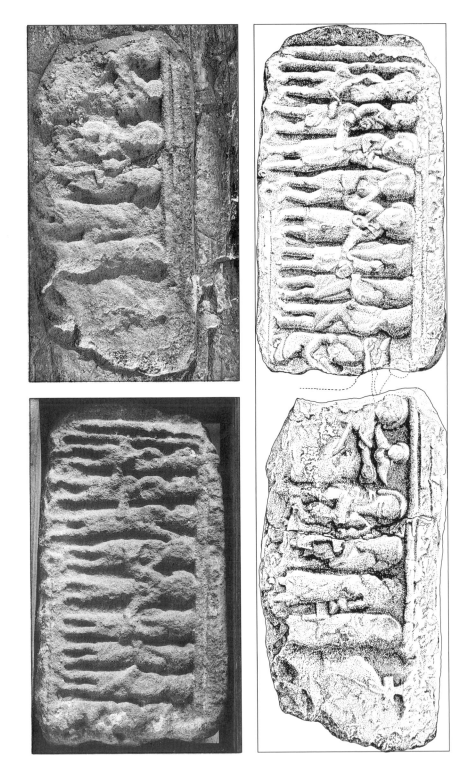

THE ROMANESQUE PASSION LINTEL
AT RAPHOE, CO. DONEGAL

PETER HARBISON

Maurice Craig, bless him, has that felicitous art, given to so few mortals, of being able to write and speak with equal mellifluousness and clarity. Indeed, those privileged enough to have been edified and entertained by Maurice's magisterial conversation will clearly hear his unmistakable voice as they read his printed works – for I know no one who writes as he speaks in the way that Maurice can and does. Yet his facility of expression is also happily combined with a great depth of learning, and his *Architecture of Ireland* of 1982 shows him to be the only architectural historian whose breadth of vision and lucid insights into detail and design span all periods of Irish building history almost down to the present day. In gratitude for all of those delighted hours spent in his company, and in joyful hope of many more, I would like to offer Maurice this essay on some richly sculptured fragments from one of those primitive Early Christian Irish lintelled church doorways which he described as 'perhaps the most distinctive and most perennially satisfying features to be found in the whole course of Irish architecture' (Craig 1982, 35).

The present Church of Ireland cathedral at Raphoe in Co. Donegal preserves two sculpted fragments which seem to be the only recognizable remnants to survive from a church which presumably preceded it on the same site. One fragment (fig.1) stands in the cathedral vestibule, and the other (fig.2) is built into the exterior north wall of the nave. When placed side by side, they can be construed as the left- and right-hand end respectively of a long rectangular stone bearing as its centrepiece a carving of *The Crucifixion,* the reconstruction of which (fig.3) shows a small piece to be missing between the two major fragments. Arthur Kingsley Porter (1931, 51 and 54) took the stone to have been the base of a cross, but Françoise Henry (1940, 182) interpreted it as the lintel of a doorway. However, Susanne McNab (1987, 30 and footnote 20), in her recent discussion, has suggested that the carving formed part of a narrative frieze, perhaps on the façade of a church, because she believed that the complete stone's original width of 255cm was too great for it to have acted as a lintel unless support-

Fig.1 – Left-hand fragment of the lintel, now in the cathedral vestibule (photos: P. Harbison)
Fig. 2 – Right-hand portion of the lintel, now built into the exterior north wall of the nave
Fig.3 – Reconstruction of the lintel (drawing by Edelgard Soergel-Harbison).

73

ed by a trumeau, of which not a single example is known in Ireland. Yet Henry (1967, 189) must surely have been right in seeing the roll moulding on the bottom right-hand portion of the fragment in the cathedral porch (fig. 1) as the upper part of a door-frame moulding. Its left-hand end is marked by a small circle, two figures to the left of which are noticeably larger in scale than those standing on the roll-moulding above the presumed door-opening. This moulded frame shows that the doorway was much narrower than the lintel itself, and unlikely to have measured more than 143 cm wide at the top. It would thus appear to have been considerably more ambitious than its nearest Irish counterpart at Maghera, Co. Derry, where the door opening is 86cm wide (McNab 1987, 20-1). The sculpture at Raphoe ought to be understood, therefore, as having extended laterally well beyond the top of the doorway, as at Maghera and on lintels beneath the tympana of French Romanesque cathedrals. The fact that the Raphoe stone has broken almost exactly in the middle, where the missing piece belonged, would only add support to the interpretation as a lintel, because this is precisely where we would expect a lintel to fracture through excessive weight from above, if not relieved by an arch above it, of the kind found for instance over the west doorway of Glendalough Cathedral (Leask 1955, 71).

The Raphoe and Maghera lintels are alike in that they both bear representations of the crucified Christ in the centre, but they differ in that the numerous figures flanking the cross at Maghera all belong to the same scene, whereas at Raphoe they illustrate separate incidents before and after *The Crucifixion.* Porter (1931, 54) interpreted the scene on the vestibule fragment (fig. 1) as *The Arrest of Christ,* with the two figures which we see to the left of Christ representing St Peter cutting off the ear of Malchus with a sword. The other figures on the same fragment would then be the multitude with swords and staves (Matthew xxvi, 47) farther to the left, as well as what we may presume (on the basis of the Maghera lintel) to be Longinus kneeling on the extreme right of the fragment, beneath the right hand of the crucified Christ. The corresponding figure of Stephaton can just be made out on the exterior wall fragment (fig. 2) kneeling beneath Christ's left arm, above which is an angel balancing another over Christ's right arm. The junction of Christ's left arm and torso suggests that he may have worn a long garment partially covering the arms.

The remaining figures on the north wall fragment were considered by Henry (1940, 83) and McNab (1987, 27) to be too damaged to allow identification. Yet a dome surmounted by a cross close to the right-hand end must surely represent Christ's tomb, which may have reached down slightly beneath the level of the top of the door-opening, as do the second and third figures on the extreme left of the vestibule fragment (fig.1). To the left of the tomb we can see a figure which may be taken to represent the angel sitting on the almost horizontal tombstone, announcing the Resurrection to a single woman (Mary Magdelene bearing spices) beside it, rather than to two or three as we might expect (compare Schiller 1971, fig. 29). The remaining two figures between this tomb scene and *The Crucifixion* appear to be bearded soldiers, presumably to be identified as those involved in casting lots for Christ's garments (John xix, 23-4). One of them may hold a knife, and both seem to hold in front of them the seamless coat (compare Schiller 1972, figs 348 and 508), symbolizing the indivisibility of the Church, as the Rev. Oliver Crilly kindly pointed out to me. Paradoxically, however, a split in the stone has fragmented the garment!

Roughly following Porter (1931, 54), Françoise Henry (1940, 183 and 1967, 189) suggested a late ninth/early tenth-century date for the Raphoe lintel, because of a similarity in sculptural style between the Raphoe lintel and the High Crosses at Donaghmore (Co. Tyrone), Armagh and Monasterboice, and the fact that MacDurnan was abbot of both Raphoe and Armagh at the time. But it is not on these crosses, but on the Cross of the Scriptures at Clonmacnoise, Co. Offaly, that we find a number of scenes which may be compared with those on the Raphoe lintel. The lower register of the west face of the base appears to bear a succession of three scenes – *Christ's Entry into Jerusalem*, *The Resurrection* and *The Holy Women at the Tomb* – which, like those at Raphoe, neatly encapsulate the events of Easter Week, while the shaft of the cross also has a panel representing the soldiers holding the seamless garment. But where the same scenes occur on both the Raphoe lintel and the Clonmacnoise cross, there is little similarity in the details of their composition, as witnessed by the soldiers holding the seamless garment, but more particularly by the representation of Christ's tomb at Raphoe, which is unique in Ireland. Such comparisons render it virtually impossible for us to derive the Raphoe sculpture from the Clonmacnoise cross. Even among the Ulster crosses, the only surviving example to offer a viable comparison is that at Arboe which, unlike all the other Northern crosses, has Stephaton and Longinus in the same respective positions which they occupy on the Raphoe lintel.

We might have been in a better position to judge the validity of High Cross comparisons if we knew more about a High Cross which is said to have been removed from Raphoe in 1441 (Chart 1940, 66), but Helen Roe (1955, 107) was justified in casting doubt on its identification with that now known as the Market Cross in Armagh, which itself is composed of fragments from two different crosses. Certainly, the existing crosses and cross-slabs from Donegal (Lacy *et al.* 1983) offer no satisfactory parallels for the sculpture of the Raphoe lintel.

While Lacy *et al.* (1983, 284, No. 1602) carefully left open the possibility of a later dating for the Raphoe lintel, Susanne McNab (1987) was the first to suggest a date in the Romanesque period, and her suggestion has much to recommend it, even if it is difficult to prove conclusively. Her conclusion was based on the similarity between the Raphoe lintel and the undoubtedly twelfth-century example from Maghera, Co. Derry, which indeed offers the best comparison. The proportions of the figures are approximately the same, and both have a *Crucifixion* as the centrepiece of a long, rectangular composition. It might also be pointed out that the hairstyle of one of the soldiers bearing the seamless garment at Raphoe, despite the poor state of preservation, may be compared to that of the figures on the bronze Crucifixion plaques of c.1100 (Harbison 1980).

In the absence of any figure sculpture on the doorways of Irish church-es which are likely to be earlier than the Romanesque period, the Raphoe lintel would fit in well with the other Irish lintels bearing figure sculpture which can reasonably be dated to the twelfth century. Prime amongst these, of course, is Maghera. Another is the pediment-shaped lintel found in the eighteenth century lying close to the twelfth-century 'Priest's House' at Glendalough, Co. Wicklow, and now built in above its door (Barrow 1972, 34-5). Although Hencken (1950, 16 with footnote 1 and Pl. V), Henry (1967, 185) and Thomas (1971, 186) all agree on an eighth/ninth-century date for yet a further lintel – with *Crucifixion* – from Dunshaughlin, Co. Meath, the forked beard of Christ and the ear placed high on his head argue much more persuasively for a twelfth-century date for it. The only other Irish figured lintels – from Carndonagh and Clonca, both in Co. Donegal (Lacy *et al.* 1983) – cannot be dated satisfactorily, though a twelfth-century date would be quite acceptable for them. A twelfth-century date for the Raphoe lintel can be seen to fit in not only with the available Irish evidence, but also with that from continental churches, where a lintel with figure sculpture makes its appearance in the eleventh century at Saint-Genis-des-Fontaines, but only becomes widespread as a type beneath the tympana of French Romanesque churches in the twelfth century (Rupprecht and Hirmer 1975). Curiously, *The Crucifixion* rarely features as part of the iconography of architectural sculpture (as opposed to internal church furnishings) much before the thirteenth century, so that it is difficult to point precisely to possible forerunners for either the Maghera or Raphoe lintels.

If Schiller (1972, 152) be correct in seeing the fresco of c.1150 at Schwarzrheindorf as one of the earliest instances of a *Crucifixion* scene showing numerous additional figures flanking the cross, then the Maghera lintel displaying this particular characteristic is likely to be slightly later – and the same may also apply to Raphoe. Unfortunately, the history – and even the nomenclature – of the diocese of Raphoe in the twelfth century is as unclear as its list of bishops. From Gwynn and Hadcock (1970, 93-5) we learn that Muiredach O'Coffey, who had apparently transferred the seat of the bishopric of Cenel Eoghain from Ardstraw, Co. Tyrone, to Maghera, Co. Derry, early in his episcopate (1152-73), was described by the Irish Annals on his death in 1173 as bishop of Derry and Raphoe, though when he did fealty to Henry II a year earlier, he was described as *episcopus Tarensis*. On that same occasion the submitting bishop of Raphoe was stated to be Gilbert, otherwise Gille-in-Choimdedh Ua Caran, who Gwynn (1959, 91-2) described as the only twelfth-century bishop of Raphoe who is more than just a name to us. He was bishop of Tír Conail when witnessing the confir-mation charter of Newry in 1156-7, and may well have been bishop of the area of the Raphoe diocese from the time of the Synod of Kells in 1152 until he was translated from Raphoe to Armagh in 1175. As Maghera and Raphoe were both listed as suffragan bishoprics of Armagh in the list which Cardinal Paparo brought away with him from the Synod of Kells, it would not be an unlikely assumption that both may have been erecting cathedrals at their respective sites some time after the Synod of 1152. On the basis of Fr Gwynn's comment noted above, the most prominent personage likely to have been responsible for the erection of a Cathedral at Raphoe would be Gilbert, *alias* Gille-in-Choimdedh Ua Caran, which could suggest a date between 1152 and 1175. Nevertheless, we cannot entirely discount the possibility of an involvement by his contemporary Muiredach O'Coffey who, however, would be a more likely candidate for the builder of the church at Maghera, perhaps early in his episcopate and, therefore, possibly earlier than Raphoe. The notion that Raphoe might be later than Maghera could find support in the larger size of the Raphoe lintel, and its more expansive Passion iconography, perhaps designed to outshine Maghera in the competition for succession to the long-lived Archbishop of Armagh, Gille mac Liag (Gelasius), on whose death Gilbert was translated to Armagh, two years after Muiredach O'Coffey had died. All that we are reasonably justified in claiming is that both the Maghera and Raphoe lintels fit best into the third quarter of the twelfth century, though we might be allowed to speculate that they may have been carved not too far apart in time, perhaps within less than a decade of the year 1160.

BIBLIOGRAPHY

Barrow 1972. Barrow, L., *Glendalough and St Kevin* (Dundalk).

Chart 1940. (ed. D.A. Chart), *A Preliminary Survey of the Ancient Monuments of Northern Ireland* (Belfast).

Craig 1982. Craig, M., *The Architecture of Ireland from the earliest times to 1880* (London/Dublin).

Gwynn 1959. Gwynn, A., 'Raphoe and Derry in the Twelfth and Thirteenth Centuries', *Donegal Annual* 4, No. 2,pp. 84-100.

Gwynn and Hadcock 1970. Gwynn, A. and R.N. Hadcock, *Medieval Religious Houses, Ireland* (London).

Harbison 1980. Harbison, P., 'A lost Crucifixion plaque of Clonmacnoise type found in Co. Mayo' in (ed. H. Murtagh), *Irish Midland Studies, Essays in commemoration of N.W. English* (Athlone), pp.24-38.

Hencken 1950. Hencken, H., 'Lagore Crannog: an Irish royal residence of the 7th to 10th centuries A.D.,' *Proceedings of the Royal Irish Academy*, 53 C, pp.1-247.

Henry 1940. Henry, F., *Irish Art in the Early Christian Period* (London).

Henry 1967. Henry, F., *Irish Art during the Viking invasions 800-1020 A.D.* (London).

Lacy *et al.* 1983. Lacy, B. *et al.*, *Archaeological Survey of County Donegal* (Lifford).

Leask 1955. Leask, H.G., *Irish Churches and Monastic Buildings*, I (Dundalk).

McNab 1987. McNab, S., 'The Romanesque figure sculpture at Maghera, Co. Derry and Raphoe, Co. Donegal' in (ed. J. Fenlon, N. Figgis and C. Marshall) *New Perspectives, Studies in Art History in honour of Anne Crookshank* (Blackrock), pp.19-33.

Porter 1931. Porter, A.K., *The Crosses and Culture of Ireland* (New Haven).

Roe 1955. Roe, H.M., 'The High Crosses of County Armagh, A Photographic Survey', *Seanchas Ardmhacha* 1, No. 2, pp.107-14.

Rupprecht and Hirmer 1975. Rupprecht, B. and M. and A. Hirmer, *Romanische Skulptur in Frankreich* (Munich).

Schiller 1971. Schiller, G., *Ikonographie der christlichen Kunst, Band 3, Die Auferstehung und Erhöhung Christi* (Gütersloh).

Schiller 1972. Schiller, G., *Iconography of Christian Art, Volume 2, The Passion of Jesus Christ* (London).

Thomas 1971. Thomas, C., *The Early Christian Archaeology of North Britain* (London/ Glasgow/New York).

1. The east entrance front

2. The south front (Walton-on-Thames Public Library)

ASHLEY PARK, SURREY

A MATTER OF SIR JOHN VANBRUGH AND
SIR EDWARD LOVETT PEARCE

JOHN HARRIS

WHEN Colen Campbell surveyed the 'adjacent Villas' from the top of
Vanbrugh's belvedere at Claremont in Surrey in either 1717 or 1725,[1] his
eye would have taken in an astonishing panorama of riverside estates. Of
course, it depends when he made his survey of Claremont gardens, but if
late in 1724, below him downstream would have been Ashley Park, the vil-
las around Twickenham such as Orleans House; Marble Hill would have
been just building, while on the opposite bank beneath the shadow of
Richmond Park, was Ham and Sudbrooke. Upstream, he would have
espied old Esher Place, Oatlands, Dorchester House, and many smaller vil-
las or farms. Except for Ashley, all have been treated to their 'biography'
and are familiar to architectural historians. In most cases the nearby parish
church contains some memorial of ownership or tenancy, and we can play
the game of assigning family tombs to the appropriate estate. So it is in the
church at Walton-on-Thames where Roubiliac's magnificent monument
erected in 1756 to Lord and Lady Shannon overshadows the interior, so vast
is it.

Richard Boyle, 2nd Viscount Shannon, died in 1740, and his widow in
1755. As a peripatetic soldier and courtier, Ashley was Shannon's main
country seat in England. In London in 1738 he employed Giacomo Leoni to
rebuild 21 Arlington Street, a house still there. At Ashley Sir Edward Lovett
Pearce is recorded as having made 'additions' at an unspecified date[2] based
upon a plan to be found in the Pearce-Vanbrugh Album at Elton Hall,
Huntingdonshire.[3]

This plan (plate 9) can be briefly discussed. It shows in outline the
north wing of the old house with semi-circular bows on the east and west
ends, and is inscribed by Pearce, 'Part of the House as it now is'. The pro-
posed extension comprises a new office and servants range the width of
the wing, a connecting corridor to a laundry and kitchen block overlooking
the kitchen garden on the west side, and a courtyard with a concave wall
on the east with the 'already built' (Pearce's notation) stable block set in the
north-east angle.

Obviously, from Pearce's reference to the main block 'as it now is', he
might only have been concerned with minor additions to a house known
to have been built from 1602. However, a rich nobleman who was a cousin
of Lord Burlington, and a soldier friend of Lord Ligonier, whose magnifi-

cent apartment at 12 North Audley Street has been convincingly attributed[4] to Pearce by 1730, might have been expected to have housed himself with some distinction. That this was so is demonstrated by photographs taken of the house before its demolition in 1925, and is one of the excitements of architectural discovery.

Today it is difficult to find the site of the house, although it is possible to follow the route that Shannon's funeral cortège would have taken from house to church. Ashley Park Avenue follows the Grand Drive that once led off Walton High Street. It is now easy to lose one's bearings, for we are apt to be confused by the intricacies of a matured housing estate laid out on two hundred acres soon after 1925. Not much can be traced of the ancestral past except for an ice house, some brick walls, and a few trees of perhaps mid-eighteenth-century date.

Ashley is only known to local historians, and especially Michael Blackman who has written a small booklet and edited the Ashley House Building Accounts.[5] The failure of Ashley to impress itself upon history is due to the ten ownerships, mostly of short duration, between 1602 and 1923. Berkeley was followed by Argyle, Villiers, Weston, Andrews, Clarges, Pyne, Boyle, Fletcher and Sassoon. The longest in possession were the Fletchers, and then only from 1786 to the 1860s. Only Berkeley (1602-11), perhaps Andrews (c.1670-c.90), and Boyle (c.1718-55) can be associated with building works.

Nothing that Lord Shannon and Sir Edward Lovett Pearce did to Ashley could disguise its origins as a moderate-sized brick manor house of traditional H-shape, with gabled wings, and with gables on the inner returns of the east front where the wings projected forward further than on the west (seen in plates 1-3). Frankly, Ashley would not deserve more than cursory attention had not the complete building accounts survived. As they demonstrate, Ashley was built between 29 August 1602 and 1 June 1605 for Lady Jane Berkeley. She had first married Sir Roger Townshend of Raynham; then in 1589, Henry, Lord Berkeley, from whom she seems to have secured a separation, hence the decision to build her own house. For just over £3119 she was provided with an undistinguished, somewhat old-fashioned design, and it matters not that the architect of the 'plott' is unknown.[6]

To elucidate what might have been effected to Ashley in the seventeenth century, it is necessary first to examine the building works of Lord Shannon. This soldier, whose military career ended with a field marshal's baton in 1739, bought Ashley in 1718. As commander-in-chief in Ireland from 1720, and one of the lords justices there from 1722 to 1723, if he improved Ashley it must have been either between 1718 to 1720, or after the tenancy of Ashley by William Pulteney, who lived here in 1724 and 1725. Shannon and Pulteney were friends and both belonged to the circle of Lord Burlington. Indeed, Pulteney had obtained a design from Burlington for a town house before 1727. However, his tenancy of Ashley did not involve him in any alterations.

What is remarkable about Ashley, and its tragedy, is that it survived, until demolition, intact as Shannon had left it. The old photographs demon-

3. The west front (Walton-on-Thames Public Library)

4. The Great Hall (Oliver Brackett)

5. The staircase (Oliver Brackett)
6. The Long Gallery (Oliver Brackett)
7. Chimney wall of room attributed to Pearce (J. Paul Getty Center for the Humanities)

strate this.[7] They show something quite extraordinary: that Lady Berkeley's old-fashioned Late Elizabethan house had been totally encased and re-fenestrated in a style unmistakably that of either Sir John Vanbrugh, or Pearce working in his style. We can recognize the bones of the 1602 house, its gables and its chimney-stacks with new-built flues where they project from the body of the house. All else has been rebuilt in an arcuated style characteristic of Vanbrugh's Ordnance manner. This is particularly the case with the east front bows, nearly full semi-circles (*cf.* plate 1), and the south front (plate 2) with massy entrance bay, blocked surround to door, and an open pediment.

The problem of attempting to distinguish between Vanbrugh and Pearce is encapsulated in the Elton Hall Album. Therein are designs clearly identified as by either, but there are many others that might be by Pearce after Vanbrugh, or by a draughtsman copying their designs. To establish when Ashley might have been given its Vanbrughian cosmetic it is necessary to consider when Pearce became professionally involved in architecture and to relate this to Vanbrugh's death on 26 March 1726.

Pearce entered the army as a cornet in Colonel Richard Morris's Dragoons in 1716; in 1723 to 1724 he was in Italy studying architecture, and from May 1725 was in Dublin for good. Therefore his connections with Vanbrugh and probable training under that architect (who was his father's first cousin) must ante-date 1723. Reference must also be made at this juncture to the Elton Album plan for additions to Ashley, for an associated 'Memorial'[8] is inscribed by Pearce, 'Arthur coppy these papers in a fair hand but wrote *sic* so small as to bring all in one sheet if possible'. This refers to Arthur, who was Vanbrugh's clerk and draughtsman. Therefore, this instruction was either given in Vanbrugh's lifetime or Pearce employed Arthur after Vanbrugh's death. This is crucial in determining if alterations were made to Ashley in two phases: one by Vanbrugh, the other by Pearce acting independently. These two phases are illustrated inside the house.

The Long Gallery (plate 6) with its Vanbrughian chimney-piece resembling a design[9] in the Elton Album seems earlier than the 'Chiswick'-styled room (plates 7-8) with its neo-Palladian chimney-piece. It is clear from a comparison of plates 2 and 6 that the gallery was on the ground floor of the south front. The gallery must belong to the arcuated exterior, for it fits the external fenestration perfectly, whereas the 'Chiswick' room accords better with Pearce's Burlingtonian tendencies after he returned to Dublin in 1725.

Many of Pearce's Irish works betray this duality of style, the one engendered by his familial relationship to Vanbrugh and training under that architect, the other by close study of the works and designs of Lord Burlington, whom Pearce must have known.

Because of this duality within Ashley it would seem likely that the Long Gallery is concurrent with the external refacing undertaken by Vanbrugh some time between Shannon's acquisition of the property in 1718 and Vanbrugh's death in 1726. In view of the Ordnance style, Vanbrugh saw this as appropriate for a great soldier, and the similarity between the east front centre and Vanbrugh's own house at Claremont may perhaps be compelling evidence to ascribe this phase to Vanbrugh. However, there is the plan to consider, for this is drawn by Pearce.

The plan shows the proposed addition of offices to the north wing which is inscribed 'Part of the House as it now is'. This north wing is shown with an eastern bow (the right-hand bow of the entrance front in plate 1) and a western bow which we know, from plates 2 and 3, to have disappeared at least when the photographs were taken. Further, since it is possible to place the 'Chiswick'-style room within this north wing, at its western end (see below), and since this room appears from the photographs unaltered, and without a bow (plate 8), we may say that the bow disappeared after Pearce's plan was drawn, and before the 'Chiswick'-style room took shape.

8. Wall with windows and aedicule mirror in room attributed to Pearce
(J. Paul Getty Center for the Humanities)

Before listing the different possibilities concerning Vanbrugh's and Pearce's involvement, let us recall that the western end of the Long Gallery was unbowed when photographed (it is the ground-floor room extending the length of the south front in plate 2); and that the memorandum among the Elton Hall drawings associated with Ashley contains a reference and instruction to Vanbrugh's clerk, Arthur.

The probable alternatives are as follows:
(i) Pearce and Vanbrugh are involved together at Ashley, with Pearce continuing to work there after Vanbrugh's death in 1726
(ii) Vanbrugh alone initiates the work and Pearce is summoned to continue, complete, or extend Vanbrugh's work in 1726.

In deciding between these alternatives, much depends on plate 9: if the 'Part of the House as it now is' shows the unaltered bowed Elizabethan house, then we know that Pearce must have been involved before the house got its Ordnance-style recasing, presumably from Vanbrugh. This recasing will have omitted the Elizabethan bows on the western front, leaving Pearce free to design a perfectly rectangular 'Chiswick'-style room after Vanbrugh's death.

On the other hand if the 'Part of the House as it now is' shows the house after Vanbrugh's intervention when – perhaps – Pearce is summoned to succeed Vanbrugh, we must explain Pearce's demolition of Vanbrugh's western bow. Surely it is improbable that Pearce would – for relatively minor gains – do away with Vanbrugh's bow (unless for compositional reasons connected with his own lengthy proposed extension of the western front)?

The solution may be along the following lines: Vanbrugh, on his own, and just before his death, designs and initiates the work which he in part executes. Only on his death, with the western front still unfinished, is Pearce summoned from Dublin. Pearce, working with Vanbrugh's clerk Arthur (no connection elsewhere between Pearce and Arthur is recorded), takes over control; completes the west front with lunette windows rather than the mullioned ones of the entrance front), and the 'Chiswick'-style room at its northern end, with the contiguous offices.

Pearce could hardly have effected interior works without visiting Ashley. He obtained permission[10] to go to England from March to June 1726, a visit that must surely be connected with Vanbrugh's death, at least initially: then from April to July 1728 and from October 1730 to January 1731. In view of the style of the one room that betrays the influence of Lord Burlington's villa at Chiswick, either 1728 or 1730 would suit. Of course, no documentary evidence exists to attach Pearce's name to the later room. Nevertheless, taken out of its Ashley Park context, Burlington's is the only name to conjure with, even if the ornamental details lack Burlington's usual rigorous resort to antique Roman and Palladian precedents.

In hastening to Ashley to witness its sad demolition in 1925, the historian would have perhaps first walked around the exterior, noting the peculiarity of the 1602 gables and roof works rising out of the arcuated Ordnance style of the ground and first floors. Speculation might have been aroused by the unusually high profile of the central part of the entrance front as to what would be revealed behind the three tall arched windows. Turning around the corner to the south front, the powerful effect of the tall semi-circular bays would have been noticed, and the south front centre between the projecting chimney breasts would be forcibly associated with the Vanbrugh Ordnance style. On the west front there had clearly been some departures from the pattern set by the east front. For example, although the 1602 gables on the entrance front and their north and south returns retained the old three light mullions, here they had been replaced by semi-circular windows, except for the south inner gable that may have been rebuilt at a later date without a light. Unfortunately, ivy prevented any detailed examination of the exterior of Pearce's office block.

Upon entering the house from the east front the unexpected experience of a two-storey hall (plate 4), set transversely across the whole width of the centre stroke of the 1602 H-plan, would evoke surprise. If the transverse hall belongs to the Berkeley house, then Ashley as of traditional plan must be reassessed. However, the arched openings and the blank arcades in the upper parts of the hall would suggest that there must be cause and effect between Vanbrugh's outside and this internal reorganization. The

painted decoration comprising *trompe-l'oeil* trophies and Gothic Revival
vaulting to the ceiling is by the painter of the trophies and the ruin compo-
sitions on the staircase, who can be confidently identified as John Devoto,
working at Burlington House in 1721.[11]

Two arches in the north-east corner of the hall opened to the stairs.
The photograph (plate 5) is taken from the first landing looking down into
the hall and up to the top landing, off which an arched opening led to the
hall's east gallery. Such stairs with panels of carved foliage only appear in
England after the Restoration, and carving of this type and quality can be
attributed to Edward Pearce, to whom has been ascribed the comparable
stairs at Wolseley and Sudbury Halls in Staffordshire, and Cassiobury Park,
Hertfordshire, all of the 1670s. Therefore the tradition that the Ashley stair
was built by Lady Angelsey, who married a Weston and died in 1662, is
incorrect. Sir Matthew Andrews (*c.*1670-90) is more probable, for as a
friend of Samuel Pepys and a co-governor of Christ's Hospital, he might
well have employed one of Wren's principal sculptors and carvers.

The Long Gallery (plate 6) seen in the only surviving photograph has
its second or matching chimney-piece hidden by the paired, fluted
Corinthian columns at the south-east end.

If the Long Gallery can be located on the ground floor of the south
front, and assumed to be a re-fitting of Lady Berkeley's one, the so-called
Burlington or Chiswick room (plates 7-8) may also be located. Plates 8 to
11 show a rectangular room. If, for temporary convenience, plate 7 is arbi-
trarily described as the north wall, it follows that plate 8 shows the west
wall. Such a room, with two round-headed windows to the 'west', and
another at the 'west' end of its 'south' wall, with doors some or all of which
connect with other interiors, must be located at the west end of the north-
ern range of the old house. In other words, it occupies the western section
of Pearce's bowed 'Part of the House as it now is', probably on the first
floor, and connecting, by means of the door on the left of plate 7, with the
extensions proposed by Pearce in plate 9. As we have already noted, this
means that the bow on Pearce's plan had disappeared by the time this
room was fitted out. Even for 1730 it is a most distinguished neo-Palladian
room. Neither Henry Flitcroft nor William Kent, nor Isaac Ware, or even
Roger Morris, were handling interiors with such refinement. If Lord
Burlington must be dismissed in view of the absence of his characteristic
ornamental vocabulary, Pearce is the only other name to conjure with.

No one would describe Ashley as a great house. It may claim our atten-
tion as a major working of an earlier house by Vanbrugh with the assistance
of Pearce, or by Vanbrugh and Pearce in consecutive campaigns. As the
few surviving photographs testify, the interior was magically evocative,
with surprise following surprise. Soon after 1925 the Burlington room and
the Long Gallery, and perhaps even the staircase, disappeared into the
maw of American decorators. In 1960 the present memorialist of this house
saw the Long Gallery dismantled and propped up in a New York ware-
house belonging to French and Company, antique dealers. Since then all
trace of it has been lost, an incredible conclusion.

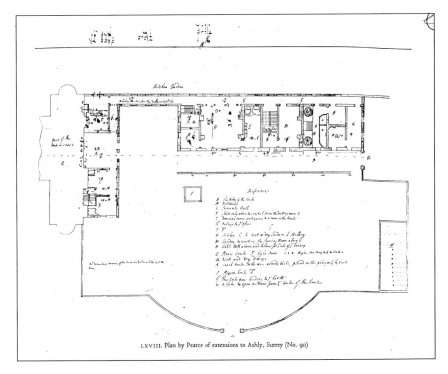

LXVIII. Plan by Pearce of extensions to Ashly, Surrey (No. 90)

9. The Elton Hall plan for additions by Sir Edward Lovett Pearce

NOTES

[1] Colen Campbell, *Vitruvius Britannicus,* III, 1725, p. 8. It has now been demonstrated that many land surveys in volume three were intended for the earlier volumes prior to Campbell's discovery of the 'pseudo'-Jones designs for Whitehall Palace.

[2] H. M. Colvin, *Biographical Dictionary of British Architects 1640-1840* (1978), pp.682-29.

[3] *Architectural Drawings in the Library of Elton Hall by Sir John Vanbrugh and Sir Edward Lovett Pearce, ed.* Howard Colvin and Maurice Craig (Oxford 1964), catalogue nos 14 (memorial) and 90 (plan). The memorial mentions 'Arthur', who was Vanbrugh's servant and draughtsman.

[4] For Ligonier's house *cf.* Greater London Council, *Survey of London* XL (1980), 100-01. Ligonier was Colonel of the 8th Horse on the Irish Establishment. He was a subscriber to architectural books and his house at Cobham in Surrey was described in *The Ambulator (1811)* as in the manner of an Italian villa.

[5] Michael Blackman, *History of Ashley Park, Walton-on-Thames,* Walton and Weybridge Local History Society, Paper no. 16 (1976); and *Ashley Park Building Accounts 1602-1607* (ed. Michael Blackman), Surrey Record Society, v, XXIX (1977).

[6] But *cf.* the later discussion of the transverse hall.

[7] These are to be found in two sources: the photo-archive of the J.Paul Getty Center for the Humanities, Santa Monica, in uncatalogued boxes, miscellaneous decorative arts; and the local history collection of Walton-on-Thames Public Library.

[8] Colvin & Craig, *op cit.,* pl. XLIII, cat., no. 231.

[9] These dates have been supplied to me by Edward McParland, to whom I am indebted.

[10] *Cf.* Edward Croft-Murray, *Decorative Painting in England 1537-1837,* v. 2 (1970), p.201.

[11] Blackman 1976.

ON THE DESIRE TO EMULATE THE ACTIVITIES OF
CAPTAIN LEMUEL GULLIVER AT BLEFUSCU,
OR SOME ANIMADVERSIONS UPON THE CREATIONS OF

MODEL-SHIPWRIGHTS

GORDON L. HERRIES DAVIES

FIFTY YEARS ago pneumonia was a serious business. One bout almost saw me into my coffin. It was early in 1937 and I was aged five. But, cared for by my parents and nurses Drummond and O'Hara, I pulled through, and during the weeks of my convalescence – weeks when my diet consisted chiefly of Brand's calf's foot jelly – books were my constant companions. There I faced a problem: I had not yet learned to read. All I could do was look at the illustrations and wonder what was being depicted therein. I still remember how deeply frustrating it was. Among the many illustrations at which I gazed in puzzlement there was one which held me spellbound. It was a colour plate in an anthology of children's stories and it showed a giant wading in a harbour where he was surrounded by a multitude of sailing ships the masts of which scarcely reached up as far as his knees. It was, of course, Lemuel Gulliver about to tow the entire Blefuscu fleet off to Lilliput but I doubt whether I then knew the story. The sight of that man surrounded by all those tiny ships nevertheless gripped and enthralled me. My life-long passion for model ships had been born.

We then lived in England on the outskirts of Manchester and as my strength returned I was removed to Derbyshire to enjoy the clean mountain air of my grandparents' home in Buxton. There, for sixpence, I acquired from Woolworth's a tin, red-funnelled tugboat and with that little vessel I became my own Gulliver at the lake in the Pavilion Gardens. Shortly thereafter my father took me down to Hunt's toyshop at the far end of Buxton's Spring Gardens and invited me to select for myself a small present. The choice eventually lay between an attractively boxed Dinky model of the L.N.E.R. train ' Silver Jubilee' and a brown and yellow model of a fishing-trawler carrying a little steadying sail aft. The train would have been the sounder investment but I walked off with the trawler. She was promptly christened the *Girl Pat* after a North Sea trawler then much in the news but she was not a good buy. Her paint flaked off after contact with water and, in nautical terms, she was crank. Far more successful was the model I received for Christmas that same year. She was a two-foot long, wooden-built, clockwork-powered cargo-boat — a kind of Clyde puffer with a hold for'ard, a working derrick, and a supplied cargo of crates and barrels. She was handsome and beautifully made. I dearly wish that she was still mine but all that I have to remember her by is a photograph which happens to sit upon my desk at this very moment. I see that she even had a brass steam-pipe running up her tall blue, white-banded smoke-stack.

So, I had begun to play Gulliver by the time the barrage-balloons made their first appearance over the distant Manchester skyline and by the time the newsboys pedalled down the road outside our home shouting 'Special. Munich conference special'. As Europe rolled towards war, my fleet of little ships grew apace. There were Dinky liners (the *Rex* was my favourite), a large three-masted, square-rigger (knowing no better I named her the *Marie Celeste*), and a clockwork diving submarine (purchased with a cash prize won in a newspaper's painting competition), but the oddity was a clockwork ship of German manufacture which came with three different interchangeable superstructures. For one voyage she could be a liner, for the next she could be a battleship, and for a third she could be a lowly dredger. I acquired this strange vessel at a toyshop in Rhyl, North Wales; it was a model which might have appealed to Anton Detmers of the *Kormoran*. But I now wanted to see model ships other than my own. When we went to Manchester I liked to go by train because on one of the platforms of Central Station there stood two glass-cased models. My recollection here is hazy but I think that one of them was a model of the Isle of Man Steam Packet Company's *Ben-my-Chree* of 1927 and the other was perhaps the L.M.S.R. steamer *Hibernia* of 1920. Under the enormous arch of that station's roof, and surrounded by the smoky exhalations of Prairie Tanks from Trafford Park and Jubilees from Kentish Town, I must have spent hours running my eyes over those two models, absorbing their every detail from their jackstaffs to their delightful counter sterns. I nonetheless had a complaint to make. Why were the saloon windows merely painted on and not properly glazed? No such complaint could be levelled at another model which was on view in Manchester. That model lay to anchor in the window of the Blue Star Line's office in Albert Square. She was huge. She was glistening white. There were quoit pitches and padder tennis courts marked out upon her decks; there were tiny chairs gathered around the blue-tiled lido swimming pool; the pool itself seemed ever so inviting; and all her scuttles and windows were properly glazed. Her name ? She was the cruise-liner *Arandora Star*. Among ships she was, frankly, no beauty. Her bows were bluff. Her bridge was too far aft. Those great blue stars emblazoned upon her two funnels were all too prescient of the decorative horrors which were to be inflicted upon ships during the second half of our century. Such blemishes in the original there might be, but for me no visit to Manchester was complete without a pilgrimage to the Blue Star office and with that model I came to possess a relationship such as I have possessed with no other ship-model. The *Arandora Star* herself fell victim to U 47 in the eastern Atlantic on 2 July 1940 but the model remained on display for several months after the waves had closed over the real ship. Then one day I went again to pay my respects to the model and her former berth was empty. She was gone. I wonder where she lies now. Real ships, if they survive some premature and catastrophic fate, eventually make that last sad journey to the knacker's yard but surely no similar end awaits those magnificent show-case models which used to grace the offices of the great shipping companies. I doubt whether my *Arandora Star* was ever torn asunder by little men wielding miniature oxyacetylene cutters, so perhaps she sits in some museum collection which I have yet to discover. Or is it possible that she has lain these fifty years in some dank Manchester cellar waiting for me to rescue her, St George-like, from her cavernous prison? Perhaps nobody wants a huge model of a forgotten ship – nobody, that is, save myself. I would be delighted to live with her. Only recently, in a curio shop in Dublin's Anne Street, I found a little lacquered dish bearing a picture of the *Arandora Star*. I suppose it was a souvenir brought home by somebody who had cruised in the ship during the 1930s on one of her regular sailings to the Mediterranean, the Norwegian fiords or through the Panama Canal to San Francisco and Honolulu. The price being asked for the dish was exorbitant, but I bought it. The dish is for me a reminder not of the ship herself – I never set eyes upon her – but of the model I once knew in one-time Cottonopolis.

My father made models of old-time sailing ships and as I approached my teens the inevitable happened: I began to spend my school-holidays building my own ship-models. An uncle had given to me a six-penny warship identification book produced by Cassandra of the *Daily Mirror* and entitled *Spot Them at Sea!* I still have it, minus its covers, and the 1:1920 – scale silhouettes therein became the plans in my earliest efforts as a model-shipwright. First I made a model of a minesweeper (I admired her nicely sheered lines), and then, in succession, I built models of the *Hood*, the *Revenge*, the *Scharnhorst* (Cassandra had included a few German ships), and the *Repulse*, before this, the first phase in my model-ship building career, came to a close with a second and better model of the *Hood*. My abiding interest in the latter, tragic ship was already clearly apparent and some words by Oscar Parkes were then, as now, deeply engrained upon my thinking.

No ship has ever before presented such an appearance of the embodiment of power and speed and no future capital ship is likely to equal her in beauty and proportion.

A just assessment, I maintain, but there does have to be one caveat: the *Hood* did not display herself to the best advantage when she was viewed on the quarter and I will always regret that *Jane's* illustrated her obituary with a photograph taken from that angle. None of my early models is now extant; they – even my second *Hood* – were just typical schoolboy creations but I was proud enough of them in their day. In building all of them I laboured under a severe disadvantage: I was forbidden the use of my father's chisels as being too dangerous in my unskilled hands. But I was working in wood and how can you reproduce the bow flare of a *Hood* or a *Repulse* without the use of a chisel? Occasionally the prohibition had to be disregarded – sometimes with unfortunate results. If I turn to page 154 in my well-thumbed 1939 edition of *The Wonder Book of the Navy* I find there a nice close-up of the bridgework of the *Renown* but there is also a large blood-stain, the result of a slip with a chisel while I was building my model of her sister the *Repulse* well nigh fifty years ago.

Gradually my skills improved and I discovered new sources of information about model-worthy ships. I used to buy plans – and very basic plans they were – from an English firm called Modelcraft Ltd; I discovered that ship photographs were to be purchased from a firm based in Liverpool; I avidly studied the nautical pictures in *The Illustrated London News* and in the writings of Eric Charles Talbot Booth; and I spent long happy hours poring over the pages of *Jane's* where the British four-funnelled cruisers of the years around 1900 held me enthralled. (Should I ever meet a kind fairy who grants me just one wish that will release me briefly from my present time-frame, then I think that I might choose to spend a few hours – with a camera – aboard the *Powerful* just after Captain Hedworth Lambton had brought her home to Portsmouth in April 1900 after her service at the Cape.) What I would then have given for the kind of reference works – the publications of the Conway Maritime Press, for instance – which are available to the modern model-builder. In my earlier days I regretted so often that a book encountered while bookshop-browsing and bearing upon its spine the title *Hood* could never be anything more than a volume of collected verse. There was, of course, one other way of developing an understanding of ships: there were real ships to be visited and explored. I had many such opportunities – the liners *Mauretania* (1938) and *Orbita*, the battleship *Iron Duke*, the Clyde steamers, David McBrayne's boats, the ships of the Liverpool and North Wales Steamship Company, and the Irish Sea ferries – but in retrospect I do dearly wish that I had created for myself many more such occasions. I do have to admit, however, that some of my visits to ships left me bewildered as to the complexity of the task confronting the marine modeller. As you pace her weather decks you realize that a ship is a complex structure which challenges the ingenuity of any magician who would seek to wave a craftsman's wand and reproduce the original in miniature. Late in the 1940s, for instance, I took it into my head to build a large-scale model of one of the modern British ' A' Class submarines and I was shortly delighted to be offered an opportunity of visiting two members of the class, the *Aeneas* and the *Andrew*. What I saw stopped me in my tracks; their hulls and casings were so replete with finicky detail that I came to doubt my ability to render an adequate reproduction. My submarine never left the stocks.

My studies of photographs and plans, and my visits to actual vessels, engendered innumerable schemes for projected models but the pressures of a busy life were soon upon me and few of my projects ever advanced beyond the drawing-board stage. In recent years I have launched only one ship: a 1:42 semi-scale model of the China river gunboat *Scorpion*, the original having been built at Cowes in 1937 by J. Samuel White & Co. Ltd. My *Scorpion* ran her trials a few years ago in the Yangtse-like setting of the Avonmore river in County Wicklow. She performed well enough but she still remains incomplete. Maybe one day I will return to her just as John Brown's men returned to Job 534 on 3 April 1934. I have just taken an early retirement so perhaps I will now have more time for self-indulgence in ship modelling. My present home certainly offers every inducement; there is ample workshop space and just across the lawn there lies a normally placid river. They tell me the river is full of trout; I am much more interested in it as a place in which to play Gulliver. From the National Maritime Museum in Greenwich I have just purchased a set of plans for the Admiral Class battleship *Howe* of 1885. She was once the portguard ship at what was then Queenstown and there she caught the eye of William Lawrence, the Dublin photographer. His splendid picture of her is reproduced in *The Irish Naturalist* for September 1907 and that, I hope, is how she will look as she rides to anchor in my river. Black hull, white upperworks, two primrose yellow funnels ... the very thought of setting my model upon the water sends a thrill of excitement surging throughout my being.

Why do I react in this manner? Why, throughout my life, have model ships so fascinated me? Why do the words 'model cruiser' or 'model paddle-steamer' have for me such a special and exciting ring? Why, in a moment of depression, can I find an antidote in either the sight of the battered Dinky model of the *Normandie* which sits upon my desk or in the pages of *Model Shipwright* ? Why do I sometimes crave for the sight of a model ship just as, I presume, the alcoholic craves for a splash of his particular poison? To all such questions I have no adequate answer. Perhaps a psychiatrist might have comment to offer. What I do know is that, while I have a very special relationship with model ships, all varieties of representations in miniature excite me. Furniture for dolls' houses, those tiny marzipan 'fruits' used for decorating cakes, displays of Britain's farm animals, minuscule books, bonsai trees – they are all to me deeply fascinating. Granted my inability to account for my taking such delight in all things miniature, there are three aspects of my passion for ship-models which I do understand. Those three aspects fall under the three headings of craftsmanship, aesthetics, and historical association.

I admire a beautifully constructed ship-model as a delicious fruit upon that tree which represents the human creative instinct. In the lines of her hull I see reflected the craftsman's hard-earned skill with his tools; in the fittings upon her decks I see her creator's meticulous attention to detail as he strives for microscopic perfection. Like a delicately carved doorway, a stained-glass window, or a piece of Chippendale, a fine ship-model is a work of art which must excite our admiration. But here there is something odd – something which is again beyond my comprehension. The subject is best approached through a musical analogy. A pianist may give a rendering of, say, Chopin's Barcarolle in F sharp major. It may be a rendering which is technically proficient but at the same time it may be a performance which is devoid of all warmth and feeling. It may leave its auditors entirely unmoved. I hold the same to be true of ship-models. A model may, technically speaking, be a brilliant rendition of the real ship and yet somehow the model may at the same time be utterly lacking in character. She may have no soul built into her – she fails to present in miniature the aura of the real ship. So many ship-models – particularly steamship models – from the early decades of the present century – lie in their show-cases like so many dead salmon laid out upon the fishmonger's slab. I first became conscious of this fact in August 1958. I was then contemplating the construction of my third model of the battlecruiser *Hood* and went to Glasgow to inspect the 3/16-inch to the foot model of the ship which lay in the Kelvingrove Museum and which had been constructed for the ship's builders at Clydebank by the famed Northampton model-building firm of Bassett-Lowke. The model is, of course, superb. It was displayed at the British Empire Exhibition at Wembley in 1924-5 and it is perfection in every detail from truck to keel. And yet it left within me a deep sense of disappointment. I had expected to be moved by the model. I had expected the model to convey to me some-thing of the spirit of the original ship. I wanted to feel that through this model I was approaching the ship which in 1923-4 had been the cynosure of international eyes during the world cruise of the Special Service Squadron, which in northern climes during 1931 had been the acting flag-ship of a mutinous fleet at Invergordon, and which in Mediterranean sunshine had in 1936 received upon her spacious quarterdeck the exiled Emperor of Ethiopia. But I was let down. I was looking at a lifeless model – a model so immaculate in her perfection that she had become sterile. In a glass case alongside the *Hood* lay something utterly different: a massive model of the battleship *Howe* of 1940 which simply exuded life. I could almost hear the roar of her ventilating fans and the sound of orders issuing from her Tannoy. I had come to Kelvingrove to pay court to the *Hood* but I instead found myself deeply in love with her neighbour. Yet, considered just as examples of the modeller's craft, the *Hood* has to be rated as far superior to the *Howe*. The builders of the model battleship have made no attempt to incorporate into the *Howe* that wealth of detail so apparent in the model battlecruiser. The *Howe's* fourteen-inch gun-houses, for instance, are reproduced in a somewhat basic form and no effort has been made to represent the varying thicknesses of armour plate upon their crowns. But the *Howe* lives; she is a real ship in miniature. Another ship model which I encountered recently and which for me possesses that same vibrant quality is one of the models aboard the preserved American aircraft-carrier *Intrepid* berthed at Pier 86 in New York. There, upon the carrier's hangar deck, sits the huge model of the battleship *Nevada* constructed for use in the making of the film *Tora! Tora! Tora!* Again, that model makes no pre-tence of being complete down to the last cleat, down to every coaming and the ship's cat, and yet for me she does possess all the spirit of her original – the only battleship which succeeded in getting under way that infamous Sunday morning at Pearl Harbour. You will perhaps protest that all such sentiments arise solely within the mind of the observer, but I prefer to think otherwise. I am convinced that in order to breathe life into his subject the ship-modeller, like the musician and the portrait-painter, needs not only his skilled craftsmanship, but also that *je ne sais quoi* of the true artist.

I turn next to that aspect of ship-models which I entitle aesthetics. My point here is simple. Ever since the Middle Ages we have increasingly learned both to appreciate and to cherish the artefacts resulting from the human creative genius. We display those artefacts in the cabinets of our museums. We position them upon the walls of our galleries. We place them in the presses of our libraries. We receive into public care follies and fortifications, mansions and mills, and of them all we make places of pilgrimage. When I wish to see the Bayeux Tapestry I cross to Normandy. When I wish to study Gainsborough's *The Blue Boy* I resort to the Huntington. When I wish to be left spellbound by the Taj Mahal I purchase a ticket to Agra. But when I wish to behold a masterpiece of naval architecture I am poorly served. Oceans cover 70 per cent of the surface of our globe yet there have been preserved only an infinitesimal proportion of the vessels which, over the centuries, we have placed upon those waters. Storms, torpedoes and the ship-breakers' hammers have wrought havoc with our maritime heritage. Had Christopher Wren designed ships rather than churches then the chances are that not a single example of his work would today survive. There have been great naval architects – Vittorio Cuniberti, William White, Vladimir Yourkevitch – but gone are the ships for which they were responsible. Their creations are now just memories. Only very recently has there dawned an understanding of the need to preserve ships just as we preserve Stonehenge or the Le Château at Versailles, and, recognizing the impoverished state of our naval architectural heritage, we have begun the task of recovering vessels from the sea-bed – the *Vasa* from the bottom of Stockholm Harbour, the *Mary Rose* from the mud of Spithead, and the submarine *Holland No. 1* from the floor of the English Channel. After thirty years as a wreck in the Falkland Islands, Brunel's *Great Britain* has been returned to her birthplace in Bristol, and after languishing for fifty years as an oil-terminal, Isaac Watts's *Warrior* has been magnificently restored and is now open to the public at Portsmouth. But so much has been lost over the centuries: the *Santa Maria*, Magellan's *Vittoria*, Drake's *Golden Hind*, Cook's *Endeavour* and *Resolution*, Darwin's *Beagle*, the *Great Eastern*, the battleship *Oregon*, Fisher's *Dreadnought*, the *Mauretania* of 1906, Beatty's *Lion*, the *Yavuz alias* the *Goeben*, the seventh *Warspite*, the submarine X 1, all the Flower Class corvettes (including the Irish *Cliona, Macha* and *Maev*), the *Jean Bart* and the *Richelieu*, the ninth *Vanguard*, and the fourth *Ark Royal*. This is impoverishment indeed and recollection of such lost masterpieces brings me back to model ships. It is to a model that we must turn if we wish to study the appearance – the lines and the fittings – of some bygone vessel. An illustration of the ship helps, a set of plans fills out the picture, but it is a large-scale model which brings us closest to the real ship herself. If I wish to recapture the essence of the *Great Michael* built for James IV of Scotland in 1511, then I have to stand before the 1:48 model of the ship in the Royal Scottish Museum in Edinburgh; if I wish to encounter the *Italia*, that six-funnelled naval freak of 1880 by Benedetto Brin, then it is to the Museo Storico Navale in Venice that I must go; if I wish to experience the *Helga*, the Department of Agriculture and Technical Instruction for Ireland's fishery cruiser which played her part in Dublin's trauma during Easter Week 1916, then I must take myself off to the National Maritime Museum in Dun Laoghaire. But frequently I am thwarted. We are told that earlier in our century British matelots would sometimes row for miles just for the pleasure of feasting their eyes upon the graceful lines of the battlecruiser *Tiger*. I would dearly love to have been able to do the same (my propensity for battlecruisers must already be fully apparent) but the *Tiger* went to the breakers within two months of my birth. The best I may hope for is a model of the *Tiger*. Strangely, however, I know of no model of that ship anywhere upon public display. The ship's motto of the *Tiger* was *Quis eripiet dentes;* it seems that if I am ever to enjoy a model of the ship I will have to begin by drawing not her teeth but her lines.

That brings me to the third aspect of my passion for ship-models – the aspect which I term historical association. I am an historical sort of person; I enjoy trying to commune with the past and in so doing I am deeply conscious of the significance of place. To visit Beethoven's birthplace in Bonn, Darwin's home at Downe, or the Lincoln homestead at Springfield, is to draw close to a giant from the past. To walk over a Connemara bog to the site where Alcock and Brown landed their Vimy, to visit the Château of Hougoumont, or to stand upon the beach at Kealakekua where Cook was murdered, is in each case to relive a moment of history. But the nautical historian who seeks such satisfaction finds himself – or herself – at a grave disadvantage. The ships which made history are mostly gone and at the places where they performed their deeds there is nothing to be seen but a watery waste. Military historians may explore the sites of the battles of Bannockburn, Blenheim, the Boyne, and Bull Run, but what maritime historian would trouble to visit the sites of such naval engagements as Texel, The Glorious First of June, Trafalgar, or Tsushima? Railway buffs make their pilgrimage to Rainhill but is there any sense in the nautical buff taking a choppy excursion over the waters of Spithead just so as to be able to observe 'It was here in June 1897 that the *Turbinia* convincingly demonstrated the marine potential of the steam turbine'? It is in helping to satisfy the desire for bridges through time that ship-models have a role to play. It is through a model that we are transported back to some historic event in which there participated her real-life namesake. Surely nobody can look at even a schoolboy's plastic-kit rendition of the *Titanic* without reflecting upon those dramatic events off Cape Race upon a night to remember in April 1912. I stand before the model of the battlecruiser *Queen Mary* in the Neptune Hall of the National Maritime Museum at Greenwich and I think of her voyage to Kronstadt with the Battlecruiser Squadron in June 1914. I think of the ship dressed for the visit to the Squadron of the Czar and Czarina. I think of Grand Dukes in full dress saluting her quarterdeck to the shrill accompaniment of bos'n's pipes. I think of her caviar-besotted, vodka-sodden officers returning on board after their latest encounter with Russian hospitality. I think of the discussion that must have taken place down below in her wardroom: did the news just received of Archduke Ferdinand's assassination at Sarajevo hold any portent for the ship? It did. By squeezing the trigger of his revolver, Gavrilo Princip had ignited a fuse which two years later was to end with the tumultuous explosion of the *Queen Mary's* magazines under a hail of shells from the German battlecruisers *Derfflinger* and *Seydlitz*. There were but nine survivors from her complement of 1275 officers and men. As the waters of the North Sea poured into the gaping hole where only seconds earlier there had stood her masts and funnels, the air pressure inside her riven hull caused a great mass of official documents to be hurled skywards from her after hatchway. I look at that hatch upon the model and I think of its strange contribution to the ship's funeral pyre. I look forward along the quarterdeck to the 13.5-inch guns of 'X' turret where Petty Officer Francis had his action station. He was one of the nine survivors and he has left us a graphic account of the *Queen Mary's* end. He tells us that after the magazine explosion ' everything in the ship went as quiet as a church, the floor of the turret was bulged up, and the guns were absolutely useless'. I look at the rear of 'X' turret to see the ladder down which Francis made his escape onto the steeply sloping deck where he was helped over the ship's starboard side and into the sea by A.Bs. Lane and Long. Neither Lane nor Long survived.

And should I one day be reunited with my *Arandora Star* what kind of temporal bridges will that model inspire within me? I will certainly try not to think of the ugly scenes that followed her torpedoing off the Bloody Foreland. She was transporting German and Italian prisoners to Canada and panic ensued as they tried to fight their way to the stricken vessel's boats. Instead I will think of her lying under a Mediterranean sun at Ajaccio, her passengers repairing on board for lunch after inspecting Napoleon's birth certificate at the Hotel de Ville down the Place des Palmiers. I will think of her lying by night off Hammerfest with the strains of the Lambeth Walk coming up from the ballroom down on 'D' deck while up on the Observation Deck a honeymoon couple from Swanage are intent upon recording the midnight sun with their new Pathe Ciné camera. I will think of her rounding Diamond Head and making course for Honolulu, her sunbathers briefly forsaking the lido pool to watch the aircraft-carrier *Lexington* and two attendant destroyers sweep past on their way to Pearl Harbour. Perhaps I will also think of a schoolboy who fifty years ago used to gaze into the window of the Blue Star Line office in Manchester and who dreamed of being able to play Gulliver with just such a model as this. Maurice Craig would understand; he and I have paddled in the waters of Dublin Bay while playing Gulliver with working model ships constructed in his own workshop.

MAN AND MODELLIST

AN APPRECIATION

JOHN DE COURCY IRELAND

I FIRST MET Maurice Craig when I was nearly as young as he was: I mean, I was older by the same large margin as now but he was somewhat alarmingly mature to listen to, and it was evident to me on that occasion – I suspect it was George Morrison who had introduced us – that he was going to go a long way without suffering any fools at all gladly while travelling.

There followed years when news trickled home from time to time of his prowess in the neighbouring island in his particular expertise. Then came the pleasure of meeting him back in his own country, where that expertise was badly needed, and has done so much to make people appreciate the architectural heritage that is our patrimony. Many battles would have been lost on this plane, to the impoverishment of future Irish generations, had he not been here.

Just after his return, when he was living quite close to me in Dalkey, I discovered that Maurice had another notable expertise. He has, I found, an encyclopaedic knowledge of many categories of ships, their origin and purpose, their history and ultimate fate. However, it has not sufficed him just to know, to be able to identify almost any ship approaching or leaving the port of Dublin, and to discourse grippingly about where she was built, her sister ships and rivals; he has also long been the finest builder of large ship-models that I have ever met outside the staffs of great maritime museums like Bremerhaven, Amsterdam, Belem on the Tagus, Madrid, Paris or Greenwich. And there are experienced professional modellists in those august institutions who would envy him his skills.

Maurice's magnificent working model of Guinness's SS *Clarecastle,* a ship familiar for many years to countless Dubliners, lying near the Custom House loading casks, now as an obsolete steam beer-carrier, is a triumph of this particular art. The man who commanded the ship for many years, when shown the model, examined it minutely and at length, and eventually pronounced it exact. This was the ultimate testimony to the excellence of the modellist, for that master mariner, Captain Meredith, whom I had the pleasure of having on Dun Laoghaire Lifeboat Committee when I was its Secretary, was celebrated among seafarers for his meticulous judgments and forthright honesty.

I have recently heard it said that Maurice has declared himself prouder of his *Clarecastle* and other ship-models than of the great standard works on architectural history by which his name is, and for the foreseeable future will be, known. Certainly the models are equally, in their own sphere, joys for ever.

Interest in ships has led Maurice Craig into activities of which admirers of his books may not be aware. He has voyaged on board a number of well-known cruise-ships to many parts of the world, and, exceptionally observant, has, on his return, always been able to pronounce shrewd and informative judgments on the places visited and on people met.

George Morrison and I persuaded Maurice to join the Maritime Institute of Ireland at a time when that body carried more weight with the community than perhaps it does now. He soon was chosen to grace the Council of the Institute where he gave much useful advice and was helpful in the installation of the National Maritime Museum, of which he is a valued trustee, in the former Mariners' Church, Dun Laoghaire. Moreover, having deservedly, and to the profound relief of the discerning, been appointed to the body set up to protect the nations architectural patrimony, he is leading the fight for the preservation of the innumerable historic wrecks around our coasts.

A MAN OF TWO CITIES

BENEDICT KIELY

MY FIRST meeting with Maurice Craig came about in the most distinguished company. Let me mention the names of some of the people who were there. Easy to remember them. Impossible to forget them.

In his favourite corner was R.M. Smyllie and with him Austin Clarke, Walter Starkie, M.J. MacManus, Seamus O'Sullivan, Cathal O'Shannon the father, Captain Tadgh MacGlinchy, splendid in his uniform but a man who could hold his own in any company of bibliophiles.

Dear shadows, now you know it all ...

The man who joined the group, at a wave of the hand from Smyllie who wised to discuss some matter with him, was tall, grave. Silent, I was about to say. But no he, rather, spoke exactly and with deliberation and everything he said was worth listening to. Who he was I knew well. He was already famous and I like to think that I was the first person to say that Maurice Craig had written the best book about Dublin and the best ballad about Belfast.

Red brick in the suburbs, white horse on the wall,
Eyetalian marbles in the City hall:
O stranger from England, why stand so aghast?
May the Lord in His mercy be kind to Belfast.

This jewel that houses our hopes and our fears
Was knocked up from the swamp in the last hundred years;
But the last shall be first and the first shall be last:
May the Lord in His mercy be kind to Belfast.

We swore by King William there'd never be seen
An All-Irish Parliament at College Green,
So at Stormont we're nailing the flag to the mast:
May the Lord in His mercy be kind to Belfast.

O the bricks they will bleed and the rain it will weep,
And the damp Lagan fog lull the city to sleep;
It's to hell with the future and live on the past:
May the Lord in His mercy be kind to Belfast.

The book, as we all know, was, and is, *Dublin 1660-1860*. Frank MacDonald who has given much thought to such matters saying a while ago about that book: 'Six months ago Maurice Craig received a letter from an eminent judge congratulating him on his masterly book, and saying how much he regretted not having read it years ago. The book was published in 1952 when Dublin City was still largely intact. And, if more people like the judge had read it, then, perhaps, much more of Dublin City might have survived the depradations which followed.

'Dublin's tragedy is that not enough of us shared Maurice Craig's vision of the city as a work of art.'

Frank MacDonald had a lot more to say on the question and he said it in *The Irish Times*, on 9 July 1988, and he was, and is, well able to speak for himself: and I, humbly, trot after him.

And here I was, some years ago, trying to grapple with another work or book, the greatest, I dare to think, by Maurice Craig.

It is neither permissible nor possible to paraphrase Edward Gibbon. Only the man's own words will serve. So here goes:

As Constantine urged the work with the impatience of a lover, the walls, the porticoes and the principal edifices were completed in a few years, or, according to another account, in a few months; but his extraordinary diligence should excite the less admiration, since many of the buildings were furnished in so hasty and imperfect a manner that, under the succeeding reign, they were preserved with difficulty from impending ruin.

All that was about the building of the second Rome: and what it suggests, I suspect, is that London Bridge and other structures might readily fall down and in ruin if not properly founded: and that Time the Destroyer could catch up on buildings that had been founded as solidly, it would seem, as the Rock of Cashel.

Meditating in *Le Médecin de Campagne* on the nature of life in a lost mountain valley somewhere near the Grand Chartreuse, Balzac thought that men could not behold any ruins, even of the humblest kind, without feeling deeply stirred: 'The though of death is called up by a churchyard, but a deserted village puts us in mind of the sorrows of life.'

And Elizabeth Bowen, in her book about the family home, Bowenscourt, built with square Roman solidity upon a conquered land, but now, that symbol, no longer there, saw the surrounding Irish landscape as peopled with the ruins, ancient and, you might ironically say, almost modern, standing up starkly out of fields, giving another character to the corner of a road.

This vast work, *The Architecture of Ireland: From the Earliest Times to 1880*, does not, by no means, confine itself to ruins: either the ruins of ill-construction or destruction, or those Ruines of Tyme about which Edmund Spenser wrote a poem. But, in the course of a journey over several thousand years, Dr Craig passes by a few ruins on the way.

He ranges from the stone-circles laid down by an unknown people to the bar-and-grocery owned by a people that we know only too well, from roundtowers to handball alleys, from great houses to railway stations, from

Norman keeps to nineteenth-century cathedrals, from many old-arched bridges to jails and gatelodges and even to the tombstones in Mount Jerome: taking in his stride everything in stone by, or through, which man has ever expressed himself on the ground of Ireland. And what a stylish stride this learned man has.The stones talk and illuminate history.

In his chapter on Cistercian Gothic he writes:

It is a paradox that the Cistercian Order, which distrusted Art as a distraction from devotion, should have promoted so much noble architecture. In practice, it was not so much Art as ornament which they distrusted and, even here, they fortunately fell short of their own ideals. The Cistercian plan was very influential in Ireland. Its transeptal chapels are to be found at Ballintubber and Athassel which were Augustinian, at Cashel Cathedral and, with a peculiarly feliticious modification, at St Canice's Cathedral, Kilkenny, also. Whether a central tower is to be called an 'ornament' or part of the architecture is, perhaps, debatable; the Cistercians legislated against such a feature as early as 1157, yet well before the turn of the century the monks of Boyle had deliberately planned a crossing tower. The stones of Boyle are *pierres parlantes*, indeed, eloquent of many contradictions ...

That is a paragraph to ponder on when you visit the old abbey by the brawling Boyle river. History re-echoes from the ancient walls, and you may meditate on what Maurice Craig has to say about the talking stones. This great book is one to bring with you on any road round Ireland if, that is, you are interested in the buildings man made to alter the landscape: made either for defence or for worship, or simply to shelter himself from the weather, or to glorify himself in grandeur, or to cross rivers or step down from trains: or for any other purpose known to him.

Before you set out, compile a small glossary. I found that even for an ignoramus like myself a list of somewhat less than twelve technical terms would be ample. Then you have with you in about 350 wide pages, and splendid illustrations, a most accomplished guide.

So often I had said about Maurice Craig that he had written the best book about Dublin and the best ballad about Belfast, that I finally began to hear my own echo. He seems, also, to have the gift for writing upon his subject the book that makes any further book unnecessary.

That road round Ireland would, for myself, begin by travelling from Dublin to Dungiven to find, with the author's help, the tomb, in Cahan Abbey, of an ancient who may have gloried in or been embarrassed by the name of Cooey na Gall: and who died in 1385. The tomb may be of a later date.

Dr Craig points out that the tracery on the tomb is of swirling flamboyance, with small cusps over a neat semicircular arch below which the occupant reposes in effigy: and then, most interestingly, the panels of the frontal are occupied by six of the mercenary soldiers or gallowglasses who gave Cooey his nickname. Dr Craig rightly finds it surprising that a petty chieftain in a remote place could be so influential that, fifteen or twenty years after his death, he could, from the earth, command a tomb of such honour. And, indeed, it is also a matter for questioning, never to be answered, how such a man could have maintained such a bodyguard or battallion of bruisers: MacDonalds possibly. Gallowglasses, whose title in time became Englished or corrupted into the name Golligley, a name common enough in that part of the world. As youngsters without Irish we called it Golliwog and thought we were very funny.

But further north at Downhill the story is well-known of that wonder, even among the men of his time, Frederick Augustus Hervey, Bishop of Derry and Earl of Bristol, who built a palace on the cliff-edge, and a bower also, for a female cousin to whom he was, it might seem, attached. He swept like a comet through Europe and left his name to a hundred hotels. Dr Craig wrote:

The siting of Downhill can only be described as Ossianic: on top of a cliff facing north across the Atlantic towards the Outer Hebrides, where only a romantic could expect to find a house, and only a lunatic would build one. The Earl-Bishop qualified on both counts.

Imagine a journey, westward the course, from Gandon's Custom House to Dun Aengus. You cannot, with comfort, go any farther. The journey must not be on a straight line. Dart north or south as the text guides you. Arrived there, you may read his laconic explanations of the famous, or monstrous, *chevaux de frise:*

This consists of the largest possible number of spike-shaped stones which can be struck into crannies in the bare rock, from which they protrude at a variety of angles; more adapted, one would suppose, to the discouragement of an armoured division or a float-down of paratroops than of the warriors who people the plays of Mr Yeats. The thought occurs again that it was because the spike-shaped stones and the cracks in the rock were there, that someone had the idea of disposing them in such a decorative way.

Finally: here is the last sentence of the first paragraph of this great book:

There are, it is true, a few categories of building which are peculiar to Ireland: such are, for example, Round Towers, spirit-groceries and ball-alleys.

Dr Craig is a grave and scholarly and bespectacled man. But quite frequently there is a glint behind the glasses.

IS THE SCREEN MIGHTIER THAN THE PEN?

A STROLL THROUGH 'VIRTUAL REALITY' AND HYPER–MEDIA

MARK LESLIE

AFFORDABLE computer-aided design – In 1986 I attended an RIBA conference in London on 'Low Cost CAD for Architects'. I was interested to discover that the general definition of 'low cost' was £50,000 per workstation. My own practice, the Leslie Fox Albin Partnership, had at that time just designed the new St Luke's Hospice in Plymouth, using no more than an Apple Macintosh microcomputer, a dot matrix printer, and some simple desk-top-publishing graphics programs; a highly effective CAD system costing less than £3000.

The microcomputing background – LFA stumbled into microcomputing in 1985 when an Apple Macintosh was installed as a replacement for Letraset as the office labelling machine. The principal activities of an architectural practice have more in common with a graphic design studio than with an engineering office. In the first few years the advantage of the Mac was that there were no cumbersome engineering CAD/CAM packages to distract one from the intoxicating possibilities for architectural drafting with cheap graphics and DTP software. By 1986 LFA had thrown its drawing boards away entirely.

Hyper-Media – Since then the personal computer industry has latched on to new terms such as 'Hyper-Media', and 'Virtual Reality'. They have become as abused as the preceding catch-cries such as 'Desk Top Publishing'. The momentum of innovation is such that solutions are usually produced well in advance of anyone clearly defining the problems. Hyper-Media is showing less sign than DTP of sweeping all before it. This is perhaps because many of the people who could most benefit from using it perceive it as some sort of specialist and time-consuming form of 'desk top *son et lumière*' involving wiring a spider's web of esoteric and expensive peripherals to powerful computer workstations.

Converging communications technologies – For years the computer, sound recording, photographic, film, television, video, printing, photocopying and telecommunications industries studiously ignored each other to produce incompatible data-communication technologies. Effectively, each invented a subtly different shape for the wheel. The idea of creating a single vehicle for marketing, design presentation, entertainment and education to which all these different-shaped wheels can at last be attached is very appealing. It is not fundamental to Hyper-Media, however.

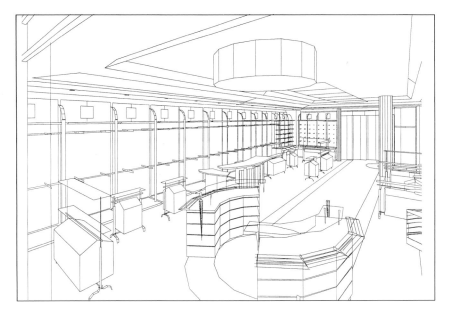

Computer walk-through – shop interior

Interactiveness as the vital quality – Stripped to its essentials, Hyper-Media is the linking of more than one type of information such as text, sound and graphics into a single seamless presentation that is interactive. A 'coffee-table' book with its semi-random combination of main text, sub-text, expanded captions, diagrams and glossy pictures nearly qualifies. The user is presented with more than one path through the material. He can skim, browse or delve at his own discretion. Clearly this type of presentation can be produced simply and dynamically on the single medium of a cheap home computer, with some digitized sound, and writing, painting, and 'slide show' software.

Microcomputers as the key technology – HyperCard, for instance, the 'do-it-yourself' information environment that comes free with every Apple Macintosh, can handle text, graphics and sound. It embodies the essence of Hyper-Media within a single software program. A wave of ever-more sophisticated 'Hyper-Media' interactive database, presentation and animation software is washing over the entire PC world, typified by products such as Guide Hypertext, Supercard, Persuasion, Sculpt-Animate Auto-Animater and Macromind Director.

The antecedents of Hyper-Media – the urge to maximize the impact of your message by addressing as many human senses as possible, simultaneously, is as old as man. There is solid archaeological evidence of exciting Multi-Media excursions into 'virtual reality' when Paleolithic men donned animal skins, painted creature and landscape symbols all over themselves and the cave walls to dance about by the light of fire brands, accompanied no doubt by chanting, music, aromatic incense and hallucinatory drugs. Equally, the notion of user-controllable, interactive knowledge retrieval systems is at least as old as the written word. So what is special about modern Hyper-Media?

Breaking the bounds of traditional presentation – Traditional multiple-sensory happenings such as religious ceremonies, concerts, ballets, plays, films, and TV programmes tend to be pre-packaged, and strictly linear, with a fixed beginning, middle and end. User-defined interactivity tended only to occur within the confines a single medium, such as a properly indexed and cross-referenced book. What is truly new and different, therefore, is the possibility of Multi-Media, combining the all-absorbing trance state induced by the audio-visual bombardment of video, with the browsability of the book.

Accessibility the key to success – For Hyper-Media to be successful in the short term it has to be seen to be affordable and easy to do. It must unlock the suppressed film director in professionals whose primary skills and interests lie elsewhere. User-friendly personal computers opened up realms that had been the preserve of a priesthood of computer specialists. Home video similarly overcame the passive nature of television, and opened up a world of viewer control, and do-it-yourself programme making. Multi-Media needs to be seen as a complementary part of this process of de-mystification and democratization. It must empower the creative individual to communicate ideas quickly, cheaply and effectively.

Slide Show Magician: Multi-Media ahead of its time – An early aquisition of LFA was Magnum Software's Slide Show Magician. With a $50 price tag and a ten-page manual this programme conformed to LFA's maxim that 'software is useful in inverse ratio to both the price and length of the manual'. Written in 1984, it already incorporated many of the features that would later make Macromind Director and HyperCard famous. One could pull in screens from any other Mac programme, overlay them with animated text captions, and both hidden and visible 'buttons' that controlled a range of dissolves, fades and wipes. The programme was bundled with a library of digitized sound effects. Pulling in images from Harvard Universities $20 CAD modelling programme 'Scheme 3D', LFA began presenting all projects to clients as a semi-animated matrix of text, sound, building plans and perspective views. The emphasis on images of ghosts, goblins and choo-choo trains in Slide Show's manual showed that its publishers saw its primary use being the creation of interactive educational and adventure-gaming environments for very small children. Clearly anything quite so affordable or easy to use would be of little interest to grown-ups. Unfortunately they were largely right.

Marketing with HyperCard – In 1987 Apple begun bundling HyperCard free with the Mac. This 'information environment constructor kit' added database search functions, and background programming, to Slide Show's presentation abilities. 'Hypertalk', the built-in programming language, had the unusual merit of being a subset of plain English. LFA could now invent invisible screen buttons by writing Hypertalk 'scripts' such as 'dissolve slowly into view of Managing Directors Office'. The commission to design the £10.5 million Labware Building for international healthcare giant

Becton Dickinson was secured in 1987 following a boardroom presentation in which HyperCard's flick-card abilities were used to show bulldozers clearing the site amidst clouds of dust, steel springing out of the ground, cladding panels flying together, and so forth. Construction was able to commence a mere eight weeks after briefing. The client had been sold a much more dynamic impression of the architectural concept than would ever be possible from mere drawings.

CAD walk through – Later, time was spent in creating a very detailed MacArchition CAD model of the administrative office area. Over one hundred perspective views were pre-processed, and saved into Hypercard and buttoned into logical looped sequences. Clicking on the left or right side of the screen might turn one in that direction. Clicking on a door, skylight or window might jump one through it. Floppy disks sent to the US let us talk the client through the building by phone from the UK. The manweek involved in creating this presentation was equivalent to the time spent setting up a single architectural perspective by hand.

Introducing colour and time, the 'fourth dimension' – A serious drawback of Hypercard is that to optimize its speed as an administrative 'filofax' it is strictly black and white. Luckily it can be buttoned to control other programs when required. LFA coloured up a number of the key views with Electronic Art's colour paint program Studio 8. This has its own slide-show utility as well as the ability to cycle colours through any of 256 shades through time. It was easy to create the appearance of night gradually falling over the building and lights coming on, as well as the reflections of passing clouds in the exterior mirror glass. The microcomputer screen presents a much closer analogue of reality than lines on a piece of paper.

Output to video – One can readily post paper to a client. Posting floppy disks requires compatible machinery at the other end. Videos are now ubiquitous, and one of the supposed benefits of Hyper-Media and Multi-Media is the linking of all forms of electromagnetic data. The invitation to produce proposals for the new *Maidstone Hospice* in competition with five other practices, in early 1989, gave us the chance to test this.

On-screen design – Receiving the brief three days before the interview left no time for pencil and paper. Paracomp's colour 3D sketching tool Modelshop was used to shuffle correctly sized, colour-coded floor slabs into an acceptable room plan. Adding the walls, furniture and fittings was an exercise in duplication. Modelling the roofs was an exercise in 'origami' using the fold and tweak commands. A single day's CAD modelling produced a file from which any number of colour shaded perspectives could be rendered.

Getting the images off the screen – Conventional wisdom requires an £8000 'Slide Maker' to generate 35mm transparencies from computer images. Not possessing one of these excellent devices, LFA's only recourse was to a bureau. To our amazement we discovered that the technology required more time to 'Image' the views than LFA had taken in designing and building the 3D model and saving seventy or so perspectives as 2D 'paint' files. Time precluded this route. A peep under the lid confirmed that

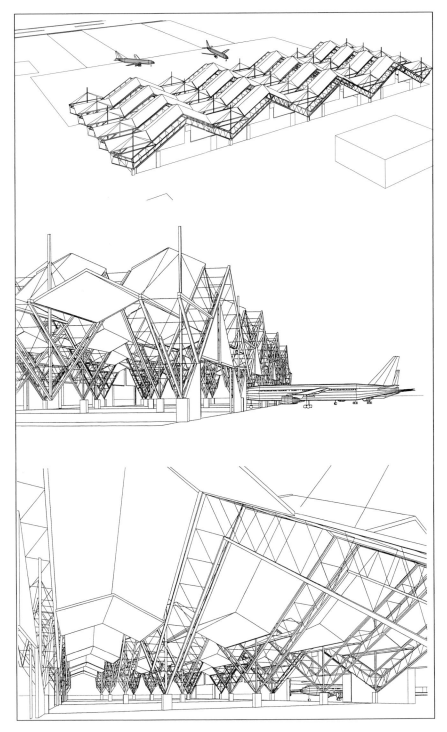

Shannon Aerospace Repair Facility

a built-in camera and LCD screen lay at the core of the Slide Maker box. LFA raced back to dust off our own slide-making machine, a 35mm reflex camera on a tripod. Trial and error established that Ektachrome HC ASA 100 produces excellent results from any Apple colour monitor at F stop 2.8 for 1/30 of a second. With the slides back from the 'One Hour' photo shop it was time to start videoing.

Imparting motion with a home video camera – Computer animations are supposed to be set up either on screen using specialist animation software, or made cinematically by filming thousands of incrementally different screens with a 'stop-frame' movie camera. Usually this involves several weeks of raw processing, even using Silicon Graphics type workstations. LFA chose to regard each still as an entire 'scene' and impart the motion by panning and zooming a home video camera onto a white wall with the slide projected on it. By exploiting the camera's built-in fades and wipes, it was easy to connect the scenes in a logical sequence. A zoom-in to an exterior perspective dissolved slowly into the same view with the exterior wall suppressed to reveal the interior, and so forth. It was easy to create a ten-minute walk through with convincing apparent motion connecting each scene to the next.

Mixing sound and live footage – Another advantage of video was the ease with which live footage of the site could be mixed and faded into computer images and punctuated with realistic sound effects, music, and a spoken commentary. LFA had very rapidly rolled over data from a CAD system, to a camera, to a slide projector and on to video, without having to hot-wire in any of the three different technologies. In the event the Hospice Committee were sufficiently startled at being presented with a TV tour of the proposal that LFA were appointed to build it the very next day.

Shannon Airport fly-through – A few months later a proposal for an £80 million aircraft repair facility at Shannon Airport was put together equally rapidly. LFA used maps and aerial photographs to create a Modelshop terrain model 32 kilometres square, centred on the airport. A model of one of the client's new fleet of Boeing 767s was used as a live template for bending roof trusses to create a four-bay structure that the aircraft could roll through. Views could be set up from anywhere within this 'virtual reality'. LFA ported in the flight deck from the MicroSoft Flight Simulator, and created a rolling series of cockpit views of flying down the Shannon estuary, touching down on runway 240 and taxiing through the facility.

Colour cycling – The benefit of saving the views into Studio 8 was that they could be linked into a convincing semi-animation using the Gallery slide-show utility. Colour cycling and slow dissolves were used to portray the sunrise over Shannon, the runway lights and homing beacons being switched on, and the winking of aircraft navigation lights. The client had Macs so the presentation was sent on disk. However, a videotape created in the same way as the Maidstone one was also sent. The video camera was bumped at the moment of touchdown. Irish pipes, seagull cries, and revving jet engines, and screaming tyres, had all been dubbed over. Once again only four man days had been required. The addition of sound and motion masked the relative unsophistication of the computer images.

Realtime computer animations – LFA now use 'true' animation software such as Studio One and Macromind Director, both for our own projects such as for a recent royal visit to Lister's City, Bradford, and in support of other people's. LFA completed a twelve-minute animated site history and 'fly-through' for the architects of Apple Computer's own manufacturing plant in Cork. This approach suggests specialist hardware such as dual frequency video-boards and monitors so that moving graphics can travel freely both ways, by wire between video-recorder and computer. The release of SuperCard, a souped-up HyperCard, with built-in animation and colour, and the interactive version of Macromind Director, along with supporting video-editing software such as Media-Maker, is consolidating the microcomputer's pivotal role as the all-purpose audio-visual presentation tool and editing deck of the future. LFA has already proved to itself that rapidly produced and effective Hyper-Media has been available for some time using no more than a little lateral thinking.

Virtual reality – Clearly in the age of marketing man when every pop song needs its video, and every product its logo, jingle, and tee shirt, 'Homo Saatchi' will yet find a million and one uses for both Hyper-Media and Multi-Media. Nonetheless Multi-Media may prove to be a very short-lived half-way house on the road to tomorrow's dreamworld of user-definable 'Virtual Reality' hinted at by current groping with head-up display helmets, and sensory clothing. As the current vogue for role-playing adventure games suggests, people's need to escape to self-defined alternative realities will grow in proportion to the grimness of the real world.

The Walkmanizing of information technology – The advertising, film, television and computer games industries have the financial muscle to ensure that marketing and entertainment will rapidly replace design presentation education, and training, as the primary foci of Hyper-Media. Miniaturization and voice activation will overcome the desk-bound nature of personal computing. Mass markets opened up by 'idiot proofing' will create the hallucination in a headset. In ten years' time disco dancers will accompany themselves on 'virtual orchestras', lone joggers pace themselves against 'virtual' marathons (through nicer surroundings no doubt), whilst would-be Rambos will down any number of 'virtual' helicopter gunships en route to work.

As an architect I can confidently look forward to walking my prospective clients through virtual realities of my own imagining, with both anticipation and dread. The anticipation is of at last being able to fully convey design ideas without fear of misunderstanding. The dread is that the sensations, degree of control and unconstrained possibilities of the world within will so outshine those on the outside, that events in the 'real' world will start to lose their significance.

PERCEVAL/EGMONT COLLECTION

ROLF LOEBER

THE EARLY seventeenth century was a period of relative peace in Ireland, which saw widespread building activities all over the country, mostly undertaken by British settlers. In the aftermath of the rebellion of 1641 and the subsequent warfare, many British settlers returned to their Irish estates. Very little is known, however, about the building or rebuilding of their residences. In several ways, the first half of the seventeenth century was a transitional epoch. Although castles were still being built, they were replaced later by country houses, often situated within fortified enclosures. In the first half of the century, the designers of buildings in Ireland were rarely more than master artisans. The architectural professional clearly emerged later, initially in the person of officer-architects and gentlemen-architects.[1] With that change, the freedom to develop alternative designs and the trappings of Renaissance classicism became more commonplace. Alongside, many patrons acquired the skills to evaluate and compare architectural designs.

The building activities of Sir Philip and his son Sir John Perceval in Munster and Leinster during this period stand out because they can be linked to a series of sometimes imaginative architectural sketches. These drawings are unique because contemporary drawings of houses and castles in Ireland prior to the 1680s are extremely rare.

The Percevals descended from a family in Somerset. Richard Perceval arrived in Ireland around the beginning of the seventeenth century. In England he had been employed at the Court of Wards, a profession that transferred easily to its Irish counterpart. At his death in 1620 he left behind two sons, Walter and Philip, who succeeded him as the court's clerk and registrar. Walter died in 1624, while Philip became the largest lessee of estates under guardianship of this court. He probably was an astute entrepeneur. By discovering concealed lands and investing in mortgages, Philip quickly amassed a vast estate, in north Co. Cork and Co. Tipperary. Up till his arrival, this area had seen few recent English settlers, and was largely inhabited by Roman Catholic landowners of Anglo-Norman descent. Philip, who was knighted in 1636, considerably improved the estate. He was said to be 'much addicted to building and gardening'. Family papers indicate various rebuilding and building schemes in north Co. Cork at Liscarroll Castle and Imogane Castle in 1640-1, and possibly at

Lohort Castle. A few years earlier he was granted the manor of Burton near Churchtown (Co. Cork), which later became the nucleus of the estate and was named after his new Somerset estate acquired in 1636. In 1639 he also undertook the rebuilding of Ballinaclogh near Golden in Co. Tipperary.[2]

The rebellion of 1641 severely disrupted settlers on the Perceval estate. Sir Philip constructed elaborate outworks in 'the modern Stile of Fortification ...' to defend Liscarroll Castle. This castle was the largest of a string of medieval castles situated on his lands. The estate was located in the centre of disputed territory; although Sir Philip placed garrisons in the several castles, eventually, they fell one by one into the hands of the Irish in 1645. He was said to have lost £20,000 as a result of the upheaval. Upon his death in 1647 his eldest son John, then still a minor, succeeded to an estate said to have been 99,900 acres, which hardly produced a bare existence.[3]

In 1652 John reached the age of majority and returned to Ireland. Helped by his good relationship with Oliver and Henry Cromwell, he successfully laid claim to his Irish property. After a brief sojourn in England he returned to Ireland to live on his estate in 1655, when he married Katherine, daughter of Robert Southwell of Kinsale.[4] John received a knighthood three years later, and a baronetcy at the Restoration.

His interest in building began in the mid 1650s when his estate had become profitable again. Between 1653 and 1657 he built at Castlewarden, Co. Kildare, on a manor dating back from Anglo-Norman times, which was the jointure of his mother. Prior to 1659, when he settled with his wife at Ballymacow near Churchtown, he had undertaken a second project – the building of 'their small nest'. Not long before his death in 1665 he started building a large country house nearby, which later became Burton House.[5]

The drawings. Several architectural sketches survive in the British Library among papers from the Earls of Egmont, the descendants of Sir Philip and Sir John Perceval. One sheet shows an adaptation of a castellated building to a country house; another sheet displays sketches for several structures, including variations of a residence on a highly unusual triangular plan. Several other sketches in Sir John Perceval's hand show unidentified structures and preliminary sketches for Burton House in Ireland, its courts and its gardens.

A small country house or castle. The first sheet (plate 1) shows two elevations and one plan, undoubtedly referring to the same building (design *a*1 to *a*3). The most imperfect elevation (*a*1) shows a three-storey house over a basement with crenellations and a low roof line. The plan (*a*2) shows defensive features with two diagonally placed towers, one for the stairs, at the corners of a basically square main structure. This plan was very typical for early-seventeenth-century Irish plantation castles.[6] The second, alternative elevation (*a*3) shows that the draughtsman omitted the crenellation. In its stead, there is a prominent roof with dormers atop the central block, while pyramidal roofs with finials crowning the two towers. The clear projection of the roofs, supported by cantilevers, became typical

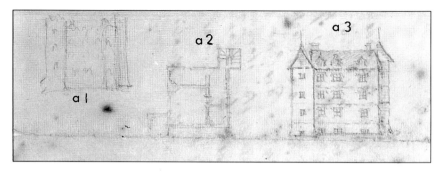

1. A small country house or castle (design *a*)

for late-seventeenth-century houses, as for example at Beaulieu (Co. Louth). But unlike such country houses, the elevation of *a*3 shows a distinctive batter to the foot of the walls, a typical feature of Irish castles.

The elevation (*a*3), aside from its roofline, deviated from castles in several ways. Judging from the plan, the walls were much less thick, and would not have accommodated a vault; also, the multitude of regularly spaced windows, even at the basement level, provided little defence. The windows were the traditional transom-and-mullion kind with a hood moulding, features which were very typical for the early seventeenth century. These sketches clearly reveal how a potentially defensible structure was adapted for a non-defensive purpose. Although it may have stood in a defensible bawn, this cannot be determined from the drawing.

The internal plan of the house shown in *a*2 (plate 1) is puzzling. Much of the space of the central building is taken up by a square room flanked by several smaller spaces, two of which probably served as living or bedrooms because they contained fireplaces. The largest room was well lit by at least two large windows. Given that the windows of each floor were spaced in the same manner (see *a*3), it is probable that the floor plan shown in *a*2 was repeated at each of the principal storeys. An unusual feature were the corner fireplaces. Introduced in London in the reign of King Charles II, they could be found in Irish buildings in the early seventeenth century.[7] A few other pencil versions of the plan are redrawn in plate 3 and will be discussed below.

The building visible in plate 1 is reminiscent of, but much smaller than, Ightermurragh in the south-western part of the same county, built in 1641 for a member of the Supple family. Like drawing *a*3, it had regularly spaced hood-moulded windows, only fewer of them for each wall surface. The building depicted in this drawing and Ightermurragh both lacked vaulting; similarly they featured string courses delineating each storey.[8]

It is unlikely that the building shown in plate 1 refers to Ballymacow, remains of which are of an almost cruciform plan. Nearby stood another of Perceval's castles, known as Imogane or Welshstown, built at an older site in 1640 for Sir Philip Perceval. A contemporary document mentioned that the house was to be '40 feet long within the walls everyway', which would be the approximate size of the square structure shown in plate 1. Imogane was burnt in 1653, when it was defended by blocking its doors and windows, which might refer to the many windows on the main floor shown in plate 1. The remains on the site, however, are too fragmentary to link it with certainty to the design of plate 1.[9]

Architectural experiments. The second sheet consists of several sketches, some in pen (plate 2) and others in pencil (redrawn in plate 3), done by an unidentified draughtsman.[10] The superimposed numbers indicate which buildings can be grouped together as versions of the same structure. One set concerns the building discussed before (designs *a*4 to *a*6); another sketch shows a keep situated against one side of a bawn (design *b*); a third set consists of drawings of a tower-like structure centrally placed in a bawn (*c* 1 to *c* 7); another group of sketches shows a complex, defensible residence (*d* 1 to *d* 6), variants of a triangular castle, an L-shaped building (*e* 1 to *e* 14), and two other structures (*f* and *g*).

Variants of design *a* are shown in plate 2 (one drawn in pen, *a*4) and in plate 3 (two pencil drawings *a*5 and *a*6). The incorporation of round flankers to the main block suggests a new structure, rather than the rebuilding of an older tower. The plans also reveal slight variations, with three and four rooms, respectively, including the corner fireplaces already mentioned.

Design *b* also shown in plate 2 is that of a bawn with two round flankers with a keep close to one of the corners of the bawn, The sketch is too incomplete to be linked to a known castle.

Design *c* consists of a few pen drawings (*c1* and *c6* in plate 2) and several pencil sketches of a building within a bawn. The elevations depict a

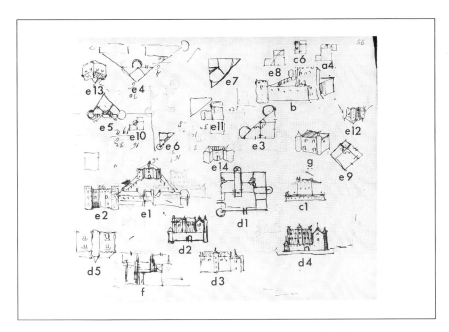

2. Architectural experiments (designs *b, c, d, e, f,* and *g*)

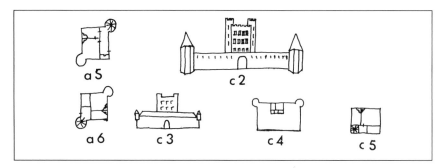

3. Further architectural experiments (other designs *a*, and *c*)

crenellated, tower-like central structure, consisting of four bays and four storeys placed within a bawn (*c1* in plate 2, and *c2* to *c5* in plate 3, *c7* not shown because it was too vague to be copied). One sketch (*c2*) shows two small towers projecting at each side of the central building, suggestive of staircases up to the roof level. The bawn wall (*c2*) was defended by two octagonal towers with conical roofs. A possible rear elevation (*c3*) shows less imposing corner bartizans.[11] A pencil drawing of a plan (*c4* in plate 3) may belong to this group of sketches. The plan of the main block is further clarified in drawing *c5* (and to a lesser extent in *c6*), showing three rooms, two with corner fireplaces, a hallway, and a stairway compactly housed within an almost square plan. This layout and the elevations may refer to an indefensible building set within a defensible bawn. In that sense, the building appears a transition between a keep and a house.

The next set of drawings refers to a complex large residence with a small bawn (design *d1* to *d4*, and possibly *d5* in plate 2), showing the front and rear elevations and its plan. This, together with the fact that the elevations do not show major variants, suggests that the sketches of building *d* all depict an existing building, which has not been identified. It consisted of a main range, at least three storeys high, with another range attached making an L-shaped plan. The remaining space was occupied by a small bawn, thus creating a rectangular layout. Two tall towers were attached to each of the ranges, one of which contained a staircase. A third, much lower, tower served to provide additional flanking fire along the two sides of the house and bawn not covered by the tall towers. Two sets of corner fireplaces echo those shown for the tower-residence of plate 1. Version *d* 1 shows one of the main ranges with its roof missing and in need of rebuilding. Version *d2* and *d3* show the building with a roof, apparently as part of a restoration plan. Unlike building *a* on plate 1, structure *d* is more defensible and appears to have been less a transition to a country house.

Another set of sketches (*e1* to *e12)* depicts the theme of a triangular or an L-shaped residence.[12] Interestingly, several of the sketches reflect draughtsman's experimentation with alternative designs. A recurring theme is the use of a rectangular room within the triangular plan (*e3* to *e6*). In one set of drawings, the remaining two spaces by necessity were triangular in shape (plans *e3* to *e6*). The plans all had one or more round towers facing the courtyard (*e*3 to *e*6). An elevation with three towers is shown in sketch *e*2, where the symmetry is broken by an entrance door on one side. The towers are slightly higher than the main block, and all are crenellated.

A second group of sketches (*e*5, *e*8 to *e*11) are also arranged around a rectangular room. Unlike the preceding designs, the two spaces adjoining the central room are rectangular, thus forming an L-plan. This change dramatically affected the appearance of the structure (*e*1, *e*12 to *e*14). Sketches *e*12 and *e*13 show two ranges at approximately 90 degrees with a round tower in the re-entrant angle. In another variant, the two ranges enclose what looks like a bolecting façade (designs *e*1 and *e*14). In this set, either a rectangular bawn (*e*7) or a triangular bawn is part of the overall design (*e*1 and *e*4). Finally, sketch *f* is hard to decipher, and may refer to a house with two rectangular towers, while sketch *g* with its two towers flanking a main block may belong to design *e* or another type of building.

Potential sources for the designs. What is striking about the drawings in plate 2 is the uncommon and whimsical nature of their designs. Despite their rarity, the designs were much more typical for early seventeenth-century English architecture than for buildings from the second half of the century. In either England or Ireland, triangular castles with towers at the re-entrant corners of their triangular courtyards were unusual. Longford Castle (Wiltshire), built in 1580, is a good example of this design. It may very well be that this castle was known to Perceval since it was located not far from his estate in Somerset. In addition, early-seventeenth-century houses on a V- or Y-shaped plan, although rare, could also be found in the West Country, as for example at Iron Acton Court (Somerset), which had an L-shaped plan and a staircase turret in the re-entrant angle. In Ireland these designs were highly uncommon; the most unusual plan of its kind is Birr Castle, rebuilt between 1620 and 1627, and possibly later again prior to 1668 for members of the Parsons family. There a main block was flanked by straight wings which, like two bent arms, projected forward.[13]

Unfortunately, none of the designs in plates 2 and 3 can be linked with certainty to one of Sir Philip Perceval's buildings. He reroofed Ballinaclogh Castle (Co. Tipperary) in 1639, but the appearance of this castle is not known. Also, building activity was going on in the winter of 1639-40 at Liscarroll, and as mentioned at Imogane (Co. Cork).[14] None of these locations, however, can be linked with certainty to the designs shown in plates 2 and 3.

Early country houses from 1657-8. The next set of sketches are more clearly datable than the preceding ones, and in all likelihood are from the hand of Sir John Perceval. They survive on the outside of letters, both dated from the winter of 1657-8, a period in which Ballymacow was being rebuilt to house Perceval's family.[15] Design *b* (plate 4) shows a rectangular bawn with one round flanker. The division of internal walls is symmetrical, forming five courtyards with the largest in front of the house. This house was sizeable, although its exact dimensions are unclear because a key is missing. The basic plan of the house is symmetrical as well, but the two right-hand spaces have been redivided.

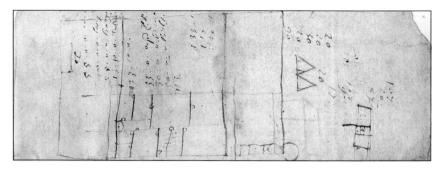

4. An early country house (design *b*)

Prior to the winter of 1657-8, Perceval had also been busy rebuilding Castlewarden, Co. Kildare, which is mentioned in several letters between February 1656 and September 1657. According to the Civil Survey of 1654-6, the 'house' of Castlewarden, dating from Norman times, was valued in 1640 at £2000, but at the time of the survey it was in a decayed state and was assessed at half its former value. The building shown in plate 4 has none of the features of a Norman stronghold; instead, its architecture with its symmetrical plan and layout of the bawn and courts is certainly innovative for that time in Ireland. On the other hand, it cannot be discounted that the sketch refers to another unidentified scheme, projected after the completion of buildings at Castlewarden or Ballymacow. Slight variations of this plan can be found on the back of another letter, not reproduced here.[16]

That letter carries a final sketch of another building (design *i*, not shown). Judging from its endorsements, it was 100 [feet] long, and had a central corridor running the full length of the building. This Italianate feature was highly uncommon in Ireland; the only house which came close was the Lord Deputy Strafford's grand residence at Jigginstown (Co. Kildare), which had rooms arranged *en filade*. Drawing *i* is reminiscent of Jigginstown in some respects, but also deviates in several other ways; therefore it must altogether refer to another, unidentified structure.[17]

Sketches presumably for Burton House Co. Cork (plate 5). The final set of sketches are in the hand of Sir John Perceval and in all likelihood concern Burton House set in the midst of courtyards and gardens, which Perceval was planning in 1665 if not earlier.[18] A first sketch, not reproduced here, shows the plan of a fortified stable yard, with a great stable, store houses, a coach house, and two towers commanding the walls 'with fire Arms' on three sides of the enclosed space. This collection of buildings was planned on one side of a fore court in front of the main residence. A second sketch, shown in plate 5, was drawn by a similarly uncertain hand, probably because Perceval suffered from the gout. The drawing shows a rectangular, not clearly defensible country house, lacking flankers. Judging from measurements in other parts of the sketch, the house was projected to be about 126 by 90 feet, making it one of the larger private residences of that time. Behind the house stretched a pleasure garden of two acres, which was separated from a long terrace walk by a 'wilderness'. On one side of the house Perceval planned 'a long walk running by ye house & Garden quite across ye Park'. At the other side of the house there was to be a bowling green, orchard, and kitchen garden. A stilling house and a garden house were planned here; the dairy and outhouses were positioned near the river,which ran in front of the house. Aside from the defensible towers along the stable yard, the only other reference to defence was made in Perceval's notes: 'The first thing to be thought of is some private Place where to hide Papers concerning my Estate & other things of Value in Cases of sudden Extremity.'

The lay-out of the house was projected more symmetrically on the second floor (drawing not shown) than on the main floor (plate 5). The latter is quite sketchy but appears to have had a central stair case placed in the rear of an asymmetrically placed hall. The principal division of rooms evident from the second floor called for two spaces – one large and one small – on each side of the stairs and upper hallway. This division was partly recognizable on the main floor, where one of the smaller spaces was taken in by a gallery. Perceval's plan for the house is likely to have been the basis for the design executed by the architect Capt. William Kenn as contractor and architect in 1665.

Kenn, like the Percevals, came from a Somerset family, seated at Kenn Court. He is first noted in 1636 in a letter by Sir Philip Perceval, who was inspecting a possible estate to purchase in that county. Kenn came to Ireland during the Cromwellian period, if not earlier, and was employed by the government to make a citadel at the church of Derry in 1653. Sometime before 1659 he probably leased lands at Cahernarry in the Southern Liberties of Limerick city, close to Sir John Perceval's brother-in-law,

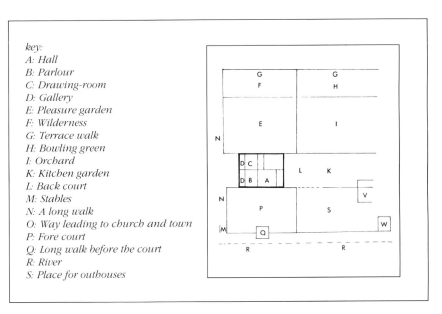

key:
A: Hall
B: Parlour
C: Drawing-room
D: Gallery
E: Pleasure garden
F: Wilderness
G: Terrace walk
H: Bowling green
I: Orchard
K: Kitchen garden
L: Back court
M: Stables
N: A long walk
O: Way leading to church and town
P: Fore court
Q: Long walk before the court
R: River
S: Place for outhouses

5. Sir John Perceval's sketch for Burton House (Co. Cork)

Colonel Randall Clayton. In the early 1660s Kenn supervised building activities at the Earl of Orrery's huge house at Charleville in north Co. Cork.[19] In 1665 Kenn was ready to proceed with the building of Burton House for Sir John Perceval. A letter by Kenn to Perceval mentions two ground plots and an elevation drawn by him, which are not known to have survived. However, only part of the foundation and at least one room were built, due to Perceval's sudden death that year when he was only thirty-six. An under-age son succeeded to the baronetcy and the estate, with Perceval's father-in-law, Robert Southwell from Kinsale, as guardian. After five years Southwell decided to proceed with the house, with Kenn again as contractor and architect. Judging form the similarity between Sir John Perceval's sketches (plate 5) and the design as executed (plate 6), Southwell largely respected Perceval's original conception of the house.[20] The executed plan, first published by Dr Maurice Craig, was slightly different: reversing Perceval's plan, it placed the principal staircase off-centre, leaving a central corridor from one side of the house to the other, and positioning the dining room at the second storey. The 'great hall' remained in its anachronistic, asymmetrical position. Perceval's original conception of the walled enclosures with the pleasure garden at the rear of the house and the kitchen garden and orchard on the side, was also preserved under Southwell's direction. Contractor Thomas Smith's plan, which shows these enclosures, protected by several defensive towers, has been published elsewhere.[21]

Contemporary documents show that Burton House emerged from the scaffolds in the early 1670s in the late Caroline style of architecture, in the same style as Beaulieu (Co. Louth), Eyrecourt Castle (Co. Galway), and Blessington (Co. Wicklow).[22] Gone was the square plan of tower houses or their successors, gone were the adjoining flankers, the batter of walls, and the hood-moulding over the windows. Instead, symmetry of design prevailed, certainly for the exterior. Even the roof rim was supported by classically inspired cantilevers, while moulding inside the house also echoed themes of Renaissance architecture. These changes certainly were a break with tradition in Irish architecture of the preceding period. Paradoxically, however, the new architecture was conventional for its time. Nevertheless, the history of Burton House and the Perceval/Egmont drawings published here make it possible to trace an unique architectural ancestry from castles exhibiting imaginative designs to the classical conventions of a late Caroline country house.

ACKNOWLEDGMENTS

The author is indebted to Rebecca Cunningham and Magda Stouthamer-Loeber for their comments on an earlier draft of the paper. Plates 1-2 and 4-6 are published with permission of the Trustees of the British Library, London. Plate 3 consists of pencil sketches from plate 2, redrawn by the author, who also redrew plate 5.

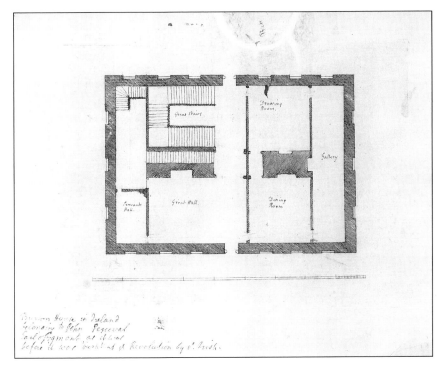

6. Burton House (Co. Cork) as executed.

NOTES

[1] M. Craig, *The Architecture of Ireland* (London 1982); N. McCullough and V. Mulvin, *A Lost Tradition* (Dublin 1987); R. Loeber, *A Biographical Dictionary of Architects in Ireland* (London 1981), pp.2-7.

[2] *Salisbury MSS* (H.M.C.), xvii, pp. 115f; H.F. Kearney, 'The Court of Wards and liveries in Ireland, 1622-41' in *Proc. of the Royal Irish Academy*, lviii (series c) (1955-6), p. 44; *Egmont MSS (H.M.C.)*, i, pp. viii, 75, 83-4, 94-5, 96-9, 202; B.L., Add. Ms 27, 988, f. 23ff; Add. Ms 47, 016, f.157, 174v-5, 182; J. Anderson, *A Genealogical History of the House of Yvery* (London 1742), i, *passim*. Note that the numbering of the Egmont MSS in the British Library has been slightly changed subsequently when they were calendared in a more final form.

[3] Anderson, *House of Yvery*, i, p. 105*n*; ii, p. 216; M. Archdall (ed.), *J. Lodge, The Peerage of Ireland* (Dublin 1789), ii, p.252*n*. An engraving of Liscarroll Castle in the *House of Yvery* (opp. p. 215) shows a ravelin in front of the main gate, attributed to Sir Philip Perceval. Four massive chimney-stacks inside the bawn, two on each side of the gate house, indicate one or two large domestic structures. If accurate, this could refer to another of the Perceval building projects. Only some of the published volumes of this book contain this and other engravings.

[4] *Egmont MSS* (H.M.C.), i, pp.541, 553; Lodge, *Peerage*, ii, pp.253-4.

[5] *Egmont MSS* (H.M.C.), i, pp.563, 575, 583, 609-10; ii, pp.14-5; B.L., Add. Ms 46, 936B, f. 24; Add. Ms 46, 937, ff. 1, 111.

[6] B.L., Add. Ms 47, 213B, f. 110; McCullough and Mulvin, *Lost tradition*, p.52.

[7] Corner fireplaces in London were noted by John Evelyn in 1671 (J. Boule (ed.), *The Diary of John Evelyn* (Oxford 1985), p.230). Earlier Irish examples were at Castle Curlews (Co. Tyrone) and Charlemont Fort (Co. Armagh).

[8] Craig, *Architecture*, p.129 shows a photograph and isometric view; J.N.Healy, *The Castles*

of County Cork (Cork 1988), pp.135-6; D. Waterman, 'Some Irish seventeenth century houses and their architectural ancestry' in E.M. Jope (ed.), *Studies in Building History* (London 1961), pp.254-5, pl. xxix. It is likely that Sir John Perceval was familiar with Ightermurragh (*Egmont MSS* (H.M.C.), i, pp.537, 540).

[9] J.N. Healy, personal communication, 1987; B.L., Add. Ms 47, 016, ff. 174v, 175, 182, 186v. Inexplicably, one of the letters in addition to the sizes mentioned, however, states that it was '20 foot broad within the Walls' (f. 175); Healy, *Castles*, pp. 365-6; *Egmont MSS* (H.M.C.), i, pp.526-7, 530.

[10] B.L., Add, Ms 47,157, f. 56. It measures about 7 by $9^{1}/_{8}$ inches. The pencil sketches apparently were drawn first, followed by pen sketches, which partly overlap. Given that some designs in plate 3 refer to the same building as plate 2, they must be contemporary. The drawing, aside from the endorsement 'margaret' on its reverse, does not carry a clue at to its authorship. It is unlikely that Sir John Perceval was their author, because known drawings by him looked very different (see below). It is hard to determine whether they are, instead, from the hand of Sir Philip Perceval.

[11] There is some similarity between this design and an engraving in the *House of Yvery* of Lohort Castle, another castle on the Perceval estate, but the engraving shows a more distinct fortification with large spear-shaped flankers. The central tower at Lohort, however, had a very different plan from that shown in *c* 5.

[12] E.g. at Killincoole, Co. Louth, is a triangular tower.

[13] M. Girouard, *Robert Smythson & the Elizabethan Country House* (New Haven 1985), p. 27; M. Airs, *The Making of the English County House, 1500-1640* (London 1975), p.7; M. Airs, *The Buidings of Britain, Tudor and Jacobean* (London 1982), p.161. See also Wormwell, Co. Dorset (*c*. 1618), Newhouse in Whitehouse, Wiltshire (*c*.1619), and Newhouse at Goodrich, Herefordshire (1636) (M. Airs, *English Country House*, pp.4-5, 10-1, 15); R. Loeber, 'Biographical Dictionary of Engineers in Ireland, 1600-1730' in *The Irish Sword*, xiii (1977-9), pl. 28; the Earl of Rosse, *Birr Castle* (Dublin 1982); M. Girouard, 'Birr Castle, Co. Offaly I' in *Country Life*, 25 Feb. 1965, pp.4-5. I am indebted to the Countess of Rosse for her advice on Birr Castle. Sir Lawrence Parsons's son William (d.1653), through his wife Dorothy Phillips, was related to Sir Philip Perceval.

[14] B.L. Add. Ms 47,016, f. 157; *Egmont MSS* (H.M.C.), i, p.114.

[15] 23 Nov [16] 57, Lieut. Beare to John Perceval, and 23 Jan [16] 57 – [8] [John Perceval] to Sir Paul Davys (B.L. Add. Ms 46, 936B, f. 105v; Add. Ms 46, 937, f. lv). Judging from his handwriting and hesitant drafting style, which can also be seen in B.L., Add. Ms 47, 113.

[16] *Egmont MSS* (H.M.C.), i, pp.575, 579, 583; B.L., Add. Ms 46, 936B, f. 105v; R.C. Simington (ed.), *The Civil Survey a.d. 1654-56, vol. iii, County of Kildare* (Dublin 1952), p.31.

[17] M. Craig, 'New light on Jigginstown' in *Ulster J. of Archeol.*, xxxiii (1970), pp.107-10.

[18] Commonplace book of Sir Philip Perceval (B.L., Add. Ms 47,113, ff. 56-7, 60). The layout of the courts and the pleasure garden at the rear of the house and the kitchen garden and orchard adjoining on the right hand side recurs in Thomas Smith's plan for Burton House (B.L., Add. Ms 46,958C).

[19] Loeber, *Biographical Dictionary of Architects*, p.6. It is clear that Kenn was familiar with the supply of building products from Bristol. He probably was the third son of John Kenn of Kenn [Court] (F. T. Colby (ed.)), *The visitation of the County of Somerset in the year 1623* (London, Harleian Society, 1876), p. 64; *Egmont MSS* (H.M.C.), i, p. 90; *Cal. S P. Ire., 1663-5*, p. 120; S. Pender (ed.), *A Census of Ireland circa 1659* (Dublin 1939), p.264; B.L., Add. Ms 46, 947B – 734C. I am indebted to Prof. Anne Crookshank for a transcript of this last document.

[20] B.L., Add. Ms 47,113, f. 56; *Egmont MSS* (H.M.C.), ii, pp. 14-15; B.L., Add. Ms 47, 157, f. 52. The executed design carries the endorsement 'Burton House in Ireland ... as it was before it was burnt at ye Revolution by ye Irish [in 1689]' (B.L., Add. Ms 47,157, f. 52).

[21] M. Craig, *Architecture of Ireland*, p. 141; R. Loeber, 'Irish country houses and castles of the late Caroline period ... ' in *Quarterly Bull. of the Ir. Georg. Soc.*, xvi (1973), opp. p.1.

[22] D. Guinness and W. Ryan, *Irish Houses and Castles* (London 1971), pp. 241-8; R. Loeber and J. O'Connell, 'Eyrecourt Castle, Co. Galway' in *The GPA Irish Arts Review Yearbook*, 1988, pp. 40-8; B. de Breffny, 'The building of the mansion at Blessington, 1672' in *The GPA Irish Arts Review Yearbook*, 1988, pp.73-7.

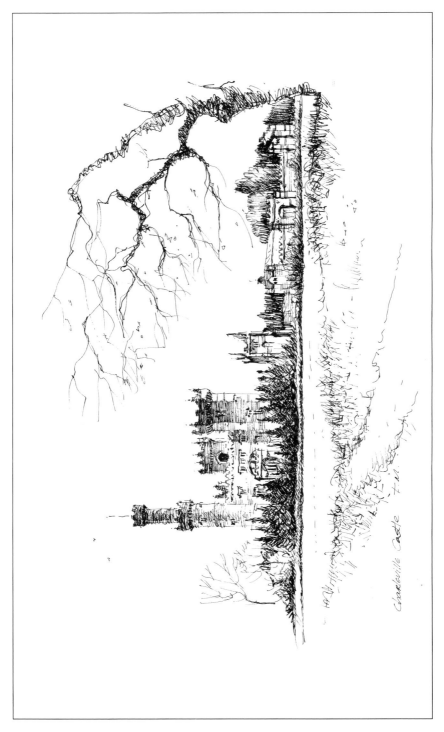

Charleville Castle – F. MacCabe

LUDWIG WITTGENSTEIN

ON BUILDINGS IN DUBLIN

W.J. Mc CORMACK

IN THE COURSE of Maurice Craig's biography of James Caulfeild, first earl of Charlemont, the author pauses over the inscription on a brass plate. Set in place when the first stone of Charlemont's casino was laid in 1761 or 1762, the text provides Craig with the opportunity to discuss eighteenth-century political terminology – 'Irish', 'British', 'English' and so forth. It is a kind of discriminating analysis which has been too rare, though instances of it are to be found in unexpected places. Architecture has provided at least one other valuable occasion for another exercise in linguistic analysis. This brief account of it is offered in homage to Maurice Craig on his birthday.

In the summer of 1934, Ludwig Wittgenstein paid the first of his several visits to Ireland. He was the guest of Maurice O'Connor Drury, formerly a Cambridge theological student but by now enrolled in the medical school of Trinity College Dublin. Wittgenstein had not only urged this change of direction but helped to finance it and Drury was to play an important part in Wittgenstein's later life, arranging accommodation for him in various remote parts of Ireland, providing a foil for impromptu philosophical discussions, and ultimately attending his death-bed. When Drury was preparing for his first MB examinations, Wittgenstein again visited him. Architecture figured in their discussions. They went to see 'the rather severe classical architecture' – Drury's phrase – in the front square of Trinity College:

Wittgenstein: Now I understand what was meant by the phrase 'the Protestant Ascendancy'. These buildings have the appearance of a fortress. But now the gypsies inhabit the castle.[1]

Wittgenstein of course had some little experience as an architect having designed a house for his sister in Vienna, and Drury's brother was a practising architect in London. In the *Philosophical Investigations,* the method of philosophy is compared to that of teaching someone to find his way round a strange city. There and elsewhere, one finds innumerable examples of Wittgenstein's close scrutiny of incidents and artefacts where language is discovered in tense or revealing relations. Drury's 'Conversations with Wittgenstein' return frequently to the topic of houses and habitations, their implications and their place in larger structures of meaning. Visiting Ely Cathedral, the two had consulted a guidebook which described a particular carving as being a humorous scene of two peasants:

Wittgenstein: That must be wrong. They would never have meant this to be funny. It is the case that we forget the meaning of certain facial expressions and misinterpret their reproduction. What does it mean to us if a Chinaman smiles?[2]

Such remarks are not confined to the recollections of students and friends; they are echoed, sometimes expanded in his own writings. Here, in the response to Ely Cathedral, we find the author of 'language-games' admitting factors of far wider implication – intention, historical change, modes of artistic production, cultural difference. It is now acknowleged, in certain quarters at least, that Wittgenstein was profoundly (if also inwardly) interested in politics; one of his closest friends being Piero Sraffa, the Italian-born and Cambridge-based economist. Sraffa, though also cloistral in habit, was a Marxist of considerable importance, not only in his academic field but also as the literary executor of Antonio Gramsci. When Drury and Wittgenstein visited Newcastle-on-Tyne and Jarrow during the Depression, the latter exclaimed 'Sraffa is right: the only thing possible in a situation like this is to get all these people running in one direction.'[3] Wittgenstein admired Lenin, visited Stalinist Russia and was a friend of several English Marxists of the literary kind, notably Roy Pascal. His own academic discipline – if indeed Wittgenstein may be called academic at all – was not remote from these considerations. 'A bad philosopher is like a slum landlord.'[4]

Drury came of an Irish family settled in Exeter in Devon. When Wittgenstein stayed with the family he read several Irish authors including Joyce and O'Casey. He admired *A Portrait of the Artist as a Young Man,* especially the account of Stephen's retreat. O'Casey he was unable to persevere with, 'no one ever talked this sort of language.'[5] *Tristram Shandy* produced a response similar to that provoked by the Ely Cathedral guidebook. It was for him quite unlike the case of *Candide* which 'was considered a very amusing book, but [he] couldn't see anything amusing in it':

You remember the incident where they are discussing infant prodigies, and after several have mentioned examples, one of the company caps the lot by saying that he knew an infant who produced a work on the day he was born. Whereupon Dr Slop replies that it should have been wiped up and nothing more said about it. Now that you could say about a lot that is written today. They should be wiped up and nothing more said about them.[6]

During his later visits to Ireland, Wittgenstein found plenty to prompt this kind of commentary, his response invariably implicating several different themes. He and Drury discussed efforts then being made to revive the Irish language, for example, by means of street-name signs:

Wittgenstein: It is always a tragic thing when a language dies. But it doesn't follow that one can do anything to stop it doing so. It is a tragic thing when the love between a man and wife is dying; but there is nothing one can do. So it is with a dying language. Though one thing is achieved by putting these notices in Irish: it makes one realize that one is in a foreign country. Dublin is not just another English provincial town: it has the air of a real capital city.[7]

Among the aphorisms gathered as *Culture and Value,* there is a similar, though less local, conjoining of the decay of historic codes and the imbalances of human passion, 'Someone lacking a tradition who would like to have one is like a man unhappily in love.'[8] This dates from 1948, most of which year he spent in Ireland – Galway and Dublin.

Drury's medical career brought him to the staff of St Patrick's Hospital Kilmainham, the institution established 'for fools and mad' by the terms of Jonathan Swift's will. (Ultimately, he became senior consultant psychiatrist.) Wittgenstein concerned himself with the problems, human as well as philosophical, posed by mental illness, and visited the hospital many times to talk to patients and staff. Much earlier in his friend's medical training Wittgenstein had asked Drury to inquire in Trinity about the possibility of enrolling himself as a medical student. Drury's tutor was properly astounded that a Fellow of Trinity College Cambridge should think of such a thing. Though nothing came of the notion Wittgenstein continued to visit Dublin: he was staying in Drury's lodgings in Chelmsford Road, Rathmines, when his homeland Austria fell to Nazi Germany's panzer diplomacy in 1938.

He became familiar enough with this strange and foreign city, became sufficiently well known in Bewley's cafe to have his regular omelette and coffee brought to the table without his having to order it. Through Drury's membership, he borrowed books from the Royal Dublin Society – generally historical works, Livy, Macaulay, Morley's life of Cromwell. He also read at this time Bismarck's *Gedanken und Erinnerungen*. The two men discussed a variety of philosophical issues while walking in the Phoenix Park, the Zoo, and the Botanic Gardens. During the later visits Wittgenstein stayed at Ross's Hotel, close to both St Patrick's Hospital and the Park. Once, he caused something of a sensation in the hotel by inviting a receptionist, who had been particularly helpful and courteous, to lunch with him in the members' restaurant of the Zoological Society. It occurred to him on at least one occasion that he might settle in Ireland. Among the three good doctors he had the good fortune to meet in his last years, he listed the Professor of Medicine at TCD.

These mundane details apart, Wittgenstein's experiences of Ireland as recorded by his friends reveal an intellect of the highest quality, a keen and painfully conscientious observer, engaged – however briefly — with the amalgam of high cultural production and social misery which was Ireland in the pre-war period. Wittgenstein was not to be deceived, nor was he ever content with a single object of attention. Though as a student Drury had begun preparations to take Anglican holy orders, he later suggested to Wittgenstein that a child brought up in 'the colourful symbolism of the Roman Catholic Liturgy' would experience a great religious awe. Wittgenstein disagreed:

When I look at the faces of the clergy here in Dublin, it seems to me that the Protestant ministers look less smug than the Roman priests. I suppose it is because they know that they are such a small minority.[9]

Being himself part-Jewish – indeed he had given Drury an astonishing 'confession' to read in which he accused himself of disguising the degree to which he was Jewish! – Wittgenstein had an eye for minorities.

Sometime in the early thirties he had written in a notebook: 'Remember the impression one gets from good architecture, that it expresses a thought. It makes one want to respond with a gesture.'[10]

One evening, in 1936 or 1937, he was walking up the Dublin quays with Kingsbridge railway station outlined against the sky. When he came nearer he shook his head, 'No, the details are poor: that cornice for example. What have I always said to you? Night is the architect's friend!'[11] This bringing together, or rather *finding* together, the human artefact and the language of response is even more vividly evident in his comment on Georgian Dublin generally: 'The people who built these houses had the good taste to know that they had nothing very important to say, and there fore they didn't attempt to express anything.'[12]

This of course is in keeping with Wittgenstein's notions of language, but its aptness in the context of Irish culture should not be missed. His deductions about 'Protestant Ascendancy' resulted from inspection of an architecture to which the phrase attaches itself. In more accessible terms, he distinguished his method by saying that:

when Socrates asks for the meaning of a word and people give him examples of how that word is used, he isn't satisfied but wants a unique definition. Now if someone shows me how a word is used and its *different* meanings, that is just the sort of answer I want.[13] [emphasis added]

Irish cultural historians might follow his example.

NOTES

[1] M. O'C Drury, (ed.) Rush Rhees, 'Conversation with Wittgenstein' in *Recollections of Wittgenstein* (Oxford 1981), pp.97-191, esp. p.137.
It will be obvious that I have derived most of the biographical information for this piece from Drury's memoir, but I hope that the implication for Irish cultural historians which I elicit from Wittgensteins's procedures will justify my own cavalier procedure here.
[2] *Ibid.* p.104. *Cf.* '(One says the ordinary thing – with the wrong gesture.)' in Ludwig Wittgenstein *Zettel,* eds G.E.M. Anscombe and G.M. von Wright (Oxford 1967), p.81. Wittgenstein's original in German; I quote here from Miss Anscombe's English translation, which is printed on facing pages. The parentheses appear in the German and English texts.
[3] *Ibid.,* p.122.
[4] *Ibid.,* p.117.
[5] *Ibid.,* p.129.
[6] *Ibid.,* p.133.
[7] *Ibid.,* p.138.
[8] Ludwig Wittgenstein, *Vermischte Bemerkungen* ed. Georg Henrik von Wright and Heikki Nyman (Oxford 1980, 2nd ed.), p.76. Wittgensteins's original in German; I quote here from Peter Winch's English translation, which is printed on facing pages.
[9] Drury, *loc. cit.,* p.166. (This appears to date from 1949.)
[10] Wittgenstein, *op. cit.,* p.22. (This is dated by the editors, *circa* 1932. *Cf.* the remark from *Zettel* quoted in note 2.)
[11] Drury, *loc. cit.,* p.137.
[12] *Idem.*
[13] *Idem.*

MAURICE CRAIG

THE CITY AS A WORK OF ART

FRANK McDONALD

EARLY IN 1988 Maurice Craig received a letter from an eminent judge congratulating him on his masterly book, *Dublin 1660-1860*, and saying how much he regretted not having read it years ago. The book was published in 1952, when the city was still largely intact – and if more people like the judge had read it then, perhaps much more of it might have survived the depredations which followed. Dublin's tragedy is that not enough of us shared Maurice Craig's vision of the city as a work of art.

Incredibly, it took 13 years to shift the first edition of 2000 copies off the shelves of the bookshops, which is a real measure of how apathetic even the cognoscenti were in those days about Dublin and its rich architectural heritage. 'Nobody cared a damn, though this was not, of course, a uniquely Irish phenomenon,' says the ever-understanding Dr Craig. 'After all, London had been pulling down the Wren churches and destroying Berkeley Square in the 1930s because of the pervasive belief that something new is always better than something old.'

Yet the English regarded themselves as civilized. 'These were the same people who would go to cities like Paris or Florence to admire their architecture. But then, nobody ever thinks of themselves as tourists. Tourism is something other people do.'

The Irish didn't travel so much and certainly not to cities, but we suffered – still do, in fact – from an almost complete absence of education in the visual arts. 'People rarely look at buildings in a street above the level of the shopfront. They don't see what's around them and the proof of that is to see what they actually *do* to buildings, with aluminium windows and all the rest of it.'

Dubliners, he feels, have a great affection for their city – but it is not an affection based on visual values. 'It's a sort of local patriotism. They like the place because they happen to live in it, the shop on the corner, the local pub where they meet their friends and perhaps sing songs about Dublin in the rare old times. But if all of the buildings are taken away, sooner or later they sit up and take notice – though, by then, it's too late. And with the buildings, a whole way of life is wiped out – the houses and the shops, the places where you can buy a needle and thread or a can of paraffin after hours. All of the little things that make up the fabric of a city.'

Dr Craig also blames our anti-urban bias ('which the English have too, by the way') – and the notion, popularized by the old saying that God made the country, but man made the town – though he insists, quite rightly, that neither of these statements is true. 'Anyone who was prosperous and living, say, in Merrion Square moved out to places like Howth or Foxrock, where they could have fresh air, gardens and even swimming pools. And, of course, none of the people who flooded into Dublin from the rest of the country would dream of living in the city centre or anywhere near it. Their attitude was that towns were essentially not a good idea and one got out of them as soon as possible.'

Dr Craig has always been fascinated by Dublin as 'a place full of buildings'. Though he was born in Belfast, he never shared John Betjeman's enthusiasm for the quintessentially Victorian city or its imposing City Hall. 'I've never been able to take it seriously. It's a ridiculous building, a rag-bag of classical tricks badly put together,' he says dismissively. 'Belfast is also a provincial town and I had an appetite for the metropolitanism of Dublin.' Dublin also had to its credit a vast stock of Georgian architecture and, as a confirmed classicist, Maurice Craig was swept off his feet by such sublime buildings as the Casino in Marino.

Typically, he had not set out to become an architectural historian, still less the most distinguished one in Ireland. 'My only qualifications are in English literature, though I realized at an early stage that this was not a good prospect. Even then, I could see that it was turning into an industry and it would eventually descend into an absurd level of specialization, like what has happened in the United States.'

Someone told him that all the papers of Lord Charlemont, for whom the Casino was built, were in the Royal Irish Academy and he immediately saw the prospects of writing a biography of this true Renaissance man. After the book was published in 1948 and 'agreeably reviewed,' he was asked to write another dealing with life in Dublin in the eighteenth century. 'The publishers wanted a book of high-grade social chit-chat about the personalities of the time, but what they got was something of a hybrid, with far more architectural history than they expected.'

In this, Maurice Craig freely acknowledges that he was influenced by Sir John Summerson's book on Georgian London, which had been published in 1945. What he wrote was a similarily definitive book on Dublin, which looked at how the city was put together by the forces – and the people – who shaped it. But when Summerson weighed in behind the ESB's controversial plan to build its headquarters in Fitzwilliam Street, blithely dismissing the Georgian terrace on the site as 'one damned house after another', Dr Craig told him this was 'totally irresponsible' to his face.

Dublin 1660-1860 is the most elegant and beautifully written book about the architecture of the city, no doubt a by-product of Dr Craig's early training in English literature. It is full of fascinating vignettes. One of my favourites, which conveys the flavour of the book, is about Dublin Castle, for long the symbol of British rule in Ireland. The upper castle yard, he writes, 'evokes to perfection the complacent Hanoverian corruption of that era. It seems to tell us that though every man has his price, the prices are moderate and have all been paid on the nail. Everything is running like well-oiled clockwork, and the clockwork soldiers are changing guard in front of the Bedford Tower.'

While researching and writing the book, appropriately, Dr Craig had lodgings in Merrion Square and made his way around the city by bicycle or on foot – 'the only way to see it'. He remembers being appalled when someone stuck a lift tower above the roofline of one of the houses though now, with all the wrecking that Dublin has suffered since then, 'one would hardly notice this little excrescence'. However, he is still appalled by the two-storey houses on Adelaide Road, which close the long vista of Georgian grandeur from Fitzwilliam Street towards the Dublin mountains. 'Whoever allowed that to happen would have no sense of how to dress for an occasion,' he says with scarcely concealed contempt.

Maurice Craig is a purist as well as being a stickler for detail. To have any intrinsic value, buildings – whatever their period – should be unsullied by higgly-piggly additions. In 1988, for example, he gave evidence at a public inquiry into plans by the nuns to demolish an old building overlooking Bullock Harbour, in Dalkey. 'It was so altered in the nineteenth century that there was almost nothing left of the original eighteenth century building and, though the local residents wanted it preserved, I said I was not at all opposed to its demolition.' At the same time, however, he regards it as perfectly understandable that ordinary people would want to save almost any old building after seeing so much destruction in recent years.

It is not that he's opposed to modern architecture – far from it. 'What I admire about the modern movement is its order and rationality, which are also features of classical architecture, of course. The problem is that so few of the modern buildings built in Dublin over the past thirty years or so are good buildings.' The ones he particularly likes include Busaras ('It's amazing how little it has aged over three decades or more'), the Bank of Ireland headquarters in Baggot Street, ('There is a real cleverness in the way its enormous size is concealed') and the US Embassy in Ballsbridge ('A very interesting modern building which is sympathetic to the scale of the area, though Queen Victoria is said to have admired the house which stood on the site.').

He regrets the destruction of so many decent houses in St Stephen's Green for speculative office developments, though he believes that this has now stopped (perhaps because there are so few houses left to destroy?). He also bemoans the whole idea of dressing up modern office blocks in pastiche Georgian clothing though, here again, he confesses his own role as one-time executive secretary of An Taisce in reaching such a compromise solution in the Hume Street saga. He is scathing, too, about the misconceived mission of Dublin Corporation's traffic engineers to remake the city to cater for cars, saying that this has done 'untold damage' to the fabric of Dublin – and all for the sake of 'a dogma which is at least twenty years out of date.'

But Dr Craig sees new hope in the emergence of community associations in the older areas of the city, like Stoneybatter, where people are waking up to the fact that there is 'something marvellous' about a street pattern which dates back through the centuries. 'This sort of community awareness would have been unthinkable 30 years ago but, instead of responding to it, the faceless men in the Corporation – most of whom seem to be from Donegal or Clare – carry on as before because they do not understand what it is that makes a city.'.

His own work ranges over a much wider area than Dublin and, indeed, he went on to trace the history of Irish architecture from the earliest times to 1880. He has also dealt with many of the more modest buildings throughout the country in his *Classic Irish Houses of the Middle Size*, which was hailed as a very important contribution to highlighting the houses which fell somewhat short of being classed as stately homes. 'Desmond Guinness jokingly refers to the book as "Maurice's Middle-Class Houses",' he says. When I interviewed him in July 1988, he was working on a semi-autobiographical series of 'jottings', running to 120,000 words, which he was hoping to 'knock into some sort of shape' at that writers' paradise, the Tyrone Guthrie Centre, in Annaghmakerrig. The working title, intriguingly, was 'The Elephant and the Polish Question'.

For a man who has passed the age of seventy, Maurice Craig leads a full and rewarding life. He is living with the actress Agnes Bernelle and, when not writing books or articles or poetry, he makes scale models of paddle-steamers and other ships of note and then takes them out for a splash in the sea of Sandymount, where he lives. The house (small Regency seaside villa, *c.* 1835) is right on Strand Road, with a view of Howth Head and the Poolbeg Lighthouse at the end of the Great South Wall and *all* of the shipping in Dublin Bay. From the flight of granite steps at the front door, there is a clear view – how could you miss them? – of the twin-striped stacks of the Poolbeg power station. Some Dubliners will probably have noticed that one of them is taller than the other, but it hadn't quite dawned on me until Maurice pointed it out that one of them is also *thicker* than the other. As I said, he's a stickler for detail. But it's odd little quirks like this that makes Dublin such an absorbing city for the undisputed doyen of our architectural historians.

EDWARD LOVETT PEARCE

AND THE DEANERY OF CHRIST CHURCH, DUBLIN

EDWARD McPARLAND

THE STORY begins with a letter from John Harris asking if I could tell him anything interesting about the Deanery of Christ Church in Dublin. His suggestive question really amounted to this: the Deanery looks as if it could be by Pearce, is it?

The long demolished Deanery stood beside the church of St John, on the west side of Fishamble Street. It is best known from the photograph of the façade in vol. 4 of *The Georgian Society Records* of 1912. This shows (plate 1) a distinguished, three-storey, five-bay, brick façade with a forecourt in front: its distinction derives from its full crowning entablature (with pulvinated frieze), and the eventful way in which its opes are dressed. The house would look perfectly at home in Old Burlington Street in London, or engraved in *Vitruvius Britannicus* and attributed, perhaps, to Colen Campbell. In other words, in the context of early eighteenth-century Dublin, it looks as if it could be by Pearce. It is.

One oddity of the building suggested a possible link with a plan (plate 2) found among the drawings of Pearce and Vanbrugh in Elton Hall, Peterborough: instead of a front door, the Deanery shows a central passage, leading into the building as if it were the *androne* of an Italian *palazzo*. The plan in Elton Hall, also for a five-bayed structure, with forecourt in front, has a central vaulted passage: it leads to a little vestibule, apparently at the heart of the plan.

The drawing is catalogued in Howard Colvin and Maurice Craig, *Architectural drawings in the library of Elton Hall* (Oxford 1964, drawing no. 39) as being a plan for a house, perhaps in the hand of Vanbrugh. It is, however, an ingenious plan for three separate houses, all entered from the centrally placed domed vestibule. Facing down the vaulted passage is the door into the house at the back of the plan. This door leads into a hall and staircase similar to that in No. 9 Henrietta Street, Dublin, a house designed by Pearce for Thomas Carter, Master of the Rolls. The other two houses are also entered from the domed vestibule. In each case the door leads into an entrance hall, with a short flight of steps. From this the visitor enters the main staircase hall. None of the three houses has a secondary staircase. (We may note in passing that the domed vestibule approached by a vaulted passage is a domestic version of the grotto Pearce built for Viscount Allen at Stillorgan, for which there are also drawings in Elton Hall.)

1. Christ Church Deanery, Fishamble Street, Dublin, now demolished
(from *The Georgian Society records of eighteenth century domestic
architecture in Dublin*, vol. iv, Dublin 1912, plate cxxi)

The link between this plan in Elton Hall and the Deanery is established
by a map of the site in Fishamble Street among the Christ Church maps in
the National Library of Ireland (plate 3), and by the chapter acts of Christ
Church which show that Edward Lovett Pearce designed and built the
Deanery between 1731 and 1733. The map 'of the old Deanery House &c
&c on the North West side of Fishamble Street ... Survey'd by Jno
Brownrigg 1799' shows three houses, disposed as in the plan in Elton Hall,
at the back of Deanery Court, one house for the dean, one for the chancel-
lor, and one for the chanter.[1] It gives no details of internal arrangement, and
no other plan of the houses has been found. Brownrigg's map differs, in
dimensions and proportions, from the Elton Hall plan, but the similarities
are sufficient to allow us to identify the Elton Hall drawing as a plan for the
Christ Church Deanery.

The chapter acts fill in the details.[2] On 21 November 1716 the chapter
decided to build houses for themselves and their successors in Fishamble
Street. The dean was Welbore Ellis, Bishop of Kildare (the two posts were
always held together); strangely, the matter did not resurface until 1731,

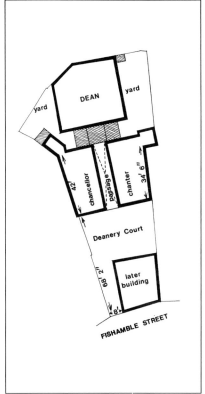

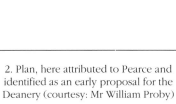

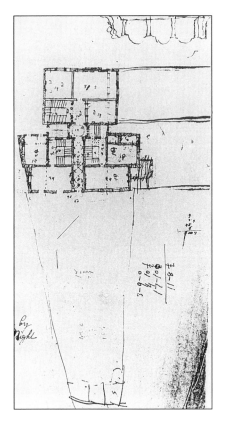

2. Plan, here attributed to Pearce and
identified as an early proposal for the
Deanery (courtesy: Mr William Proby)

3. Plan of site redrawn from a map of 1799
in the National Library of Ireland (maps of
Christ Church estate, Ms 2789, fol.12)

just before Ellis was translated to Meath. On 12 August 1731 'A Plan drawn
by Capt. Edward Pearce Surveyor General of three Houses ordered to be
built for the Habitation and residence of the Dean Chanter and Chancellor'
was approved. The houses were finished within two years: on 15
November 1733 the proctor was ordered to pay fifty guineas to Pearce 'for
his trouble and Care about the buildings in Fishamble Street ...'

The chapter acts give a little more information than this. They throw
light on how Pearce conducted such a commission. On the day his
plan was approved, 12 August 1731, it was agreed that he be 'Impowered
to agree with and Employ Artificers and Workmen for the carrying on and
finishing the said Buildings and to buy necessary materials for the same,
and that the Proctor shall sign Articles with the respective undertakers and
pay the Workmen from time to time according to Capt. Pearce's Directions,
and also that the Proctor shall Employ a person to look after and take care
of the Materials which shall be laid in for the carrying on of the said Work.'
Pearce's rôle, therefore, was somewhere between that of modern building
contractor and modern architect: he arranged the supply of materials, and

engaged workmen, but was not responsible for the security of the materials on the site, and left payment – probably for materials and certainly for labour – to his clients. On completion of the work, his client paid him a gratuity (fifty guineas); it is probable that the eighteenth century considered it proper for him to receive considerations from the firms of craftsmen and suppliers he engaged (though did not pay). Such professional practice left one interest unprotected: that of the client – the cathedral chapter – who needed to know that their architect had not instructed them to pay for more materials than were actually needed for the erection of their building. In cases of dispute they would call in other builders for an opinion. It is also quite possible that a client would forgo a system of checking, particularly if their architect was Captain Pearce, surveyor general.

The procedures seem to be the same as those involved in 1716 in the employment on a non-governmental commission of Pearce's predecessor as surveyor-general, Thomas Burgh.[3]

Welbore Ellis was translated to the see of Meath before his new Deanery was complete. Charles Cobbe, the builder of Newbridge, was therefore the first occupant. One of his neighbours was Patrick Delany, chancellor from 1728 to 1744. Early in 1743 Cobbe became Archbishop of Dublin and his successor in the Deanery was George Stone. Stone immediately decided the Deanery was inconvenient.[4] He moved to Derry in 1745 where he stayed for an equally short time, settling into the Primacy early in 1747. His successor at Christ Church, Thomas Fletcher, also found the Deanery inconvenient 'on account of his bad state of health': like Stone, he settled for an allowance of £60 a year in lieu of occupying the house. By 1765 we hear of Thomas Johnson, apothecary, already in arrears of rent for the Deanery, taking a lease of the three houses for forty years at an annual rent of £103.

And so John Harris's question is answered, if only in part. What of the final shape of Pearce's plan? What of the interiors? When was it demolished? Were records made of it other than the single photograph published in 1912 by the Georgian Society? Let us hope so, now that we know, at least, that it was an ingeniously planned building by the greatest resident architect of early eighteenth-century Ireland.

NOTES

[1] National Library of Ireland, 'A book of maps of the several estates of the ... Dean and Chapter of Christ Church Dublin, partly survey, & partly copied by Brownrigg, Longfield & Murray 1800', Ms 2789, fol. 12.
[2] Representative Church Body, Dublin, copy chapter acts of Christ Church Cathedral, vol. iv, 21 Nov. 1716; vol. v, 12 Aug. 1731 and 15 Nov. 1733.
[3] Patric Judge, 'The state of architecture in Ireland, 1716', *Irish Arts Review,* vol. iii, no. 4 (winter 1986), p. 63.
[4] For details in the rest of this paragraph see Representative Church Body, Dublin, copy chapter acts of Christ Church Cathedral, vol. vi, 17 Oct. 1743, 25 June 1748 and 12 Nov. 1765. I am grateful to Dr R. Refaussé, Librarian and Archivist of the Representative Church Body Library, for his help with the preparation of this paper.

A MEDALLION OF
JOHN'S LANE CHAPEL IN 1840

WHODUNNIT AND WHY?

F.X. MARTIN, O.S.A.

EVERYONE LOVES a whodunnit. The scholars, in addition, love the whydunnit.

This volume of essays in honour of Dr Maurice Craig gives me an opportunity to combine a whodunnit and a whydunnit on a problem within his own specialist field of buildings and architecture in Dublin. It is a brief expression of my admiration for his signal contribution to modern Irish cultural history. It has been written at very short notice and under high pressure to meet a publisher's immoveable deadline.

My contribution concerns a fascinating and for many years a puzzling item, literally illustrating the emerging Roman Catholic Church of the eighteenth-century Penal Days, but not yet the triumphant Roman Catholic Church of Paul Cardinal Cullen, as Archbishop of Dublin, 1852-78.

It involved me personally forty-six years ago, but left me with a nagging question mark to which I have found the answer only recently.

Early in 1946 Fr J. C O'Driscoll, O.S.A., editor of *Good Counsel,* a popular pious monthly magazine published by the Augustinian friars at 'John's Lane' church, was given a drawing of the exterior of the church as it was in the late eighteenth and early nineteenth centuries. It was based on a clear representation of the two-storeyed church as found etched on what was described as a 'medallion of the year 1840'. He decided to publish the etching but needed background information on the Augustinians at 'John's Lane'.

I was then seriously ill, an impatient patient in the open-air sanatorium huts of the Richmond Hospital, just across the Liffey from the 'John's Lane' church. With time on my hands. Though I was then merely a student of philosophy I was credited with special knowledge of the Augustinians in Ireland. So Fr O'Driscoll called to the Richmond Hospital and asked me to supply a popular account of the Augustinians at John's Lane.

I did so, in the *Good Counsel* of Jan.-March 1944, pp.5-7, with a just-adequate illustration of the 1840 chapel. The legend, supplied by Fr O'Driscoll, stated, 'Through the courtesy of the Irish National Museum, we reproduce from a medallion of the year 1840, a sketch of the John's Lane Chapel, with the old tower in the background.' In fact that tower was not, as I had thought, the late medieval Augustinian tower of the Crutched (i.e. Cross-bearing) friars but was that of St Patrick's Cathedral across the river

134

Poddle. This oblique view of St Patrick's shows that the John's Lane chapel was tucked away in the north-west part of the medieval property of the Augustinian Hospital.

'John's Lane' holds a unique tradition of continuity in Dublin. It represents, almost without a break, an Augustinian presence in Dublin since the year 1198, when Aildred, an Englishman, established a hospital at the west gate of Dublin for men, while his wife organized beside it a hospital for women. There was sex equality in medieval times!

The men, under Aildred, became Augustinian Hospitaller Brothers, officially described as Crutched friars. The women, under Aildred's wife, became Augustinian nuns.

The hospital was the biggest in Ireland, running to over 200 beds before the Protestant Reformation in the sixteenth century. It was officially closed by the government of Henry VIII in 1541 but it continued to give service for many more years. Hospitals cannot close overnight, as we know from present-day experience in Ireland and Great Britain.

Nevertheless, the Augustinian cross-bearing friars, being an independent Irish group, had no international organization and died out in Ireland, as did their accompanying hospitaller sisters.

However, the Augustinian presence re-surfaced almost by arrangement in the early seventeenth century when the Augustinian mendicant friars (O.S.A.), who had been banished from Dublin town at Cecilia Street by Henry VIII in 1541, returned to Dublin. They were not welcome and were banished abroad by Cromwell (1649-50) and William of Orange (1690), but would not take 'no!' for an answer. They returned quietly in the 1690s and settled on the rear part of the medieval St John's hospital site of the cross-bearing Augustinians.

The head of the Augustinian friars in Dublin, disguised under the grandiose title of 'Colonel Byrne', arranged for a hay-barn at 'John's Lane' to be acquired by the Augustinian order. It was rapidly converted into use as a 'Mass-house' – a description dictated by the English officials in Dublin.

That hidden Mass-house has continued in varying improved forms up to the present day. In the late nineteenth century it emerged flamboyant as French Gothic, described by Ruskin as 'a poem in stone', with the highest steeple in Dublin, 223 feet. Its awe-inspiring exterior is well matched by its interior, with striking Munich stained-glass windows and Harry Clarke windows which can only be appreciated in the sunlight of dawn.

Let us now return to that puzzling 'medallion' which became available in 1946, was then described as belonging 'to the year 1840', and whose outlines were reproduced through the courtesy of the Irish National Museum. It had, and has, special importance for the history of the Roman Catholic Church in Dublin and for Irish architectural records.

My initial inquiries drew a blank. The medallion escaped the otherwise admirable catalogue of *National Gallery of Ireland – illustrated summary of drawings, watercolours and miniatures*, compiled by Adrian Le Harivel and introduced by Homan Potterton in 1983.

In my haste and scepticism I even began to suspect that the 1946 information might be a spoof – we were in the time of the bogus Piltown Man! Fortunately I called upon the expertise of John Teehan of The National Museum of Ireland. He and his assiduous colleagues first conducted a search among all the normal items in the museum. That too drew a blank.

Then, by a stroke of genius, they decided – don't ask me why – to examine the National Museum items on Temperance Societies. Eureka! There it is – The record in the National Museum states:

'St Augustine Total Abstinence Society, 1840. Medal by Isaac Parkes. Bronze.
Obv. Greek cross with trefoil ends and across PLEDGE/I PROMISE/TO/ABSTAIN/FROM ALL/INTOXICATING DRINKS &c/EXCEPT USED MEDICINALLY/AND BY ORDER OF A MEDICAL MAN/AND TO DISCOUNTENANCE/THE/CAUSE &/PRACTICE/OF/INTEMPERANCE. Above, between inner circle and rim, ST AUGUSTINE TOTAL ABSTINENCE SOCIETY. and below, VERY REVd C STUART, PRESIDENT.
Rev. St Augustine standing, wearing robes and mitre, holding a crozier in his left hand, a flaming heart in his right hand, to the right a Gothic church with spire and cross, a building behind. To the left an open book on the ground, a small temple with palm trees in the background. Above, FOUNDED THE 26th DECEMBER/1840. In exergue, a cross. Signed, I PARKES to the left, DUBLIN to the right.
Diameter 2.1'

This medal is of interest because it commemorates Father Charles Stuart, 1797-1853, a distinguished member of the Augustinian Order in Ireland, and recalls the old building of the Augustinian Priory in John's Lane. On the reverse, showing the great St Augustine, Bishop of Hippo in North Africa, the flaming heart is his emblem; the open book a symbol of his writing; and the palm a symbol of the North African coast where his see was sited. He was the founder of the Augustinian Order. This Temperance Society was established in 1840 at the Augustinian Priory in Thomas Street. The chapel to the right represents the one which was built in 1781 and demolished in 1860 to make way for the present-day church.

NATIONAL TREE

RICHARD MURPHY

The flowers of the ironwood
Last for a day.
Opening at sunrise
They fall when the sun goes down.

Their little white flags
With yellow hearts
Flutter in a state
Of carnival and terror.

Yesterday's petals
Lie beheaded on the ground.
There are buds in hiding:
Tomorrow these will explode.

Above the low scrub jungle
Seething in hot air
The young leaves turn
Transparently blood-red.

A king cobra demon
Stays hoodwinking on top.
The ironwood grows high
Exuding festivity.

10 January 1989, Kandy, Sri Lanka

THE ARCHITECTURAL METAPHOR

EILÉAN NÍ CHUILLEANÁIN

The guide in the flashing cap explains
The lie of the land:
The buildings of the convent, founded

Here, a good mile on the safe side of the border
Before the border was changed,
Are still partly a cloister.

This was the laundry. A mountain shadow steals
Through the room, shifts by piles of folded linen.
A radio whispers behind the wall:

Since there is nothing that speaks as clearly
As music, no other voice that says
Hold me I'm going ... so faintly,

Now light scatters, a door opens, laughter breaks in,
A young girl barefoot, a man pushing her
Backwards against the hatch –

It flies up suddenly –
There lies the foundress, pale
In her funeral sheets, her face turned west

Searching for the rose-window. It shows her
What she never saw from any angle but this:
Weeds nesting in the churchyard, catching late sun,

Herself at fourteen stumbling downhill
And landing, crouching to watch
The sly limbering of the bantam hen

Foraging between gravestones – Help is at hand
Though out of reach:
                        The world not dead after all.

138

REBELLION IN THE ARTWORK

O TUAIRISC, *DÉ LUAIN* AND THE CRAIG CONNECTION

PROINSIAS O DRISCEOIL

CONOR CRUISE O'BRIEN has described 1916 Republicanism as 'the official ideology of the Irish state' in the de Valera years.[1] However, by the time the fiftieth anniversary of the Rising came to be commemorated the ideological force of the cult had waned, undermined by the consumer capitalism promoted by Seán Lemass, a Taoiseach who 'spoke little of unity, less of the Irish language'.[2] A policy document issued by Fine Gael in the very year of the commemoration advocated 'the preservation of the language by means of realistic policies', rather than revival.[3] A 1965 pamphlet by David Thornley entitled *Ireland: the End of an Era?* spoke of Irish politics and social habits taking on

a flavour that is ever more urban and, as a consequence, ever more cosmopolitan. And this in turn will sound the death-knell of the attempt to preserve any kind of indigenous Gaelic folk culture in these islands.[4]

For most intellectuals, independence had led to a deep sense of disillusionment. A special Easter Rising edition of *The Dublin Magazine*, containing material by important future writers, carried an editorial on the commemoration:

it seems appropriate to detach ourselves briefly from the celebrations in order to reflect on what forty-five years of autonomy have done for Irish culture ... If we are prepared to confront realities, we must surely admit that from the cultural point of view Ireland is a disgrace. For sheer philistinism it is hard to match Ireland among European nations. We are profoundly unappreciative of the arts of civilized living ... Architecturally Dublin is well on the way to becoming an eyesore ... an interdict should be placed on the oft-repeated phrase 'land of saints and scholars'. We no longer have the right to pronounce it ...[5]

Similar antagonism to the official celebration of the fiftieth anniversary was felt among committed language revivalists, but on utterly different grounds. Máirtín O Cadhain lashed out at the state's failure to preserve the language and said that Ireland was more anglicized in 1966 than it had been in 1916. His followers in the radical *Misneach* organization went on hunger strike during the official celebrations.[6] Eoghan O Tuairisc, in an essay published the preceding year, shared O Cadhain's reverence for the ideals of Patrick Pearse but equally shared the disillusionment felt by *The Dublin Magazine* at the state's failure to develop artistic life:

Thuig an Piarsach níos mó ná duine ar bith eile an tsaoithiúlacht ... Seans go bhfaca sé an díseart ina mairimid ó shin — na blianta fada beadaí beagintinneacha, 1922-65 ... An tsaoirse gan saoithiúlacht, an tír gan teanga, an Phoblacht gan phobal ...'

The publication by O Tuairisc of his novel of the Rising, *Dé Luain,* in time for the commemoration represented an attempt to posit a glorification of Pearse and the Rising against the developing (and combining) strength of consumerism, anglicization and historical revisionism. The novel made little impact[8] and has not yet been assessed at length, yet it constitutes an intellectual and stylistic experiment which, if only for its singularity, deserves wider attention. The death of his wife during the period of its composition (which runs as a motif through the work) and the need to have it published in time for the commemoration, led to careless proof-reading and lack of revision, faults to which O Tuairisc (for whom the book evoked the most tormented part of his difficult life) often publicly alluded, thus hardly aiding the work's reputation.[9]

The novel is in three section – An Oíche, An Mhaidin, Meán Lae – and deals with events from the preceding night until the outbreak of fighting on Easter Monday. Originally planned as an epic on the events of the entire week, the traces left by the abandonment of this ambition constituted the novel's principal faults – a rather arbitrary ending and a tendency to include extensive details of military positions which would only be of value to the reader in a description of the actual fighting. What gives the book its merit is the tension between intellect and emotion (often in the form of great classical architecture and the people moving though it), between the Rising as an act of will and an act of fate, between violence and thought, and between the permanence of the city and the immediacy of the action. The city is simultaneously a living artwork initiated by the first Duke of Ormond and an amphitheatre in which a Greek tragedy, dominated by fate, is about to be enacted: theatre and architecture in *Dé Luain* are indivisible.

The Rising is conceived of as an intellectual event led by poets on the insurgent side and by intellectual sophisticates (and Platonists) in the Castle administration. A consciousness of Greek thought and civilization permeates everything: Gaelic or Celtic references are rare and the Cúchulainn myth, normally associated with 1916, is foresworn, apart from an oblique reference in a metaphorical passage where a *cú* or hound is killed in the chase. Stylistically, too, the classical influence is paramount and Alan Titley has referred to the way in which O Tuairisc's work is 'tectonically organized with a sense of classical proportion which is wholly appropriate to the patterned articulation of his style'.[10]

The outstanding intellectual influence on the book is Plato's *Republic.* This allows O Tuairisc to avoid having to justify the undemocratic nature of the Rising, an attempted coup d'état without popular support. Like Plato in his simile of the large and powerful animal, he distrusts contemporary democracy and instead sympathizes with what Richard Crossman in his *Plato Today* called 'the dictatorship of the Virtuous Right'.[11] This is not to implicate O Tuairisc in the kind of fascist sympathies sometimes evident in the work of the novelist Diarmaid O Súilleabháin,[12] or the life of the poet

Liam S. Gógan,[13] but it is to acknowledge his acceptance of the right of the individual to revert to violence if, subjectively, he must. In his 1981 *Innti* interview he put forward a notion of violence as a human necessity and of the hero as the one uniquely prepared to stand for what he values until the very end:

Is riachtanas é ... Caithimid cogadh a dhéanamh. Ní mór don duine a bheith cróga, spiridiúil ... tá sé de choinsias ag gach uile dhuine an fód a dhéanamh amach dó féin ... Má chreideann tú go diongbháilte ionat féin·go bhfuil sé le déanamh, go bhfuil an fód seo le seasamh go deireadh ... sin é an laochas ...[14]

But complexity is intrinsic to O Tuairisc's work and he undermines what might appear to be an easy acceptance of violence in *Dé Luain* by regularly evoking a phrase already familiar from his 1962 novel, *L'Attaque,* 'cailltear gach cath', every battle is lost. Violence is thus a symbolic, almost intellectual, response to extreme circumstance.

For O Tuairisc, the poet and soldier are complementary and in his 1962 lecture *Religio Poetae*[15] he put forward the view that the poet, the soldier and the priest are necessary intermediaries between the quotidian world and 'another world beyond the womb of time and space':[16]

(Tá) an Sagart, an File agua an Saighdiúir ag teastáil uainn, mar níl slí ar bith eile chun an *Religio,* an seannasc idir an dá shaol, a amisiú, a léiriú, agus a chur i bhfeidhm ar an phobal ach amháin tríd an Phaidir Phoiblí, tríd an Iobairt (Iobairt an Aifrinn nó Iobairt na Cásca), tríd an tSacraimint agus trí shaothar Ealaíne an duine ...

Pearse is a soldier and poet, and through the confusion of Easter as date of insurrection and resurrection and through the transformation of the GPO into a sacrificial altar, has become a quasi-priest and potential intermediary between the worlds; in Platonic terms he is the Philosopher Ruler-Apparent of Ireland. But he cannot, in spite of O Tuairisc's best efforts, go from the fallibility of opinion and belief into the realms of the higher intelligence, not even when elements of Yeats are incorporated into the Pearse persona (Pearse can even quote from Yeats' 1927 poem, 'In Memory of Eva Gore-Booth and Con Markiewicz'). Perhaps only Eoin Mac Néill with his great powers of reasoning could have fulfilled this role but, with Douglas Hyde, he has been placed beyond the arena of action through the deceit practised by his inferiors. This fact is constantly tugging at Pearse's conscience and he acknowledges them as the true revolutionaries: 'Mac Néill, de hÍde, ba iad siúd na réabhlóidithe'.

The style of the novel represents a compromise between drama and conventional narrative technique. Although not consisting entirely of dialogue, it is set out in the manner of a drama script but without the characters being attributed. Each of the cast consciously prepares to come on to the revolutionary stage. For Connolly, Liberty Hall has become a green room where he asks his bodyguard to fetch him a mug of hot water but then wonders if a revolutionary can be cleanshaven! The plot of the tragedy moves inevitably towards its culmination when the masks must be removed: 'Caitear an aghaidh fidil i leataobh ag deireadh an dráma agus brúitear é. Suas.' The individual will is powerless to resist the fated end determined by the poets: 'bhí an tordú tugtha ag na filí, ní raibh dul as'. The most convincing of the minor characters are Abbey actors playing the role of revolutionaries – Peadar Kearney, Helena Moloney, Seán Connolly – and the members of the cast resort regularly to stage metaphors: 'mhothaigh sí an straidhn intinne ar an láthair sin, an doicheall agus an mhífhoighne, mar a bheadh ar ardán roimh eirí don bhrat'. The GPO is a theatre within the wider amphitheatre of the city and when Helena Moloney brings a vital message from the Castle to the GPO she is ignored by Connolly and Pearse. She has strayed on to their stage and must retreat in embarrassment. Finally, the individual minds of Pearse and Connolly are themselves theatres, but on to these stages only the reader can stray.

The novel culminates with Pearse reading the Proclamation on the steps of the GPO where, elitist that he is, he stands between the neo-classical columns and above the audience of passers-by, enacting the tragedy which must be enacted again and again: 'an traigéid le gníomhú arís agus arís eile don slua'. He thinks of himself as on a Greek stage before the king's palace: 'mar a bheimís ar ardán Gréagach os comhair phálás an Rí '. By the culmination of the tragedy the GPO has become both a set and the sarcophagus of martyrs ('Labhraimidne as an uaigh'). Pearse is the tragedy's hero – but in the Greek manner rather than that of the Gaelic *laoch*.

The outbreak of the rebellion is made to carry a heavy symbolic load. Thus the conception of Christ and the Rising are linked though having the Angelus bells ring as hostilities commence; and both are linked to the conception in Greece of the idea of the republic: 'Sa Ghréig a d'eascair an bodsmaoineach as fréamhacha na bunteanga.' Verbal associations and the power of words, rather than strategy have brought the Republic into being: 'Polaitíocht, polis, póilíní, pole, col, colún, baile. Níl éalú againn ó chuibhreann na bhfocal, mar bhí an focal ann ó thús.'Consider also: 'An Rialtas, Rí, Náisiún, natus sum' – this verbal association runs through Pearse's mind as he stands on the steps of the Irish Parthenon, its three classical statues – Mercurius, Fidelitas and Hibernia – emphasized by O Tuairisc, presumably because of the message the faithful Pearse is now sending to the risen Hibernia.

History for O Tuairisc (who was a keen student of *Finnegans Wake*) moved through cycles of gods, heroes and demons. Now, according to Nietzsche, God is dead (Tá dia marbh, fuair sé bás den trua. Nietzsche) and so only heroes and demons remain. The GPO as temple of commerce has become the temple of heroes. In direct contrast to modern historiography, O Tuairisc in his *Innti* interview, denying any claims to being an historian, said that for him, as for the classical writers, the attraction of the historical story was the myth it offered to contemporary man. This contrasts with his description of himself in the 1962 lecture already referred to as speaking 'mar stairí agus mar chritic ealaíne', as historian and artistic critic. Thus it can be inferred that he is attempting in *Dé Luain* the role of both historian and novelist.

While the accuracy of O Tuairisc's research is remarkable,[17] it remains true that the manner in which he mythologizes the rebellion would not be difficult to deconstruct. Considerations of mundane political strategy, such as the possibility of sustaining the rebellion long enough to obtain belligerent status at a peace conference following the war, never arise nor do the frequent passages on the Citizen Army ever doubt the wisdom for Irish socialism of its participation. Pearse's mystical approach to politics makes such evasions easy but it is to be doubted if the interpretation of the Rising in classical terms would have appealed to its leader:

When the Gaelic revival reached its full strength towards the end of the nineteenth century, classical quotations and appeals to classical precedent became rarer. One can see evidence of the change in the writings of Patrick Pearse. Now Cúchalainn and Finn have supplanted Leonidas and Scaevola as exemplars of heroic patriotism. In his essay on 'Some Aspects of Irish Literature' in 1912 Pearse speculated on what might have happened if there had been a renaissance of Celtic, rather than of Greek and Latin, literature in the fifteenth century. Something would have been lost, he observed – 'the Greek idea of perfection in form, the wise calm Greek scrutiny'. But more would have been gained from the Celtic tradition – 'a more piercing vision, a nobler, because a more humane inspiration, above all a deeper spirituality.[18]

Surprisingly, the Gaelic revival itself was not much in evidence during Easter Week, notwithstanding Pearse's claim in the novel to be able to savour the rebellion only through the medium of Irish. In one of O Tuairisc's principal sources for the events of Easter Week, the memoirs of the Volunteer intellectual Liam O Briain, it is pointed out that no Irish at all was heard either by himself or by a fellow revivalist, Piaras Béaslaí, during the week:

I gceann tamaill thug Piaras ar leataoibh mé agus dúirt: 'An gcuala tú aon Ghaeilge i rith na seachtaine?' 'Ní chuala, ná focal', a d'fhreagair mé, 'ní raibh aon Ghaeilge chor ar bith ag na daoine a raibh mise leo.' 'Ní chualas-sa focal ach chomh beag, agus ní raibh an leith-scéal sin agam mar bhí Gaeilgeoirí sna Ceithre Cúirteanna ...[19]

Few modern historians are likely to accede to the notion which dominates *Dé Luain* that the rising is the culmination of history, even the culmination of the history of Ringsend! Maurice Craig, whose extensive influence on *Dé Luain* we shall shortly discuss, had drawn attention in his book *Dublin* to the way in which 'post-reformation Irish history is at almost every point backward-looking: a series of pretences that history has just stopped happening'; but this astute observation was not accepted by O Tuairisc, at least for the purpose of his novel. While his research was impeccable and his abilities as a novelist very considerable, his interpretation of the Rising, while original, is at the very least debatable and unlikely to find adherents at the present point on the cycle of historical writing.

In a famous entry from the diary which ends *A Portrait of the Artist as a Young Man* James Joyce gives an insight into his attitude to the civilization of the west:

April 14, John Alphonsus Mulrennan has just returned from the west of Ireland. 'European and Asiatic papers please copy'. He told us he met an old man there in a mountain cabin. Old man had red eyes and short pipe. Old man spoke Irish. Mulrennan spoke Irish. Then the old man and Mulrennan spoke English, ... I fear him, I fear his red-rimmed horny eyes. It is with him I must struggle all through this night till day come, till he or I lie dead, gripping him by the sinewy throat till ... Till what? Till he yield to me? No. I mean no harm.

In what reads like an inversion of that passage, Patrick Pearse in *Dé Luain* recalls approaching a cabin door and being given a drink of buttermilk by a woman who brings it to him from the freshness of her kitchen. What he tastes is freedom:

I gConamara dom, Lá brothaill, bheannaigh mé go briotach thar leathdoras isteach, tháinig sí chugam, aghaidh roicneach le deoch bláthaí ó úire na cistineach ... Bhlais mé den tsaoirse ar an tairseach sin.

By contrast he has nothing but hatred for the Dublin which has formed him:

Mo bhaile dúchais. Is fuath liom gach cloch agus gach smúit agus gach casadh di. Tógtha ag sclábhaithne do sclábhaithe ...

Only through blood can the city's streets be redeemed:

Tá doirteadh fola ag teastáil ón tsráid, go mbaistfear í, go mbeidh ainm dá cuid féin aici os comhair an tsaoil.

For Connolly also, urban life is alienating even if his alienation is that of the working-class poor rather than that of the bourgeois Gaelic revivalist:

Foirgnimh dhubha arrachtúla gach taobh de, chomh hard is a bhí siad, bhí sé ina chime ...

O Tuairisc, however, does not share the attitude he has his heroes adopt. Eoghan O hAnluain has examined the attitudes adopted towards Dublin by those who have written of it in Irish, and has found O Tuairisc uniquely sympathetic to the city.[20] Fortunately for O Tuairisc's purposes, the insurgents decided to occupy key public buildings rather than resort to the street-fighting which was to prove so effective at Mount St Bridge. This allowed him to utilize the symbolic possibilities of great architecture in an exploration of his own philosophical stance. Always greatly attracted by the Book of Kells, O Tuairisc follows its example by including in the novel highly wrought passages on the Four Courts, Dublin Castle, St Stephen's Green and the Ringsend area of the city.

His information on these areas derives from Maurice Craig's *Dublin* and Weston St John Joyce's *The Neighbourhood of Dublin.* Joyce's unique work was first published in 1912 and is itself a source for Craig's 1952 work, so that in the Ringsend passage it is not always clear whether O Tuairisc is drawing on Craig or on Joyce, but in the main for that passage he uses the latter's description of the development of the Pigeonhouse (O Tuairisc derives from Joyce the form, 'Pidgeon'), the South Wall, the development of 'New Holland' and the glories and decline of Ringsend port.

The details of the Rising apart, most of the historical information in *Dé Luain* derives from Craig's *Dublin*, which he ransacks literally from start to finish, and it is from this source that he takes all of the considerable information incorporated into the novel on buildings and their history. Craig's book is preceded by a quotation from Logan Pearsall Smith beginning, 'the growing splendour ... of the age of Reason, the *Enclaircissement* ...'. In O Tuairisc's passage on Dublin Castle we find: 'in *enclaircissement* an Octhú hAois Déag', and forty pages later, 'Ag deireadh Aois an Réasúin, 1795 ...'.

At the very end of Craig's text we find in its final sentence the phrase, 'Moses who, carved by Edward Smyth, stands on the pediment of the Four Courts holding the Tables of the Law, with the great dome behind him ...', which O Tuairisc utilizes in his description of the Four Courts: 'Sheas Maois i lár baill ar an bpeidiméid agus Táblaí an Dlí ar a bhacán cloiche.'

The elements of *Dé Luain* deriving from Craig are randomly scattered throughout the text and there is no sense in which O Tuairisc is being mechanical or plagiaristic. Instead he found in *Dublin* and *The Neighbourhood of Dublin* reliable secondary sources which could be moulded to his own purpose and which rendered original research in certain areas unnecessary. O Tuairisc derives from Craig his sense of the city as a work of art, and it is from Craig that major passages on the Four Courts (p.127), Dublin Castle (p.144), and St Stephen's Green (p.172) derive, as well as the references to the Duke of Ormond and his achievements, to the GPO, City Hall and the William of Orange statue in College Green. Such information in these passages as cannot be traced in Craig, can normally be attributed to direct personal observation. The Ringsend passage (beginning p.183) can similarly be traced through the pages of St John Joyce with some additional material deriving from Craig.

The way in which O Tuairisc uses these sources varies considerably. Sometimes a sentence is almost directly translated:

the Castle stood on a landward corner, with the miserable trickle of the Poddle river serving as a ditch round two of its sides ...

tá an Caisleán ag bun an chnoic i gcúinne thoir theas bhalla na cathrach, silín uisce an Phodail thart ar dhá thaobh de ...

Sometimes Craig, the witty Grattanite rationalist, is translated into the terms of O Tuairisc, the republican mystic; on other occasions the alteration is much more slight. Thus a mystical passage on page 144 and a factual passage on page 145 can both derive from the same Craig source:

Atógtar an íomhá arís is arís eile. Túr Bhermingham. Túr Bhedford. Cuireann gach aois lena chaisleanú, lena chuimhní ...'

Sa Chlós Uachtarach folaítear ceann de gheataí an tseanChaisleáin faoi Oifig na nGinileach agus tógtar túr álainn Bhedford os a cionn ...;

Two of the medieval towers ... were visibly incorporated in the new scheme while one of the original northern gatetowers is embedded in what is now the Genealogical Office and supports the delightful Bedford Tower with its cupola ...

Further examples would be tedious in the present context but could form part of a properly amended and annotated edition of *Dé Luain,* a project which should be undertaken.

Reference has already been made to the indivisibility of architecture and theatre in the novel, particularly in the passages dealing with the GPO. It is, however, in the Dublin Castle passage (from which our examples have derived) that we gain the clearest insight into O Tuairisc's architectural interpretation, an interpretation derived largely from Plato's *Republic.* The passage opens with the sentence, 'Ní áit í an

Caisleán ach íomhá a leanann dínn' – a sentence which would present considerable difficulties to a translator. While Dineen gives his habitual long list of meanings for *Iomhá* none fits in this context. O Dónaill confines himself to 'image, statue', already on Dineen's list.

The negative *ní* is a significant opening word for the sentence and corresponds to the negative opening of a related sentence later on: 'Níl suíomh ró-chinnte faoina charnán ailtireachta', the latter suggesting that the site of the castle is uncertain, the former that the castle is not a place but 'Iomhá' and both alluding to the illusory nature of human existence. O Tuairisc spoke of Plato's simile of the Prisoners in the Cave as 'an image of the unreality of human life: the other world, the real world, is behind us, out of our ken and all we are aware of is the shadow of reality flickering in the things that we see'.[21] Thus while the Castle is constantly being altered and added to by 'An Normanach, an tAngevin duairc, an Plantagenet, an Tudorach, an Stiobhart', the concept 'castle' remains intact and is continually being reinterpreted while remaining essentially unaltered: 'Atógtar an íomhá arís is arís eile'. Thus the *Iomhá* is what remains unaltered – it is in fact the Platonic 'form' and it is thus that the word *Iomhá* must be translated with the opening sentence being accurately, if inelegantly, given as, 'The Castle is not a place but a form which adheres to us.' The Castle is thus but the 'shadow of reality' built on the belief of the colonial administration in its own right to rule but indicating a world of which, in O Tuairisc's view, we can know almost nothing.

If what we see is illusion, then it is also true that what the characters see is selected by their subjective concerns, a metaphor for their state of mind. When Arthur Griffith travels along Dublin bay by tram he sees the symbols of former industry and of future prosperity under Sinn Féin: The South Wall, reclaimed land, grain stores. For the Volunteers on the roof of the GPO, its architectural features are merely a matter of military possibilities, while for Pearse architecture and even urban life itself are repugnant, and consequently he is oblivious to the buildings around him.

It was those who claimed to be Pearse's legatees, and who held the views on urban life attributed to him in *Dé Luain,* who dominated the independent state, rather than those who, while acknowledging the fact that the architecture of Dublin was colonial, could see in the work of Gandon, or the Duke of Ormond, great human achievements. This latter is a recognition which permeates the pages of *Dé Luain.* O Tuairisc would have endorsed the words of Gandon's contemporary, the eighteenth-century German art historian, Johann Joachim Winckelmann, and applied them to the neo-classical architecture of Dublin as well as to its Greek inspiration:

To those who know and study the work of the Greeks, their masterpieces reveal not only Nature in its greatest beauty but something more than that, namely, certain ideal beauties of Nature which, as the old commentator of Plato teaches us, exist only in the intellect.[22]

NOTES

[1] Conor Cruise O'Brien 'Ireland: The Shirt of Nessus' in *Passion and Cunning and other essays* (London 1988), p.223.

[2] Dick Walsh, 'Between Populism and Conservatism', *The Irish Times,* December 1989.

[3] Fine Gael, *Irish Language Policy* (1966), pp.2,9.

[4] David Thornley, *Ireland: The End of an Era?* Tuairim Pamphlets 12 (1965), p.16.

[5] It included work by Eavan Boland, Derek Mahon, Seamus Heaney and Brendan Kennelly. It was edited by Rivers Carew and Timothy Brownlow.

[6] An tSr. Bosco Costigan, *De Ghlaschloich an Oileáin* (Conamara 1987), pp.115, 117.

[7] Quoted in Máirín Nic Eoin, *Eoghan O Tuairisc Beatha agus Saothar* (Baile Atha Cliath 1988), p.208.

[8] Máirín Nic Eoin, *op. cit.,* p.221.

[9] Interview with O Tuairisc in *Innti* 7 (1981).

[10] Alan Titley, 'Contemporary Irish Literature' *The Crane Bag*, vol. 5, no. 2.

[11] R.H.S. Crossman, *Plato Today* (London 1959).

[12] See, for example, his novel, *Ciontach* (Baile Atha Cliath 1983), p.122.

[13] John P. Duggan, *Neutral Ireland and the Third Reich*, (2nd edition, Dublin 1989), pp.xiv, 167.

[14] *Innti* 7 (1982).

[15] Máirín Nic Eoin (ed.), *Religio Poetae agus Aistí Eile* (Baile Atha Cliath 1987), p.16.

[16] *Poets Choice*, RTE Radio, 29 August 1982.

[17] O Tuairisc's painstaking approach to his research greatly impressed his publisher, Allen Figgis, at the time. (Conversation with the writer.)

[18] W.B. Stanford, *Ireland and the Classical Tradition* (Dublin 1977), p.219.

[19] Liam O Briain, *Cuimhní Cinn* (Baile Atha Cliath 1951).

[20] Eoghan O hAnluain, 'Baile Atha Cliath i Nua-litríocht na Gaeilge', Scríobh 4 (1979).

[21] *Poets Choice.*

[22] Quoted in H. Osborne (ed.), *The Oxford Companion to Art* (Oxford 1970).

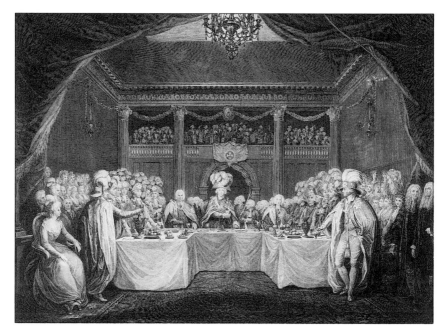

1. Inaugural Investiture of the Knights of St Patrick in 1783, engraving after John Keyse Sherwin (proof, 4th state), *c*.1803. [National Gallery of Ireland.]

2. State Ball at Dublin Castle, the Duke and Duchess of Dorset presiding. Traditionally dated 1731 and ascribed to William Van der Hagen, it is more probably the work of Joseph Tudor, *c*.1753. [Colonel L.G. Stopford-Sackville, photo E.T. Archive.]

THE BALLROOM AT
DUBLIN CASTLE

THE ORIGINS OF ST PATRICK'S HALL

FREDERICK O'DWYER

DISCUSSION OF the architecture of St Patrick's Hall, Dublin Castle, has tended to concentrate on the ceilings painted by the Italian-born artist Vincent Waldré between 1787 and 1802. The only previously recognized view of the pre-Waldré room is an engraving of the inaugural investiture of the Knights of St Patrick, held in 1783.[1] It was from this event that the room, hitherto known as the Ball Room, acquired the title St Patrick's Hall. Authorities have disagreed as to when the Ball Room was constructed, and whether it was purpose-built or adapted from an earlier structure. There are descriptions of this earlier 'Old Hall' being fitted up by the surveyor-general (Sir) Edward Lovett Pearce for a State Ball (presided over by the Duke and Duchess of Dorset) in 1731, and of it being used again for functions in 1732 and 1733. 'What happened to the room after that,' wrote John Cornforth in *Country Life* in 1970, 'I have been unable to discover, but it seems likely it was altered or reconstructed between 1746 and 1753.'[2] John Gilmartin, on the other hand, wrote in *Apollo* in 1972 that St Patrick's Hall 'was built c.1730 and stands on the foundations of a medieval hall'.[3]

The years 1731 and 1746 are important, the first being the putative date of a painting (the oldest of a Dublin Castle interior) depicting a State Ball presided over by the Duke and Duchess of Dorset; the second the year in which a later lord-lieutenant, the 4th Earl of Chesterfield, petitioned the Treasury for funds for a major reconstruction of the south-west corner of the Upper Castle Yard – the area in which St Patrick's Hall is located. The painting appears to show the decorations provided by Pearce for the 1731 ball and described by the letter-writer Mrs Delany at the time: 'On Monday at eight o'clock went to the castle. The room where the ball was to be was ordered by Captain Pierce [sic] finely adorned with paintings and obelisks, and made as light as a summer's day.'[4] In an account of a subsequent ball, held on 1 March 1732 NS, Mrs Delany wrote, 'We were all placed in rows, one above another, so much raised that the last row almost *touched the ceiling!*'[5] The link between the painting and Mrs Delany's account was first made by Anne Crookshank and the Knight of Glin in their catalogue of the Irish Portraits exhibition (1969).[6] The connection was taken up by Cornforth (1970) and was further discussed by Crookshank and Glin in *The Painters of Ireland* (1978), where they attributed it to William Van der Hagen (*fl.* 1715-45). The painting has since been reproduced in other

3. Investiture of the Knights of St Patrick in 1888, as illustrated in *The Graphic*. The view shows the room after its final late-Victorian remodelling, which gave it its present appearance. [Photo Dr Peter Galloway.]

books with the attribution to Van der Hagen and the date 1731. This plausible connection between painting and letter is apparently reinforced by the provenance of the picture which has been passed down among the Duke of Dorset's descendants, and by the survival of some of the canvas drops, seen in the picture, in an attic at Knole, the family seat.[7]

THE OLD HALL AND THE NEW BALL ROOM

The Ball Room depicted in the painting appears to have approximately the same internal dimensions as St Patrick's Hall, and though the ceiling is different, the columnar screen at the end is similar to that of St Patrick's Hall, albeit of a different order – Ionic as opposed to Corinthian. The differences between the picture and the present hall can certainly be explained by remodelling; the tiered seating, for instance, appears on a floor plan of 1767, but by 1783 survived along two sides only, while the present coved ceiling (in situ by 1783) can arguably be dated to the documented re-roofing of the hall in 1769.[8] The absence of windows in both the painting and in the 1783 and later Victorian views has been taken to indicate that the room was originally top-lit. This is incorrect – the four large windows in the south wall are clearly shown in Alfray's survey of 1767 – they were probably hidden behind painted screens during evening functions.[9]

If, as Gilmartin stated, the present hall dates from *c*.1730, that is just prior to the 'Pearce ball', then it would follow that its most likely designer was either Pearce himself or his predecessor as surveyor-general, Thomas Burgh, who died in December 1730. However, accounts of the 1731 festivities indicate that the ball was not held in a new room, but an old one. The lord-lieutenant, the Duke of Dorset, said of the occasion, 'It was resolved to make use of the old hall,which had long been disused and very much out of repair ... the walls were all covered with canvas painted in perspective.'[10] Pearce, therefore, can be credited only with the decorations, not the structure. Although Mrs Delany confusingly refers to the second ball held some months later, in March 1732 NS, as being in the 'old Beefeaters'Hall', Dorset's name for the room is confirmed by plans of the 1680s (attributed to the surveyor-general Sir William Robinson), on which it is marked simply 'Old Hall'.[11] Other references of the sixteenth and seventeenth centuries refer to it simply as the Hall.

In 1728, three years before the 'Pearce ball', a view of the Upper Castle Yard was published as a plate (one of a series of views of public buildings) on Charles Brooking's map of Dublin. The engraving appears to be quite accurate, the older buildings conforming with a survey plan of 1673, attributed to Robinson,[12] while the newer buildings, built after designs pre-

4. View of the Upper Yard 1728, by John Brooking. Note the unfinished south-west range. The building behind it was the Old Hall, precursor of St Patrick's Hall. [Photo PDI.]

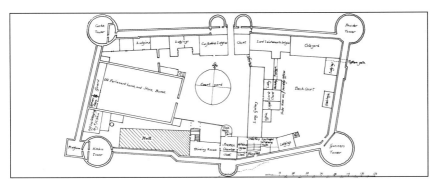

5. Ground Plan of Dublin Castle 1673, attributed to William Robinson. Tracing from a copy of the original in the Dartmouth Collection, Staffordshire Record Office. The Old Hall is indicated by cross-hatching.

pared by Robinson following a major fire at the Castle in 1684, accord with surviving architectural drawings and the evidence of the present façades. Only one of the buildings envisaged in Robinson's master plan was actually built during his term of office, the main block of State Apartments (1687-8) corresponding to the present south-east range of the Upper Yard.[13] The other two 'new' blocks seen in Brooking's view – the Upper and Lower Cross Blocks – were erected by Burgh in 1712-17. The south-west range (designed to match the 1687-8 building) was begun by Burgh after 1712, but was halted in 1716 and left in the unfinished state seen in Brooking's illustration, which shows only the arcaded ground floor of the façade erected. Behind this arcade Brooking shows the Old Hall as an insignificant low, dormer-roofed building, its eaves being no higher than that of the arcade itself, that is about 15 feet. While it might be argued that the Old Hall could have had an open-work roof with an effective ceiling height of more than 15 feet, the Dorset painting shows a room with a flat ceiling. Scaling the height of the figures in the tiered seating in the painting would suggest a ceiling height of about 36 feet, which is close to the actual height of St Patrick's Hall (given as 38 feet by James Malton in the 1790s). On this point there would appear to be a significant discrepancy between the painting and the probable height of the Old Hall, even allowing for artistic licence by Brooking. Further study shows that there are problems with regard to the width also.

The 1673 plan and Brooking's view show the Old Hall to have been on the site of the present St Patrick's Hall, or rather below it – at ground floor level as opposed to first floor level. This is borne out by Robert Ware's description of the Castle in 1678: 'On the right hand [of the 'Entrance into the Palace'] are the Hall, on the ground, the kitchen and other places belonging to the offices below stairs, reaching as farre as *Berminghams Tower*.'[15] The entrance to which he refers is the rusticated archway, surmounted by the royal arms, which had been erected by Captain John Paine, surveyor-general, for the Duke of Ormonde in the 1660s. It can be clearly seen in Brooking's view. Unfortunately Ware, who dates most of the Castle buildings he inspected, gives no indication as to when the Hall had been built. The researches of J.B. Maguire and Dr Rolf Loeber have corrected the old belief that the Hall was synonymous with the building known as 'The Old Parliament House', built by Henry III and destroyed by fire in 1671.[16] The survey of 1673, made just before the burnt-out ruin was demolished, shows that the Old Parliament House stood in what is now the middle of the courtyard, whereas the Hall was to the south of it, against the curtain wall. The origins of the Hall or Old Hall have yet to be determined. It is referred to in a report of 1585 – 'the castle wall is weakest in the south side by means of the hall windows, and other windows'.[17] Its relationship with the old State Apartments, which were at first floor level, was essentially that of a hall to the great chamber of a later medieval building. The sequence of rooms at Dublin Castle was described by an English visitor Sir William Brereton in 1635: 'Here we saw the hall, a very plain room and the dining room where is placed the cloth of estate over my Lord Deputy's

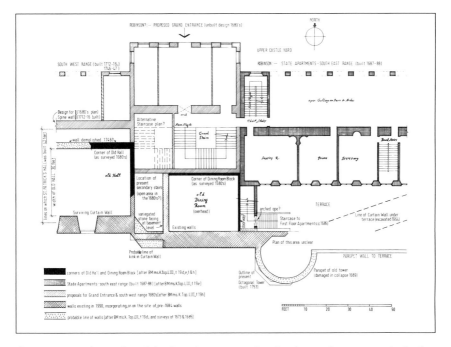

6. Reconstructed Part-Plan of the State Apartments, showing the south-east range, built after the designs of William Robinson in 1687-8, and the proposals, attributed to him, for building a new Grand Entrance beside it. [Drawing – Author.]

head, when he is at meat. Beyond this is the chamber of presence, a room indeed of state; and next to this is the withdrawing chamber.'[18]

A study of the various drawings, combined with the evidence of surviving old walls at ground and basement floor levels beneath St Patrick's Hall, suggests that the Old Hall was a rectangular structure (not boot-shaped as shown on the 1673 survey), its south wall being the surviving eight-foot thick calp limestone curtain wall of the medieval castle, which was reduced in height when the much thinner outer wall of St Patrick's Hall was built on top of it.[19] The east wall of the Old Hall, clearly marked on the 1680s plans, coincides with the east wall of St Patrick's Hall. The location of the west wall of the Old Hall is unclear. The 1673 survey shows it some distance from the Bermingham Tower, but it probably abutted it, since Ware noted that the basement beneath the Hall connected with the tower, where the Great Kitchen of the Castle was situated. The north wall of the Old Hall no longer survives, but it is marked on the 1680s drawings and can be plotted with reference to its proximity to surviving walls. The internal width of the Old Hall can thus be established, scaling at 30 feet, some 12 feet narrower than St Patrick's Hall. The length of the Old Hall, which scales at 80 feet on the 1673 survey, may have been closer to that of St Patrick's Hall (93 feet 10 inches) if it abutted the tower. The length, though, is not critical in establishing which hall the painting depicts – but the width is. The ladies in the picture are shown seated twenty-five abreast. In anthropometric terms they could not fit into a room 30 feet wide, whereas they could be accommodated in the 42-foot width of St Patrick's Hall. The dimensional discrepancies call into question the dating of the painting, suggesting that it could not depict the Old Hall used for the 1731 ball, but shows, rather, the Ball Room which replaced it, now known as St Patrick's Hall.

When did the Old Hall give way to the Ball Room? Was it 'altered or reconstructed between 1746 and 1753' as Cornforth speculated? Are there other descriptions or plans of the new Ball Room that might tally with the picture? Documentation showing that the Old Hall was, in fact, taken down and a new Ball Room built in 1746-7 appears to have been overlooked by historians. So has the possibility that the picture shows the Duke of Dorset, not in 1731, but during his second term as lord-lieutenant in 1751-5. This would explain the discrepancies in reconciling the picture with the Old Hall – the dimensions, columnar screen, tiered seating and balustrade (across the floor) all accord with the known appearance of the *new* Ball Room, as described by Chief Baron Willes in 1757 and as recorded in Alfray's survey drawing of 1767.[20] The disposition and number of seating tiers seen in the picture coincides with those given by these sources. Opinion, however, is divided as to the date of the costumes depicted in the picture – which some experts consider *retardataire* for the 1750s.[21]

The use of tiered seating, described by Mrs Delany in 1731, was by no means unique to that occasion. There was, for instance, similar seating in the Ball Room at St James's Palace as early as 1729.[22] Nor were obelisks unusual as a decorative motif. They were used in both theatrical design and as architectural ornaments in Dublin right through the 1740s and 1750s. It is recorded that at least one obelisk was supplied for the King's Birth Day celebration at Dublin Castle in 1753 by the painter and scene-designer Joseph

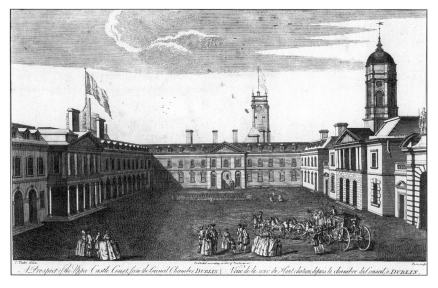

7. View of the Upper Castle Yard 1753, by Joseph Tudor. [National Library of Ireland.]

Tudor.[23] If, as seems likely, the painting is of one of the State Balls presided over by the Duke of Dorset during his second term of office (1751-5), then Tudor must be considered a serious candidate for attribution. Van der Hagen, to whom Crookshank and Glin attributed the picture, had died in 1745, and had been succeeded by Tudor as a scene painter at Smock Alley theatre. Tudor was extensively employed on decorations and the construction of stage props (known as 'machinery') at the Castle from the mid-1740s and was one of the contractors involved in fitting out the new Ball Room. In 1753 he published a view of the Upper Castle Yard which incorporated the Bedford Tower, not then built, suggesting that he had access to official plans. He had enjoyed the patronage of the Duke of Dorset since his first lord-lieutenancy. Tudor dedicated to him a view of the Site of the Battle of the Boyne, published in 1736.[24] Whether Tudor reused canvasses and props from the Old Hall, one cannot say, but as the resident scene-painter at the Castle he would surely have wished to be associated with such a picture, particularly if it depicted his own handiwork.

LORD CHESTERFIELD

A clue as to what happened when the south-west corner of the Castle was rebuilt in the mid-eighteenth century is contained in a slim volume, *Historical Reminisences of Dublin Castle* (1896) by F.E. Ross, who noted that St Patrick's Hall 'was built during Lord Chesterfield's Viceroyalty', that is in 1745-6. A description of Dublin Castle published anonymously in *The Irish Builder*, also in 1896, refers to St Patrick's Hall as a 'large red brick building'.[25] This cannot have been a reference to its appearance since the external wall was rendered with stucco 'in imitation of stone' as early as 1810.[26] Beneath the stucco is calp rubble but this is faced internally with red brick bonded into the stonework, while the internal walls are also of brick. While no brickwork is normally visible internally, renovations in 1989 confirmed the extensive use of brick which clearly differentiated St Patrick's Hall from the old Castle which was built of calp limestone, and suggests a purpose-built structure rather than the adaptation of an old hall.

Philip Dormer Stanhope, 4th Earl of Chesterfield, was arguably Ireland's most popular eighteenth-century viceroy. An intellectual, remembered today for his letters, he managed to cultivate both sides of Irish political opinion, polarized as the Government and the Patriot parties. A patron of the arts, he was a regular attender at the Dublin theatre. Although a *bon viveur*, he banned gambling at the Castle and instituted a number of projects designed to give employment, such as the planting of the Phoenix Park, commemorated by the Phoenix Monument, which he inaugurated in April 1746. He also commissioned a chapel for the Royal Barracks. Chesterfield was appointed lord-lieutenant of Ireland on 12 January 1745 NS, but did not arrive in Dublin until the following July. He was not impressed by the condition in which he found the Castle. In March 1746 NS, at the start of the financial year, he wrote to the Treasury in London:

the Great Staircase, Battle Axe Hall, Chaplains Apartments and other necessary rooms comprising the principal Entrance into the Castle are not only in a most ruinous condition but in immediate danger of falling to the Ground although continually propped ... and all that space of ground between the said Principal Entrance and Bermingham's Tower containing one hundred and fifty four feet in front and eighty three in depth, forming more than one half of the Chief Side of the Court of the said Castle, now lieth in one Great Ruin although necessary to be employed as well as for the dignity as for the Convenience of his Majesty's Governors.[27]

These dimensions encompass all of the south-west corner of the Upper Castle Yard between Robinson's south-east range and the Bermingham Tower and Upper Cross Block. Chesterfield enumerated the various apartments at the eastern end of the space – the Great Staircase, Battle Axe hall, Chaplains Apartments etc., comprising the then Principal Entrance. The entrance front and staircase had been built by Paine for Ormonde in the 1660s, together with the Battle Axe Hall. However, the latter is not shown on the 1673 survey, though its function as the hall of the yeoman guard protecting the viceroy suggests that it must have adjoined the staircase. Certainly Chesterfield's new Battle Axe Hall was to be at the head of the staircase. The room in this position on the 1673 plan was the Dining Room, which Robinson rebuilt and raised for the Earl of Essex in 1674-5. The obligation to retain both the Dining Room and the Old Hall were major determinants in restricting Robinson's replanning of the Castle after the 1684 fire. It may be that the Battle Axe Hall was synonymous with the Dining Room or occupied the floor beneath it. It is interesting that the substructure of the Dining Room survives at basement level, beneath the present main staircase, as do portions of the south wall of the Old Hall (including its window embrasures) beneath St Patrick's Hall.

While Chesterfield's petition did not specifically mention the Old Hall, which was the main reception room in the space between the Principal Entrance and the Bermingham Tower, the warrant for the final account, paid by the Treasury to the Irish surveyor-general Arthur Jones Nevill in January 1748 NS, lists the 'Servants'Hall' as one of the rooms that had been rebuilt.[28] That the Battle Axe Hall is also mentioned appears to suggest that the Servants'Hall was the other main hall in the south-west range, and it is probable that *that* was the term by which the Old Hall was then known. There are references in the *Irish House of Commons Journals* to the Servants'Hall at Dublin Castle being fitted up for the King's Birth Day celebrations in 1743 and 1745. Aside from such special occasions, the Hall was probably indeed used by servants, in line with contemporary practice – the use of large halls for regular dining having passed out of fashion. A contemporary plan of Portumna Castle, for instance, shows that the great hall there was known as the Servants'Hall.[29]

THE BUILDING

Chesterfield departed for England on 23 April 1746, the day after the issue of the King's Letter which sanctioned his request to rebuild the Castle. Although no doubt kept abreast of developments by his officials and by

Irish friends like George Faulkner and Thomas Prior, Chesterfield is not known to have returned to Dublin and probably never saw the results of his representations. Things moved quite quickly. The main social event of the Dublin season was the State Ball at the Castle, which took place on alternate years when the lord-lieutenant was in residence. It was held in late October or early November and marked the King's Birth Day, the celebrations beginning with the delivery of an ode in the Castle in the afternoon, the ball being held later that evening. Building operations at the Castle were usually planned so as to be completed during the eighteen months or so while the viceroy was in England – that is between about April in an even-numbered year and September of the next year. This meant that the works initiated by Chesterfield would have to be completed by the autumn of 1747. The task was entrusted to Nevill, who had been appointed engineer and surveyor-general of fortifications and buildings two years earlier, in 1744, on the recommendation of his predecessor Arthur Dobbs. Like Dobbs, Nevill was neither an engineer nor an architect, but a placeman, a political figure entrusted with high office. The post did, however, carry responsibility and accountability beyond that of a mere sinecure.

No plans survive, nor indeed has any document been located recording the name of Nevill's architect for the Castle additions. Maurice Craig has written: 'During Nevill's tenure his clerk of works was George Ensor, and in the absense of any evidence that Nevill was an architect, Ensor is the likliest candidate for government designs between 1744-51.'[30] Ensor and his brother John, who was assistant to Richard Castle and successor to his practice, are believed to have come originally from Coventry. Whatever the role of the clerk of works, it was not unknown for viceroys to engage their own architects in special cases, and there is more than a hint in the quality and sophistication of Chesterfield's improvements at the Castle to suggest a hand other than Ensor's.

Nevill submitted an estimate of £5205. 4s. 7d. for the works, a warrant for the first £2000 being issued on 5 May 1746.[31] That it had been calculated down to shillings and pence would suggest that plans had already been prepared. Progress payments for the actual building works can be traced in the Irish *Commons Journals* which reveal that Nevill was simultaneously building a new stable block for the Castle Horse Guard at the recently opened entrance from Cork Hill. On 29 August 1746 Nevill was paid a further £2000, effectively drawing down most of the £5202 estimate. The next payment, £1000, was not made until 18 June 1747, leaving just £205 unspent which was paid out on the following 30 October, the King's birthday. The job had, in fact overrun the budget, but the extras, amounting to £1938. 15s 4s., were not paid out until 9 February 1748 NS. The final cost, £7143. 19s. 11d., was some 30 per cent over the budgeted figure. This did not include fitting-out costs, nor refurnishing, but Nevill's achievement in completing so much in such a short space of time must surely have been recognized. *Faulkner's Dublin Journal*, in a piece on the King's Birth Day celebrations, referred to the 'ball at the grand stately room in the Castle.'[32]

The room, which we now know as St Patrick's Hall, had been inaugurated.

All payees of £23 and over are listed in the *Commons Journals*. No trades nor addresses are given, but it is possible to identify most of the individuals. It can be seen from the figures that of the £7143 expended, almost 60 per cent was paid to just two individuals, John Chambers, £2927, and Simon Hammond, £1270. Chambers was a timber merchant, but must have acted more as a general contractor, employing allied trades like carpenters and joiners. Hammond, who described himself as a master builder, was a bricklayer by trade. Three stone cutters/masons can be identified, David Sheehan (£341), Richard Morgan (£278) and Hugh Darley (£209); a plumber, William Lewis (£444); an ironmonger, Timothy Turner (£33); and the carver, John Houghton (£28). John Wilkinson, who was paid £401, was Nevill's 'Clerk in the accompts' rather than a tradesman. The payment of £200 to Joseph Tudor, the scene-painter, is of interest, and may relate to the decorations seen in the Dorset picture. If the figure seems low for such an extensive scheme, it should be viewed in the context of a further £487 (the third-largest individual payment) given to the herald painter, John Seymour, who appears to have been entrusted with much of the general painting at the Castle. That Seymour and Tudor were collaborating in some way can be taken from the further payment of £104 to them jointly for the fitting out of the new apartments for the Birth Day celebrations. Other payments at that time included £95 to the brazier Samson Theaker – possibly for brass chandeliers. The lighting of the new Ball Room proved difficult. In 1751 *Faulkner's Dublin Journal* reported that 'The large Branch that hung in the Ball Room is taken down, and replaced by one of a smaller size and four fine Glass Branches are fixed up, one at each corner of the Room, which greatly adds to the magnificence of the Place.'[33] The provisions of 'lustres for the Ball Room' at this time is confirmed in the *Commons Journals*. The Dorset picture shows ten chandeliers, apparently of brass, indicating yet another arrangement.

On 21 April 1749 a balance of £1669 was paid for expenditure during the previous two years, which included 'refurnishing the new Addition to the Castle, for the reception of the Earl of Harrington' (i.e. in 1747-8). This sum included £62 paid to Nevill for pictures, £399 to Mark Forward (probably for furniture), £262 to Theaker and £222 to Chambers.

THE DESIGN

The scope of the building works incorporated in this 'New Addition' related to a replacement of the old accommodation more or less on a room-for-room basis.[34] In place of Capt. Paine's rusticated entrance of the 1660s the Castle got a grand portico in Portland stone, apparently based on Palladio's Palazzo Chiericati. Robinson had planned a grand pedimented entrance at this point in the 1680s, also of five bays, which may perhaps have been the genesis of the design for the new centrepiece. The south-west range having been built somewhat closer to the south-east range than Robinson had projected, the new entrance was narrower than the one he had proposed.

Behind the portico, the colonnaded entrance hall, based on Italian examples and originally open to the courtyard, leads to a grand imperial staircase, probably the first such staircase to be built in Dublin. At first-floor level, over the entrance hall, was the Battle Axe Hall, now the Throne Room. The unfinished south-west arcade, seen in Brooking's view, was completed with a new Supper Room above it, running the length of the first floor behind the courtyard façade. The top floor was a dormer storey matching the south-east range except in that it had a modillion stone cornice rather than the old-fashioned bracketed cornice of the Robinson building.[35] The dormer storeys were replaced with a full attic storey in the nineteenth century, visually reducing the impact of the portico and pedi-

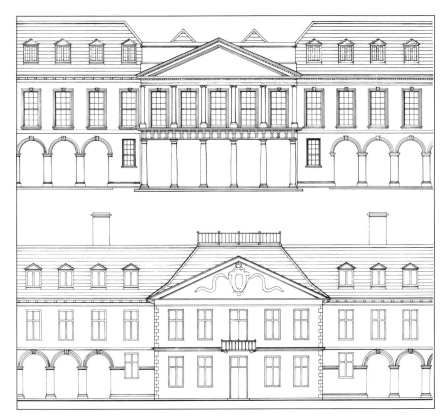

8. Comparative Elevations of the State Apartments, as envisaged in the 1860s (bottom) and as completed in 1746-7 (top). The 1860s elevation is based on two drawings attributed to William Robinson which are not consistent in all details – note the plinth and impost moulding. The carving in the tympanum is conjectural – a note on the original drawing simply indicated that the Royal Arms were to be placed in this position. The 1746-7 elevation is taken from Tudor's view of 1753 and from nineteenth- and twentieth-century survey drawings. Chimneys have been omitted as their location and form are not entirely clear. The south-west range, as built, differed from the south-east range in cornice detail and in the spacing of the windows nearest the portico. The dormer roofs were replaced by brick-fronted attic storeys between 1819 and 1826. The portico was rebuilt with some alteration of detail in 1825-6. [Drawing – Author]

ment. On the ground floor, behind the open arcade, the remains of the Old Hall were divided up as servants' quarters.[36] The back wall of the arcade appears to date from the abandoned works of 1712-16, and to have been later buttressed at basement level to take the superimposed load of the three-foot thick brick wall that separates St Patrick's Hall from the Supper Room (now the Picture Gallery) and the storey above. The new Ballroom, the heart of the development, was favourably compared with that at the English court. Mrs Delany, who, of course, had known the Old Hall, attended the 1751 Birth Day celebrations and thought 'the ballroom ... very fine, much better than that at St James's'.[36] Chief Baron Willes was similarly impressed in 1757: 'The ballroom upon the King's Birthday is a prodigious fine sight. Tis a noble room Much larger than the Ballroom at St James.'[37] Such comments were not mere hyperbole, the new Ball Room was about 30 per cent larger than its London counterpart. Although Chesterfield, in exchanging posts with his kinsman, Lord Harrington, the secretary of state, in October 1746, effectively severed his connection with Dublin Castle just as his project was getting underway, his name remained linked with its success. His association with the Castle has today largely been forgotten, although his bust, by Roubiliac, still surveys the Hall from a niche at the east end. In all the lists of tradesmen in the *Commons Journal* there is no record of payment to an architect. Chesterfield was the man who caused the new addition to be built, but did he perhaps do more than sign a petition to the Treasury in London? According to one contemporary account he did.

THE ARCHITECT?

Benjamin Victor was deputy manager and treasurer under Sheridan at the Smock Alley Theatre. Originally a London barber, he had run an Irish linen warehouse in the metropolis, with, he claimed, the support and encouragement of the Duke of Dorset, then (1734) in his first term as viceroy. After the collapse of this venture in 1746, Victor moved to Dublin, took up the theatrical post and established himself, in his own words, as 'an Officer of Importance' in Dublin Castle circles. As such he attended a Birth Night celebration shortly after the completion of the new Ball Room, and described the occasion in a letter to Colley Cibber, the London actor and dramatist. The letter was subsequently published by Victor in his memoirs where it is dated 17 November 1748, but as there are references to a lord-lieutenant and a ball, in a year when Ireland was governed by lords justices, it is more likely to have been written in 1747, when the new rooms were inaugurated. Balls were apparently only held when the lord lieutenant was in residence; there are no newspaper references to a ball in 1748. Of the occasion, Victor wrote:

Since I have accidently fallen on this courtly subject, I cannot quit it, in Justice to the present *Lord Lieutenant,* without informing you, that nothing within the memory of the oldest Courtier living, ever equalled the Taste and Splendour of the Supper-Room at the Castle on the Birth-Night. The Ball was in the New Room, design'd by Lord Chesterfield, which is allowed to be very magnificent. After the Dancing was over, the Company retired to an apartment form'd like a long Gallery, where, as you pass'd steady through, you stopp'd by the way at Shops elegantly form'd, where was cold Eating, and all sorts of Wines and Sweetmeats; and the whole most beautifully disposed by transparent Paintings, through which a Shade was cast like Moonlight.[38]

Was Chesterfield then an amateur architect? He certainly did not claim to be. In one of his celebrated almost daily letters to his natural son, Chesterfield wrote, on 7 August 1749:

It would not be amiss, if you employed three or four days learning the five orders of Architecture, with their general proportions: and you may know all you need to know of them in that time. Palladio's own book of Architecture is the best you can make use of for that purpose, skipping over the lowest mechanical parts of it, such as materials, the cement etc.

In a further letter, two months later, he added,

You may soon be acquainted with the considerable parts of Civil Architecture; and for the minute and mechanical parts of it, leave them to masons, bricklayers, and Lord Burlington; who has, to a certain degree, lessened himself by knowing them too well.[39]

Chesterfield clearly saw himself as an informed patron rather than an amateur architect. There are certainly Palladian influences (as noted) in the design of the Castle additions, but then Palladianism was the prevailing style of the day, particularly in Ireland, where there had been no serious threat from a baroque school. At the time the Castle additions were contemplated or just begun, Chesterfield was also planning to build a new town house in Mayfair, then an undeveloped part of London. The exact date of its commencement is not known, but it is believed to have been early in 1747 NS. Chesterfield had returned from Ireland in April 1746. Significantly, Chesterfield did not design his town house, but chose as his architect Isaac Ware, a protégé of Burlington's, and ostensibly an arch-Palladian. Ware had published a translation of Palladio's *Four Books of Architecture* in 1738. In 1736 he had succeeded Hawksmoor as secretary to the (English) Board of Works, but he also carried on a private practice. Various theories have been expounded as to why Chesterfield should have gone to Ware, 'a Palladian of the second rank', for designs for his new house. It has been suggested that a so-called star architect might have had reservations about the French rococo decoration with which Chesterfield proposed to challenge London architectural fashion,[40] but whatever Ware's 'reservations about the style to be adopted, [he] would work with the reliability and professionalism that came of an Office of Works training'.[41] Chesterfield moved into the new house in March 1749, although internal decoration was not apparently completed until a couple of years later. In his magnum opus, *A Complete Body of Architecture,* which came out in weekly instalments from 1756, Ware described and illustrated Chesterfield House, but attempted to distance himself from the use of French rococo motifs, which were a feature of some of the main rooms. Is it possible that Ware was Chesterfield's architectural advisor prior to the commencement of the London house in 1747, and might he have been involved in the design of the Dublin Castle additions also?

It is not recorded when Ware and Chesterfield first met, but they would certainly have had the opportunity of meeting before Chesterfield left for Ireland in July 1745. The two men had a mutual acquaintance in the sculptor Louis François Roubiliac, for whom Chesterfield had sat prior to his departure. Although the bronze bust of Chesterfield in St Patrick's Hall is dated 1746 on the socle (the full inscription is 'Philippus Stanhope Comes. [Ch]esterfield Prorex Hiberniae. Anno 1746 – Rubillac [*sic*] F[ecit]'), there is an earlier version, in marble, dated 1745.[42] The St Patrick's Hall bust seems to have been set up in its present niche in the 1840s, but it is mentioned as being at Dublin Castle in Dr Maty's edition of Chesterfield's letters, published in 1777. A plaster bust, similar to the Castle bronze, was among the pieces Maty purchased for the British Museum after the sculptor's death in 1762. Ware himself sat for Roubiliac on at least two occasions, the first time in 1741.[43] Both men were members of the Beefsteak Club, a circle of artists in London, and were associated with the St Martin's Lane Academy and Old Slaughter's Coffee House. Another member of the club was Benjamin Victor's friend, the dramatist Colley Cibber.

While documentation connecting Issac Ware to the Castle additions is lacking, his official post in the English Office of Works, cited above as an asset in obtaining the Chesterfield House commission, would have been doubly so in a commission at Dublin Castle, in that he was already employed in the public service and had an intimate knowledge of English court practice, being responsible for the maintenance of St James's Palace. There was apparent precedent for this in the employment by Ormonde of Hugh May, comptroller of the King's Works in England, on Irish projects in the 1670s and 80s, while the practice of unofficial appointments continued in the Irish public works establishment.[44] Recent research by David Griffin has revealed that Ware had an Irish practice and a patron in the Earl of Kildare, who was appointed by Chesterfield to his privy council. Kildare was made a lord justice in 1756, by which date Ware had already produced designs for a bridge on the earl's estate at Carton, illustrated (though not identified) in the *Complete Body of Architecture*.[45] By 1759 Ware was working on Kildare's Dublin town house (now Leinster House) and was probably also the architect for the remodelling of the reception rooms at Castletown for Thomas Conolly, who married Kildare's sister-in-law in 1758.

There is no mention of Dublin Castle, nor any design connected with it, in the *Complete Body of Architecture,* though it would appear that Chesterfield's additions conformed to the ideals expounded by Ware in its pages. These include the use of an imperial staircase, an innovation in Dublin, the method of wall construction seen in the brickwork of St Patrick's Hall, and the type of compartmented ceiling and plaster decoration in the room, as seen in the Dorset painting. Ware included a detailed plate of the portico of Palladio's Palazzo Chiericati, the apparent model for the portico at the Castle. While little in the way of interior decoration survives from the 1740s, there is in storage at the Castle a carved overmantle that can be connected to Ware. This stood over a chimneypiece on the

Battle Axe landing, taken down when a doorway was knocked through into the Throne Room in 1952.[46] However, this was not its original location since there had been a doorway at this point up until the 1780s when the room was replanned. Drawings in the collection of the Office of Public Works appear to indicate that the overmantle was removed c.1888 from above the chimneypiece of the Ante-Drawing Room, which adjoined the Throne Room to the east[47] This room, the Presence Chamber in Robinson's 1687-8 block, had been enlarged and remodelled in 1750-1, the work being undertaken as a consequence of the Chesterfield additions of 1746-7, in particular the construction of the Battle Axe staircase and Battle Axe Hall which improved the internal circulation of the State Apartments. The Ante-Drawing Room was unfortunately destroyed by fire in February 1941. The room, completed for the return of the Duke of Dorset as lord-lieutenant in September 1751, was something of an architectural hybrid, with engaged Doric columns around three walls, a frieze incorporating garter stars (a reference to Dorset's membership of the order?), and a remarkable baroque coved ceiling.[48]

The overmantel, in carved pine and oak, derives from a design by William Kent for the chimneypiece in the hall at Houghton Hall, Norfolk, while the actual chimneypiece appears to have been based on that in the Saloon at Houghton. The centre panel of the Castle overmantel is carved with a scene from the life of Marcus Aurelius. A similar overmantel, different in detail, with a panel depicting a scene from the Iliad, survives in the hall at Iveagh House, St Stephen's Green. Both may be the work of the celebrated Dublin carver John Houghton, who was employed both on the

9. Chimneypiece and overmantle formerly in the State Apartments. The chimneypiece (destroyed by fire in 1941) appears to have been erected in the Presence Chamber (later called the Ante-Drawing Room) in 1750-1. The overmantle probably stood above it before being moved to the Battle Axe landing c.1888. The design of both chimneypiece and overmantle appears to have been inspired by plates in Isaac Ware's *The Plans, Elevations and Sections of Houghton in Norfolk*, published in 1735. [Drawing – Author]

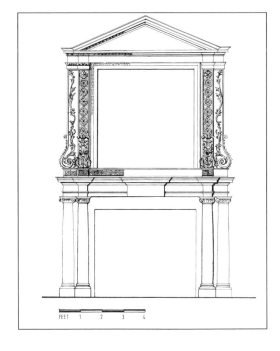

Chesterfield additions at the Castle and for fitting out the Ball Room and Council Chamber for the 1749 Birth Night. The centre panel of the Iveagh House overmantle, depicting 'The Achaeans offering a sacrifice of bulls and goats to Apollo', is copied from a panel by Rysbrack in the chimneypiece of the Marble Parlour at Houghton. While the official guide to Iveagh House gives William Kent's *The Designs of Inigo Jones, with some Additional Designs*, (1727) as the source for the overmantel there,[49] this is unlikely since the Rysbrack panel was not completed until 1732 and was not illustrated by Kent.[50] All three Houghton Hall chimneypieces (from which the Dublin chimneypieces are derived) were, however, illustrated in Isaac Ware's *The Plans, Elevations and Sections of Houghton in Norfolk*, which was published in 1735. Indeed portions of all three can be traced in the Castle example since the Greek fret decoration on its base is taken from the Marble Parlour design. Ware had probably worked on the construction of Houghton Hall himself during his apprenticeship to Thomas Ripley, who was executant architect there. While the derivation of the Castle chimneypiece from plates in Ware's book does not prove that he designed it, just as the use of Garter stars in the room decoration is not necessarily linked with similar decorative motifs at both Houghton Hall and Chesterfield House, it does indicate that Ware was being used as a source, which the Chesterfield connection and the design of the 1746-7 addition might suggest is more than coincidence. Balanced against this is the fact that Ware makes no reference to Dublin Castle in the *Complete Works*. It may be that his role was that of consultant, with the Irish surveyor-general's office, in the person of the clerk of works, George Ensor, formulating the detailed proposals, perhaps with an input from Chesterfield himself.

SUMMARY

Apart from the panelling in the Supper Room (now the Picture Gallery), no significant internal decoration survives from the 1740s. The Ball Room, as noted, was re-roofed in 1769, while the present pilasters appear to date from Waldré's time. The mirrors and cove decoration are late Victorian, while the niche and screen framing Chesterfield's bust appear to have been erected by Jacob Owen in the 1840s. Owen's hand can also be seen in both the Picture Gallery and the Throne Room, the roof of which he raised on screw jacks, earlier improvements having been carried out to the room in the 1780s and the 1820s. The Battle Axe staircase shows the imprint of Owen and more recent architects. The absence of contemporary internal decoration makes it difficult to reach any definite conclusions about the authorship of the works initiated by Chesterfield. Isaac Ware, who was working for Chesterfield in London, was certainly the right person at the right time to have been consulted. Chesterfield, who was credited by a Castle courtier with the design of the Ball Room, on the other hand disapproved of Lord Burlington's descent to the level of tradesmen in practising as an amateur architect. Did Chesterfield perhaps obtain a sketch scheme from Ware and pass it on to Nevill for detailing in his office? The near-contemporary overmantel at the Castle can be linked to Ware's book on Houghton Hall, while other themes in the design accord with the philosophies and recommendations enunciated by him in the *Complete Works*. Shortly after the completion of the Chesterfield additions to the Castle, Ware was employed by the leading Irish political figure of the day, the Earl of Kildare, at both Carton and Kildare (now Leinster) House.

Regarding the painting of the State Ball, a strong case can be made for redating it from 1731 to about twenty years later, and consequently for reattributing it, Van der Hagen having died in or before 1745. It is clear that the disposition of the old buildings on the south side of the Upper Yard, particularly the Dining Hall and the Old Hall, was a major factor in dictating the planning of the Castle Apartments in the 1680s and in planning the completion of the south range and the construction of the new Ball Room in the 1740s, portions of the medieval structures as well as the abandoned arcade of 1712-16 being incorporated in the fabric.

NOTES

The suffix NS is used to denote new style for years before 1753 when, under the Julian calendar (old style), the year started on 25 March.

[1] The engraving was begun in the 1780s by the English draughtsman and engraver John Keyse Sherwin but was unfinished at the time of his death in 1790, and not published until 1803. An early proof, dated 1793, shows the architectural detail less complete, but an oil sketch by Sherwin would suggest that the plate is based on a contemporary study by him, but with some changes of detail. My thanks to Adrian Le Harivel, National Gallery of Ireland, for showing me the Sherwin studies in the collection.

[2] John Cornforth, 'Dublin Castle', Part II. *Country Life*, Vol. CXLVIII (6 August 1970), p.344.

[3] John Gilmartin, 'Vincent Waldré's Ceiling Paintings in Dublin Castle', *Apollo*, vol. XCV (January 1972), p. 42. For further information see also Edward McParland, 'A Note on Vincent Waldré', *Apollo*, Vol. XIV, (Nov. 1972), p.467.

[4] Lady Llanover (ed.), *Autobiography and Correspondence of Mary Granville, Mrs Delany* (London 1861-2), vol. I, p.308.

[5] *Op. cit.*, pp.337-8.

[6] Catalogue no. 24, p.37.

[7] The surviving canvasses are of some of the giant figures from the side walls. Information of the Knight of Glin.

[8] *Journals of the Irish House of Commons*, vol. VIII, pt. 2, p.ccclvi. In a warrant dated 20 September 1769, Hugh Henry Mitchell, treasurer to the Barrack Board, was paid for 'taking down the old Roof, and new roofing the Ball-Room in his Majesty's Castle of Dublin'.

[9] Alfray's survey, collection the Office of Public Works, Dublin. There are contemporary references to window screens in the adjoining Supper Room. Although Sherwin's engraving shows no windows, the outline of a window is discernible in his oil sketch of the view (National Gallery of Ireland no. 396).

[10] Quoted in Cornforth, n.2 above.

[11] British Museum, Ms K Top LIII, f.19.

[12] Dartmouth Collection, Staffordshire Record Office.

[13] For Robinson, see Rolf Loeber, *A Biographical Dictionary of Architects in Ireland 1600-1720* (London 1981), pp.88-97. Although planned by Robinson, the execution of the south-east range was entrusted to his collegue William Molyneaux, Robinson having departed to England for the duration of the Jacobite administration (1687-90).

[14] A report of the Privy Council Committee, dated 16 June 1738, refers to stonework carried

out at the Castle by the mason John Whinrey, which included 'the Piazza where ye Stewards and other Officers Apartments are', a reference to the unfinished arcade. Public Record Office, Kew, T1/308/108. Information Dr E. McParland.

[15] Robert Ware, 'History and Antiquities of Dublin' (1678), collection Central Municipal Library Dublin, Ms 1678.

[16] J. B. Maguire, 'Seventeenth-Century Plans of Dublin Castle', *JRSAI* (1974), Vol. 104, pp.5-14; 'Dublin Castle: Three Centuries of Development', *JRSAI* (1985), Vol. 115, pp.13-39. Rolf Loeber, 'The Rebuilding of Dublin Castle: Thirty Critical Years, 1660-1690', *Studies* (Spring 1980), pp.45-69.

[17] Quoted in James J. Hughes, 'Dublin Castle in the Seventeenth Century – A Topographical Reconstruction', *Dublin Historical Record*, Vol. 2, No. 3 (March 1940), p.85. Hughes confuses the Old Hall with the Old Parliament House.

[18] Sir William Brereton, 'Travels in Ireland', quoted in C. Litton Falkiner, *Illustrations of Irish History and Topography* (London 1904), p.380.

[19] The evidence of surviving walls at basement level suggests that the irregularly shaped east end of the Hall on the 1673 survey was not part of the room but represents an open area dividing it from the Dining Room block, and occurring at a point where there was a kink in the curtain wall. The outer wall of St Patrick's Hall averages from three to four feet in thickness, about half the width of the old limestone wall on which it stands.

[20] Letter from Willes to the Earl of Warwick, quoted in Thomas and Valerie Pakenham (eds), *Dublin – A Traveller's Companion* (London 1988), pp.68-9. Information John Redmill.

[21] See Mairead Dunlevy, *Dress in Ireland* (London 1989), pp.92-3.

[22] Plan after Henry Flitcroft of St James's Palace, 1729, reproduced in Hugh Murray Baillie, 'Etiquette and the Planning of State Apartments in Baroque Palaces', *Archaeologia*, Vol. CI (1967), p.177. Information Dr E. McParland.

[23] *Faulkner's Dublin Journal*, 13-17 November 1753. 'Emblems of Royalty resting on a pyramidal Pillar', part of the fittings supplied by Tudor for the Supper Room at the direction of the surveyor-general's office. See also W. G. Strickland, *A Dictionary of Irish Artists*, Vol. 2 (Dublin and London 1913), p.462-5. The 1753 Birth Day celebrations were particularly lavish, George II being the first monarch, it was believed, to reach his seventieth birthday. Unfortunately no details are given of the Ball Room decorations on the occasion.

[24] The date of publication given by Strickland, 1746, is erroneous. A painting of the same scene by Tudor is reproduced in *The Painters of Ireland*, p.65.

[25] *The Irish Builder*, 15 February 1896, p. 38. Information David Griffin.

[26] Public Record Office of Ireland, Board of Works Minute Book, 1809-11, p.213.

[27] Public Record Office, Kew, T1/322/14.

[28] Public Record Office, Kew, SO.1.20 f20.

[29] Collection the Royal Irish Academy, reproduced in David Newman Johnson, 'Portumna Castle: A little known early survey and some observations', in *Settlement and Society in Medieval Ireland* (Kilkenny 1988), fig. 24.3.

[30] Maurice Craig, *Dublin 1660-1860* (London 1952), p.166.

[31] *Commons Journal*, Vol. IV, pt. II, p. cclxxix. The warrant was issued on foot of a King's Letter of 22 April 1746, Public Record Office, Kew T14/12/484.

[32] *Dublin Journal*, 27-31 October 1747.

[33] *Dublin Journal*, 14-17 September 1751.

[34] As analysed by Bailie (n.22 above), the State Apartments of English palaces conformed to certain planning protocols, the sequence of rooms being Stairs, Great Chamber (Yeomen Guard), Presence Chamber, Drawing Room, State Bedchamber and Closet (Study). A similar sequence was maintained in Dublin Castle and at the conclusion of the rebuilding in 1751 was as follows – Battle Axe Stairs, Battle Axe (Yeomens') Hall, Presence Chamber, Lord Lieutenant's Drawing Room, Lady's Drawing Room, with the State Bedchamber and Study in adjoining rooms to the rear.

[35] Robinson's block probably had a timber cornice, as at the Royal Hospital. The discrepancies between the eaves details of the south-east and south-west ranges were faithfully recorded by Tudor in his view of 1753, and by James Malton in his view of 1792.

[36] The arcades were filled in in the early nineteenth century. The present open arcade in the south-east range dates from the rebuilding of that block in 1964-8.

[36] Llanover (n.4) above, vol. III, p. 31.

[37] See n. 20 above.

[38] Benjamin Victor, *The History of the Theatres of London and Dublin*, vol. II (London 1761), pp.216-17.

[39] Quoted in Barrington Kaye, *The Development of the Architectural Profession in Britain* (London 1960), p.46.

[40] David Pearce, *London's Mansions* (London 1986), p.71.

[41] Roger White, 'Isaac Ware and Chesterfield House', *The Rococo in England – A Symposium*, (Charles Hind ed.) (London 1986), p. 182. For Chesterfield House (demolished 1937) see also Christopher Simon Sykes, *Private Palaces* (London 1985), pp.116-28.

[42] Katharine A. Esdaile's *The Life and Works of Louis François Roubiliac* (London 1928), which makes no reference to the Dublin Castle bust, noted the inscription on the back of the pedestal of the marble bust, then in the collection of Colonel Sir E.A. Brotherton, Bart. It included among Chesterfield's titles, Lord Lieutenant of Ireland, and was inscribed by Roubiliac 'Sct. ad vivum MCCXLV'. From her description, it would appear to be similar to the Dublin bust. There were two terracotta and three plaster busts of Chesterfield in the sale of Roubiliac's effects in 1762. The Castle bust was presumably cast from one of these, but exactly when is not known. Nor is it clear how the sculptor's name came to be misspelt. According to the Knight of Glin, a bronze bust, similar to that at the Castle, survives in a private collection, while a slightly different version is in the collection of the Victoria and Albert Museum.

[43] See Howard Colvin, 'Roubiliac's Bust of Isaac Ware', *The Burlington Magazine*, vol. XCVII (1955), pp.151-2. A bust of Ware, believed to be the 1741 example, acquired in the 1980s by the Detroit Institute of Arts, was illustrated in *The Burlington Magazine*, vol. CXXX, no. 1023 (June 1988).

[44] The case of the London architect Henry Keene is relevant. Having been employed on the College Green front of Trinity College in the 1750s, he was brought back to Dublin in 1761 by the newly appointed lord-lieutenant, the Earl of Halifax and 'appointed by him Architect of the Kingdom of Ireland for his Majesty's Works there' (letter quoted by Howard Colvin, *A Biographical Dictionary of British Architects 1600-1840* (London 1978), p.48. Keene's post was subsequently formalised when he served as architect to the Barrack Board between 1762 and 1766. No official works by him have been identified. A notice in *Sleater's Public Gazetteer*, 27 April 1762, recording Keene's appointment, refers to him as 'Henry Keene, architect, a gentleman of the greatest ability in that science'. Information David O'Connor.

[45] See David Griffin, 'Leinster House and Isaac Ware' above.

[46] Information Oscar Richardson FRIAL.

[47] A lighter overmantel with an inset mirror was substituted, probably to brighten the Ante-Drawing Room, and the old overmantel erected above a new wooden chimneypiece on the Battle Axe landing.

[48] Accounts in the *Commons Journals*, vol. V, p. ccxxxvi *et passim*, indicate that this room dates from 1750-1, rather than the 1730s as was previously believed.

[49] Nicholas Sheaff, *Iveagh House, An historical description* (Dublin 1978), p.33, no.5.

[50] H. Avray Tipping, 'Houghton Hall', part IV, *Country Life*, vol. XLIX (22 January 1921), p. 98.

[51] John Harris, 'Who Designed Houghton?', *Country Life*, vol. CLXXXIII (2 March 1989), pp. 92-4.

BINDING MEMORIES OF
TRINITY LIBRARY

WILLIAM O'SULLIVAN

WHEN I joined the staff of Trinity College Library in 1949 from a back-
ground of work for the Irish Manuscripts Commission, I may have been
well grounded in reading the most difficult seventeenth-century hands but
I was scarcely aware of the excitements of bibliography. Delightful as many
of my new colleagues were, they failed to inspire me with a zest for the
finer points of my calling perhaps because they had served through a time
which left no room for such interests. Although one of the great libraries of
the world, the Trinity library was chronically short of money and at that
time it was probably at the lowest ebb of its fortunes since its foundation at
the end of the sixteenth century. Josiah Gilbart Smyly, who became
Librarian in 1913 and died in 1948, had presided over this sad period. A
brilliant papyrologist and potentially a brilliant librarian, he was totally
hamstrung by the absence of all resources, itself a reflection of the penury
of the College which had come to have a semi-twilight existence in the life
of the country.

    Into this dusty world, literally too because there was no money to clean
the books, Maurice came to my rescue. We already knew each other and
had many friends in common, notably the poet Geoffrey Taylor, who was a
source of inspiration for both of us. Maurice's widely acknowledged book
on Lord Charlemont had been published in 1948[1] and his laurels were still
fresh, but more importantly that work had set his future course on the
study of eighteenth-century architecture. Charlemont, moreover, had built
up the greatest private Irish library of his day, and Maurice shared his love
of fine books. By my standards he was extremely knowledgeable about
bibliography and my education began when he joined the Friends of the
Library, the society of which I was secretary, and launched me into setting
up an ambitious exhibition on the history of printing. The object was to dis-
cover and display the resources of the Library to illustrate 'the early
development and spread of printing, fine printing with a special section on
fine printing in Dublin and the history of Gaelic typography from the fount
used in Queen Elizabeth's Gaelic prayer-book to Mr Colm O Lochlainn's
monotype Colum Cille'.[2] The operation exposed the extraordinary riches of
the Library but of course also threw up some notable gaps. I can still
remember Maurice proposing to my dismay that we include a modern
reproduction from Aldus Manutius' 1499 edition of the *Hypernotomachia*

Poliphili for lack of the original, because it represented too important a step in the ultimate triumph of roman over gothic type to be omitted.

Maurice was to serve on the committee of the Friends from 1950 to 1952, when he had to leave for London to earn a living for his family. During these years he was exploring a new field but one that seemed to grow naturally out of his previous interests, the history of Dublin book binding in the eighteenth century. Although a certain aura surrounded the finer examples of these bindings which had already been of interest to collectors, little research had been done on them since in the early years of the century Sir Edward Sullivan had made a tentative beginning. There was still only a minimum of solid information, but this situation was to change with the publication of Maurice's work in 1954.[3]

When he generously gave me a copy of his book he inscribed it 'in recollection of the Long Room'. The Long Room contains all the books that were in the Library by 1800 and Maurice was remembering our searches along the shelves on long summer evenings after the visitors had gone. All special bindings of all periods, and not merely eighteenth-century Dublin, were our quarry, though the latter were his special interest and many of our finds were to be listed and illustrated in his book. The new Librarian, H.W. Parke, was encouraging and sheltered our discoveries in a splendid seventeenth-century armoire in his own room. The object was to give some measure of protection to a few of the better-preserved fine bindings, which like those on all the Long Room books had suffered severely from the polluted atmosphere of the city since Victorian times. I can still remember my surprise at the contrast provided by the bindings on the books bought by David Webb for the Library at the Carton sale in 1949.[4] Coming as they did from only a few miles west of Dublin but in the clean air of County Kildare, they were still in splendid condition. The finer Long Room bindings, being for the most part of morocco tanned in the traditional way, had stood up to the pollution rather better than the ordinary calf bindings, though vellum bindings had weathered it best of all. It was noticeable, too, that the less refined seventeenth-century leather of books bound for Archbishop Ussher had survived where that of the eighteenth-century bindings for Vice-Provost Gilbert had crumbled. Many of the finest bindings in the Library belonged to a single but splendid collection, that of Henry George Quin, an eighteenth-century Irish bibliophile. This is, however, curiously weak in Dublin bindings. Quin, like other great collectors of his day, preferred to patronize the English binder, Roger Payne, or the Paris binder Derome le jeune. Even his set of the Hawkey classics printed at the University Press, which was certainly bound in Dublin, is of very modest grade and he did not deem it worthy to form part of the *Bibliotheca Quiniana* which he bequeathed in its bookcase to the Library. Ironically it is now kept in that bookcase. His copy of the Baskerville *Virgil* is the exception, but since that came to him as a gift, the elegant binding in olive green morocco from the William McKenzie bindery would not have been of his choosing.[5]

It was probably Smyly's predecessor, T.K. Abbott, who added to the permanent Long Room exhibition most of the examples of Irish, English, continental and oriental fine bindings. In his time, on 2 May 1907, four bindings were chosen from the Library's holdings for display at the Irish International Exhibition at Herbert Park. They were 'Commons Journal iii 1796', a specimen from the splendidly bound set of the fourth edition presented by John Foster, the last speaker of the House, now sadly ruined by constant use, 'Keil's Trigonometry 1726, 00.1.44', a Harleian type Dublin binding, perhaps by McDonnell's Worth binder [26], 'a George Mullen about 1835, V.1.1. Pompilius by Sir Edward Sullivan, Press A.5.42'.[6] Sullivan, who was much influenced by the French eighteenth-century mosaic style, presented several examples of his skill to the Library, and he had already shown a large selection of his work at the Dublin Arts and Crafts Exhibition in 1895. His researches on the history of Dublin binding for the catalogue of that exhibition may very well have inspired Abbott's Long Room selection.[7]

The last years of Smyly's reign over the Library were justly troubled by the attempts by a few of the younger academic staff to introduce some desperately needed reforms into his feeble administration. One of their targets spearheaded by H.W. Parke, who eventually succeeded as Librarian, was the permanent exhibition in the Long Room. Parke began by listing what had over the years become an amazing collection of many things besides books. Unhappily and almost uniquely his report does not list the bindings individually. He notes: 'At present 44 books are exhibited for their bindings in different cases. A selection of about 15 should be made and put in a single case.' Although I may have entered the Library shortly before him, by the time I became aware of the bindings he had already reformed the exhibit. Wisely, however, instead of returning the books to their shelves, where they would have been at serious risk of damage, he held them in the armoire in his room, where they were shortly to be joined by the discoveries that Maurice and I were to make. All of these books now occupy vacant space in the Quin bookcase.

Parke's librarianship was to be one of far-reaching reform which radically changed the whole character of the Library. One of the earliest of his reforms was my appointment to take charge of the manuscripts in 1953, the first such appointment. This had the effect of transferring my attention from bindings on printed books to bindings on manuscripts, and from an admiration for fine examples to a study of what they might reveal about the history of the individual manuscripts. For instance, it seems most likely that the large number of additional manuscripts belonging to the collection of Archbishop Ussher added by Samuel Foley, when he began the re-cataloguing in 1680, had been omitted from the previous catalogue, dating from about 1670, largely because they were unbound and so unable to stand in numbered sequence on a shelf.[8] Judging by the number of these additional manuscripts that were bound by John Exshaw during the period 1741-4, it is unlikely that there was any great campaign of binding, certainly of manuscripts and probably also of printed books, in the late seventeenth century. The only manuscript whose binding we know of in this time was that of the Book of Durrow, which had been given to the Library by Bishop

Henry Jones in its original silver shrine. This disappeared during the Williamite war when the College was occupied by troops and the now-naked manuscript needed the protection of a binding. In 1699 Archbishop Marsh described it as bound 'in a plain rough brown leathern cover'.[9]

The Exshaw rebinding of about half of the manuscripts[10] was a late part of the large-scale effort which began with the printed books in 1732, its purpose being to dress them in a manner worthy of their new and splendid setting in Thomas Burgh's Long Room. The Manuscripts Room, being hidden from the general view, with the manuscripts themselves locked away in their oak cupboards, could afford to wait a further ten years. Theirs was strictly a duty binding with the Book of Kells costing only three shillings and sixpence, the same amount as a seventeenth-century volume of copies of Connaught inquisitions, probably because they were of about the same size. Some of the service books like the Armagh antiphonal cost up to eight shillings because they were taller. No distinction seems to have been made between vellum and paper books in the charges, unhappily reflecting the absence of distinction in the treatment to the detriment of the former, which were subjected to very heavy glueing of the spines. This made it difficult to open the books and cockled the membrane. Combining several smaller manuscripts together, which is a feature of Exshaw's work, cost more per volume as it would have involved re-sewing. Thus MS 196 (B.4.2) in calf, which included MSS 355, 387 and 695 in the seventeenth-century numbering, cost two shillings and sixpence, whereas the eleventh-century saints' lives from Salisbury of a size and shelved next door, MS 174 (B.4.3), in parchment was twopence cheaper. Exshaw's general rule seems to have been to bind parchment manuscripts in calf and paper manuscripts in vellum, but there are plenty of exceptions. In every case the hinges of the calf bindings have broken down and many were re-backed in the nineteenth century. Those in vellum have survived intact for the most part.

The second George Mullen, the most prestigious of the Dublin fine binders of his day, was responsible for the re-backing, or vamping as it was known in the trade, and the wholesale rebinding in the second quarter of the nineteenth century of the half of the manuscripts not touched by Exshaw. George Mullen, father and son, were College binders for much of the first half of the century. The father's earliest surviving bill is dated 13 December 1808[11] and the son's connection ends in June quarter 1848.[12] In signing the receipts the son uses a looped tail to the capital G and from about 1818 an epsilon-shaped 'e'.[13] The Dublin Directories show the firm moving from the Temple Bar to Nassau Street, to William Street. On 4 May 1821 the Board of the College agreed to continue the widow of the late J. [sic] Mullen as bookbinder jointly with Devoy as her husband was.[14] The Dublin directories, being one step behind as usual, still register both father and son at 38 Nassau Street in 1822, but only the son in 1823. Besides acting as binder, the son was later to be also a bookseller to the Library on a large scale.[15]

Franc Sadleir, who is described by the most recent historians of the College as a good administrator if not a scholar, was Librarian from 1821 to

1837, when he became Provost.[16] To his initiative we owe the Mullen campaign of rebinding. That he was a man of considerable taste is shown by two manuscripts, among the finest in the Library, that formerly belonged to him: the deservedly well-known Dublin Apocalypse (MS 64) and a beautifully painted Book of Hours (MS 105).[17] Both manuscripts are splendidly bound in straight-grained crimson morocco elaborately tooled in blind. Prominent among the tools is the paschal lamb, which is not, however, the Sadleir crest.

The first surviving Mullen bill for work on the manuscripts shows a charge of three shillings and fourpence for 'repairing old manuscript books' on 3 Feb. 1815.[18] On May 15 the Board ordered that the manuscripts were to be examined to see if they needed repair.[19] H.J. Monck Mason's work on cataloguing the collection for the Record Commissioners at this time would have thrown their needs into relief.[20] When the Persian ambassador called on 16 Nov. 1819 he pronounced the Persian manuscript of the Koran from Tipu's library (MS 1549), which had been presented by the East India Company, to be worth £1000.[21] This clearly made an impression in the College and, the book's condition leaving something to be desired, Mullen was called in to repair it in the presence of the Librarian. He gave it a characteristic new spine and a cedar case was ordered to keep it in.[22] By then George Mullen junior had already described himself as binder to the lord lieutenant and several bindings he made for Lord Whitworth, who held the office from 1813 to 1817, are known.[23]

Most of his work on the Trinity manuscripts came later. The main Mullen campaign on the manuscripts seems to have taken place between 1825 and 1831. On 17 Oct. 1825 the Board ordered the bursar to 'have sundry books carefully repaired and it was agreed that the expence in this case and on like occasions be charged in the extra expences of the quarter'.[24] Up to this point, Mullen's charges appear on the Library account and they return there in the December quarter 1831 with three bills for 'binding etc. manuscripts', but in the interval they appear under 'extraordinaries'.[25] The Manuscript Room bindings are in reddish-brown crushed russia or in pale calf, a few in light grey calf, all simply decorated in blind using twenty or so different rolls in various ingenious and beautiful combinations and generally with marbled paper end-leaves. Despite their relatively sheltered existence in the Manuscripts Room, most of these bindings are in an advanced state of decay and can no longer be said to be fulfilling their primary tasks of protecting the contents.

Nowadays other libraries are inclined to envy the Bodleian, which perhaps for very lack of resources at that time escaped the Exshaw-Mullen type of large-scale rebinding and as a consequence a proportion of their medieval manuscripts retain their early bindings. Trinity probably saw its greatest prosperity in the decades before the Great Famine and this was a period of lavish spending on the Library.

The Mullens' general work is one index of this expenditure but advantage was also taken of the second George Mullen's great skill as a fine binder. During his time the practice developed of fitting the covers of the manuscripts to the contents and this is shown to some extent even in the Mullen duty bindings of the manuscripts, where the more highly regarded tend to have more elaborately decorated covers, while remaining on a certain general level. Above this level, George Mullen the younger was clearly allowed to have his head, and great manuscript treasures were fitted out with very fine bindings and great liberties were taken with them in the process. As is well known, he trimmed the edges of the leaves of the Book of Kells so that he could gild them, but he also washed the margins of some of the leaves to their lasting detriment and painted over defective places in water-colour, besides filling up every hole with new vellum, regardless of whether it was structurally necessary, and tinting it to match. Such a wholly new approach to binding a fine manuscript may I think have been inaugurated with Kells itself. Because of a statement[26] by J.H. Todd, perhaps the greatest of the College Librarians but still only an undergraduate at this time, the work was thought to have been done in 1821. The accounts, however show Mullen receiving £22.15.0 'for repairing Columb Kills manuscript' in the March quarter of 1826.[27] This was the name by which the manuscript was still known and it appears on the extant spine of Mullen's binding as 'Liber S. Columbkille'. Kells was bound in diced russia, the fashionable leather of the time costing as much as the best morocco, its propensity to early decay still unrecognized. It was provided with clasps to keep the leaves under pressure. The tooling was, however, very simple and the binding[28] is undeniably dull, only the bold 'T' roll on the turn-in recalling some of his stronger designs. Later, a box was provided to keep it in, dated by its patent lock to Victoria's reign. His work on the Book of Durrow and the Garland of Howth, both in rich brown calf, is on a different plane, with vigorous all-over designs in blind. The most sumptuous of his works on the manuscripts was for the Fagel missal, a large and handsome fifteenth-century service book from a convent in Delft. Here he pulled out all the stops in a heavily tooled design in dark purple-crushed morocco, blind but just barely lightened with a very minimum of gilt lines. The doublure is almost more elaborate, in the same skin, with a very characteristic central panel of lines and small 'feathers' gilt, and a border enlivened with inlays of red sub-rectangles and citron discs, two of the latter on each cover carrying different flower arrangements in several colours on pointillé grounds, a feature that will find echoes in Sir Edward Sullivan's bindings. Mullen signs it *Compactus Georgio Mullen Dublinensi MDCC-CXXXI*. His leather-tooled ticket in the Garland of Howth is from the same year. In a border of interlaced shamrocks it announces boldly: 'Restored, cleaned, rebound by Geo. Mullen. William Street, Dublin. August, 1831'. His best work for the printed books like the specimen sent to the 1907 exhibition is in crushed dark-green morocco decorated in a panel of lines relieved with a few small 'feathers'. Very similar is the fine binding he made for the two volumes of Bodoni's *Manuale tipografico* (Parma 1818), but here small spirals instead of 'feathers' relieve the lines. In this case a pencil note inside the front cover shows that he charged six guineas for the binding.

My appointment to take charge of the manuscripts in 1953 coincided with another rebinding of the Book of Kells, this time by the leading English conservation binder of our day, Roger Powell. However, because I was almost immediately sent to the British Museum to learn my trade, I was to see little of the actual operation. Fortunately the still more difficult binding of the Book of Durrow took place in the Museum shortly after, while I was still there, and as a result I came to know Roger as a friend and to develop a deep appreciation of his work. Over the following years he was to bind a succession of the most important of the College manuscripts[29] and I came to rely on him for advice on conservation matters in which his importance as a pioneer was coming to be more widely recognized. As elsewhere, the craft of the Dublin binder declined steadily in the nineteenth and twentieth centuries and the very materials used became more and more suspect. In 1950, simply for the protection of the manuscripts, the Librarian ironically had to suspend all binding and repair. Meanwhile the need for restoration became ever greater as the use of the manuscripts increased. Roger advised that no commercial house could offer a standard that would be satisfactory and that we must establish a conservation bindery in the Library. Although older printed books continued to be sent out to commercial binders, they too, even if not as desperately as the manuscripts, needed expert care and the quantity involved was enormous. Gradually the College authority came to accept the Library bindery as inevitable.

Its feasibility, however, owed a lot to the interest of Rollin McCarthy, an American industrial engineer, at that time working in New York on the new headquarters building for the Ford Foundation, which had subscribed most generously towards the New Library then rising in the College Park. He had already provided the temporary Manuscripts Room housed in the Magnetic Observatory, a little temple in the Fellows' Garden, with an air-conditioning plant. In 1967, when the staff of the printed books department moved into the New Library, the project for reconstructing the West Pavilion of the Old Library for the use of the manuscripts was initiated and he threw himself into planning the still unauthorized bindery. He visited Roger and various libraries with pretensions to conservation binderies and they were few, because in most ways the Trinity Conservation Laboratory, as he wished it to be called rather than bindery, was to be a pioneering institution. He also tried to raise a fund to float the project, but in this he failed. However, his professional skill in drawing the plans and estimates was invaluable in giving the novel proposal an air of reality, not only for the College authorities but for the architects and engineers to whom they had to be submitted. Most fortunately, the planning for the West Pavilion coincided with Denis Roberts's short term as Trinity's Librarian. A manuscript librarian from the National Library of Scotland, whither he was to return as director in 1970, he was very much aware of the difficulties under which the manuscripts department laboured, and before his departure the major structural alterations to the third floor of the Old Library for the projected laboratory had been completed.

The furnishing and personnel still remained to be found. His plan to have a young art-school graduate trained at Roger's studio failed with the young man's resolution. Roger then proposed Anthony Cains, who in the event was to become the first director of the laboratory. At the time he was in charge of the international project to restore the books damaged in the National Library in Florence by the great floods on the Arno in 1966. I had visited him there in the following year to see his work, already with the possibility of the Trinity bindery in view. Roberts's successor as Librarian, Peter Brown, who had previously served in both the British Museum and the Bodleian Library, although neither yet boasted such a convenience, readily grasped the importance of the conservation bindery project in its pioneering aspect and knew that if well handled it must redound to the prestige of the College. To him then it fell to finalize the plan, to persuade Anthony Cains to undertake the directorship and encourage him to plan and equip the laboratory to his taste.

In all, perhaps, a somewhat surprising outcome of the spin Maurice gave to my professional career in 1950, from the decoration of book covers to the restoration of the very structure of the books. However, the programme of Cains and his team includes also the care of the fine bindings, and many of those we rescued together and that were then so desperately in need of attention have now had it, I am sure that it could not but gladden his heart to see those bindings, once so forlorn, now well groomed again, each in its own protective slipcase, with only such minimal repairs as were necessary most skilfully and tactfully performed.

NOTES

[1] *The Volunteer Earl* (London 1948).
[2] *Friends of the Library of Trinity College Dublin: Annual Bulletin 1950*, 6.
[3] *Irish Bookbindings, 1600-1800* (London 1954).
[4] *Friends of the Library of Trinity College Dublin: Annual Bulletin 1949*, 10.
[5] V. Morrow, 'Bibliotheca Quiniana' in *Treasures of the Library, Trinity College Dublin* (Dublin 1986), p.193; J. McDonnell and P. Healy, *Gold-tooled Bindings Commissioned by Trinity College Dublin in the Eighteenth Century* (Leixlip 1987), p.250.
[6] TCD Mun. Lib. 2/7, p.76.
[7] McDonnell and Healy as cited in note 5, p.xiv.
[8] See my introduction to M.L. Colker's forthcoming Catalogue of the medieval Latin manuscripts in TCD.
[9] *Original Letters of Eminent Literary Men*, (ed.) Sir Henry Ellis for the Camden Society, vol. xxiii (London 1843), p.298.
W.O. Sullivan, 'The eighteenth-century rebinding of the manuscripts' in *Long Room*, no. 10, Spring 1970, pp.19-28.
[10] TCD Mun. V. 57/11
[11] TCD Mun.V. 11/1.
[12] TCD Mun. Lib. 11/1.
[13] TCD Mun. V. 5/6.
[14] TCD Mun. V. 5 a/1.
[15] TCD Mun. Lib. 11/1/2.
[16] R.B. McDowell and D.A. Webb, *Trinity College: Dublin, 1592-1952, an academic history* (Cambridge 1982), pp.98, 177.

[17] B. Meehan, 'A note on the Dublin Apocalypse', *Scriptorium* 38 (1984), pp 82-3.

[18] TCD Mun.Lib. 11/1/2.

[19] TCD Mun. V. 5/6.

[20] See note 8.

[21] TCD Mun. Lib. 2/2.

[22] TCD MS F.6.33,f.48.

[23] *D.N.B.*; C. Ramsden, *Bookbinders of the United Kingdom (outside London), 1780-1840* (London 1954, repr. 1987), p.244.

[24] TCD Mun. V. 5/6.

[25] TCD Mun. 57/18.

[26] TCD MS 1826a, f.12. Todd was Assistant Librarian from 1835 and Librarian 1852-69.

[27] TCD Mun. 57/18.

[28] TCD MS 58*.

[29] For Roger's ninetieth birthday the accomplished scribe and my former colleague in Trinity Library, Miss Máire Kelly, inscribed a roll of his work, over the years 1953 to 1981, on Dublin manuscripts, including those of the Royal Irish Academy as well as those of Trinity. This was presented to him during a ceremony in the Victoria and Albert Museum on 17 May 1986. The year after this was written, Roger Powell died, 16 October 1990.

PLAIN CALF FOR PLAIN PEOPLE

DUBLIN BOOKBINDERS' PRICE LISTS OF
THE EIGHTEENTH CENTURY*

M. POLLARD

THROUGHOUT the eighteenth century the public were offered their new books in a number of binding styles, but books continued to be issued in sheets, especially in the earlier years, and sometimes the customer was given no choice in the matter. The price asked in proposals for publication by subscription was frequently for the book in sheets; occasionally an alternative price for binding in calf was offered. In 1725, for example, subscribers to 'All the Drapier's Letters, Poems, and Songs' paid '18*d.* per Book, stitch'd, or if bound 2*s.*'[1] Ten years later it was proposed to reprint Burnet's *Life of William Bedell* in twenty-six octavo sheets for the sum of 3*s.* 4*d.* in sheets; when published it was sold to non-subscribers at 4*s.* 6*d* bound.[2] In the 1740s subscribers could sometimes be offered their books stitched in blue paper or, less often, in marbled paper. The University Press's Hawkey classics, for instance, were to cost 2*s.* 6*d.* each in the common half-binding.[3] Plain calf, lettered on the spine, however, remained the standard covering until the end of the century, and was what the bookseller kept on his shelves as an alternative to the sheets stitched in wrappers, with sheepskin for the cheaper school and chap-books.

Binders were perhaps the most anonymous members of the Dublin book trade and it was a trade not as clearly segmented as in London; some booksellers were also printers, printing their own publications, while both booksellers and printers might run their own binding shops.[4] Others, however, did not, and by the 1740s the trade was sufficiently polarized for the master binders to have joined together to issue a printed list of terms for the booksellers: 'Whereas the Bookbinders of the City of Dublin at a meeting ... did unanimously agree, that from and after the 29th of [September] no books are to be bound ... for booksellers, under the following prices.'[5] That the prices are terms for the trade only is underlined by the statement: 'By unanimous Consent, it was the Day aforesaid further Resolved, That all Octavos shall be charg'd Ten Pence, Twelves Eight Pence (at least) and so in Proportion for Books of larger Size, as rated underneath, to all Gentlemen, Authors or others.' Calf is here understood.

No copy has yet been found of the second – or possibly third – scale of prices which was issued in 1766. Its existence is known through the row that developed in which the booksellers accused the master binders of raising their prices 'for a second Time within these few Years'.[6] The booksellers apparently successfully resisted the new prices for a time and in 1768 the master binders informed the public that because of the 'excessive Rise of Calf Leather (owing to the constant Export of raw Skins to Great Britain)', they could not 'bind any Duodecimo in Calf and lettered, under 10d. nor any Octavo under 1s. 1d. per Vol. and all other Sizes in proportion'.[7] The booksellers replied with an exhortation to gentlemen to 'have their Books done up in Boards, or sewed in blue Paper'.[8] This provoked an informative letter from an anonymous binder:

In the Year 1743, certain *Rates* were then agreed to by the MASTER-BINDERS, which have ever since been the Standard between them and the BOOK-SELLERS. At that Time, Calf leather could be purchased from Twelve to Eighteen Shillings per Dozen, seldom above Twenty Shillings; Journeymen's Wages [were] from Seven to Ten Shillings per Week. Within these Ten Years, the Leather has been extremely fluct[u]ating, and still on the Rise every Year, according as the demand was from Great Britain ... so that on the whole, Leather is now from Twenty-four to Thirty Shillings per Dozen, Journeymen from Ten to Fifteen Shillings per Week, together with a proportionable Advance on other necessary Articles used in that Branch of *Trade;* besides these, the great Advance on Provisions within these last Twenty Years, cannot escape the Notice of any Individual.[9]

The writer ends by advising gentlemen to take their books straight to the binder without 'applying to Booksellers'. This letter not only gives some idea of the cost of the binder's most expensive material, leather, but also shows that the journeyman's top wage had risen to 15s. a week from the 10s. paid when the 1743 price list was drawn up.

The contending parties must have reached agreement long before 1774 and in this year a short price list was included in the earliest co-operative Dublin bookseller's catalogue: 'A complete catalogue of modern books (printed in Ireland) ... Also, The prices of the different bindings of books.'[10]

Its lay-out differs radically from the 1743 list but is the same as that followed in the official scale of seventeen years later. It must therefore be a link between 1791 and some undiscovered list issued before 1774, but because it is part of a catalogue presumably intended for the use of the reading public the prices cannot be compared directly with the trade terms given in the official lists.

The second extant official list appeared nearly fifty years after the first: 'A regulation of prices agreed to by the Company of Bookbinders of the City of Dublin, for work done for booksellers only.'[11]

The new prices came into effect from 1 December 1791. This time dissensions had been ironed out in private and the list was 'revised and corrected by a Committee of the Company of Booksellers'.

In order to see these lists in action we need copies of the bills charged to both private customers and to booksellers. Unfortunately I have found no records of the prices paid by members of the book trade; however, it can be shown that the two institutions I have cited as examples of private customers were charged trade terms for binding in bulk. In shelving the book stock of Trinity College Library in Thomas Burgh's magnificent new building very considerable quantities of new and tidy bindings were required; the work went on through the 1730s and into the 1740s and many of the binders' bills survive. At the end of the century the work was naturally much less extensive; it chiefly entailed the binding of new acquisitions and the occasional repair or rebinding of older books. Marsh's Library accounts were less meticulously kept than Trinity's and much less binding was done; I quote from these only as a sort of extra footnote.

Extracts from the Dublin bookbinders' list of trade prices, 29 September 1743, and from customers' bills, 1732-45

Price list, 1743
'Books bound in Calve's Leather and Letter'd only'

	Folios	Quartos	Octavos	Duodecimos 'Without Distinction'
	s. d.	s. d.	s. d.	s. d.
Imperial	8-0	4-0		
Super-Royal	6-6	3-3		
Royal	5-0	2-6	1-2	0-7
Medium	3-6	1-9	0-9	
Demy	2-10	1-5		
Propatria	2-4	1-2		

Sept 1743	(a) TCD: J Leathley's bills before 29/28 Sept. 1743	after	(b) Marsh's Library before 29 Sept. 1743 (unspecified)	(c) TCD: J. Exshaw's bills before (sizes unspecified)	after 29 / 2 8
	s. d.	s. d.	s. d.	s. d	s. d.
Folio					
Imperial	5-6				
Super-Royal	4-6			4-6	4-6
Royal	3-6	5-0			
Medium	3-0	3-6		3-3	4-0 / 3-3
Demy	2-6	2-10	2-8½		2-10 / 2-8½
Propatria	2-0	2-4		2-4	2-6
Quarto	1-4	1-6	1-4	1-6	1-8 / 1-4 / 1-2
Octavo	0-9	0-9	0-7	0-7½ / 0-6	0-10 / 0-8
Duodecimo	0-7	0-7		0-5	0-6

(a) TCD, MS MUN/LIB/10/45, Joseph Leathley's bill for work done May – Nov. 1732, passed for payment 5 Dec.; and, MUN/LIB/10/169, for work done 1744-5, receipted 30 Dec. 1745.
(b) Marsh's Library, Account book 1731-1953, fol. 3, c. 1740.
(c) TCD, MS MUN/LIB/10/161, fols 20-28, John Exshaw's bill for work done April-July 1743 and Nov. 1743 – Jan. 1744; MUN/LIB/10/164, for work done Jan. – April 1744, both bills receipted 13 April 1744.

The theory that when a bookseller/binder undertook to bind large quantities for a private customer such as Trinity College he charged trade rates is confirmed by the binder Joseph Leathley's method of billing.[12] No individual titles are given; entry is simply by the number of volumes bound in each format and paper-size group, in the same designations as in the official scale. Leathley's prices can thus be compared directly with the scale and the 1744-5 bill shows agreement with it in all sizes, though quartos are lumped together, undivided by size, and charged for at a single rate. The price charged for duodecimos is another indication of trade terms for the College. The master-binders state categorically that private customers will be charged eight pence 'at least'; both Leathley's and Exshaw's prices were well under this sum.

In contrast to Leathley John Exshaw priced his bindings individually, listing each book by short title and very seldom giving format or size. Most of his work on printed books was done after the price list was issued but from 1741 to 1744 he did a major job on the Library's manuscripts and his bill for this includes a number of printed books bound before October 1743.[13] In view of his lucrative manuscript binding it seems likely that he allowed the College trade terms for printed books but his later prices rarely match the price list. Exshaw's short titles make it possible to find on the library shelves an example of a book bound at each of the various prices, but it is still difficult to identify the original paper group from the cut-down binding. There was no standard size of sheet; dimensions varied, not only from one end of the century to the other but also according to the country in which the paper was made. Even at the same time and place measurements could vary; for instance, demy sheets made at the same time in England could differ by several centimetres.[14] Nor are watermarks a reliable guide; the French grapes appear in royal, demy, crown, and propatria. As I have not been able firmly to assign the examples I examined to their particular groups within each format I have tried to arrange their binding costs to fall at or between the most likely group or groups.

Exshaw's first bill provides an indication of what a journeyman binder's wage was at about the time the master-binders issued their price list. He charged 2s. 6d. per day for work done in the Library in 'pasting cleaning & sewing the Manuscripts'.[15] Of the 15s. charged for a six-day week probably at least a third would be due to the master, leaving at the most 10s. for the man. If this represents the top of the wage scale it agrees with the scale of 7s. to 10s. referred to in 1768 as operating at this time.

Comparing the 1743 price list with Leathley's bill of ten years earlier, the steepest rise had taken place in the cost of folio bindings: the larger the book the greater the rise. For imperial folios there was a 45.5 per cent increase, for propatria 16.6 per cent. A rise in the cost of leather is presumably reflected here rather than in the cost of wages, the other heavy expense to the master. Quarto prices cannot be compared in detail but Leathley's single charge for all sizes had risen by 12.5 per cent in 1744. His smallest bindings, octavos and duodecimos, remained unchanged. Exshaw, on the other hand, whose smaller bindings were originally cheaper than Leathley's, had increased his charges for these by 1744, though duodecimos were still 1d. less than the 7d. laid down in the price list.

Unlike Trinity College Library, Marsh's Library was not committed to up-dating its book stock and indeed had no funds for large-scale purchasing, but some books were bought and more were given. The only bill for binding in even moderate quantities to appear in the Account Book can be dated as about 1740;[16] the binder is unnamed but may have been John Watson who in 1731 had bound three small folios for 2s. 8d. each.

	£-s-d
15 Books in Folio of Pamphlets & Mss bound at 2s-8½ p. Vol: in calf skin	2-1-3½
8 Do in sheep skin or half binding at 1s-8d p. Vol:	12-8
67 Books in 4to bound at 1s-4d p. Vol: in calf skin	4-9-4
39 Do bound at 10d p. Vol: in sheep skin	1-12-6
40 Do bound at 5d p. Vol: in half binding	16-8
5 Do bound at 7d p. Vol:	2-11
15 Books bound in 8° at 7d p. Vol: in calf skin	8-9
49 Do bound at 5d p. Vol: in sheep skin	1-0-5

In view of the quantities bound it seems likely that the Library was given trade discount; the charge for quartos in calf was the same as both Leathley's and Exshaw's, and for octavos cheaper than either. The particular interest of this bill lies in the plainer than plain bindings in sheepskin and in half-binding. In 1743 the price list gave the cost of a demy folio in sheep as 2s. while the smaller propatria cost 1s. 8d., a demy quarto in sheep cost 1s. and an octavo 7d. Half-binding was not listed as one of the options offered by the Dublin bookbinders in 1743, and quarter-binding was actually forbidden: 'no Quarter Book of any Sort whatsoever to be allowed'. Technically a half-binding was given a calf or sheepskin spine and corner pieces with paper-covered boards, and according to newspaper advertisements it was used quite frequently in the late 1730s and 1740s. Certainly some quartos with marbled paper boards exist in Marsh's Library that could have been bound at this time.

In the middle of the fifty-year period between the two known price lists evidence for the cost of binding is scanty and difficult to interpret. We lack not only a good supply of binders' bills but also the master-binders' official scale issued in about May 1766 and the probable later revisions. Instead of these we have prices that must be assumed to be for the private customer rather than the trade: the binders' statement of 1768 and the list in the booksellers' *Complete Catalogue* of 1774 already referred to.

Prices for the private customer of plain calf bindings

	Folio s. d.	Quarto s. d.	Octavo s. d.	Duodecimo s. d.
1768			1-1 (medium)	0-10
1774				
Imperial	10-6			
Super Royal	8-9			
Royal	7-0	3-0	1-5	
Medium	5-6	2-3	1-0	0-10
Demy	4-4	1-10	0-11	
Propatria	3-3	1-6		

I at first thought that the shortened scale of 1774 was intended for the trade because the cost of a medium octavo (1s.) was lower than the private customer's price (1s.1d.) in 1768. However, as it is impossible to know what effect the booksellers' resistance may have had on the earlier price it is safer to assume that the 1774 list was addressed to the book buyer. It, however, certainly reflects whatever trade list had already been issued. It is abbreviated, but its method of arrangement is the same as that used in the official scale of 1791, and is a complete departure from the pattern set in 1743. The various styles and changes are outlined below.

The only relevant surviving bill in Trinity College's muniments for this middle period is Anne Leathley's, Joseph's widow, and is dated 1766. It is chiefly for stationery, new books and periodicals but includes seven folio volumes bound at 4s. 6d. each, twenty-nine octavos at 1s. and 143 duodecimos at 9d.[17] Prices for the smaller books were lower than the binders' later charges to the public and, considering the quantities bound and the Leathleys' past relations with College, these were probably trade terms.

When Mr Byrne bound three books for Marsh's Library in 1783 and 1785 he is unlikely to have given trade discount. Two quartos cost respectively 3s. 9½d. and 2s. 8½d. and were expensive according to the 1774 price list, but the binding on volume two of Benjamin Kennicott's Hebrew Bible (Oxford 1780), a medium folio, was good value at 5s. 5d., in panelled calf to match the first volume, with covers rolled and tooled in blind and red and black labels rolled and tooled in gold.[18]

The second printed price list to survive, *A regulation of prices agreed to by the Company of Bookbinders,* took effect from 1 December 1791, and it again made clear that these prices were for work done for the book trade only. The various binding styles now on offer were the same for all formats from folio to duodecimo, with the addition of 'blue paper' for the smaller books. Duodecimos were considered in one size only as usual and the 'eighteens' and 'twenty-fours' were priced separately, as they were in 1774. A medium octavo, for example, could be bound in the following styles:

	s. d.
Medium, in Turkey, gilt over	15-00
Ditto, – gilt	10-10
Ditto, in Calf, gilt	3-09½
Ditto, – plain	1-01
Ditto, in sheep	0-10
Ditto, in half-binding cut and lettered	0-10
Ditto, – not cut or lettered	0-06½
Ditto, blue Boards	0-05
Ditto, blue Paper	0-03

Example of prices charged at this time are again taken from Trinity College muniments and Marsh's Library accounts. In contrast with the 1740s binding in bulk, these bills are for new and old books bound as they were bought or needed repair. Both McKenzie's and Mercier's for Trinity listed the books by author and short title and priced them individually; it cannot, therefore, be assumed that the trade terms applied, though both men were official booksellers to the College.[19]

Plain calf bindings extracted from the price list 1791, and from customers' bills, 1791-1802

Price list, 1791

	Folio	Quarto	Octavo	Duodecimo	Eighteens	Twenty-fours
	s. d.	*s. d.*	*s. d.*	*s. d.*	*s. d.*	*s. d.*
Imperial	11-4$\frac{1}{2}$	5-5	2-10			
Super-Royal	9-9	5-0	2-2			
Royal	8-8	4-4	1-9			
Medium	6-0	3-6	1-1	0-10	0-9	0-8
Demy	4-4	2-8$\frac{1}{2}$	1-0			
Propatria	3-6	2-2				

	(a) TCD: W. McKenzie's bills		R.E. Mercier's bills	
	before	after	(b) TCD, 1796	(c) Marsh's Library
	1 December 1971			1801-02
	s. d.	*s. d.*	*s. d.*	*s. d.*
Folio	11-4$\frac{1}{2}$ [Imperial?]		16-3 'Imperial'	
			8-8 [royal?]	8-1$\frac{1}{2}$
	7-7	7-7	7-7 [demy?]	
Quarto	4-4 [medium?]	4-4	6-6 [medium?]	
	3-3 [medium?]		5-11$\frac{1}{2}$ [medium?]	5-5
	3-9$\frac{1}{2}$ [demy?]	3-9$\frac{1}{2}$	4-10$\frac{1}{2}$ [medium?]	
Octavo		1-7$\frac{1}{2}$	2-0 [medium?]	
			1-10 [medium?]	
			1-6 [medium?]	
			1-1$\frac{1}{2}$ [demy?]	
Duodecimo		1-1		

(a) TCD, MS MUN/LIB/10/177, bill for work done Feb. 1791, receipted 3 May, and MUN/LIB/10/179, 7 July 1791, receipted 9 Aug. MUN/LIB/10/187, Jan.-June 1792, receipted 4 Aug., and MUN/LIB/10/195, 7 Feb. 1793, receipted 21 Nov.
(b) TCD, MS MUN/LIB/10/211, bill for work done Apr.-Oct 1796, passed for payment 20 Oct
(c) Marsh's Library, Account book 1731 – 1953, fol. 17.

It is difficult to make much sense of the prices in relation either to paper group or to materials and treatment. Both sprinkled calf and tree calf were used by McKenzie for quartos charged at 4*s. 4d.*, marbled and poor quality laid endpapers were used with tree calf, and the cheapest quarto was not the smallest and was bound in tree calf with marbled endpapers. The new price list appears to have made little difference in his charges.

By 1796 when Mercier was binding for the College the cost of living in general and of paper and other materials in particular had started to spiral upwards, largely due to war with France. It was unfortunate for the binders that their new scale was issued early in the decade, but it seems that Mercier for one paid it little attention. As with McKenzie's bills, it is difficult to reconcile size with price. For instance, we know from Philip Gaskell's bibliography that the Foulis Press *Aeschylus* of 1795 was printed on 'post' (crown) paper.[20] Crown in size fell between demy and propatria; it was unrecognized by the Dublin binders at this date and was probably counted as demy, the second smallest group. The book was plainly bound in sprinkled calf for which the 1791 price was 4*s. 4d.*; Mercier charged 7*s.7d.* By the end of the century when Mercier worked for Marsh's Library prices had risen further but the charge of 5*s.5d.* for the medium quarto *Transactions of* *the Royal Irish Academy* in calf seems not unreasonable. The increased costs of the 1790s are clearly demonstrated by William Sleater's charge for binding in boards the folio *Journals of the House of Lords of Ireland.* This rose from 2*s.*9*d.* in 1792 to 4*s.*4*d.* in 1799, an increase of 57.5 per cent in seven years.[21]

A comparison of what these price lists offered in the way of treatment, covering materials, and ornamentation illustrates the changes that took place in Dublin in the last half of the eighteenth century. Goatskin (although it was certainly used for bespoke bindings), half-binding, boards, and paper were not in such general use as to be listed in 1743. On the other hand, by 1774 vellum, used for all formats in 1743, had disappeared from the list for everything except pocket and account books. There was little change in the various grades of decoration offered. The 'Gilt Work', gilt back, filleting, rolling, tooling and lettering of 1743 all appear in 1791, with the addition of 'colouring edges and burnishing' and stamping the King's, College's, or other arms on the covers. By this time the binders could also supply 'wooden backs for deceptions'; books, and pretence books, had evidently become fashionable as a wall or door covering in the libraries of the gentry.

In 1802 James Draper's charges for two bindings for Marsh's Library appear excessive, but examination of the demy folio, Holinshed's *Chronicles,* and the propatria folio, Dugdale's *Monasticon Anglicanum,* volume two, shows that these calf bindings were not plain but ornamented. The style is similar with the same tool used on the spine panels. Both are in tree calf with spines tooled and boards and edges rolled in gold. Holinshed has suffered a nineteenth-century rebacking with remains of Draper's spine preserved, but Dugdale shows the 1802 marbled endpapers. According to the 1791 list 'calf, gilt', i.e. with the spines 'filletted only', cost 13*s.* for a demy folio and 10*s.* for propatria; extra decoration in these sizes included 'tooling and filletting' at 4*d.*, 'rolling the edges' at 10*d.* and 'rolling round the boards' at 1*s.* 8*d.* Draper charged 16*s.*3*d.* for the larger volume and 14*s.*1*d.* for the smaller.[22]

In half a century binding costs had changed more radically than styles. Broadly speaking, by 1791 for octavos and duodecimos there was an increase of between 40 and 50 per cent over 1743 prices, and a much greater increase, sometimes of over 100 per cent, for folios and quartos. The increase is as marked for sheepskin as for calf and was probably due as much to wages and higher cost of living as to expensive leather.

Price increases for the booksellers

	Bound in calf			Bound in sheep		
	1743	1791	% increase	1743	1791	% increase
	s. d.	*s. d.*		*s. d.*	*s. d.*	
Medium folio	3-06	6-00	71	2-06	4-04	73
Medium quarto	1-09	3-06	100	1-03	2-08$^{1}/_{2}$	116
Medium octavo	0-09	1-01	44	0-07	0-10	43
Duodecimo	0-07	0-10	43	0-04	0-08	100

For the plain book buyer there is less information, and prices for the smaller formats only can be quoted. Octavos and duodecimos represented by far the greater proportion of Dublin's own book production so, considering the relatively small increase in price – and in profits – shown below, it is understandable that the master-binders found them the least profitable part of their business.[23]

Price increases for the private customer 1743-74

	1743	1768	1774	% increase
	s. d.	*s. d.*	*s. d.*	
Octavo	0-10	1-01	1-00	20
Duodecimo	0-08	0-10	0-10	25

The book buyer who could not afford bespoke bindings was sometimes offered his new book in a variety of styles and prices, especially when the nature of the text made it a suitable present. George Faulkner, for example, advertised his *Memorandum book* for 1750 as available stitched for 6*d.*, bound in parchment at 13*d.* or in green vellum as 1*s.*4*d.*[24] By 1790 the choice of styles was wider; the buyer of *The young lady's library; or, Parental monitor* was faced with no less than six, all but one aiming to sweeten the pill of the contents for the recipient:[25]

	s. d.
Plain binding	3-3
Elegantly gilt [calf], silk strings, etc.	3-9
Green Turkey leather, "	3-9
The same, gilt over, "	4-4
Red Morocco leather, "	5-5
The same, gilt over, "	6-6

Where are all these grand bindings now?

NOTES

* I am grateful to Mirjam Foot of the British Library and to Anthony Hobson for some helpful comments and corrections.
[1] Faulkner's *Dublin Journal*, 1 May 1725.
[2] Pue's *Occurrences*, 12 June 1736; *Dublin Journal*, 24 December 1736.
[3] *Dublin Journal*, 14 July 1744.
[4] An advertisement for auction of the bookseller Luke Dillon's stock shows that besides his books and printing materials he owned 'Tools for Book-Binders': Reilly's *Dublin News-letter*, 19 July 1740.
[5] *Whereas the Bookbinders of the City of Dublin at a meeting the 15th day of September 1743, then held, did unanimously agree, that from and after the 29th of the said month no books are to be bound ... for Booksellers, under the following prices* ([Dublin]: printed by Edward Bate, [1743]) The only known copy of this broadsheet is pasted into the notebook of an Irish bookbinder who worked in London; see H.M. Nixon, 'The memorandum book of James Coghlan', *Journal of the Printing Historical Society* (1970), 39-41. The list is printed in Mirjam M. Foot's 'Some bookbinders' price lists of the seventeenth and eighteenth centuries', in *Economics of the British Booktrade 1605-1939*, edited by Robin Myers and

Michael Harris, 'Publishing History' occasional series, 1 (Cambridge 1985), pp.124-75 (162-5), where she explains some of the more uncommon terms used in the list.
[6] *Dublin Gazette*, 31 May 1766. See also James W. Phillips, 'The origin of the publisher's binding in Dublin', *Transactions of the Cambridge Bibliographical Society*, 2 (1954), 92-4.
[7] *Dublin Gazette*, 30 April 1768.
[8] Faulkner's *Dublin Journal*, 28 May 1768.
[9] *Freeman's Journal*, 7 June 1768.
[10] *A complete catalogue of modern books (printed in Ireland) ... With prices affixed, ... also, the prices of the different bindings of books* (Dublin, printed for the Booksellers, 1774), pp.38-41. Royal Irish Academy copy.
[11] *A regulation of prices agreed to by the Company of Bookbinders of the City of Dublin, for work done for booksellers only. Commencing the 1st day of December, 1791*. Revised and corrected by a committee of the Company of Booksellers ([Dublin 1791]). 8⁰. pp.12. The only copy known to me is in private hands.
[12] Joseph Leathley's work for Trinity College is discussed in Joseph McDonnell and Patrick Healy, *Gold-tooled Bookbindings Commissioned by Trinity College in the Eighteenth Century* (Leixlip, Irish Georgian Society, 1987), pp.41-55.
[13] Exshaw's manuscript work has been discussed and the bill transcribed by William O'Sullivan in 'The eighteenth century rebinding of the manuscripts', *Long Room*, no. 1 (1970), 19-28.
[14] Philip Gaskell, *A New Introduction to Bibliography* (Oxford 1974), pp.73-5.
[15] TCD, MS MUN/LIB/10/161, fols 1, 29, 1741, 1743.
[16] Marsh's Library, Account book, fol. 3.
[17] TCD, MS MUN/LIB/10/173, A. Leathley's bill, Aug.– Oct. 1766, receipted 2 May 1767.
[18] Marsh's Library, Account book, fol. 15, Dec. 1783 and Feb. 1785.
[19] For a general account of McKenzie's and Mercier's relations with the College see J. McDonnell and P. Healy, *Gold-tooled Bookbindings*, chapter V.
[20] P. Gaskell, *A Bibliography of the Foulis Press*, second edition (Winchester 1986), no. 699.
[21] *Journals of the House of Lords of Ireland*, VII (1799), 61; VIII (1800), 298.
[22] Marsh's Library, Account book, fol. 17, 11 May 1802. R. Holinshed, *The third volume of chronicles* (London 1587), STC 13569, shelf mark N2.1.21: Sir William Dugdale, *Monastici Anglicani volumen alterum* (London 1661), Wing D 2484, shelf mark D2.1.19.
[23] 'The second memorandum, 1787' of James Fraser, a London bookbinder, printed in Ellis Howe, *The London Bookbinders 1780 – 1806* (London 1950), p.161.
[24] *Dublin Journal*, 6 January 1750.
[25] Advertisement of John Archer, bookseller, in the *Dublin Chronicle*, 27 November 1790.

GLIMPSES AND LONGER VIEWS

FROM *LA COLLOZIONE GUGGENHEIM*

DACHINE RAINER

'Cézanne would have regarded Picasso as an obnoxious pseudo-Hottentot crossed with a crooked necromancer.'

— Wyndham Lewis, Tarr (1918)

I
Sortoportega Corte Venier dei Leoni

From an Eleventh-Century stable at *S. Vio* (my house) on the *Sortoportega Corte Venier dei Leoni,* next door to where Henry James, untroubled by Guggenheim, composed
the Aspern Papers, I stare out upon this dispensary — contents, staff
and patrons — in a fortunate position to give it all my particular attention:
from each southern window across a low wall into the Guggenheim garden.
At the rear of a loft where once sweet hay was stored, I lie in bed wakened not long
after false dawn to birdsong warm from Africa, by way of the Adriatic.

Rose-coloured winds pass through my window. Breathing becomes a conscious pleasure.
I regain the use of eyes and ears, reminded that to the flavour of spring water
as to the scent of air, we are undeserving heirs. From my bed, the wall, draped with sedate braids of small, green black ivy. The old sycamore, bare branched still, where few burrs cling; the peeling bark of its trunk patched in muted tones of sophistication, leans upon my vision. The background beyond and above it, a cubist pastiche of roof tops is as Cézanne might have struggled

to arrange! One cannot ask for more masterpiece to wake to! I have no companionship other than these merry small birds whose songs denote feathery pleasure in air, trees, light and silence. They and I share *Venezia.* Sometimes a branch or two will stir to reveal the particular blue of an old Italian sky. Swift, bright birds and I, scrutinizing wisely, see it is the sky Giotto knew.
Sometimes, mists blow in from the sea to hide my sycamore or sail closer into the room with a scented cargo of fog.

II
At Rear Window Overlooking Guggenheim's Museum and Peggy's Garden Grave

The most admirable mobile in the Guggenheim Collection is in the garden.
Few bother to look, although the sycamore knows beyond talent of men
how to prepare itself for admiration. Large masterpiece of trunk,
stylishly patched with such tans and greys as Braque worked not so well.
Forms differ each from each, regard! like designs of the zebra, no two alike,
never repeated: repetition is abhorrent to nature, anathema to men
avoiding boredom, the same path, task, lover. Branches ornamented

with prickly burrs, merrily sway in perfect design, joyous like a Calder
mobile, like Miro. Upon gravelled paths this sad stomping ground
for rabblers. To its right, a sister tree, less brave, roots restricted
to contain the bulging. Root and stone rise mysteriously, like Lazarus,
from the grave. In the foreground laburnum and beyond, a beech,
straightest of tall trees (lopped beneath a silver birch) so straitened!
huddled in its jacket of air. A fierce cypress looms, black green

backdrop: tinned music pounds imprecisely against the tourist uproar.
They are engaged in what they presume to be Kultur.

One dares hope, late in winter's transition to an early spring, to enjoy
the quiet of these trees, listen to birds singing themselves to sleep.
Twilight softens the Guggenheim terrain, air is astir still but tramping
has receded from *fortissimo* to *diminuendo*. I hold my breath, sigh
tentatively. From dusk's gentle imprecisions high voltage discs,
unnoticed in daylight, scream an abomination of florescence, glare
in all directions. Draped with black rubberized lengths of thick wire

dangling like obscene tubes, the sycamore hangs from the bloodstreams
of life. Nature drugged, high, and modernized, gardens hooked
on electric lights loud as noise. The sycamore whose burrs remind
me, all winter, of spring, beckons until I stray from work. What can I *do?*
These lights are heavy as noise. They pound the night like an artillery
attack. They drum through the garden with insulting accusation of theft!
Is a Guggenheim worth stealing? — or this, paranoia of chronic mistrust?

Light sinister through these Eastern skies stray upon neighbour's roof
tiles and panes, arrogantly, creating an airport, or an institution
for the deaf and mad, overseeing no man's land. Although
I am not persuaded to run across, will be machine-gunned if I do?

III
Architectural Origins

Even the building is wrong, squat and institutional, suburban ogre,
a veritable bungalow of a *palazzo* in a city of grandeur.
History of its single storey is narrated in various hues of malice:
First, that its growth was arrested four centuries ago by the *palazzo*
across the *Canale Grande* opposite, whose nobles bribed masons
to stop before second and third storeys would interrupt their view!
Second, that the city issued an edict to prohibit its rise

for motives of envy. It is also rumoured this noble family
became decadent, or succumbed to misfortunes of war, or both;
losing its money, making do with a half house. No one has added
the second storey in four hundred years. (Think of *Palazzo* nobles
as poor! Yet, I never know where money starts from; that is, where
it admits an origin. Whatever the official line, it erupts, flows
like volcanic lava, but not over the poor. I know it accrues —

usuria — and adheres to the wrong 'uns.) The museum pays no tribute
to its location in this centre of Western civilization: that
would be humility, require a sense of gratitude and an awareness
of European history. *Guggenheim* is *echt* Twentieth-Century arrogant,
and conforms. Inside and out, edifice and surround suit a twice-swept
collection. What has hygiene to do with art? Would old Solomon G.
have complained? One enters the clinical courtyard, mockery of a garden.

In all *Venezia*, it is said, *Guggenheim* is the largest tourist attraction.
A circus could not call forth larger crowds or a football match
vastly dissimilar ones. One season's entrance fees and picture-postcard
sales surpass the billion lira mark. Even as tourism goes
in *Venezia, Guggenheim* is Big Business, a multi-national.
It is intended we receive from this institution
an unhappy conviction that all *Venezia* could do with modernization.

ON THE CULTIVATION OF
THE COMPASS ROSE

TIM ROBINSON

PROUSTIAN TRIANGULATION

Is IT by chance that Proust twice uses a trio of uprights and their apparent motions as examples of the type of impression that seems to him the most significant? Let me briefly summon up remembrance of the two passages:

Certain sensations seem to the narrator to impose an obligation on him to discover the reason for the intense but obscure pleasure they give him, but usually the distractions of the succeeding moments provide him with an excuse for evading this duty of consciousness. However, on the drive back from Martinville circumstances leave him facing the memory of such an experience and he begins to consider it deeply. Phrases form in his mind which wonderfully augment the initial pleasure, and he writes a description of the changing appearances of three belltowers he had observed from various distances and angles during the drive. On finishing this, his inaugural work of literature, he is filled with happiness in having acquitted himself of his obligations to the impressions and what they hid.

But we do not learn what they hid. Instead we have two descriptions, one almost objectively topographical and the other full of metaphors and similes in which the towers are shamelessly anthropomorphized.

Later, near Balbec, the narrator recognizes this unique pleasure again in the sight of three trees near the road he is being driven along. But this time he lets the moment slip away without the necessary effort of analysed consciousness and as the trees fall into the distance he feels as sad as if he had lost a friend, died to himself, denied a ghost, or failed to recognize a god.

The back-reference from the pattern of three trees to the pattern of three towers, the possibility that it is a submerged memory of the latter that is stirred by the former, is latent in the passage; indeed the narrator wonders if it is because they remind him of something that the trees are so potent, but he soon drops this line of enquiry. And it would merely bring one back to the question of what was so significant in the earlier experience itself. I suggest that since the narrator himself never knew what it was that the trees wanted to bring him, we are at liberty here to look around from this space in the great work, and turn away from the infinite regression of Time Past, to a rarer realization, that of Space Present. The towers are described as close neighbours, three birds alighted in the plain, arms waving farewell, three golden pivots, three maidens in a legend: the trees become a round-dance of sorcerers, lost friends waving their arms in despair. But if all these charming clusters of images are blown off them, what terrain may be triangulated, starting from three bare poles?

Sometimes, changes in the relative position or apparent size of objects, caused by our own motion, reveal that motion to us at an unaccustomed level of consciousness, and bring the bare fact of motion, of position itself, into the light of attention. We rush to humanize the perception: the trees are watching us go; the towers are withdrawing resignedly into the night. But we are left with an uneasy notion that something else is hidden in the experience, and hidden the more deeply by our added layer of interpretation. It may be forced upon us that such kinetic geometries are not merely an endlessly reinterpretable stuff for the expression of the cloudwork of the soul, that the world is not just a Rorschach blotter to soak up the projections of our hopes and fears, not just a bottomless well of metaphor; that behind whatever social or personal significances we read into them such impressions carry a reminder of something so obvious that to state it seems absurd, so basic that it rarely intrudes into consciousness, so overwhelming that its realization might be profoundly therapeutic or psychically crushing. We are spatial entities – which is even more basic than being material entities, subject to the laws of gravity. The barest of bones of the relationship between an individual and the world are geometrical: on the landscape scale, topographical. Our physical existence is at all times wrapped in the web of directions and distances that constitutes our space. Space, inescapable and all-sustaining Space, is our unrecognized god.

I once wrote about a man who consciously obeyed the laws of perspective, an absurdity that points to its opposite banality; like Carroll's sundial we stand in the middle of a 'wabe'. The totality of geometric relations between the individual and the world is more than infinitely dense, and even the mere set of directions from me to other things or places forms an uncountable continuum. Consciousness at its richest can only hold an infinitesimal proportion of them, and so the image of a web is acceptable not as referring to the totality but to the miserable selection from it that our minds can handle. The relationships are always there, constituting our geometrical existence, which is a component of our physical existence and hence of every other level of individual and social existence. The most rudimentary element of geometry, the relationship of topographical inclusion, is the kernel of all the complexities of social and ecological belonging. At such higher levels the geometrical is usually generalized out of mind, though there is always the possibility of unusual circumstances imposing primacy, as in the ballistic space of the battlefield. Perhaps the duty of consciousness in this regard is to be open to a maximal realization, a delicate and precise awareness of one's spatial relationships to the world. (Try it when watching branches swaying in the breeze, one behind another.) But this awareness if it becomes strained and muddled soon subsides into the indiscriminate welter of 'being at one with Nature'. Like love, it flourishes best on the very edge of loss of identity, of merging with the object; it is a dangerous leaning over the brink of the blissfully all-dissolving Oceanic, or of the seasick existential shudders. A cliff-edge experience.

FIGURE IN A MAP

The topographical sensations (arising, for instance, from crossing a pass, completing the circuit of an island, or walking out to an island accessible at low water) are privileged moments of spatial awareness, able to bear the heavy vestments of symbolism. The exhilaration of crossing from one valley to another through a pass comes partly from such a journey's being a metaphor for threshold moments in which successive life-stages are simultaneously graspable, and past and present support the moment like two giant stilts. But the ground of this feeling is the geometrical configuration of the saddle-point, combining the highest and the lowest into a highly defined point of unstable equilibrium, so that you, here, are highly defined as a figure in a landscape. The landscape itself focuses on you, pinpointing a precise 'sense of place'. Such eruptions of the meaningful into the plains of geometrical existence are themselves distractions from the quotidian inevitability of emplacement, the humble submission to the laws of perspective. It is fitting that, on a map, such singularities and discontinuities of topography as mountain summits, coastlines and passes occupy an area tending to zero with increasing fineness of drawing.

The general utility of a map resides in its being a conceptual model of the terrain projected onto paper, a representation of spatial relationships in a symbolism that facilitates calculations; i.e. the map is a visual calculus for topography. In my own maps this aspect only arises incidentally and inescapably, the web of self-centred spatial relationships, which one might symbolize by the compass rose, being inextricable from the totality of directions from point to point. We could not use or even bear to look at a map that was not mostly blank. This emptiness is to be filled in with our own imagined presence, for a map is the representation, simultaneously, of a range of possible spatial relations between the map-user and a part of the world. The compass rose represents the self in these potential relationships; it is usually discreetly located in some unoccupied corner, but is conceptually transplantable to any point of the map sheet. Its meagre petals are a conventional selection of the transfinity of directions radiating from the self to the terrain. It is a skeletal flower, befitting our starved spatial consciousness.

This irreducible nub of topographicity is my emblem as map-maker. I present the exiguous mystic bloom of the compass rose to the one who unfolds my map and finds herself a point upon it. It comes from a god unrecognized, a ghost denied, a lost friend, a self to whom you had died. Alternatively it comes from something as crashingly obvious as an Ox, and I, imitating the Rosenkavalier, have cheekily appropriated it for my own wooing of the world's wide spaces.

For I do not know that I understand what I have written. No; I am writing blind, as a pilot has to fly blind in fog or cloud, sustained by faith in a compass course rather than by vision of a destination. But this much is clear: the recommended site j3for cultivation of the compass rose is on the very edge of the cliff.

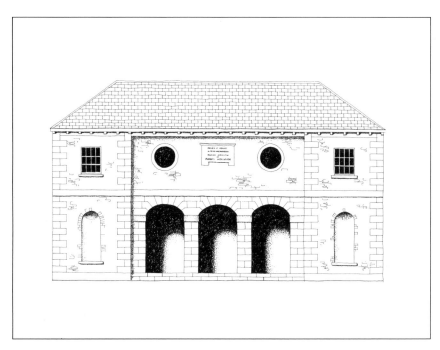

1. Ballyjamesduff Market House, Co. Cavan, 1813 (drawing by S. Rothery)

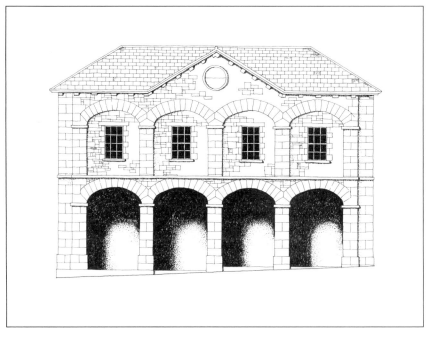

2. Newtownbutler Market House, Co. Fermanagh, *c*. 1830 (drawing by S. Rothery)

COURT HOUSES AND MARKET HOUSES

SEAN ROTHERY

'IRISH provincial towns are not just relatively but also absolutely rich in public buildings, and particularly in court houses, which are amongst the best productions of the period.'

These were the words of Maurice Craig and the Knight of Glin in their introduction to the catalogue for the Irish Architectural Drawings Exhibition of 1953. Twenty years later, in his monograph, *Court Houses and Market Houses of the Province of Ulster,* C.E.B. Brett said:

Today only about a third of the court houses, and hardly any of the market houses, are used for their original purposes. Many have been demolished; some have been turned into shops; some into masonic halls, or orange halls, or parish halls, or bingo halls, or cinemas; one houses the village hearse, another the school bus; too many have simply been allowed to moulder into dereliction.

Thirty-nine years on, while undoubtedly more losses have occured of this almost unique Irish traditional building type, there is a new awareness of the value of preserving the buildings of the past. This awareness has been largely achieved by the work of these writers. Appropriate new uses, such as the conversion of the court house and market house in Dunlavin, Co. Wicklow, for community needs, can rescue these lovely little buildings and demonstrate their strong architectural character.

The drawings are of two market houses, described in C.E.B. Brett's book, and are conjectural reconstructions of particularly beautiful buildings. Each has had its arcade built up, and in the process the most splendid architectural feature has been spoiled.

The closed form over an open arcade has always been seductive to architects; from the Doge's Palace in Venice to Le Corbusier's Villa Savoye. Revived historicism today ensures the continuation of the tradition which can be seen in Philip Johnson's post-modern A.T.&T. building with its great Roman arcade on Madison Avenue, New York.

DÚN AENGUS

AND SOME SIMILAR CELTIC CEREMONIAL CENTRES

ETIENNE RYNNE

'The great fort of "Dún Aenghus" on Inis Mór, on the edge of its cliff, with the Atlantic boiling and snarling 300 feet below, as though seeking to devour what remains of the fort, is a scene of Miltonic grandeur, deservedly famous.'
– Maurice Craig, *The Architecture of Ireland from the earliest times to 1880*
(London & Dublin 1982), p.20.

MAURICE CRAIG, now there's a name which conjures up a multitude of images: of stone upon stone, building up forts, castles, towers, churches, cathedrals, houses, towns and other Irish monuments from the distant past to recent times; of a man pushing off home-made steamships as he paddles in the sea near his home; of a to-all-appearances benign, amiable young/old gentleman endowed with a sharp wit; of an irresistibly eccentric but brilliant scholar.

To illustrate the point. As my term of office as President of the Royal Society of Antiquaries of Ireland (1985-8) was drawing to its close, I approached him with the suggestion that he might allow his name go forward for the following term, wondering all the while why he had not long previously become the Society's President. With a cheerful, rather proud laugh he gave me my answer: as he had enjoyed informing all the others who had approached him with a similar suggestion, he clearly enjoyed telling me that he was not, nor had ever been, a member of the said Society! He obviously thrived on catching out all of us who dared to presume that membership/fellowship of such an august Society was a *sine qua non* for *gelehrter* such as himself! Regrettable, nonetheless, as he would undoubtedly have made a good President, one who would have stood for no nonsense or lowering of standards and who would have brought honour to the Society by being in its presidential chair.

With this non-event in mind, therefore, I wish to pay my respects to my friend, Dr Maurice Craig, by offering in his honour the following slightly revised version of my 'Presidential Address' to the Society in question, an address which he missed due to his non-membership but which I dare to think he, as a possessor of such wide-ranging interests, would have found interesting – if only for the odd bit of kite-flying involved!

I know nothing in any county more stimulating to the imagination than the problem which these extraordinary fortresses present to the archaeologist. Huge structures stand on those barren islands, and we ransack tradition and history in vain for the smallest ray of light as to their origin. We find nothing but vague tales of Fir Bolg refugees – tales highly improbable,

196

for the forts do not look like the sort of buildings that refugees would be able to construct.
  – R.A.S. Macalister, *Ireland in Pre-Celtic Times*, (Dublin & Cork 1921), p.268.

The Partholon-Nemed-FirBolg legend meets us next ... The last of these three names must not be translated 'Belgae', as has sometimes been done. It means 'Men of Bags', and its most reasonable explanation reveals the people so designated as wearers of breaches.
  One tale ... makes the Fir Bolg avoid oppression by a flight to Aran, to Islay, and to other islands on the outskirts of the British Archipelago. Here at once we see an explanation, which is actually given us in this story – and the only reasonable explanation available – of the most perplexing buildings in Ireland: namely, the colossal stone fortifications in the West, which are especially conspicuous upon those very Aran Islands ... Protected behind the great walls which they built for themselves, they managed at least to keep body and soul together, on the bleak and economically unattractive islands which afforded them an asylum.
  ... Who could have thought it worth while thus to fortify a group of barren rocks, miles out to sea? No one: except people who feared that, even there, ruthless, gold-greedy plunderers might find them out ... If those mighty walls had proved unavailing to keep out the invaders, armed with their irresistible glaives, the refugees would have had no prospect other than to be hurled, over the towering cliffs of their island sanctuary at the end of the world, into the boundless, fathomless ocean.
  – R.A.S. Macalister, *Ancient Ireland* (London 1935), pp.57-8.

The above opinions strongly contradict one another, albeit both by the same noted authority. From the quotations we can appreciate two things: (1) the courage of good academics to change their minds, and (2) the mystery of the Aran forts. But is there really need for such mystery? Are they really inexplicable monuments rising out of the mists of a Celtic Twilight? A new, more analytical approach seems justified, one which suggests an altogether more tenable and commonsense solution to the problem.

For generations countless people from all parts of the globe have been visiting the Aran Islands, those three rocky outcrops rising out of the Atlantic Ocean and strung diagonally across the entrance to far-famed Galway Bay in the west of Ireland. And still they go there, now more than ever before, thanks not only to new, easier and more readily available methods of transport such as luxury motor vessels and small passenger aircraft, but also because of improved, more efficient, more extensive, attractive and appealing tourist propaganda advertising those romantic islands. Where a thousand tourists might have visited the islands in a whole season a hundred years ago, or in a summer month of the inter-war years, or in a week of July or August during the last few decades, that many probably arrived almost daily last summer.

The appeal of the Aran Islands is strong and multi-facetted. It extends to romantics be they poets, painters, photographers or just dreamers, to lovers of nature be they geologists, botanists, ornithologists, or even lepidopterists, to linguists be they Gaeilgeóirí (speakers/learners of Irish) or searchers after quaint turns of phrase in English such as those heard by John Millington Synge and used by him in his plays, and of course their appeal extends to anthropologists, antiquarians and archaeologists, not to mention the merely curious tourist looking for something strange, different and wonderful. And no matter for what purpose he or she goes to Aran, no visitor can fail to see, and few fail to visit, at least a handful of the many fine ancient ruins strewn generously over all the three islands. Though the

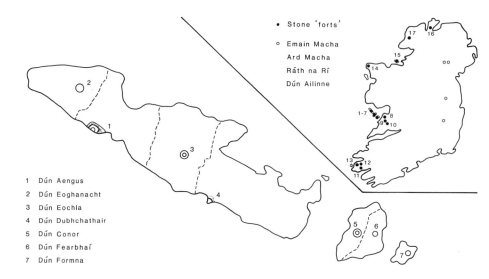

1. Distribution map of the 'forts' on the Aran Islands – the broken lines indicate the town-land boundaries; *inset:* map of Ireland showing the stone 'forts' discussed in this essay and the four major earthen-enclosed royal residences.

ancient, prehistoric, Early Christian and medieval monuments on the Aran Islands are many and important, none are more noteworthy than the massive stone forts, of which none is more famous, better known and more visited than Dún Aengus.

Seven massive stone-built forts are on the Aran Islands (four on Inishmore, two on Inishmaan, and one on Inisheer), ten or more similar well-known monuments are in counties Donegal, Sligo, Mayo, Clare and Kerry, and also others less obvious and well-known elsewhere (Illus. 1). All are invariably described and thought of as fortresses, an interpretation which has seldom been queried and which *seems* acceptable enough. But is it? Another interpretation seems more reasonable when the various sites are examined individually and collectively. All these ancient monuments are clearly related to one another and therefore it can be argued that they were most probably all built for much the same purpose. It would seem justifiable, therefore, to select the finest, most military-looking and best known of them all, Dún Aengus, for detailed examination with a view to interpreting them, always accepting that whatever was the reason for Dún Aengus probably was the reason for the other related monuments also.

Sited on the top of a cliff almost three hundred feet above sea-level on the south-western edge of Inishmore, the largest of the three Aran Islands, Dún Aengus is undoubtedly one of the most impressive and best-known ancient monuments in Ireland, perhaps even in Europe (Illus. 2). Everyone recognizes the site even if they have never been there, as so many photographs and accounts of it have been published and, furthermore, because of its very distinctive appearance. First of all, it has a huge, strong, semi-circular stone rampart built on the very edge of the near-vertical cliff rising high above the roaring Atlantic; secondly, there are two other fine stone ramparts, lower and weaker perhaps but neither insignificant, around the main inner citadel, and thirdly there is a fine *chevaux-de-frise,* a wide band of sharp-edged slabs stuck into the ground like spikes, between those two outer ramparts. All three ramparts have terraces, giving them a stepped appearance from within. Generally forgotten in most plans and descriptions, however, is a naturally formed rectangular rock platform sited on the very edge of the cliff, roughly in the centre of the whole monument. It averages about 75cm. in height, and about 11.50m. in length by 9.50m. in width, forming a perfect stage should one require a stage at that place – and when one thinks about it maybe a stage would be required exactly there.

There are four main reasons why monuments are built, namely, for living purposes, for burial purposes, for military purposes, or for ceremonial purposes. The first two alternatives can be eliminated without much trouble insofar as Dún Aengus is concerned. The place is in no way suitable for either living in or for burial: there is not enough earth there for even a shallow burial and, furthermore, it fits into no known funerary monument-type, while anyone who has ever been there in wet and windy weather conditions, which are by no means infrequent on the Atlantic coast of Ireland, knows that living there would be out of the question – one does not try to

2. Aerial view of Dún Aengus (photo: D. Pochin Mould)

3. Dún Aengus, showing entrance into central area and late nineteenth- century buttresses
(photo: Commissioners of Public Works in Ireland)

rear a family on the edge of a high cliff, a permanent danger to children
and even to adults, and where there are no adequate facilities for normal
living, there being not enough soil to grow food for humans or pasture for
cattle (though O'Donovan in 1839 argued that the 'fort' would hold 1050
cows!), not to mention the lack of a source of fresh water on the site.
Despite these drawbacks, the late Professor M.J. O'Kelly gave it as his opin-
ion that 'Even the very impressive sites are not military structures – they are
merely 'big houses' of the time, their snobbish owners manifesting their
wealth by building great stone walls late in the Early Christian Period'
('Problems of Irish Ring-Forts' in *The Irish Sea Province in Archaeology
and History*, D. Moore [ed.], Cardiff 1970, p.53); however, he puts forward
no reasons to support either the *raison d'être* or late date he suggests for
these monuments.

The third alternative, the military one, is less easy to dismiss. Should it
have been built and used for military purposes then it could only have
served as a place of refuge which, *ipso facto,* implies siege warfare. Quite
apart from the fact that the ancient Irish did not normally engage in siege
warfare, the site is unsuitable for such on many points. There is, for
instance, no fresh water, no escape route, and the terraces of the inner
citadel are not suitable for looking over the ramparts for defensive or other
such purposes (the top rampart is mainly a reconstruction carried out in the
1880s by the Board of Works and originally was at least 1m. higher). The
missing stones are probably those now in the large buttresses (which give
the monument a decidedly medieval and military appearance) added to the
wall by the Board of Works at that time (Illus. 3).

By a process of elimination, therefore, one is left with the fourth and last alternative, that Dún Aengus was conceived, built and used for ceremonial purposes. Already just over a hundred years ago there were some who realized that there was an alternative solution to the question as to the purpose of these huge fort-like monuments other than the apparently obvious military one. Margaret Stokes gives' in one short, almost throw-away but inspired comment, a solution which has for the most part been ignored to the point of rejection by most subsequent scholars:

These forts are amphitheatres, encircled by outer walls, rather than towers.
    – M. Stokes, *Early Christian Art in Ireland* (1887, reprinted 1928), part II, p.27.

But does Dún Aengus really fit the bill? It surely does, but to show why, we should perhaps not examine it in total isolation but alongside the many other related sites. On the Aran Islands these include Dún Eoghanacht, Dún Eochla and Dún Dubhchathair on Inishmore, Dún Conor and Dún Fearbhaí on neighbouring Inishmaan, and Dún Formna on the third of the islands, Inisheer, while elsewhere in western Ireland to be included with them are such well-known monuments as the Grianán of Aileach and O'Boyle's Fort (on Lough Doon, near Portnoo), both in Co. Donegal; Ballykinvarga, Caherdooneerish and Cahercommaun (see Appendix I), all in the Burren, Co. Clare; Staigue Fort, Cahergal, Leacanabuaile and others in Co. Kerry; Doonamo, on the Mullet Peninsula, Co. Mayo; and even the stone 'fort' enclosing the Early Christian monastery on Inishmurray, off the coast of Co. Sligo; there are several other less well-known stone-built 'forts' which might be included too, but it is not necessary to list them all here. All are similar though not identical, are clearly related and can be reasonably confidently dated to the pagan Celtic Early Iron Age, that is to within a couple of centuries on either side of the birth of Christ. By the same process of elimination as used regarding Dún Aengus, all these related monuments can be interpreted as having been built for ceremonial purposes, purposes such as inauguration ceremonies, or for the annual or seasonal *aonach* (assembly/celebrations*) of the *tuath* (tribe), where and when payment of tribute, making of treaties, arranging important marriage contracts, holding ritual games, promulgating laws, receiving honoured guests, etc., would have taken place.

One might be forgiven for imagining that ceremonies associated with sun-worship may have taken place within these structures, though any possible connection with significant positions of the sun may be either fortuitous or, if not, then with calendrical feasts rather than with sun-worship. Such exotic ideas are·perhaps excusable when one remembers that already in 1821 F.C. Bland pointed out that the entrance to Staigue Fort faces exactly towards the midday sun and 'Whether ... it goes to show, that

---

* Of course the usual translation 'fair' is quite inadequate for 'Oenach', as in Greece 'Agora' was a place of assembly and also a market. It is not only a 'fair', but an assembly for legislation, musical contests, races, and games, and it is probable, even in later times, that chariot races, as well as horse races, prevailed ... Tirechan uses the Greek *agón* for the 'Oenach of Tailltiu' – T.J. Westropp, *Proc. Roy. Irish Acad.*, 25, c (1920), 371, fn. 2.

the people who erected the building were fire-worshippers ... It certainly affords a strong presumption, that they were not entirely ignorant of Astronomy' [*Trans. Roy. Irish Acad.,* 14 (1825), Antiquities p.25], while in 1909 Captain H. Boyle Somerville, who rather specialized in mooting the deliberate astronomical orientation of ancient Irish monuments, suggested that the Grianán of Aileach served as a focal point for the November (Samhain) sunrise as seen from what he considered to be a 'prehistoric circle' at Ray Point [*J. Roy. Soc. Antiqs. Ireland,* 39 (1909), 224-5]; more recently still, a snippet in *The Irish Times* of 21 June 1989 stated that '... there are theories that some Irish stone monuments, notably Dun Aengus on Aranmore, may be aligned to the summer solstice and discreet celebrations may take place there today'.

When all of these sites are viewed as possible ceremonial centres, one readily appreciates their suitability. They are all most impressive, one might even say majestic, structures, just as are all ancient temples and contemporary cathedrals, ranging from Stonehenge in England, to the Parthenon in Athens, to St Peter's in Rome. These ancient 'forts' are not only impressive in themselves but are sited in positions which immediately command attention and respect, generally in prominent places overlooking vast areas and thus eminently suitable as meeting-places for the people of the surrounding regions. Furthermore, their stepped and terraced walls are much more suitable for looking *inwards* than for looking *outwards,* indicating that these monuments should more fittingly be regarded as amphitheatres rather than as forts – nobody ever thinks of Rome's Colosseum as a fortress of the terraced sports stadia from Olympia in ancient Greece to Croke Park in Dublin to the Polo Grounds in New York as places built for defensive purposes!

Another thing, there are no annalistic or other records of any of these sites ever having featured in war or battle. Indeed, the only historical associations any of them have are with ritual or ceremonial functions. The very fact that the massive stone enclosure of this type on Inishmurray was used secondarily as a *vallum monasticum,* the enclosure of an Early Christian monastery, surely supports a belief that it was originally a place of ritual – after all, Christian monasteries are more likely to succeed and replace pagan sanctuaries than former military forts, *cf.* Armagh Cathedral built on Ard Macha, a proven pagan ritually enclosed hilltop. The Grianán of Aileach, furthermore, still served until at least the twelfth century as the royal seat and assembly place of the Cinél Chonaill, rulers of the O'Neill kingdom of Aileach.

But Dún Aengus of itself provides several good reasons to be regarded as a monument specifically built for ceremonial purposes. The natural platform centrally placed on the cliff's edge would serve as a perfect focal point for ceremonies, surrounded as it is on three sides by the terraced rampart. The *chevaux-de-frise* is normally a military feature used as an obstruction against charging chariots, cavalry or even foot-soldiers, but is so totally unnecessary on Aran (at Dún Aengus and Dún Dubhchathair, and indeed also at Ballykinvarga in the Burren and Doonamo in Co. Mayo) for such purposes due to the natural irregularities of the virtually earthless limestone terrain, that it can best be considered as a prestige or status feature, erected to give the monument a sense of awe and importance, just as are the turrets, battlements, crenellations and machicolations on numerous nineteenth-century 'castles' such as those at Ashford, near Cong, and Dromoland, near Shannon – or even on the early twentieth-century bath-house at Enniscrone, Co. Sligo, and the strange, relatively recent town house in Balla, Co. Mayo, or the brash White Castle Hotel built within the present decade near Lisdoonvarna, Co. Clare. Indeed, the *chevaux-de-frise* could well have served some useful practical purpose too: it would have effectively prevented cattle or other animals from approaching too near to the inner sanctuary – if, as is quite possible, cattle which were brought to the site as tribute or payment to the chieftain were temporarily kept for reckoning in the outer enclosure. The suggestion 'that it was because the spike-shaped stones and the cracks in the rocks were there, that someone had the idea of disposing of them in such a decorative way' (M. Craig, *op. cit.*, p. 24) is far-fetched in the extreme and quite unnecessary.

That Dún Aengus is only one, albeit the largest and most impressive, of seven such monuments on the Aran Islands can also be argued as supporting a ceremonial or prestige interpretation for it. Each of the seven monuments is located in a different townland, of which there are only seven altogether on the islands. These townlands are each topographically distinct from one another and, furthermore, may well owe their origins to fossilized land-divisions, sub-divisions of long-forgotten Celtic *tuath* (tribes).

The great landscape continuity provided by Townlands ... allows the reconstruction of large segments of the past social landscape ... the Townland may prove one of the the richest legacies of past settlement evidence in the Irish landscape.
– T. McErlean, *BAR*, 16(1983), 336.

Each Aran 'fort' should perhaps be looked upon as the 'temple' of the local community, just as each diocese has its own cathedral, each parish has its own church, and each political entity (town, city, county, state) has its own meeting-place (Town Hall, Mansion House, County Buildings, Parliament).

The stupendous works, involving such outlay in labour and materials, are not the structures that a decaying race, beaten to the very ocean brink, on a barren island, would think of raising. They are more the strongholds of a powerful and aggressive people, having great resources at their command.
– P.J. Lynch, *J. Roy. Soc. Antiqs. Ireland*, 29 (1899), 10.

Part of the explanation for their existence may well be that which accounts for the network of drystone field-walls in so many areas: that there is nowhere else to put the stones, and no field until the stones have been somehow disposed of. Yet even if there was more soil-cover in ancient times than there is today, it is difficult to see an adequate economic basis for structures so demonstrative as these.
– M. Craig, *op. cit.*, p.23.

These massive monuments required considerable motivation to build, motivation, however, which is not easily provided by 'a decaying race' of refugees or by forced slave-labour, such as is most likely to have been the case where they build for military purposes. Voluntary labour would, however, readily account for their building – men throughout prehistory and history have always willingly co-operated to erect magnificent monuments to their gods, be they the temples of South-East Asia, the pyramids of Central America, the nuragi of Sardinia, the henges and stone circles of Great Britain, or the cathedrals of medieval Europe. In such circumstances 'an adequate economic basis' need not be invoked – idealism and religious fervour would replace any such inadequacy.

Just as stone-built ringforts (cashels) present no problems of relationship when compared with earthen ringforts (raths), one being the equivalent of the other but constructed of different material, so should one find no difficulty in equating the massive stone-built 'forts' under discussion with the large earthen 'hillforts' such as those at Emain Macha (Navan Rath), Co. Armagh, Ard Macha (Cathedral Hill, Armagh), Rath na Rí on the Hill of Tara, Co. Meath, and Dún Ailinne, in Co. Kildare (Illus. 1, inset), not to mention numerous other less well-known examples throughout Ireland (*e.g.* Dind Rí in Co. Carlow, and Fahy's Hill at Grannagh, in south Co. Galway, which latter was excavated some years ago). These huge earthen enclosures are generally accepted without question as having been constructed for ceremonial rather than defensive purposes; indeed, historically some of the better-known examples are recognized as royal residences and as places where *aonachs* were held in ancient times. Local conditions can surely be accepted as ordaining the type of construction, whether for field-walls/banks, ringforts, hillforts (compare Mooghaun, near Shannon, Co. Clare, with 'The Pinnacle', Rathcorran, near Baltinglass, Co. Wicklow), or for ceremonial centres: stone in the more barren Atlantic western regions and earth in the richer midlands and other regions.

When visiting Dún Aengus, therefore, one should not think of it as a place where desperate men held out in a forlorn last stand against ferociously attacking enemies, *Fir Bolg,* if tradition/folklore is to be believed, who were prepared to leap to certain death in the raging ocean almost three hundred feet below rather than to surrender to invading forces.

Nothing but massacre, or drowning in the Atlantic deeps, awaited them outside their island fortresses: in desperation they heaped them up these vast walls, to shield them from the fury of the tempest that had burst upon their country and their kindred.
– R.A.S. Macalister, *The Archaeology of Ireland* (2nd ed., London 1949) p.281.

But Dún Aengus was no Masada.

Instead the visitor should conjure up an image of druids, ollavs, bards, kings and nobles, all processing formally through the Dún's impressive entrance, some to perform rituals on the stage-like platform, some to assist in the innermost enclosed area, and others to stand on the surrounding terraced wall chanting incantations or signing sacred songs while viewing the solemn proceedings taking place against the dramatic backdrop of the wild Atlantic ocean whose waves sonorously thunder against the rock-face far out of sight below.

APPENDIX I
ANTIQUITY AND PURPOSE OF CAHERCOMMAUN

The triple-ramparted site of Cahercommaun, Co. Clare, resembles Dún Aengus in some ways, not least in that it is sited on the edge of a high cliff-like precipice (Illus. 4), and for this reason it demands comparison with it. It was excavated in 1934 by the Third Harvard Archaeological Expedition in Ireland, under the direction of Hugh O'Neill Hencken who argued that it dated from the ninth century and that its massive innermost wall was 'definitely defensive' while 'the two outer enclosures were mere kraals for cattle'.[1] More recently, however, Dr Barry Raftery has suggested that Cahercommaun should perhaps be classed as a hillfort and dated some 500 years earlier,[2] while Dr Seamas Caulfield has suggested that it 'could potentially have a BC rather than AD date for its construction and initial occupation'.[3] The present writer has likewise indicated acceptance of a primary Early Iron Age date for it and, indeed, perhaps also for some other apparently related Co. Clare sites.[4]

4. Aerial view of Cahercommaun, Co. Clare
(photo: Cambridge University Collection)

Among arguments for the earlier date one might include some of the stratigraphical evidence and also the presence of saddle querns (as argued by Caulfield) and a glass dumb-bell bead among the excavated finds. Similarities with other sites discussed in this essay include not only the massiveness of the inner wall but also its impressive, processional entrance and the terracing, albeit slight but not less so than at Caherdooneerish and Leacanabuaile, within – interestingly termed 'benches' by Hencken.

Also of significance, as suggestive of a ritual nature for the site, is the skull found in Souterrain B which the excavator claimed had been 'intentionally buried' totally independently of any skeleton or other human bones; he even suggested that it may 'previously have been displayed' on an iron hook found immediately underneath it.[5] It would appear that such a skull-burial must be ritualistic and, as such, indicative of some form of head-cult which in turn suggests a pagan Celtic date for it – as argued for a somewhat similar skull-burial, likewise found lacking its lower jawbone, at Ballinlough, Co. Laois.[6]

[1] *Cahercommaun: A Stone Fort in County Clare,* Roy. Soc. Antiqs. Ireland Extra vol. (Dublin 1938), p.1.
[2] In C. Thomas (ed.), *The Iron Age in the Irish Sea Province,* CBA Research Report 9 (Lon-

don 1972), pp.51-3.
³ In D. O Corráin (ed.), *Irish Antiquity: Essays and Studies presented to M. J. O'Kelly* (Cork 1981), pp.210-1.
⁴ *Nth Munster Antiq. J.*, 24 (1982), 6-9.
⁵ *Op. cit.*, p.23.
⁶ E. Rynne, *J. Kildare Archaeo. Soc.*, 15:4 (1974-5), 430-3

APPENDIX II
THE NAMES OF THE 'FORTS'

Mainly due to the fact that most of the 'forts' have been known for generations by their Irish names, verbally rather than in the literature, the resultant written versions tend to be misspelt phonetic renderings, pseudo-Gaelic attempts or crude anglicizations. As a consequence, not only do a wide variety of different spellings occur throughout the nineteenth and twentieth centuries but some of the 'forts' have been graced with totally different alternative names. The more popular and commonly known versions (*e.g.* Dún Aengus rather than the more correct Dún Aengusa) are those used above, and which are given underlined in the lists below, though they may not necessarily correspond exactly with either the 'official' names given on the relevant Ordnance Survey six-inch scale maps or with those most frequently encountered in the literature. Below are listed most of the various versions to be so met with – the first in each case, given in italics, is the 'official' one on the Ordnance Survey maps; in the case of those on the Aran Islands and in the Burren the second version given is that on Tim Robinson's excellent maps of those areas (*The Aran Islands, Co. Galway: a map and guide*, Roundstone 1980, and *The Burren, Co. Clare: a map of the uplands of North-West Clare*, Cill Rónáin, Arainn 1977), being the maps most likely to be used by the antiquarian or discerning tourist. The numbers for the sites listed below correspond with those of Illustration I.

THE ARAN ISLANDS, Co. GALWAY

Inishmore/Inish Mór/Aranmór/ Arran-More/ Arainn
1. *Dunaengus*; Dún Aonghasa; Dún Aonghusa; Dún Aonghus; Dún Aongusa; Dún Aongus; Dún Aenghusa; Dún Aenghus; Dún Aengusa; <u>Dún Aengus</u>; Dún Oengusa; Dún Oengus; Dún Angus; Dún Engus – John O' Donovan in 1839 met an old man who remembered 'that the old people were accustomed to call it Dun Innees', but that 'all the other inhabitants style it Dunmore' (Dun Innees is the correct Connacht Irish pronunciation of the ancient name; Dunmore merely is the Irish for Big Fort).
2. *Dun Onaght;* Dún Eoghanachta; Dún Eoghnachta; Dún Eonaghta; <u>Dún Eoghanacht</u>; Dún Onacht; Dún Oonacht; Dún Onag.
3. *Oghil Fort;* <u>Dún Eochla</u>; Dún Eocla; Dún Eoghla; Eochala; Dún Eochail; Dún Eochaill; Dún Ochil; Dún Oghil; Dún Oghill; Oghill Fort; Oaghill.
4. *Doocaher;* Dún Dúchathair; Dún Dubhcathar; <u>Dún Dubhchathair</u>; Dún Dubh Cathair; Dún Cathair; Dún Caher; Dubh Chathair; Dubh Cathair; Dubh Cahir; Duvcaher; Duchathair; Dhu Caher; Black Fort.

Inishmaan/Inismain/Inis Meáin/Inis Meádhoin
5. *Doonconor,* Dún Chonchúir; Dún Chonchobhair; Dún Conchobhair; Dún Chonchubhair; Dún Chonchuirn; <u>Dún Conor</u>; Dún Connor; Duncraggadoo.
6. *Doonfarvagh;* <u>Dún Fearbhaí</u>, Dún na Fearbhaí; Dún Fearbhaigh; Dún Fearbaigh; Dún Fhearbhaigh; Dún Farvey; Dún Farvagh; Dún Múr; Dún Mohr; Dún Moher; Mothar Dún; Dún an Mhothair.

Inisheer/Inishere/Inishiar/Inis Oírr
7. *Great Fort;* <u>Dún Formna</u>. (Within this 'fort' is a castle known as O'Brien's Castle and generally called Caisleán Uí Bhriain locally – the 'official' name on the O.S. map is, however, Furmina Castle.)

THE BURREN, Co. CLARE.

8. *Caherdoonfergus;* Cathair Dhúin Irghuis; <u>Caherdooneerish</u>; Caher Dún Fergus.
9. *Caherballykinvarga;* Cathair Bhaile Cinn Mhargaidh; Caher Ballykinvarga; <u>Balykinvarga</u> (pron. Ballykinvarriga); Caherloughlin; Caherloghlin.
10. <u>*Cahercommaun;*</u> Cahercommane; Cahircomaine; Kaherekamon.

Co. KERRY

11. <u>*Staigue Fort;*</u> Staigue Pound; Staige; Steague Fort; Steag Fort; Staic Fort; Póna na Stéige.
12. <u>*Cahergal;*</u> Cahergall; Cahergel; Cahir Gel; Cahergheal; Cathair Geal.
13. Not named on O.S. map – <u>Leacanabuaile</u>; Lecanabuaile.

Co. MAYO

14. <u>*Doonamo;*</u> Dunnamoe; Erris Downan.

Co. SLIGO

15. *Cashel;* <u>Innishmurray Cashel.</u>

Co. DONEGAL

16. *Greenan Fort;* <u>Grianán of Aileach;</u> Grianán of Ailech; Grinán Ailigh; Grianán Aighligh; Grianán Oiligh; Greenan Elly; Greenan Ely; Greenan Elagh; Greenan Gormly; Aileach.
17. *The Bawan;* <u>O'Boyle's Fort;</u> The Doon; The Doon Fort.

Postscriptum

Because of their names, one might even find reason to believe that some, if not all, of these monuments may have been used as cattle enclosures. For instance, Caher Ballykinvarga (no. 9) derives from *Cathair Baile Cinn Mhairgidh*, meaning the 'fort of the town of the head of the market', while *Leacanabuaile* (no.13) derives from *Leaca na Buaile*, meaning 'the flagstones of the cattle-enclosure', and Doonamo (no. 14) derives from *Dún na mBó*, meaning the 'fort of the cows'. The best example would appear to be O'Boyle's Fort (no. 17), so-called after the long-time local land-owners, which is 'officially' called The Bawan, a name derived from *Bádhbún* which in turn is sometimes thought to derive from *Bó-Dhaingean*, meaning 'cow-fortress/enclosure/pound', but which could equally derive from *Badbhdhún*, in turn derived from *Badbhh* (a cattle-goddess) + *dún* (a fort) – *anglice* Bawn.

However, very few of these massive 'forts' would have proved practical as places in which to enclose cattle: while cattle might be corralled in some of them for a short while, the lack of fresh water in or near most of them would preclude detention for any worthwhile length of time. The above-mentioned four 'forts', moreover, would be extremely difficult of access by cattle because of their very siting. Either way, not only would anything so massive and impressive as these 'forts' be constructed for cattle but in enclosures built for such a purpose stairways and terraces would be unnecessary, and lintelled doorways would be superfluous. No, they were not originally, if ever, used for enclosing cattle.

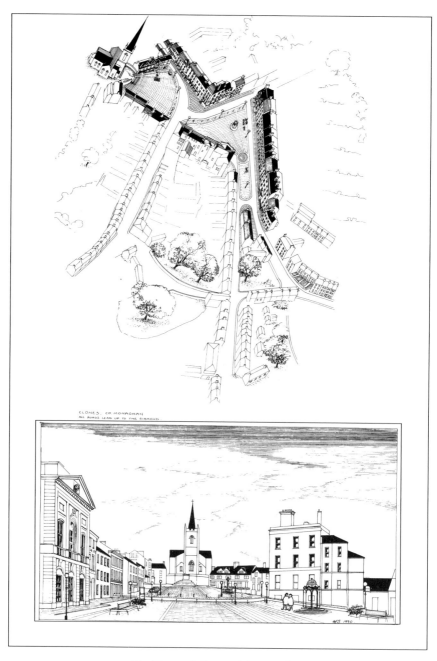

The Diamond, Clones, Co. Monaghan

Among the finest of urban spaces: (a) perspective view, (b) bird's eye view. Illustrations suggested improvements to the Diamond; traffic organized; the space paved and furnished for pedestrians; the jubilee fountain is reconstructed on its original location; the Market Cross is undisturbed; lamp standards and bollards, while performing their own functions, act to articulate the space.

PUBLIC SPACES

AN INTEGRAL ELEMENT OF URBAN ARCHITECTURE

PATRICK AND MAURA SHAFFREY

IN IRELAND, concern for architecture was biased in favour of round towers, castles, monastic ruins, together with a few great towns and country buildings. Maurice Craig's classic and pioneering book, *Dublin 1660 -1860*, established fresh architectural perspectives, which, over the years, were gradually widened and intensified. Later writers, the work of organizations like An Taisce – The National Trust for Ireland – and the many battles fought to protect well-loved buildings under threat, all contributed to a new outlook on architecture.

Today, architecture is no longer considered unimportant or of elitist interest only. In particular, classical architecture, both in town and country, is now recognized as an important element in the architectural heritage. Architectural conservation and protection assumes a wider rôle in national and local government policies, but does not yet approach that of other European countries in terms of legislation and financial assistance. Nor do we have an adequately comprehensive approach to conservation in cities and towns where the pressures on the architectural heritage are complex and challenging.

Urban conservation has a number of different aspects:
– The quality of the individual buildings, including their design, craftsmanship, historic and cultural associations, and their standard of presentation and maintenance.
– The civic qualities of groups of buildings, whether they consist of broadly similar architectural styles as in a Georgian square, or more varied building types to be found in the typical main street. In many cases the aesthetic character of the group is more important than the qualities of individual buildings.
– The design, quality and presentation of the public spaces created by the disposition of the buildings, including streets, squares, footpaths, open parks, etc.

The interaction between these three elements gives towns and cities their essential qualities. How they are managed in a comprehensive way will form the basis of a meaningful conservation policy. Public spaces are most often the forgotten components of our town centres, despite their important effect on a town's sense of place and identity. An approach to conserving these spaces is the subject of this essay.

The essential character of Irish towns owes a great deal to the quality of the public spaces. One thinks of spacious main streets in Cookstown, Castleisland, Gort, Naas, or the potentially great squares in Clones, Newcastle West, Dundalk, Athy and Portaferry. The influence of the Dublin Wide Street Commissioners, the body largely responsible for establishing Dublin's civic design, was not lost on the builders of provincial towns. We have inherited a great urban legacy in which the public spaces of our cities and towns are the central focus. Unfortunately, over the years their spatial qualities and aesthetic potential were totally ignored. Signs of every description were erected on streets, footpaths and buildings without the slightest aesthetic consideration to their positions. The provision of modern services – electricity, telecommunations – caused a rash of unsightly poles and wires that remain a blot on the visual character of most towns and villages. Public utility companies are much too financially demanding of local communities who earnestly wish to rid their streets of visual squalor. It is high time they were more public spirited on this particular matter. In particular, as we approach the end of the century, the ugly timber poles should be removed as a matter of urgency and public responsibility, without any prodding from local communities.

Streets and squares have been considered primarily as traffic routes or parking lots, and aesthetically important buildings at the end of streets removed to allow cars to travel a little faster. Fine buildings which dominated small squares, such as the Market House in Mountrath, were demolished to make way for roundabouts. In Dublin City entire streets are still earmarked for demolition to provide traffic highways. Georgian squares have been turned into day-long parking lots, and pleasant front gardens replaced by patches of crude tarmacadam. The ubiquitous security shutter has turned town centres into 'no-go' areas at night and at weekends. In addition, the shopkeeper, professional person and artisan – for so long the leaders of urban communities – have departed for their new bungalows and mansions on the outskirts. City and town centres were dying as an historic heritage was being eroded. Even new developments turned their back on the traditional street with the concept of the internal shopping mall, generally closed at nights and on Sundays.

This decline in the aesthetic qualities of the public spaces was accompanied by a growing perception that town centres were undesirable places to live, really only suitable for shopping, offices and associated traffic requirements. The decline of Dublin city centre was the epitome of this process and widely recognized as a national disgrace. The main problem was not necessarily a low standard of new architecture, but the total decline in the appearance and presentation of the public spaces. In Dublin, the perceived image of O'Connell Street was of a 'fast-food, amusement parlour strip', rather than the most important street in the country containing some of its finest buildings.

One of the few positive notes in this sad period was Bord Fáilte's National Tidy Towns Competition, which for many years has encouraged local communities to be more concerned about the appearance of their public spaces, even though its lasting achievements were confined to an all-too-small number of committed communities.

The importance of public spaces, as an integral part of urban conservation, has however been acknowledged in Europe for many years. Among the first cities to pedestrianize their traditional centres was Copenhagen during the fifties. In recent years this trend has accelerated dramatically, influenced not necessarily by new architectural ideas but by the growing economic importance of tourism and the knowledge that old cities and towns can be significant tourist resources. There is a recognition that this requires not just the conservation of individual buildings, or groups of buildings, but the total ambience of a town, including the streets, footpaths and public spaces. Like other cultural attitudes this understanding of historic town centres is only now being taken up in Ireland, influenced no doubt by increasing contacts with Europe.

Tourism has become the world's greatest industry, and visiting old cities and towns is among Europe's most popular activity. The idea of 'theme towns', mooted by Bord Fáilte, recognizes this activity as a growing interest among the public. The emphasis on tourism, however, must be approached with caution. It would be a pity if, in the interest of developing tourism, many of our more historic towns were turned into 'folksy theme parks'.

The decline in the appearance of Dublin city centre, and the impact of new ideas from outside, prompted the establishment of The Dublin Metropolitan Streets Commission in 1986. The Commission was also inspired by the legacy of the earlier Wide Street Commissioners, and the modern area of concern coincided largely with the main spine of streets originally laid out by their predecessors. In a few short months of activity, the Metropolitan Streets Commission brought a fresh approach to urban renewal and their ideas and plans have influenced greatly what has happened in Dublin and elsewhere since.

In a new era of public space improvement, streets and squares must be seen as an essential component of a town's aesthetic quality. There will be many opportunities to improve them with sensitive widening of footpaths; curtailing of unnecessary traffic; carefully considered tree-planting schemes; and, not least, a suitable choice of paving materials, which generally should acknowledge the character of the adjacent buildings, reflecting their materials rather than competing with them.

The simple classical qualities of Irish towns, with their predominance of stone and plaster, could be eroded if streets were over-prettified with fussy brick paving and flower boxes, 'olde-world' signs and light fittings. Multi-coloured brick treatment could demean towns whose main aesthetic characteristics stem from the simplicity of their buildings and the pleasing proportion of their public spaces. In the more important streets, stone or reconstituted materials are appropriate, while colour brick patterns may be acceptable in narrow secondary streets and laneways. Access and servicing of buildings can be taken into account and provided for when carrying out improvement schemes.

Considered tree planting could also lay the foundations for fine tree-lined streets and public spaces as a potential source of pride to future generations. The tree-lined street of Castlecomer is an example of such an investment by our forefathers. Market squares could again become appropriate settings for public activities and exhibitions.

The Urban Improvement Programme, initated by the International Fund for Ireland, has begun most promisingly. The market square in Cavan has been transformed from a semi-derelict parking lot into a friendly public space, which acts as a focus for the entire town. The space outside the courthouse in Carrick-on-Shannon has been upgraded, highlighting the importance of this fine, long-neglected building, and in the process ensuring its long-term protection. The visual qualities of Monaghan town centre are now more evident following the removal of poles and wires, and widening of footpaths. Work is begun on the Diamond in Clones, arguably one of the most importact spaces in the country.

In Dublin the radical ideas suggested by the Metropolitan Streets Commission for widening the pavements in O'Connell Street, Westmoreland Street and D'Olier Street, or paving large parts of College Green, should be implemented as a matter of urgency. In the process Dublin would become an exciting city in which the high architectural qualities of its buildings would match the equally fine appearance and presentation of the public spaces.

In all major developments the concept of 'public domain' should be foremost in planners' minds. There will be opportunities where derelict and underused lands in city and town centre are developed to create new squares and streets integrated into the existing fabric; where the bleak appearance of many recent commercial developments can be softened by new urban approaches.

Public art works and sculptures are an important additional aspect of urban improvement. Every town, village and city district now wants its public sculpture. The standards achieved are uneven – there is too much poor quality work. New art work should be considered integral to public space, not an incidental afterthought. Artist and urban designer should co-operate in the development of the entire space from the beginning.

Urban design presents exciting challenges, and if public spaces can be seen as integral to city design, we can bequeath a valuable legacy to future generations, combining the best ideas of our day with a distinctive Irish style.

POWERSCOURT AND
ENNISKERRY

THE ARCHITECTURAL DEVELOPMENT OF AN ESTATE

JEANNE SHEEHY

THE STORY OF Powerscourt as a planned estate begins about 1741, the date
of completion of the new house built for Richard Wingfield, to the design
of Richard Cassel. From the beginning the house was admired for its own
sake, but perhaps even more for the magnificence of its situation. The sur-
rounding area included all of those features – rivers, deep wooded glens
and one of the tallest waterfalls in the British Isles – considered necessary
for a romantically landscaped park. Richard Wingfield was praised for his
taste, and also for his charity in affording labour for large numbers of peo-
ple, at a time of great famine and hardship. 'A poem occasioned by a view
of Powerscourt House, the Improvements, park etc', was published in
Dublin in 1741. The poem was anonymous, but internal evidence suggests
that the author was a clergyman of the Mr Collins sort.
     He begins:

> The muse forgetting, by the Muse forgot,
> And what I relish least become my Lot,
> Doom'd to a country church remote and poor,
> And what is still more dreadful, serve the Cure.

and goes on,

> O let my rapt imagination trace,
> The Site, the Sylvan Genius of the Place,
> Where Nature varies, yet unites each Part,
> And Chance reflects Advantages to Art;

It is ART whom he addresses next:

> Here gushes down steep Steps a ductile Rill
> There spreads in fluid Azure, broad and still.
> So mix'd the Views, so exquisitely shewn,
> Each flow'ry field and Valley seems your own,
> While Nature smiles, obsequious to your Call,
> Directs, assists, and recommends it all.
> At last she gives (O Art how vain thy Aid)
> To crown the beauteous Work, a vast Cascade.

213

The author has less to say about the house, though what he says is fulsome.

> The finished Seat demands the Founder's praise,
> Where Taste sets off and dignifies Expense,
> Neat without Glare, Magnificent with Sense.
> Thus in Improvements shines the Attick Taste,
> Thus Eden springs where once you found a Waste.
> Sketched in your House the candid Heart we view,
> Its Grace, Strength, Order, all reflecting you.

He also praises the social benefit of the undertaking:

> Hence, from this Taste are numbers pleas'd and fed,
> The Wise have Pleasure, the Distress'd have Bread,
> Thus taste brings Profit, and improves with Sense,
> And through a thousand Channels turns Expense,
> Benevolence in num'rous streams imparts,
> And ends in Virtue what began in Arts,
> Removes sharp Famine, Sickness and Despair,
> Relieves the asking Eye, the rising Tear,
> Such Woe, as late o'er pale Hibernia past,
> — And such (ye guardian Powers) we wish the last.

From the beginning the house, the waterfall, and the Dargle valley were tremendous tourist attractions, and many travellers echoed the sentiments of our anonymous clergyman:

> Lo! down the Rock which Clouds and Darkness hide
> In wide Maeanders spouts a Silver Tide;
> Or sprung from dropping Mists or Wintry Rills,
> Rolls the large Tribute of the Cloud-topp'd Hills;
> But should the damp wing'd Tempest keenly blow
> With whistling torrents and descending Snow
> In one hugh heap the show'ring Whirlpools swell
> And deluge wide the Tract where first they fell.

This kind of exaggerated view of the Dargle became very common – Thackeray made fun of it in his *Irish Sketchbook* of 1842. Such descriptions of roaring cascades tended to raise expectations which were not always fulfilled, many travellers remarking on the thin trickle of water, though all agreed on the magnificence of the setting.

The most illustrious visitor was George IV, who was entertained by the 5th Viscount to a great banquet at Powerscourt in September 1821. Mindful of adverse criticisms of the summer, Lord Powerscourt and his staff decided to ensure that the king had a good show:

The King was invited to visit Powerscourt Waterfall, a dam having been constructed above the fall, to confine the water, so that His Majesty might see it in full flood. Time, however, did not permit of the King going there, which was fortunate, for the wooden bridge, which had been erected at the foot of the fall on which His Majesty was to have stood while the dam was being blown up by a mine to let the water down, was carried away by the force of the water when the mine was afterwards exploded, so that a fearful catastrophe was averted.[1]

Richard Wingfield was created Viscount Powerscourt (this was the third creation of the title) in 1743. During the ensuing period not a great deal was done at Powerscourt, or in the village of Enniskerry, until the succession of the 5th Viscount, in 1790. Development under the 5th Viscount consisted of a number of solidly built terraces of Regency-vernacular appearance, with fanlights, panelled doors, sash-windows, rendered walls and slate roofs, 'Tastefully built in the cottage style', to quote Lewis's *Topographical Dictionary*. These formed the basis of the triangular layout of the village, and many are still recognizable. The 5th Viscount and his wife built schools, one in the village and one on the Dublin road, and contributed towards a fever hospital (on Kilgarron Hill) and almshouses.

The nineteenth century saw a great deal of activity at Powerscourt, though there were periods of stagnation, owing to the long minorities of both the 6th and 7th Viscounts. Richard, the 6th Viscount, succeeded in 1823, when he was only eight, and came of age in 1836. He died in 1844 at Rochester on his way back from Italy. Though he had a short life, and was abroad a lot towards the end of his life, he put in hand a great deal of work at Powerscourt and in the village of Enniskerry, and he used his time in Italy buying sculpture for the house and gardens. The accounts to do with the winding up of his estate include payments to Mr Pisani of Florence for cases of statuary – it cost £45-17-6 to ship the copy of the *Laocoön* that is now on the terrace – and £225 to Laurence MacDonald, sculptor, of Rome.[2] In 1836, the year of his majority, he married Lady Elizabeth Jocelyn, daughter of the 3rd Earl of Roden, a celebrated beauty of her day. She was described in 1841 as being:

In the bloom of such unparalleled loveliness that the people would crowd on the staircase of the hotels where she stayed on her journeys between Powerscourt and England, to watch her pass.[3]

Disraeli published a poem about her: 'Lines on Ross's Portrait of the Viscountess Powerscourt'. Inevitably, he begins with a description of the waterfall, then continues:

> Fair scene, but fairer at this noontide hour
> When from the stately palace of her race,
> Fresh as the fragrance of some unculled flower
> That is not half so sweet as her bright face,
> Forth comes in all the pride of beauty's power
> The gentle POWERSCOURT with airy grace,
> Bearing some treasured tome with pensive mien
> To muse upon its music, 'mid the scene.[4]

They seem to have been a glamorous pair, very much figures of international high society. He was a keen yachtsman, and she spent hours on board his boat, *The Antelope,* in the Mediterranean, doing needlework with which she filled Powerscourt.

About 1842 he brought in Daniel Robertson to lay out the gardens. Robertson is an interesting figure. He was one of the two most active architects in the eighteen-twenties in Oxford, where he designed the University

Press building. He left Oxford rather suddenly, perhaps pursued by bailiffs – the 7th Lord Powerscourt, who was a boy when Robertson was working at Powerscourt, said they used to hide him in one of the domes when the bailiffs came looking for him.

He also had what would nowadays be referred to as a 'drink problem' – perhaps that made Ireland an attractive place to pursue his career, which he did very successfully.

He drew best when his brain was excited with sherry. He suffered from gout, and used to be driven about in a wheel-barrow with a bottle; while that lasted he was always ready to direct the workmen, but when it was finished he was incapable of working any more. Nevertheless, his drawings in the books of plans show what a clever artist he was.[5]

The terraces were begun to Robertson's design, the first stone laid by the heir, Mervyn Edward, on his seventh birthday, 13 October 1843. The chief stonemason was Matthew Noble, of Glencree. Labour was cheap, and a lot of the work was done, but it ceased at the death of the 6th Viscount in 1844.

The 6th Viscount also began to develop the village of Enniskerry, outside the gates of the demesne. The original form of the village had been one long, meandering street, leading from the bridge at the beginning of the Dublin road to the demesne gates – this is how it appears in Rocque's map of 1760. By the time of the Ordnance Survey of 1840 the Dublin road had been joined by the road leading down Kilgarron Hill from Glencree, forming a triangular open space where the three roads met, which was used for fairs, and around which 'The neat rustic cottages ... erected by Lord Viscount Powerscourt from designs by Mr Morrison' were arranged.[6]

In 1843 the village received its centrepiece, the clock-tower, to mark the centenary of the third creation of the Viscountcy.[7] The tower, square in plan, is built in three stages, with triangular pediments on each face of the top stage, and a little dome. At the bottom are curved troughs into which the village water supply once drained, and the whole edifice rests on a trefoil-shaped base. It is not clear who designed it, but it was probably John Louch, who was architect to the estate, and to whom payments are recorded at the time of construction.[8] When the 7th Viscount collected the estate drawings together in 1893 he attributed the design to George Moyers, but Moyers only seems to have designed the curious little dome, added in 1860. Sir George Moyers was an eminent Dublin builder, and onetime Lord Mayor. He had a very grand manner, and was nicknamed 'Duke of Memel', his son being 'Viscount Scantling'. The stonework was by Matthew Noble of Glencree.[9]

The death of the 6th Viscount in 1844 occurred when his son Mervyn Edward was only eight. During his minority, from 1844 until 1857, the estate was administered by his guardians, his great-uncle, the Hon. and Rev. William Wingfield, rector of Abbeyleix, and his maternal grandfather, Robert, 3rd Earl of Roden. Wingfield kept a strict eye on the morals of the village – when, in 1851, it was decided to adapt the clock-tower as a fountain he wrote:

This I consider a very necessary item of expenditure, both in order to carry out, at least a part of Lord Powerscourt's plan of carrying water to the town, and to get rid of the present well, which being in a lane near the school ... is quite a nuisance from being the gossiping place of idle and improper persons, and a great annoyance to the respectable neighbours.[10]

In 1853 the guardians went to Richard Turner, the pioneer of wrought-iron construction, for a bridge over the river on the Dublin side of the village. Unfortunately his design proved too expensive, so they had a wooden one, from E. W. O'Kelly of Bray. This was replaced in 1865 by the present stone bridge, to the design of H. Brett, the county surveyor.

The next addition to the village, in 1855, was the picturesque forge, with its horse-shoe entrance, broad forecourt and blacksmith's cottage. Like the clock-tower, but unlike the rest of the village, these are built of granite. The forge cost about £150, the house about £200. They were probably designed by E.W. O'Kelly of Bray – it seems to have been the habit of the estate at this time to get designs from O'Kelly, and have them approved by John Louch. At the same time the scheme for re-modelling the village began, giving it its very un-Irish appearance. At the top of the street leading to the demesne gate is the old almshouse, probably contemporary with the forge. Then comes the police station or barracks. This is a detached build-ing, but it establishes the vocabulary of asymmetrical façades, finial-crowned gables, squared hood-moulds and ornamental barge-boards which continue to be used in the terrace which curves down towards the centre of the village. Most of these seem to be remodellings of the original houses – farther down the hill the houses revert to their original Regency vernacular, and the little court-house, with a gable suggestive of a pedi-ment and round-headed windows, still has a vaguely classical effect, though there is a design giving it a 'Tudor' façade like some of its neigh-bours. All of the designs for this 'tudorization' of the village are signed E. W. O'Kelly of Bray.[11] O'Kelly seems to have moved gradually from builder to architect. By 1861 he was being referred to in the building press as 'architect', and had designed a 'monster hotel' after the American fashion near the new railway-station at Bray.[12] The last change to the centre of the village was the rebuilding of the Powerscourt Arms Hotel, which was burnt down in 1894. It was erected to the design of Cecil Orr, architect, of Dublin, not very different from its predecessor, except for the addition for a few extra gables and barge-boards, and a gothicized wooden porch. The builders were Sutton and Doyle of Enniskerry, and the cost was £1083-18-10.[13]

The 7th Viscount, when he gained his majority, devoted himself to the completion of the schemes left unfinished at the death of his father. Under him several new roads were built, and Catholic and Protestant churches were begun in the village. Until about 1860 Catholics in Enniskerry attend-ed Mass in a barn attached to a farm outside the village. They had wanted for some time to build a new church, but had difficulty obtaining a site. During the minority of the 7th Viscount, one of his guardians had been his grandfather, the 3rd Earl of Roden. The Earl of Roden was a strong evangel-ical Protestant (he published a pamphlet on *The Progress of the*

Reformation in Ireland in 1851) and seems to have put up opposition to the granting of a site for the Catholic church. When asked to sanction a site at Enniskerry he is said to have replied that '*one* chapel in Ireland was one too many'.[14] However, on the day he came of age, 13 November 1857, Lord Powerscourt gave the Catholics a site for a church and priest's house near the bridge at Knocksink, at a rental on one shilling a year. The Catholics of Enniskerry had already begun to raise money. Designs were obtained from Patrick Byrne, one of the leading Catholic architects in the Dublin diocese, plans were submitted to Lord Powerscourt on 20 November, and the foundation was blessed by Archbishop Cullen on 4 April 1858. The trowel used in laying the foundation-stone was of silver from the Wicklow mines, the handle made of yew from a tree said to have been planted by St Kevin at Glendalough. The parish also owns the mallet used on the same occasion, and a chalice, which was given by the Emperor Napoleon III on 17 January 1860.

The Church of the Immaculate Heart of Mary was dedicated on 12 October 1859, and, complete but for the spire, was inaugurated with Pontifical High Mass on 17 June 1860. It is a rather dull barn of a building with the conventional middle-pointed detail south porch, chancel-arch. Its best feature, the plaster vault, once charmingly painted with vine garlands on a blue ground, suggests that Byrne had not fully assimilated Pugin's lessons about 'truth', though he is said to have been converted to Gothic by Pugin's essays in the *Dublin Review*. The parochial house is also to the design of Patrick Byrne, the foundation-stone laid by Archbishop Cullen, on 25 August 1861.

At the other side of the village, nearer to the demesne gates, and on a rather more elevated site, stands St Patrick's Powerscourt, the Church of Ireland church. The rivalry of the two religions is reflected in the building history, as well as in the site. Though the Protestant church was begun first, the delays in its building meant that the Catholic one was finished first. During the minority of the 7th Viscount there were already plans for a new church:

A few years before the year 1857, when I came of age, in consequence of the demesne being on Sundays filled with people attending Divine Service, who used to tie their horses to the trees in the avenue, and whose carriages filled the old stable-yard, my mother, and her husband, Frederick, 4th Marquess of Londonderry, determined as my guardians to build a new Parish Church outside the demesne, nearer to Enniskerry and more conveniently situated for the parishioners, also to make the Demesne more private.[15]

The church was paid for, as a parting gift to the village, by Lady Londonderry. The architect was John Norton of London. The foundation-stone was laid by the 7th Viscount on the day he attained his majority, 13 October 1857.[16] Though completed by 1859, it was not consecrated until 1863, owing to objections made by the Ecclesiastical Commissioners to the spire being slated. It was eventually covered in copper, which makes it very identifiable as a landmark from the surrounding hills. It is not clear why Norton was chosen as architect, though it may have been because he could be trusted not to design anything too outrageously polychromatic or muscular.[17] This was especially important in Ireland, which did not take to High Anglicanism because of the danger of confusion with Roman Catholics. As it was, there was trouble over the stained glass at Powerscourt church. The glass was ordered from O'Connor of London in 1860, three panels containing the twelve apostles, at a cost of £100. It had been installed about two years when several of the windows were smashed, and a note pinned to the churchyard gate:

if the parish wishes to spare expense and more of trouble they will keep down what images are broke and take down the rest as soon as convenient.

NO SURRENDER

a daub of blue a piece of orange peel

This was apparently the work of some parishioners who were 'Orange men and extreme low Churchmen', who objected to what they regarded as 'emblems of popery'. In spite of the threat, the windows were packed and sent to London for repair, and are still to be seen in the church.[18]

The 7th Viscount continued his father's work on the garden and park, and on the estate buildings. He embellished the main gate, now known as the Eagle Gate, with an eagle designed by the Dublin sculptor Thomas Kirk, and he set up a picturesque new entrance on the Dargle at Tinnehinch. There is a pretty 'Tudor' lodge, designed by Sir George Hodson of Hollybrook, a neighbour; it was paid for by the 4th Marquis of Londonderry, whom Lady Powerscourt had married in 1846. The gates, known as the Golden Gates, were put up in 1869. They had been exhibited at the Paris Exhibition in 1867, and bought by Lord Powerscourt from the manufacturer, J. Leroy, Avenue de la Grande Armée, Paris. The piers were to a French design, supplied by the manufacturers, but executed in Wicklow granite by Matthew Noble, the mason from Glencree.[19]

He also built a lot of less picturesque estate cottages.

Outside the Kilmolin Gate I built eight blocks of Labourers cottage. The first were constructed after a plan from the Board of Works, but they were rather large for labourers, two stories high, and these are now inhabited by a mason, a carpenter, etc. The next two blocks were also built two stories high, one half of each cottage being a kitchen with an open roof; the other half being divided into two bedrooms on ground floor, and two over them, with an open wooden staircase in the kitchen leading to the two upper bedrooms. Some years after these were built I went into one of them and remarked that the staircase had disappeared. On enquiring what had become of it, the occupants said: 'Ah! sure we burnt it for firewood long ago!' I said 'Then how do you get to the upper rooms?' 'Ah! sure, the fowls live up there!' After that I did not build any more two-storied cottages.[20]

The 7th Viscount lavished a great deal of attention on the terraces, extending and embellishing the scheme begun by his father and Daniel Robertson:

There were a quantity of poor people on the estate up at Glencree who were wanting employment, and we put them to work at this terrace, at about six shillings a week ... I had upwards of one hundred men on it at one time, with carts and horses, and they were very glad of the employment.

He was a great traveller, and always on the lookout for objects for the house and garden, and he noted meticulously the sources of his various finds, from Mrs Brady, a dealer in Liffey Street, to Prince Napoleon in the Palais Royal, Paris. He had a plaster model of Bernini's Barberini Fountain made by Laurence Macdonald, who had a studio on the Piazza Barberini, in Rome. He then got Sir Thomas Farrell, PRHA, to make a copy in cement of the upper part (he thought the whole would be too big), and put it in the lake as the *Triton Fountain*. He set up the Pegasus on the terrace above the lake in 1869. They are by Professor Hagen of Berlin, and made of zinc, painted to look like bronze.

He decorated the perron, with black and white cobbles from Bray, and made a fountain, incorporating two colossal figures of Eolus. These are seventeenth-century Italian, and had originally come from the palace of the Duke of Litta at Milan, but Lord Powerscourt bought them in Paris, where they had adorned Prince Jerome Napoleon's apartments in the Palais Royal. There they had gas jets issuing though their mouths, and water between their legs.[21]

The owners of Powerscourt from the 1st Viscount on seem to have had an eye to Versailles. It is therefore fitting that the terraces should have received, as a last embellishment, a set of bronze urns copied from the ones on the terraces at Versailles. These were obtained by the 7th Viscount through Sir Richard Wallace, whose father, Lord Hertford, had had permission to make copies of them for Bagatelle. They look very well at Powerscourt, and we may well agree with our anonymous clergyman of 1741, that the site is *better* than Versailles:

> Let grand Versailles her liquid landskips boast,
> Pure scenes of Nature here delight us most.

NOTES

[1] M. E. Wingfield, 7th Viscount Powerscourt, *A Description and History of Powerscourt* (London 1903), p.43.
[2] Powerscourt Papers, National Library of Ireland.
[3] Mabell, Countess of Airlie, *Lady Palmerston and her Times* (London 1922), Vol. II, p.48.
[4] Quoted in M.E. Wingfield, 7th Viscount Powerscourt, *Memorials of the Family of Wingfield* (London 1894) p.48.
[5] *Description and History, op.cit.,* pp. 60ff.
[6] Wilson and Lawson, *A Descriptive View ... of Ireland,*(c.1842), p.414.
[7] Rev. A.E. Stokes, *The Parish of Powerscourt'*, *A Centenary Lecture* (1963).
[8] Powerscourt Papers, *loc. cit.*
[9] *Description and History, op. cit.*, p.86.
[10] *Minutes of the Guardians,* 22 February 1851. Powerscourt Papers, *loc. cit.*
[11] The designs are in a series of albums collected by the 7th Viscount, the property of The Powerscourt Trust.
[12] *Dublin Builder,* 1 February 1861, p.412.
[13] *Irish Builder,* 1 June 1895, p. 134.
[14] John O'Toole (Rev. C.P. Meehan), *The O'Tooles of Feracualan* (Dublin), p.99. *Battersby's Catholic Directory* (1858), pp.244ff.
[15] *Description and History, op. cit.*, p.71.
[16] *Illustrated London News,* 21 November 1857, p.508.
[17] Gomme, Jenner and Little, *Bristol, an Architectural History* (Lund Humphries 1979). 'He

designed more churches in Bristol than anyone else, being accounted a "safe man" who could build the "regulation church" without exposing clients or worshippers to architectural or theological extremes.'

[18] Papers, St Patrick's Church, Powerscourt. I am grateful to Canon Stokes for access to these papers.

[19] *Description and History, op. cit.,* p.102. Albums of drawings, *op. cit.*

[20] *Ibid.*

[21] For an account of all of this see *Description and History, op. cit., passim.*

(Photo – P. Starling)

FOR MAURICE CRAIG WHO FIRST INTRODUCED ME TO ISLINGTON, THE NEW FACADE
AT THREE THORNHILL ROAD BY. SAM STEPHENSON! '90.

Three Thornhill Road. Islington, London

RUSKIN, MORRIS

AND THE 'ANTI–SCRAPE' PHILOSOPHY*

JOHN SUMMERSON

JOHN RUSKIN, William Morris, Philip Webb, and W.R. Lethaby all held very nearly if not absolutely identical views on the subject of the preservation of ancient buildings. Ruskin announced his views in 1849; Lethaby died in 1931. So I think we may say that for about eighty years a distinct philosophy of preservation was upheld. It was passionately upheld by these men and less passionately by great numbers of their followers. I much doubt if any living person adheres to it now. I also much doubt if many living people have a very clear idea of what this philosophy was. In the context of present conditions and problems it may appear rather curious; but it still has power.

The philosophy was invented – that is not too strong a word – by Ruskin, and here is a key passage from 'The Lamp of Memory' in *The Seven Lamps of Architecture*:

For, indeed, the greatest glory of a building is not its stones, not in its gold. Its glory is in its Age, and in that deep sense of voicefulness, of stern watching, of mysterious sympathy, nay, even of approval or condemnation, which we feel in walls that have long been washed by the passing waves of humanity. It is in their lasting witness against men, in their quiet contrast with the transitional character of all things, in the strength which, through the lapse of seasons and times, and the decline and birth of dynasties, and the changing of the face of the earth, and of the limits of the sea, maintains its sculptured shapeliness for a time insuperable, connects forgotten and following ages with each other, and half constitutes the identity, as it concentrates the sympathy, of nations: it is in that golden stain of time, that we are to look for the real light, and colour, and preciousness of architecture; and it is not until a building has assumed this character, till it has been entrusted with the fame, and hallowed by the deeds of men, till its walls have been witnesses of suffering, and its pillars rise out of the shadows of death, that its existence, more lasting as it is than that of the natural objects of the world around it, can be gifted with even so much as these possess, of language and of life.

The music of this passage is the music of a seventeenth-century sermon, as so much of Ruskin's earlier writing is: it is elevated, metaphysical, almost theological in tone, and floats across to us with tremendous dignity the quite monstrous paradox that the emotional effect of a piece of architecture arises not from its form or the quality of its materials but from its antiquity. It is important that this declaration is made not as a plea for the conservation of buildings already ancient but as a fundamental truth about

*Read at a conference on Preservation at Williamsburg, Va., USA, in 1965 but unpublished..

architecture. New buildings must be built to last indefinitely and must not depend for their impressiveness on anything that is perishable. In course of time they will acquire the marks of age and in those marks themselves there is meaning which, says Ruskin, 'nothing else can replace and which it is our wisdom to consult and to desire'.

In other words the art of architecture is the art of building ancient monuments; or, rather, of building structures which after several hundred years of experience will be received as such by an unknown generation of men. 'I think', says Ruskin, 'a building cannot be considered as in its prime until four or five centuries have passed over it; and that the entire choice and arrangements of its details should have reference to their appearance after that period.' He goes at considerable length into the question of 'the picturesque', which he calls 'parasitical sublimity'. In modern jargon this might, I think, be paraphrased as 'romantic overtones'. Ruskin seeks to distinguish between these romantic overtones which arise from attention being given to accidents of decay, to the extent that these accidents acquire an emotional meaning entirely their own, and those which remain inherent to the building and ennoble it by expressing what is, to Ruskin, its chief glory – its age.

It is very important to understand this position of Ruskin's. I called his attitude, just now, a monstrous paradox, and it is not very difficult for us to dismiss it at once as pure nonsense. But wait. It may be nonsense to us in our material circumstances and intellectual climate. But consider Ruskin in his. He was living in an England many of whose institutions had scarcely changed since the time of Queen Elizabeth and the centres of whose towns consisted in very many cases entirely of medieval and Tudor buildings. When *we* think of such a town we think at once of obsolescence, of the 'problem' of the city centre, and of the rescue of parts of it as museum pieces. Ruskin in the 1840s did not see it so. These old buildings were not, technologically, much inferior – and, indeed, in substance and workmanship were often superior – to new buildings. The fact that they had stood for a very long time seemed only to confirm their excellence, and their capacity to stand for a good deal longer. The rate of change in English towns and villages in the 1840s was still, by our standards, incredibly slow. A huge vista of change, such as we are conscious of every moment of our lives, was then inconceivable.

Now these ancient time-resistant buildings had, at Ruskin's date, gradually been acquiring a new interest. A new sensibility towards them had developed through the writings of antiquaries and the engravings of illustrators: Sir Walter Scott, Carter, Britton, the elder Pugin, and Rickman. The younger Pugin they had utterly transported, even to a sort of mania. In Ruskin, too, the new sensibility was heightened to an extremity. Here were these buildings – neglected, despised, mutilated, but shining through everything and across four or five centuries as models of sound construction and exquisite ornament and sculpture. Once their ideal excellence was recognized it was not surprising that the sheer fact of age should carry overwhelming emotional significance. Had not something of the sort happened among the humanists of the fourteenth century, newly awakened to the architectural perfections of Rome?

The pattern of ideas in the passage we have just been considering is curiously logical. Ruskin has searchingly examined the sources of his love for medieval buildings. At the very centre of them he has discovered, with absolute honesty and absolute conviction, the consideration that these building are old, that they have lasted. He has found that he cannot separate the mere intellectual certainty that they are old from the emotions induced by the presence of the buildings themselves, emotions which lead him to call them beautiful. The buildings look old. It is, in fact, the marks of age which certify their antiquity and it is through these marks that he has leaned to discover them as beautiful. Such has been, quite authentically, the pattern of appreciation. Then he takes the whole of this pattern and turns it upside down. Because the sheer age of buildings is, to Ruskin, the most moving aspect of them, therefore for a building to become moving as architecture it must be built with a view to becoming old; and it must be built of materials which will strongly and sympathetically take the marks of age. Of the actual forms which might accompany the application of this principle Ruskin declines to give any indication. There are, after all, the other six lamps to guide the architect in the way he should go.

Now, from this standpoint what view did Ruskin take of preservation? For the actual demolition of ancient buildings he would admit of no valid excuse whatever. 'A fair building', he wrote, 'is necessarily worth the ground it stands upon, and will be so until Central Africa and America shall have become as populous as Middlesex: nor is any cause whatever valid as a ground for its destruction.' In ratification of this uncompromising attitude he argued that there were positive moral obligations both to the dead and to posterity. 'It is ... no question of expediency or feeling whether we shall preserve the buildings of past times or not. We have no right whatever to touch them. They are not ours. They belong partly to those who built them, and partly to all the generations of mankind who are to follow us.' In an Addendum to one of the *Lectures on Architecture* (1853) he developed this argument with quite fantastic ingenuity:

Putting aside all antiquarian considerations, and all artistical ones, I wish that people would only consider the steps and the weight of the following very simple argument. You allow it is wrong to waste time, your own time; but then it must be still more wrong to waste other people's; for you have some right to your own time, but none to theirs. Well, then, if it is thus wrong to waste the time of the living, it must be still more wrong to waste the time of the dead; for the living can redeem their time, the dead cannot. But you waste the best of the time of the dead when you destroy the works they have left you; for to those works they gave the best of their time, intending them for immortality.

So much for the ethics of demolition. But in Ruskin's mind there was a threat to ancient buildings much more terrible and much more evil than demolition. This was restoration. Demolition was the work of the ignorant mob – barbarous and crude. Restoration was the work of educated and responsible people, people who should know better. The indictment of restorers is one of the famous passages in the 'Lamp of Memory':

Restoration ... means the most total destruction which a building can suffer: a destruction out of which no remnants can be gathered: a destruction accompanied with false description of the thing destroyed. Do not let us deceive ourselves in this important matter; it is *impossible*, as impossible as to raise the dead, to restore anything that has ever been great or beautiful in architecture.

What Ruskin mainly understood by restoration was a process very frequently employed in the 1840s and 1850s which consisted in the tooling away at decayed stone to reach a new, firm, and smooth surface. Naturally in this process mouldings were distorted out of recognition, while all marks of handling and age were lost. And this loss of the visible marks of antiquity was to Ruskin the most dreadful fate which could befall any building.

If it were urged that restoration was often a physical necessity, Ruskin's answer was that proper care should prevent that necessity:

Take proper care of your monuments, and you will not need to restore them. A few sheets of lead put in time upon a roof, a few dead leaves and sticks swept in time out of a watercourse, will save both roof and walls from ruin. Watch an old building with an anxious care; guard it as best you may, and at *any* cost, from every influence of dilapidation. Count its stones as you would jewels of a crown; set watches about it as if at the gates of a besieged city; bind it together with iron where it loosens; stay it with timber where it declines: do not care about the unsightliness of the aid: better a crutch than a lost limb; and do this tenderly, and reverently, and continually, and many a generation will still be born as pass away beneath its shadow. Its evil day must come at last; but let it come declaredly and openly, and let no dishonouring and false substitute deprive it of the funeral offices of memory.

In all this, of course, we recognize the beginnings of the conservation ideology of William Morris's Society for the Protection of Ancient Buildings, the Society he founded in 1877, twenty-eight years after the publication of the *Seven Lamps* and which, in reference to current restoration methods, he called the 'Anti-Scrape'. It was in 1877 that Ruskin, writing to Count Zorzi about the havoc that was being wrought at St Mark's, Venice, put the principle that the Society was to embrace as its own:

The single principle is, that after any operation whatsoever necessary for the safety of the building, every external stone should be set back in its actual place: if any are added to strengthen the walls, the new stone, instead of being made to resemble the old ones, should be left blank of sculpture, and every one have the date of its insertion engraved upon it.

For the internal support of St Mark's Ruskin suggested the use of sculptured and gilded wood. Iron bands, too, could have a picturesque effect; monastic ruins in the private grounds of English noblemen, he told the Count, with perhaps just the slightest hint that rank might count a little in this matter, were held together in this honest, practical way.

The idea of preservation by the propping and tying together of collapsing structures is somehow grotesque. It is interesting that in the letter to Zorzi, Ruskin lets slip the word 'picturesque' without, this time, intending anything very precise and it suggests that this rough mode of preservation may have been sanctioned for him by the pictorial use of such devices, perhaps in the water-colours of Samuel Prout whom he so much esteemed.

Anyway, here was the beginning of S.P.A.B. method, rationalized in the course of the Society's later activities and still upheld in principle, in all circumstances where its adoption is practicable, by most reputable restorers. The main difference between the modern attitude and Ruskin's is that the modern restorer preserves old material so far as possible as a matter of scientific conscience, because to replace old material with new is 'bad archaeology'. To Ruskin preservation of the old was something more spiritual; to bedevil old work by renewing it was a crime against the dead and the unborn. Perhaps it is only the words which are different.

Now if Ruskin was the author, as he certainly was, of the S.P.A.B. philosophy of restoration, he was also the grandfather of the Society itself. In the year that the Crystal Palace was reopened at Sydenham (1854) he published a pamphlet suggesting the formation of just such a Society, a society to watch over the welfare of ancient buildings and to publish at regular intervals reports on what was happening to them. Another twenty-three years was to elapse before William Morris took the steps which led to the formation of the S.P.A.B., and perhaps that interval of time was necessary for Ruskin's vision to descend into the air of practical politics, to become something capable of realization without inviting ridicule or contempt. In that interval, of course, restoration of the hated kind proceeded at headlong speed, with Sir Gilbert Scott overhauling cathedral after cathedral and far less competent architects than Scott massacring country churches by the dozen.

To William Morris, Scott was the villain of the piece, and it was the news that this architect was about to 'restore' Tewkesbury Abbey that sparked off his resolve to make concrete proposals for the new Society. We should perhaps pause here to consider how much of a villain Scott really was. The answer is quite simple. When Scott approached the restoration of a church he did so as a professional architect whose duty it was to remove decay, replace missing parts, and render the structure secure. He preserved old work when it was sound, replaced it when it was not. He had immense knowledge and if his restorations were a little harsh they were never ignorant. But *restorations* they certainly were. In his handling of old churches Scott saw them most decidedly as medieval buildings which required that they be rendered back so far as possible to their original condition. This is where Morris so profoundly disagreed with him. For what was their 'original' condition? At what precise point in time were they perfect and complete? Could one, by stripping off accretions and restoring missing parts, return the building to some ideal condition of completeness? Obviously not. The notion was philosophically unsound. A building was a long-drawn event in time and in that very fact lay its essential value to the present.

This was Morris's belief. He stated it first in a letter to the Athenaeum in whose correspondence columns the subject had already been receiving attention. A month after the publication of the letter the new Society had held its first meeting, Morris himself acting as secretary, and an eloquent statement by him had been issued.

In the course of this statement Morris had to face what was to him a slightly embarrassing problem. If it was necessary to plead for the protection of ancient buildings, it was necessary to give some indication of what, in point of time, made a building ancient. Morris's own loyalty was to the Middle Ages but to plead exclusively for the medieval would have cut the ground from under his own philosophy and authorized that process of stripping ancient buildings which he so much deplored. His solution was slightly evasive:

If ... it be asked us to specify what kind or amount of art, style, or other interest in a building, makes it worth protecting, we answer, Anything which can be looked on as artistic, picturesque, historical, antique, or substantial: any work, in short, over which educated artistic people would think it worth while to argue at all.

'It is for these buildings,' he continued, committing himself rather more deeply, 'of all times and all styles, that we plead.' All times and all styles. Was the odious seventeenth century, was Sir Christopher Wren, then, to be admitted? Under pressure, yes; and the pressure came immediately from Thomas Carlyle. Carlyle was approached to join the new Society through William Morgan. He was skeptical of its value, but one thing that caught his interest was the possibility of preventing the destruction of Wren's city churches, then under a grave threat from the Ecclesiastical Commissioners. He accepted membership on the implied condition that the Society interested itself in Wren. Morris was not pleased.

This intervention on behalf of Wren somewhat distorted Morris's intentions. His Society was to stop the restoration of buildings, not to stop their demolition. 'It seems to me', he wrote in a letter intended for Carlyle's eye, 'not so much a question whether we are to have old buildings or not, as whether they are to be old or sham old.' Actually to prevent the demolition of buildings, and seventeenth-century buildings at that, opened the door to a very different field of endeavour. It was one to which the Society soon became committed and to which it has been committed ever since. What, I wonder, would Morris have felt if he could have known that in 1962 his Society would be in alliance with an attempt to stop the demolition of the Greek Doric portico of Euston Station!

The ethics of preservation which Ruskin and Morris established was wholly concerned with the treatment of buildings of great age, the protection of their substance and their strictly honest repair. When the Society went into action this protective treatment had to be seen in a more technical light than either Ruskin or Morris understood, and it was on this plane that Philip Webb made his great contribution. Webb was three years older than Morris; he had designed for him the Red House at Upton and was closely associated with him in all his ideas and many of his projects. But he was, of course, what Morris was not, a professional architect; a very professional architect with a love and knowledge of the crafts unequalled in his time. It was Webb who took Ruskin's romantic and technically rather horrifying ideas of wooden props and iron hoops and devised more seemly, permanent, and effective, but also no less frank and honest substitutes.

The main difficulty [Lethaby tells us] was how to deal with obviously weak and fractured walls without pulling down and rebuilding. This Webb accomplished by mining into a patch of the wall on the inside and filling with strong new work; then by forming another hole next to the filled part the work could be extended by degrees in a band throughout a wall. In this way chains of blue brick in cement strong as steel may be inserted into a shaky wall.

That was the kind of practical interpretation of Ruskin which Webb was good at inventing; and some of his devices are still recommended. All the time he was concerned with an old building he was working as an artist as well as a technician. Lethaby puts this well:

The best repair is a sort of building surgery which aims at conservation. A building properly cared for will be all the more lovely because it bears the evidence that it is understood and valued. Such principles open up a whole new art of building conservation. A well done, unaffectedly modern piece of building cannot be offensive, and a study of old art should teach that every manner of building belonged to its own day only. Right understanding of the ancient would make us modern and produce a form of building art proper for today.

Thus there was a connection by way of honest, simple craftsmanship between the repair of old buildings and the design of new. Not merely the *act* of conservation but the *art* of conservation became an aspect of the Ruskin-Morris-Webb philosophy.

As participants in and critics of the preservation movements of today we must, I think, regard this philosophy as something belonging irrevocably to the past. Even if, in part, we subscribe to the same principles we do so for different reasons. I think it must be said that we have not the same passionate, almost religious, reverence for the ancient; we have a much wider and more exact knowledge of the past and we study it as doctors rather than as lovers. The sheer age of a building is something which, in our studies, we are constantly trying to discount. We argue on grounds of architectural quality and/or of historic interest. We are even beginning to want to preserve buildings not as old as ourselves (I speak as someone born five years before the Robie House was built). This is right. But open the pages of Ruskin; read the life of Morris or the letters of Webb. How strongly the magic of antiquity still works! How very nearly one agrees with Ruskin that the next best thing to preserving ancient monuments is to build them!

MIS-QUOTING YEATS
ON LOUGH ERNE

COLM TÓIBÍN

I WAS WARNED about him. The main thing is, I was told, don't misquote any-thing. And be careful with facts, because he has spent a long time getting them right, and he hates other people getting them wrong.

It was St Patrick's Day, 1985. Bernard Loughlin and I were to take a trip on Lough Erne with Maurice and his son, Michael. Michael, I discovered on the journey from Dublin, laughed at my jokes. But his father was making his own way to Bellinaleck from where we would pick up the boat, and there was a strong possibility that Maurice didn't like those sort of jokes. He had a sense of humour, I was told, but it was his own. And please, once more, don't misquote anything in front of him. Michael seemed to agree on the importance of this, and Michael was his son.

When he came in his neat French car he looked at everybody carefully. And after a while two things became clear; he liked words and he liked things. The boat, for example; he seemed to take great pleasure in the boat, and he expressed his pleasure with great precision, but there was nothing dry or cold about the way he spoke. He enjoyed words for their own sake, but at the same time would not be given to flights of fancy.

He didn't lecture us about the lakes, he simply presumed that we knew as much as he did, and when he discovered that we didn't, then he told us. He pointed a few times at buildings in the distance, a house where he had once stayed, or something he remembered. He had just written an intro-duction to a book by Hubert Butler and that was on his mind; he mentioned it quite often ('Hubert's book'). Getting it right meant a great deal to him.

Things were going fine until I told him that I was considering writing a book called 'Walking Along the Border'. He considered this for a moment, and then proceeded to remind me, with mock seriousness and heavy irony in his voice, that I would have to walk along a great deal of water. Did I know that? He asked this with deep concern.

I didn't really know what to say. Then things got worse, because the subject of Schubert came up. This was fine for a while: the trios, the quar-tets, the quintets, the piano sonatas, the songs, the symphonies, all these could be gone through. This was fine. But what about the Masses? I didn't know the Masses. Maurice looked shocked. It was as though some desper-ately important ingredient had been left out of the stew I was preparing.

Oh, you should listen to the Masses. Wonderful. You really have to listen to them.

Revenge was not planned. It just happened that we were standing at the edge of the boat when we saw swans.

'Oh, look, Maurice,' I said, 'swans.' And I quoted mock-poetically: 'Upon the brimming water among the stones are fifty-nine swans.'

He looked at me immediately, aghast.

'I think that's wrong,' he said firmly. 'I think it should be nine and fifty.'

'No, no,' I insisted. 'It's fifty-nine.' And I repeated the quote as though I had been saying it all my life. 'Upon the brimming water among the stones are fifty-nine swans.'

Our two companions were consulted, but neither was sure. And I insisted that it was fifty-nine. This, I soon realized, was his nightmare: somebody has misquoted a poem, and not just that, but is insisting he is right, when he isn't, and we are on a boat, far from the land where books can be consulted and the truth established.

Over the next while he regarded me regularly, a look of deep suspicion on his face. Was I going to say something else? What further outrage had I planned?

When we stopped at White Island he changed. He was clearly in his element now, examining stone, watching how it curved, delighting in angle and elevation. He know his way around, paying no attention to brambles, briars or wet grass, more interested in the pleasures of the Hiberno-Romanesque tradition. He seemed content on Devenish. He simply knew each thing, how it was made, when it was made, its place in our line of buildings. We were merely watchers, tourists. His eye was different, and the delight he exuded was wonderful.

Now I desperately wanted him to know that the fifty-nine swans was a joke. I asked him if he knew the opening verse of 'Elegy in a Country Churchyard' and, of course, he did. I told him I knew a version of it with no adjectives or adverbs, which was better:

The curfew tolls the knell of day
The herd wind o' er the lea
The ploughman homeward plods his way
And leaves to darkness and to me.

He grinned for a second, and then frowned in mock disapproval, realizing with a glint of humour in his eye that the Yeats mis-quotation was part of a similar process of up-dating old poems, rather than a mistake. He seemed satisfied, and cheered up. The world was still as he had always known it: everything, once more, was in its proper place.

WORK IN PROGRESS

BEING THE FIRST AND SECOND CHAPTERS OF AN UNFINISHED NOVEL PROVISIONALLY ENTITLED 'THE ODIOUS GENERATION'

MERVYN WALL

JOHN CHRISTIAN, Professor Emeritus of English Literature, stood before the kitchen sink dreamily washing the luncheon plates, saucers and cups, and meticulously placing each dripping piece of delph into the draining rack, one behind the other in order of size. He carefully put the knives, forks and spoons upright in the respective compartments to which he had mentally allotted them. From time to time he glanced through the open window at his wife Kristin and his son and daughter only a few yards away on the lawn outside. Kristin was seated very upright at her little table pensively reading and making an occasional correction mark on the German exercises of the students to whom she lectured three times a week in the university. His grown-up daughter Sinéad in a crimson bikini lay on a rug on the lawn, her supple body a-glisten with oil and her eyes protected by dark glasses from the strong afternoon sunlight. His twenty-four year old son Leo lay sprawled in a deckchair, his shirt open to the waist, disclosing the carpeting of auburn hair on his chest. Dr Christian, gazing at the young man's moist lips between the untidy ginger moustache and beard, smiled slightly as the thought came to him that his son's face was like that of Judas as traditionally represented in medieval art.

'The worst thing about the old man', he heard his son remark, 'is that he has no sense of humour.'

His daughter answered: 'Gawd! Messing in there with a lot of dirty dishes on a lovely day like this! He's a real old woman. Right?'

Dr Christian saw his wife sharply jerk her head. 'I won't have you criticizing your father,' she said in the same acid tone which was so effective in bringing restless students to order. 'He washes to help me. The two of you never raise a hand to give the slightest assistance in the house. Anyway, he's a brilliant scholar, and on that account alone he's entitled to respect.'

His son grinned. 'Call that brilliant! Eight years on a bloody seventeenth-century book that no one will buy anyway. I call that stupid.'   .

'And talking all the time,' put in his daughter, 'like a bloody Anglican divine. Right? Dean Swift or someone. Gawd!'

Dr Christian noticed the annoyance in his wife's voice.

'Your father gets so involved in what he's doing that he's in another world. There's nothing strange in his falling into phrases from the period he's working on.'

'Is that why they fired him from the university?' jeered his son.'Because they couldn't understand a word he said.'

'He wasn't fired from the university', snapped Kristin.'They just felt that he wasn't a good lecturer, that he wasn't good at hammering knowledge into the dull heads of the young. The university recognized that he was a great scholar and were glad to keep him on as an emeritus professor at the same salary. Look, I have sixteen essays to correct. If you two don't stop your silly chattering, I'll have to bring my papers inside.'

Dr Christian smiled and, turning away from the open window, made his way quietly out of the kitchen and up the stairs to his study. Inside in his sanctuary he glanced at his desk where a few papers lay in a neat bundle beside his typewriter, and at the bookshelves which lined the three walls, every book in its proper place. Then his eyes fell on the two great piles of newspapers on the floor, those which he had skimmed through and placed on their faces to be put in the refuse bin, and on the larger unread bundle which he had still to tackle. He sighed and, stretching himself on the old leather couch which stood beyond his desk, closed his eyes. The depression which had afflicted him for the month since he had completed his great work on Bunyan and delivered the typescript to the university press descended on him again, seeming to press down upon him like a great burden.

During the eight years which he had devoted to the life and work of the great seventeenth-century evangelist, Dr Christian had hardly read the newspapers. He had done little more than look at the headlines and glance down the death columns to see whether he might perhaps have a funeral to attend or a letter of condolence to write. When he noticed an article or detailed account of some matter which he thought he should know about, he had marked the page with red pencil, and it was the accumulated newspapers so marked that he had spent the last month going through and reading with ever-increasing gloom. Seemingly during the years he had been struggling with John Bunyan's life and thought mankind had been behaving with far more than its usual historical stupidity.

The slow train of his thought was interrupted by a remonstrative miaou and a paw laid on his elbow. He opened his eyes and found himself looking into the expectant eyes of his cat, Johann Wolfgang von Goethe. He put his hand on its head, stroked each ear and rubbed with his forefinger the hard, thin bones of its lower jaw. The cat's eyes, sensuously half-closed, continued to watch him.

He stood for a moment and thought of the day he had accepted it as a gift from his colleague, the Professor of Palaeontology, a tiny kitten which he had brought home snuggling beneath his overcoat. He remembered with a smile the furore when he had announced that its name was to be Johann Wolfgang von Goethe, saying that it was fitting to honour the cat and a great man at the same time, the angry incredulity of his son and daughter and the contemptuous laughter of Kristin. The family had abbreviated the name to'Joe' despite his protest that such a name was offensive to feline dignity and was, at a remove admittedly, disrespectful to a great philosopher-poet.'Don't mind him. He's mad', his son had shouted.

His wife was in the hall, her arms full of students' exercises.

'I'm going into the sitting-room,' she said.'I can't stand that pair outside. I don't know where we got them.'

He followed her and watched her seat herself at he desk.

'You're their mother. Could you not talk to them and try to wean them away from their deplorable mode of speech?'

Kristin stopped fussing with her papers and, putting her elbows on the desk, gazed at him with tolerant amusement.

'You've been living in another world. They all talk like that nowadays.'

'But why? We sent them to a good school?

'You've had your head stuck in your books for too long. you don't realize what's been happening in the world. The young are anti-establishment. They like to shock their parents and respectable people. That way they assert their independence. As for their misuse of language, they know it annoys the older generation. "It", and I quote, "subverts the linguistic universe of the establishment." They feel they don't belong to our society, and they want to indicate their scorn.'

'Do you really think that, Kristin?'

'You should get out more. Look up some of your old friends and colleagues. Start now. Go out and have a drink.'

'Indeed I think I will. I'll have a snack somewhere. I might look in to the University Club.'

Back in his study Dr Christian took from a shelf the large notebook he called his Diary, in which he made occasional entries. The last was dated a month before when he had recorded the delivery of his typescript. Kristin is wrong, he thought as he opened it, the revolt of youth is not peculiar to this age. It's a constant in human affairs. Didn't Horace say something about it? He thought of his daughter Sineád and recalled the night she had set up a howl that brought him bouncing out of bed and hurrying to her bedroom. When he had switched on the light, he had seen her sitting upright in her cot, her face streaming with tears.

'What's wrong, Sineád?'

'There's a cwocodile under my bed.'

He had gone down on his knees to look. 'There's no crocodile under your bed. Look for yourself.'

She had hung over the side of the cot to satisfy herself. He had dried her tears, kissed her, squatted down in his pyjamas on the floor to tell her a story, and finally crept out of the room, leaving the light on.

He brooded on Sineád as she now was, twenty years older. He took his biro from its upright position in his waistcoat pocket, mentally composed a few lines and wrote them into his Diary:

All children die, or perhaps their friends, the fairies spirit them away and leave in their places changelings whom we at first call teenagers and adolescents, and finally adults.

Professor Christian did not go out for a drink or to see his academic acquaintances as his wife had suggested, but stayed in his study during the succeeding weeks going through the accumulated newspapers. Their continuing presence offended him: they were a mute accusation that here was a task commenced, but uncompleted, so he set himself determinedly to go through them all, skipping those items of which he felt that he knew enough already, but reading carefully what was new to him or of which he thought that he should be more fully informed. His wife and children noticed his increasing moroseness, his silence during meals, and that he had begun to go for long solitary walks. Several times while washing up, articles of crockery had slipped from his hand on to the floor where they re-arranged themselves in irregular fragments. At last his wife Kristin commented to the two children.

'What on earth is wrong with your father? Never a smile or a joke this last month. He's too old for all those long walks he takes. Where does he go anyway? Comes back exhausted, good for nothing except to fall into bed.'

Sinéad raised her eyes momentarily from the transistor set from which she had been trying to coax a desired programme but which had obstinately been producing staccato bursts of pop music and unintelligible singing in a sham American accent. 'He wasn't always that way,' was her only comment. 'I can remember him as quite a normal father, but now, Gawd!'

Kristin glowered at the two of them and rising abruptly went into the kitchen. Her husband was leaning against the sink staring in front of him, apparently at nothing.

'What's wrong with you, John? Are you not well?'

'I'm all right.'

'I'm worried about you. I don't think you realize how much your behaviour has changed. For a month now you've been going round like a zombie, scarcely speaking. You're stuck in your study all day reading those old papers. It's not as if you were writing.'

'I suppose I'm depressed. I think I'll take a walk. I need a breath of air.'

She gestured impatiently. 'Don't go too far,' she called after him as he passed her on his way into the hall. She glanced at her wristwatch. 'It's very late. You'll tire yourself out.'

She had no sooner seated herself in her accustomed armchair in the sitting-room than he too came in and sank into his own chair on the opposite side of the fireplace.

'Not going out after all?' she asked.

'No. I've changed my mind.'

'In God's name, John, what *is* wrong with you?'

'I've been reading those newspapers that I've neglected for the last few years, and I'm saturated with them, and —.'

'Well?'

She noticed the lack of lustre in his eyes as he stared across at her. She was suddenly alarmed.

'Tell me, John.'

'I'm disturbed,' he burst out, 'more disturbed than I ever remember having been in my whole life.'

'At what?'

He swallowed, and then his words burst out and surged about her like the waters from a broken dam.

'I've realized what's been going on in the world. Between fifty and a hundred thousand nuclear bombs exist at this very moment, each a thousand times more powerful than the one they dropped on Hiroshima. One intercontinental missile can scatter ten or more bombs of Hiroshima size on its target, and can travel half-way round the world to do it, and it can be released by pressing a button. Mankind is racing towards suicide. Forty thousand tonnes of explosive power exist for each individual on this earth, and if that isn't enough, a million dollars a minute is being spent in adding to the stockpile.'

'But that's all old news, John. Everyone knows that.'

'And does nothing about it!'

'What can we do? You've been so dug into John Bunyan that you've been living in an unreal world.'

'Unreal! It has all been foretold in the first chapter of *The Pilgrim's Progress* – the city will be destroyed by fire from heaven in which all will perish, unless some ways of escape can be found.'

Kristin rose authoritatively to her feet. 'You're going straight to bed. It seems to me you're on the verge of a nervous breakdown. Get a good night's rest, and I'll phone Doctor Pillory in the morning.'

'But, Kristin, I can't sleep. I hardly got any sleep these last few nights – turning and tossing all night long.'

He let her take him by the arm and lead him into his bedroom. 'I've still some of that Sodium Amytal that was prescribed for my insomnia last year,' she said. 'It worked for me. You take a spoonful, and you'll sleep.'

She returned a few moments later. 'Here, take a double dose.'

But he did not sleep. He tossed restlessly for an hour, his mind a turmoil of elusive thoughts. He rolled despairingly from beneath the bedclothes and sat for a time on the edge of the bed, his head in his hands. He remembered an old remedy of his to induce slumber, a glass of whiskey while sitting up in bed. He switched on the bedside lamp and made his way to the wardrobe, hoping that the bottle of whiskey was still there. It was. He poured himself a stiff glass, climbed back into bed, and slowly drank it. He wondered would it work this time. He began to doubt it. 'I will sleep,' he said fiercely and noticing that the little bottle of Sodium Amytal was not empty, he uncorked it, poured the remainder into the empty glass and tossed it off. He turned off the light and settled himself in the bed.

'A prayer mightn't be any harm,' he thought, and tried to concentrate on the Godhead. It was difficult to visualize the Almighty. Professor Christian had always thought of Him as a giant intellect permeating all things, the intellect that had created the intricate clockwork of the universe, of life, and even such miracles as the human digestion which his friend the Professor of Medicine had once sought to explain to him. He remembered Einstein's assertion that so complicated was the universe and all it contained; distant nebulae, the veritable universe within the atom, man and beast, that it could not have come into being without the operation of a mighty intellect to conceive, set in motion and sustain it. Chance can have played no part in such incredibly ingenious mechanisms. 'God does not play at dice.'

Professor Christian's thoughts floated quite out of his control. He could not visualize a Godhead. Obstinately there came to his mind again and again a small bowed figure, seated with great volume open on his knees, a quill in his hand with which he was inditing. Professor Christian stood behind him and read over his shoulder, '... there shall be great tribulation such as there was not since the beginning of the world to this time. Immediately after the tribulation of those days shall the Sun be darkened, and the moon shall not give forth her light.'

Professor Christian became suddenly aware of a great blinding flash of intense white light. It faded. He felt himself lifted and flung against a building. He was showered with broken glass. Thick dust filled the air, and he was aware of great objects, buildings flying through the air and disintegrating. As he struggled to his feet and stumbled into the roadway, a little girl, a doll clutched closely to her breast, ran by him, her clothes and head of golden curls on fire. He stood in a street and heard the screams of people coming from the piled rubble. Grey figures staggered blindly past him, naked, the skin peeled from their bodies from head to toe, the skin dragging behind them, still attached to their heels. Human arms, moving, still alive, protruded from heaps of rubble. He turned and ran staggering from the horror. He suddenly felt himself lifted by a hurricane-force wind and swept across an infinity of ruined streets and tumbling houses. Where was he? He only knew that a mighty city seemed to have been destroyed utterly. The sky was pitch-dark and all beneath it was covered by a yellow-brown fog. Something towered above him. A giant condemning figure pointed upwards at the black sky which had vomited this horror on to the earth. He glanced up fearfully.

Cleopatra's Needle! My God, it's London! He was on the Embankment. He turned and leaned upon the wall overlooking the river, but drew back hastily as he felt the heat of the stone and heard the sizzle as the arms of his jacket caught fire. He tore the jacket off, flung it from him and stared across the Thames. The entire farther bank as far as he could see in each direction was a hell of raging fire. On the bank thousands of hideous figures with white, mask-like faces were moving slowly, a broken army of pallid ghosts. With difficulty they scrambled up on to the Embankment wall and let themselves fall into the river. He turned away, stumbled past burning trees and a patch of smoking grass. Then an intense blackness intervened, and he could see no more.

Dr Pillory sat in a chair beside the bed, a smile on his face. 'Aren't you the foolish man? Sodium Amytal mixed with whiskey! Of course you had a nightmare. And all this brooding on things you don't understand. Kristin tells me that you've hardly gone out at all for seven or eight years, writing a book or something like that, and that you haven't mixed with any of your colleagues in the university.'

'I've encountered them, but only occasionally. I give a lecture to post-graduate students once a year.'

'Great God, man, you must go out and mix with people again. There's nothing physically wrong with you. There must be a Professor of Science or of Nuclear Studies whom you know in one of the colleges. Talk to him. He will allay your fears.'

'I used to be addicted to walking in the countryside and in the mountains. Maybe if I got my old rucksack out and went off for a few days by myself it might do me good.

> I'd like to experience again:
> The lowing of Moynalty's kine,
> The larks loud carol all day long,
> And borne on evening's salted breeze
> The clanking seabird's song.s

'There's solace in poetry,' grinned Dr Pillory.'Even if it's not of the highest order.'

Professor Christian returned the smile.'You stick to pontificating about medicine, and I'll stick to judging what's good in literature.'

'Good man,' said the doctor.'You're your old self again. That nightmare of yours may have had a purging effect. Do as you say. Go for a few days' hike in the countryside. It can't do you any harm; it might do you good.'

'I used to be a regular swimmer,' said Professor Christian thoughtfully.'I could take up my old habit of going for a daily dip in the Forty-Foot Hole.'

Dr Pillory frowned:'No,' he said,'I wouldn't do that. There are plenty of indoor swimming-pools. The Irish Sea is not thought to be safe. It's very polluted, thick with sewage as well as chemical and nuclear wastes. It has the highest concentration of radioactive discharges of any area of similar size in the world. They come from the nuclear reactors at Sellafield in Cumbria. The radiation pollution levels are within safety levels, but who knows? Radiation has no acceptable safety level. I hope you don't eat fish caught in the Irish Sea. Badly malformed fish have been found.'

'I don't know. You would have to ask Kristin.'

'I don't eat fish', said Dr Pillory,'unless I know where it comes from.' He rose from his chair by the bedside and smiled benignly at his patient.'As for your worries about a possible nuclear disaster; none of us could go on with our everyday lives if we worried our little heads about such imaginary dangers. You must deny such possibilities to yourself. Denial is the most appropriate and effective of psychological defences. In our world with its ever-increasing need for power, there's no practical alternative to nuclear energy, so why worry about it?'

He turned at the open bedroom door to glance back at his patient.

'I wouldn't like you to be too disappointed', he said,'but I'm afraid that you'll find all the kine imprisoned in stalls nowadays, the skies as birdless as Italy, and such seabirds as there are strewn dead along the beaches.'

'Why? What do you mean?'

'The needs of intensive agriculture and industry,' smiled the doctor.'Resultant pollution of land, sea and sky – the price of economic progress.'

WILLIAM ATKINS
1812-1887

A FORGOTTEN CORK PRE–RAPHAELITE

JEREMY WILLIAMS

A CORK evening newspaper congratulating itself at Kerry's expense is the only time that William Atkins received due recognition from his contemporaries. The only other evidence that he designed Oak Park, his masterpiece, is 'W.A.' carved on a medallion matching one inscribed with the date in the semi-darkness of the inner porch: 1860.

He was born in Cork, the year 1812. He was intended by his family to be a landowner, having inherited half of his maternal grandfather's estate, Fountainville, now known as Hazelwood, just north of Mallow. But his father's sister had married George Pain, the younger of the two Pain brothers sent across by John Nash to supervise the Irish commissions. George settled in Cork, his elder brother James in Limerick, and they both set up a practice independent from their master. George may not have been the better architect, yet he was the more gifted artist, and it would seem that he was responsible for William's early training and passing on his skills as an architectural renderer. But George died in 1838 and his commissions were completed by James. In the Pain output there is no mention of Atkins. Nothing is recorded until 1845, the year of his marriage, when he won a competition against eleven competitors for a new chapel at Mount Jerome Cemetery in Dublin. His church still stands, a simple Gothic structure, one of the earliest churches in Ireland to reveal the influence of Pugin.

His next known commission was also to reveal the influence of Pugin, but to be quite different in other ways, the Cork Lunatic Asylum, his largest work, and his most prominent: too prominent for a society concerned to house its victims with more discretion; an interminable façade and a panoply of spires, spectacularly sited to dominate the valley of the Lee. The endlessness at least is not in the original scheme. As first built, three separate blocks linked by low arcades which serve also as entries to a chapel and refectory, sited further back but on an upper level, the gable end of the rectory and the spire of the chapel, would have been clearly visible from below. At each end of the façade the ground falls away to reveal a battered basement. The composition is further enlivened by six staircase towers, lit by double-height windows that set up a counter rhythm to the horizontal emphasis of the fenestration elsewhere. The weakest feature of the design is the centre, where a heavy brick and stone steeple straddles a conventionally pitched and slated roof. The same steeple, more securely positioned, marks the centre of each wing. In contrast, his deployment of chimneys as vertical features in their own right, and the irregular spacing of the windows as dictated by the internal layout, are evidence of his receptivity to Pugin and a more reflective reaction to the monotonous and souless workhouse architecture of the previous decade which had given the architecture of the Board of Works a bad name. The desire of the Board to update its image must have been why they appointed a relatively young and inexperienced radical, as would be the case today; also crucial was the intervention of the Cork expert on mental health, Dr Osborne.

There would have been two further reasons for their choice: Atkins was a local man, secondly he was not Sir Thomas Deane. Deane had built up the largest architectural practice in Cork against the competition from the Pains and the Hills through his talent spotting in the arts that he combined with well-judged political interference. The apogee of Deane's career came with his election as Lord Mayor and ensuing knighthood. He was also on the Board of the Asylum and resigned, so he would be deemed eligible for the ensuing commission. But the Deanes were involved in the construction of Cork's newly founded university college across the river, and to have received another vast commission from the government would have led to charges of corruption. The Deanes were fobbed off with the Lunatic Asylum in Killarney. Here we find the conventional workhouse formula handled with such subtlety and variety by Deane's gifted young assistant Benjamin Woodward as to make Cork's three separate blocks with their changes of material, their towers and spires, extravagant and impractical. Indeed the cost of Cork, £85,000, was double that of Killarney, and in 1861 Atkins was forced to increase the accommodation by joining his three blocks together. By then also the architecture of the asylum would have compared with Sir John Benson's masterful Lombardic waterworks on the river bank below, to its detriment. *The National Gazetteer* (1868) called it 'a hideous structure like an overgrown cruet stand'. Its quasi-religiousness, as detected by that hostile critic, has since been emphasized by the public lighting of its approaches, designed as an illuminated rosary of beads, a device that must have shocked many Cork Protestants back into their sanity. It has now been removed.

The Ecclesiologist singles out the Church of Ireland, Clonbur, a tiny church sited to look across a wooded valley towards the mountains, and there is just enough of its interior left to see the reason why. Although Atkins had just been appointed to design the largest lunatic asylum in Ireland for his native city, one suspects he had lavished greater care on this more congenial commission, adapting the ideals of Pugin to the needs of the Church of Ireland. Looking upwards from the altar to a rose window above a triple lancet with just enough stained glass surviving to decipher a triumphant resurrection, it is difficult to grasp that one is not in a cathedral, and that one would be crowded out by a congregation of forty. The church is just a single cell of five bays with a lean-to vestry to the north dominated by a monumental boiler chimney that challenges the pre-eminence of the western bellcote. On the south side, the base of the trefoiled windows is progressively raised to reflect the floor within rising to the altar.

Inside, timber transverse arches corbelled out on colonettes brace the open roof. The corbel under the last colonette squirms into a twisted root above a recessed credence niche: Atkins knew his Irish medieval friaries well. Like the English Catholic churches of Pugin, this is also the architecture of a minority searching for their justification in the past.

Atkins was one of the last Church of Ireland architects to cross the religious divide and work for the Catholic Church. His next commission was a convent, St Marie de l'Isle on Crawford Street in Cork. The chapel is here linked to the main structure by a tower with intended spire, balanced at the farther end by another tower with a projecting oriel, its corner bays not windows but unexpected niches enshrining statues. Niches and statues snuggle also into the splayed buttresses of the chapel. The neighbouring orphanage is also freely treated and reveals a deepening understanding of Gothic architecture and Pugin. At the same time Atkins completed the interior of the Trinity church for the celebrated Father Mathew who advocated temperance but dismissed architect after architect, Pain and Deane alike. Atkins seems to have been able to cope with his formidable client, but his interior has been recently disfigured, its columns stripped to expose their iron cores in order to give the side aisles an unobstructed view of the celebrant; yet the church survives redeemable. The Greenmount orphanage in Cork at the same time was deplorably demolished. There is no evidence that Atkins was the architect but he must be the likeliest where sensitive details and delicate polychromy contrast with to its overall chunkiness. The clients here were the Christian Brothers and one of them, Brother Townsend, was an architect, whose adjoining buildings in a more traditional idiom still remain.

The Cork Dominicans on Popes Quay commissioned the neo-classical St Mary's from Kearns Deane in the early 1830s that remained incomplete until Sir Thomas Deane added the portico a generation later. In the meantime they asked Atkins to build for them an adjoining monastery. The result is his most eclectic composition, neo-Romanesque but enlivened by a Flemish pediment and an Italianate campanile, all built out of a ruddy red sandstone with silvery limestone dressings. After his first foray into Romanesque, Atkins returned to it with not always such happy results. A characteristic example is Lindville, a private lunatic asylum in Cork built for a founder of the Cork Lunatic Asylum, Dr Osborne, out of the money made through patenting a method of feeding patients who refused to eat. His institution has a grimness that accords with the invention, and remained unfinished until after Atkins's death.

The 1850s in Ireland marked a time of architectural expansion, with a growing number of competitions every year. Atkins entered three of them. He won them all but nothing was ever built: the most important was that for Cork City Hall. Atkins won with a classical scheme, defeating the neo-medieval scheme of Deane and Woodward. Woodward's drawings survive and his scheme was realized with modifications as the Oxford Museum. Nothing survives of the drawings for the winning entry, and the present

City Hall, albeit in a classical style, is the result of a competition held after a fire in 1921. The next competition won by Atkins was for the Great Southern Hotel in Killarney. In this case the building was erected shortly afterwards but the architect was Frederick Darley. The third successful competition was for the New Markets, Limerick. The job went to John Ryan. There must have been other disappointments. Some years ago his exquisitely rendered scheme for St Columba's College in Rathfarnham came to light. The job went to the protégé of Lord Dunraven, the younger Hardwick.

Atkins was also unlucky with his country house practice. He missed out on the first era of castle building before the famine. The country seat that he built for his cousins the Franks's near Scarteen, Castle Ryves, demolished in 1956, proved to be a castle only in name, after my search for it ended before a faded photograph. As architect of Anner Castle near Clonmel for the Mandevilles, he acted as executant after the emigration of the architect Charles Anderson to the United States. The client's mother was Sophia, the younger sister of the diarist Dorothea Herbert. Dorothea described her sister as marrying into a family long decayed into extravance and eccentricity. Castle Anner was built with Nicholas's wife's money. She was the child of Dorothea's great love, John Roe, who had entered into an 'execrable Union with a Common Drab of the city, a mere street-strolling Miss'.

Dorothea's father had been born in Muckrus, the principal family seat of the Herbert family, where the Herberts had just commissioned William Burn to rebuild the original house as a neo-Elizabethan manor house. But they retained Atkins to embellish the estate: the main entrance gates, the farm and adjoining church; also a porte cochère for the main house, carefully designed not to look part of the original design. When Henry Herbert died in 1866, Atkins designed his memorial, an Irish high cross with a view of the entire property that the family were soon to lose to their creditors after a disastrous attempt to mine copper from their lakes.

John Leahy, whose estate Coolclogher or Whitehill bordered the Herberts to the east, gave Atkins his first opportunity of building a country house in a personal style. The house is conceived as two parallel sequences; the entry porch, hall and axial staircase to the rear, dining room, double drawing-room and conservatory to the front. The spatial progression through the interior is carefully devised to focus first on the staircase, then the bow window of the drawing-room with its panorama of the Killarney Lakes and McGillicuddy Reeks, and finally on the conservatory with a sun terrace and garden beyond. The architecture is an engaging blend of Romanesque and Neo-classical.

Coolclogher is the prototype for his most important country house, Oak Park (1856-61). His client Maurice Fitzgerald Sandes (1805-79) had been Registrar General of Calcutta and had amassed a fortune in indigo before returning to Ireland to settle near Tralee and marry Ellen Dennis from Fort Granite, in Co. Wicklow. He decided to build a completely new house on a more elevated site. The setting, while lacking the drama of

Coolclogher, faces south across the vale of Tralee towards the Dingle Mountains. Again Atkins devises two parallel sequences, that to the rear with the entry and the stairs, that to the front with the principal reception rooms opening on to a terrace and taking full advantage of the sun and view. But here the scale is more imposing, and there are far more surprises, within rather than without. Instead of an entry porch, there is a far-flung porte cochère and the front door is framed by a series of trefoiled arches, with the arms of Sandes impaling Dennis. A flight of steps leads to the vestibule with front hall and staircase hall beyond. The stairs themselves, balustraded with sheaves of corn in glinting brass, are first glimpsed through a columned screen of purple marble. The walls are treated and marbelized with a sombre olive and ceilings are lined with darkly varnished timber as a foil to their patterning in luminous red, green and gold. The staircase hall is the architect's most spectacular interior. It is double height with the stairs ascending to a timber-galleried structure braced tautly to the walls. The far wall is perforated with arcades lighting service corridors off hall and landing. This allows the staff to supervise new arrivals, and to be sighted in return. 'That is not Juliet waiting on the balcony, but the assistant housekeeper wondering if there are enough hot water bottles.'

The sequence of reception rooms is arranged symmetrically along the garden front, to terminate with two contrasting conservatories.

The craftsmen involved in the interior decoration were Thomas Dixon and Frederick Taylor. Dixon (late of Dublin) advertised in Laings' *Cork Mercantile Directory* (1863): 'Imitations of woods, marbles and plain painting will be executed in the best manner and at prices that will be found to suit the prevailing economy of the day.' Interiors similar to Oak Park survive at Dunkathel and Ballinatray. Taylor is registrared as a painter in the same directory. To him must go the credit for the painted ceilings. They are inspired by the French Renaissance and are without counterpart in Ireland. On the other hand, the door cases with their poppy-head terminations are copied from *The Ecclesiologist* and appear in Pugin's interiors at Adare Manor executed ten years earlier. The brass-work hinges, locks, bolts, bell pulls and fingerplates are also Puginesque.

However, the dominant influence on the design of Oak Park is not Pugin but Ruskin, the Ruskin of *The Stones of Venice* and *The Seven Lamps of Architecture* who had not yet lost faith in the regenerative powers of art. Ruskin believed that the domestic architecture in medieval Venice came the nearest to perfection. How to adapt that style to the requirements of the day was not his concern. He showed little interest in the architects who tried to put his ideas into practice. He made only one exception, Benjamin Woodward. Woodward's Curator's House in Oxford dates from the same year as Oak Park, and ogee arches, quatrefoils, columns without pedestals, polychromatic banding, and windows underplayed behind delicate arcades of stone occur in both commissions, or rather did occur since the Curator's House was demolished between the Wars. It is a curious reflection on the values of academia that the Oxford Museum authorities destroyed Woodward's masterpiece, while its obscure Kerry counterpart survived the struggle for independence and civil war to be lovingly cared for by a novitiate of Presentation nuns, most of whom were unaware when they were instructed by their order to sell up that their convent had ever been a country house. The new owners are the County Committee for Agriculture. While Woodward's work has an intensity that his contemporaries never equalled, he never received a comparable commission, unconstrained by cost, time, or the limitations or a pre-existing house.

Atkins himself never received a comparable country house commission after Oak Park. There is no official record that he ever built another country house, but is possible to make four attributions: first Aghadoe House, Killarney, for the third Lord Headley, from an English family who adopted Ireland with such enthusiasm that his brother built another house in Kerry. The fifth Lord Headley suffered a double disaster during the Troubles when both houses he had inherited went up in flames. Seeking consolation, a convert to Islam, he went off on a pilgrimage to Mecca where he was given permission to be addressed as Al'Haz. Aghadoe was rebuilt and it is now a youth hostel. While there are no photographs of its original appearance, it must never have been an architectural success. Certainly when Lord Headley's brother decided on a second Irish seat, Glenbeigh Towers, the commission fell to Edwin Godwin, a choice that may well have been regretted. So much damp came in that Godwin was sued and his career never recovered.

The second house is Parknamore, Ballincollig, for the Green family, the third Streamhill, Doneraile, for a cousin of the Crofts Lysaghts, Cavanaugh Murphy. They are all vaguely Italianate: asymmetrical with wide eaves and round-arched fenestration. The last of these domestic commissions was Velvetstown for Sarah Lysaght, his cousin and co-heiress to Fountainville. She had married a neighbouring landowner Christopher Crofts in 1861, and the decision of the family to build a large new house in 1875 is surprising. Perhaps it was a gesture of support for their cousin on the eve of his retirement. He built it of discordant red and yellow brick set in forceful horizontal bands, with segmental windows making the minimal concession to the picturesque. After a long career of adjusting his romantic visions to the requirements of his clients, for the first time he loses his equilibrium and reveals his discontent. The house was lived in for twenty years, destroyed by fire in 1895, and not restored. The Crofts retired to their original eighteenth-century house that they still inhabit. The ruin is used as a silo, but even still appears more appropriate to a north London suburb than to an Irish farm.

Atkins still continued to enter the principal competitions of the time. St Peter and St Paul, St Finbarr's Cathedral and St Luke's, all in Cork, St Andrew's in Dublin, Belfast City Hall. Only in Limerick Gaol was he successful with alterations that still exist but are impossible to visit. His alterations to the prison in Cork have been destroyed, including his chapel.

If he was unsuccessful in major competitions, in what he was able to build his materials became more varied, his detail more delicate, his polychromy more daring. In Cork this phase is best seen in the Diamond Hill

Memorial put up by Alexander McCarthy in honour of his Milesian ances-
tors. Local vandals of long ago have made off with the bronze
commemorative plaques at the base, before they won unanimous accep-
tance from rival claimants to the lost title of the McCarthy Mór. The bronze
medallions above have also lost their names but are still inset in contrasting
coloured marbles. The plinth he built for the statue of his erstwhile client
Father Mathew is appropriate but a minor work, interesting as evidence
that Atkins was able to cross the religious divide in 1864. But now on his
principal patron was to be the recently disestablished Church of Ireland,
and only what he built for them attains to what he achieved in Oak Park.

Disestablishment led to an upsurge of religious feeling among Irish
Protestants, long lulled into apathy by officialdom. They raised their own
money to build again. Their inspiration was the Irish Celtic Church assert-
ing its independence from London and Rome out of snug little churches in
remote wooded valleys that resounded loudly with their hymns. In a series
of churches, Atkins gave them what they wanted: East Ferry near Midleton,
Leighmoney near Kinsale (dem. c.1960), both date from 1865. These are
followed by Roosky beyond Bantry, Ardfert beside the ruins of Kerry's
medieval cathedral (dem. 1937). Both date from 1868. The following year
he built Killarney, set on fire in 1888, restored by the ubiquitous James
Franklin Fuller, and now credited in its guide to one of the Hills. The last of
these rural churches was St Michael's, Whitegate, overlooking the estuary
of the River Lee, started in 1881 and completed posthumously.

The most happily preserved is East Ferry, beautifully sited on a wooded
promonotory above an inlet off Cork Harbour. The design is based on thir-
teenth-century Fench Gothic prototypes with a simple nave, a polygonal
choir, and adjoining tower with a dormered spire of banded stone.
Leighmoney, sited to overlook the Bandon and built in a more English
style, its octagonal spire upheld by tiny columns, is one of the more serious
casualties of the Church of Ireland's policy for redundant churches.
Likewise Ardfert, an example of his more abrasive later manner. One feels
that Roosky, a simple cell built of brick and rubble, has only survived by
being so tiny and remote.

In 1869 R.W. Edis, an English journalist visiting Killarney, wrote that a
Mr Atkins of Cork had just completed the new church, 'a carefully thought
out design, with some good detail but thoroughly French in general feeling
and giving the idea that the architect had studied Mr Burges's new cathe-
dral rather than the ecclesiastical buildings of his own country'. The
influence of Burges has been lost in the rebuilding, but is very evident in
the refitting that Atkins carried out in the chancel of the Cathedral of
Cashel, elaborately marbled and gilded but totally at variance with
Morrison's Georgian interior. Within sight of Burges's Cork Cathedral,
Atkins added a tower and spire to St Nicholas. But here there are no
changes of material, no parapets or pinnacles to arrest the soaring upward
movement of silvery limestone. Cork has the best neo-Gothic spires in
Ireland, and St Nicholas ranks among them. St Michael's, Whitegate, reveals
the disillusion of his later manner. There is no apse or spire, and the exter-

nal polychromy is underplayed with a certain grimness, but the brick interi-
or reveals a religious intensity unequalled by his Irish contemporaries. The
porch, tower and the decoration of the chancel date from 1892, five years
after his death.

In 1873, after being asked to extend his lunatic asylum yet again, he
was accused by the site engineer Dr Edwards of making unauthorized
changes to the contract drawings, and dismissed unpaid. In the *Irish
Builder,* he bitterly defended himself claiming that the changes had been
demanded by the Board, and that he did not deserve this treatment after ·
twenty-six years of service. He was only fully paid after he had been
replaced as architect by Robert Walker, and Edwards had died. Atkins him-
self died in 1887. His obituary mentions a large attendance at his funeral
but fails to list his architectural achievements.

The last person to remember him was the architect Arthur Hill. Writing
in the 1909 *Irish Builder,* Hill remembers him as the chief exponent in Cork
of the Romantic School. Today he is remembered only for the Cork Lunatic
Asylum. His ability to absorb the influence of his great contemporaries and
yet to develop a personal idiom has been forgotten. His centenary passed
unnoticed. He is recorded in *Burke's Landed Gentry,* but not as one of
Cork's most gifted architects, only as the co-heir with his cousin Sarah to
the estate of Fountainville.

In the church of Clonbur, still inset among the Minton tiles, the
dedicatory slab lies before the altar: 'in memory of H.R.S. whose example
encouraged the building of this church and who died before it was com-
pleted' and deconsecrated and abandoned. As in the mausoleum of
Drumacoo immortalized by Betjeman, among shattered fittings, broken
glass, slipping slates with roof and windows open to the sky, 'another
extinguished family waits a Church of Ireland resurrection', and the reputa-
tion of their architect slips ever deeper into oblivion.

WILLIAM ATKINS: A CHRONOLOGY

1812   Birth to Ringrose Atkins M.D. (1738-1818) and Sarah *née* Atkins d.1854
1832   Design for a temple to the Fine Arts. Exhibited RHA.
1838   Death of the architect George Pain, uncle by marriage.
1844   Residence at 11 Morrison's Island, Cork.
1845   Marriage to cousin Louisa Gelston (1812-1904).
        Chapel, Mount Jerome, Dublin, won in competition (E'46, p.124).
1846   Church, Clonbur, Co Mayo.
1847   Inherits half the estate of his maternal grandfather William Atkins (1757-1847) at
        Fountainville (now called Hazelwood and Curraghkerry) near Mallow.
        Cork Lunatic Asylum (1847-52). (B'50, p.473, B'52, p.481, p.755, illus.).
1849   Restoration Castlecomer Church (E'49, p.265).
1850   Convent, Sisters of Mercy, St Marie de l'Isle, Cork (B'50, p.582).
        Completion of the interior, Father Mathew or Holy Trinity Church, Cork, (B'50,
        p.568), and the Dominican Friary, Cork (B'50, p.28).
        c.1850 Additions to St Columba's College, Rathfarnham, unexecuted drawings in
        possession of Ml. Scott and Partners.
1852   Address in Adelaide Terrace, Cork.
        Competition City Hall, Cork. First prize to Atkins and Johnston (B'52, p.481).
        Unexecuted.

1853	Cork Art Exhibition. Study for Virgin and Child (catalogue).
1854	Gives up farming at Fountainville.
1855	Greenmount Orphanage, Cork. Attribution, demolished.
	Ryves Castle, Knocklong, Co. Limerick, for Mr Franks.
	Demolished 1956. (B'55, p.502, *Vanishing Country Houses of Ireland*, p.104).
	Streamhill Doneraile. Mr Cavanaugh Murphy (attribution).
	Private asylum for Dr Osborne, Blackwall, Cork. B'55, p.502 (*Cork and County* by Pike, p.101, illus.).
1857	Completion of Anner Castle for Rev. Nicholas Mandeville.
	Castle started c1845 by Charles Anderson (BGCHI, p.5, and information from Geoffrey Mandeville).
	Muckrus, Co. Kerry, Gate Lodge, Chapel for Colonel Herbert and Coolclogher, now Whitehill, Killarney for John Leahy (DB'61, p.387).
1857-61	Oak Park, Tralee, for Maurice Sandes (DB'61, p.387 and BGCHI)
1859	Unsuccessful competition entry, St Andrew's, Dublin (DB'60, pp.247,267). P. McCarthy Memorial, Diamond Hill, Cork (CAJ 1926, p.103).
1861	Extensions to Cork Lunatic Asylum (DB'61, p. 688).
1862	Aghadoe, Killarney, for Lord Headley. Attribution (BGCHI).
1863	Winning entry competition, alteration to Limerick Gaol (DB'63, p.101) Executed.
	Unsuccessful competition entry St Finbarre's Cathedral, Cork (DB'63, p.101) (R.H.A. Exhibition Book 1863. Nos 458, p.478).
1864	Base, Father Mathew Statue (DB'64, p.206).
1865	Office 39, South Mall, Cork. Mention of competitions won in England and Ireland (DB'65, p58).
	Church, Leighmoney, Kinsale, demolished 1960. Plans RCB. (DB'65, p149 Nos B67, p32, illus.)
	Church Garrane now East Ferry, Midleton. plans RCB (DB'65, p.223 illus p.228).
1866	Cross Muckrus, in memory of Col. Herbert. (IB'67, p.328)
	Chancel, Cathedral of Cashel. Plans RCB.
	Chapel added to Cork Gaol, and alterations, demolished c.1960 (B'66, p.964, IB'68, p86).
1868	Church of Roosky, Bantry.
	Church of Ardfert, Co. Kerry. Demolished 1937. Plans RCB (IB'68, p.209).
1869	Church, Killarney. Burnt 1888 and rebuilt by J.F. Fuller. (IB'68, p.220, A'69, p.870)
	Chapel, Convent St Marie de l'Isle, Cork (IB'69, p.165).
	Competition, Belfast City Hall. Placed 5th. (IB'69, p.107).
	Spire, St Nicholas, Cork. Plans RCB.
1870	Parknamore, Ballincollig, Co. Cork, Mr Green. Attribution porch, Muckrus House. (*Ireland Observed*, Maurice Craig, Knight of Glin)
1872	Unsuccessful entry limited competition St Luke's, Cork.
1873	Extensions Cork Lunatic Asylum (IB'73, p.140).
1875	Termination of work on Lunatic Asylum after dismissal (IB'75, 76, p.17, p.140, p.159. 76).
1875	Velvetstown, Buttevant, Co. Cork, for Christopher Crofts, husband of Sarah Lysaght, cousin and co-heiress of Fountainville. Attribution. Burnet 1895 (BCGHI).
1881	St Michael's, Corkbeg, now Whitegate, Co Cork.
	Tower, porch, choir decoration 1892 (IB'81, p.142).
1887	5 Jan., death, aged seventy-four, leaving widow, daughter, three sons.
	He left £5000 in Ireland, £500 in England. Obituary, *Cork Constitution* Jan. 10th (IB'87, p.31).

DNB	*Dictionary National Biography*	B	*Builder*
E	*Ecclesiologist*	BGCHI	Burke's *Guide to Country Houses:*
A	*Architect*		*Ireland*, Mark Bence-Jones
DB	*Dublin Builder*	RCB	Library, Representative Church
IB	*Irish Builder*		Body, Rathgar

I am grateful to Frederick O'Dwyer for drawing my attention to *The Ecclesiologist* and the unexecuted scheme for St Columba's and for information on Charles Anderson. Also to Mr John Leslie, a relation of the Colles Sandes family, and to the late Mrs Ingeborg Atkins.

SUBSCRIBERS

BRUCE & MAVIS ARNOLD
LADY ARNOTT
ASSOCIATION OF IRISH ART HISTORIANS

THE ALFRED BEIT FOUNDATION
MARK BENCE-JONES
NICHOLAS BIELENBERG
BRIAN BOYDELL

DAVID CABOT
MAUREEN CAIRNDUFF
FLANN & MARY CAMPBELL
SIMON CAMPBELL
ANDREW CARPENTER
MAUREEN CHARLTON
HAROLD CLARKE
LEWIS CLOHESSY
JOHN COSTELLO
BRIAN COYLE
THE LATE ALAN F. CRAIG
BEATRIX CRAIG

BRIAN FITZELLE
CHRISTOPHER & ANNE FITZ-SIMON
ROY & AISLING FOSTER

JOHN GILMARTIN
HERR & FRAU HANS GRABERT
CALLA GRAVES-JOHNSTON & RODERICK
  WINGROVE
LYDIA GRAVES-JOHNSTON
MICHAEL GRAVES-JOHNSTON
THE LATE BENJAMIN GUINNESS, EARL
  OF IVEAGH
THE LATE BRYAN GUINNESS, LORD
  MOYNE
DESMOND & PENNY GUINNESS
KIERAN & VIVIENNE GUINNESS
THE TYRONE GUTHRIE CENTRE

DIANA HAMILL
MARGARET E. HAMILL
DAITHI HANLY
SHEELAGH HARBISON
CHARLES J. HAUGHEY
FRAN HAUGHEY
RICHARD G. HAWORTH
KEVIN & ANTONIA HEALY
JAMES J. HICKEY
KIERAN HICKEY

THE IRISH ARTS REVIEW

PENELOPE J. KAVANAGH
ANGELA & JOSEPH M. KELLY
LORD KILLANIN

COMMANDER WILLIAM KING

DESMOND LESLIE
SIR JOHN LESLIE, Bt
NORA LEVER
JOSEPH LONG
CHARLES LYSAGHT

FERGAL & BRÍD MCCABE
JOE & NUALA MCCULLOUGH
ROBERT J. MCKINSTRY
ANNA MANAHAN
THE LATE CON & PAMELA MANAHAN
F.X. MARTIN
MARY C. MOON
EILEEN, COUNTESS OF MOUNTCHARLES
SEAN & ROSEMARY MULCAHY
ROSALEEN MULJI

DAVID NORRIS

CHARLOTTE & TOM O'CONNELL
BRIAN & CONSUELO O'CONNOR
TIM O'DRISCOLL
MAUREEN O'FLANAGAN
ANDREW O'MAHONY
F.J. O'REILLY
K.P. O'REILLY-HYLAND
ANTONY O'RIORDAN

VINCENT POKLEWSKI-KOZIELL

DACHINE RAINER
ANN & JOHN REIHILL
LUNIA RYAN
PHYLLIS RYAN

LESLIE SCHEPS
PHYLLIS SEIGNE
JONATHAN SHACKLETON
DAVID P. SHAW-SMITH
ANTONIA SHELLEY-SMITH
DESIRÉE SHORT
DOREEN E. SLATTERY
COUNTESS SLIWINSKA

A.D. TOMLINSON

THE UNITED ARTS CLUB

W.E. VAUGHAN
PAUL & GLYNIS VOORHEIS

THE LATE ROBIN & DOROTHY WALKER
BRENDA & DONALD WEIR
HENRY A. WHEELER
BRIDGET WILKINSON
JONATHAN WILLIAMS